HISTORIC PHOTOS OF
MISSISSIPPI

TEXT AND CAPTIONS BY
ANNE B. MCKEE

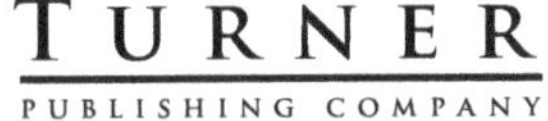

The Big Black River Station, located near Vicksburg in Warren County, is shown here in 1864 as wagons hitched to mules await the next tiresome journey. Supply sheds can be seen to the left and right of the mule teams. The Civil War would not end before another year of travail had elapsed.

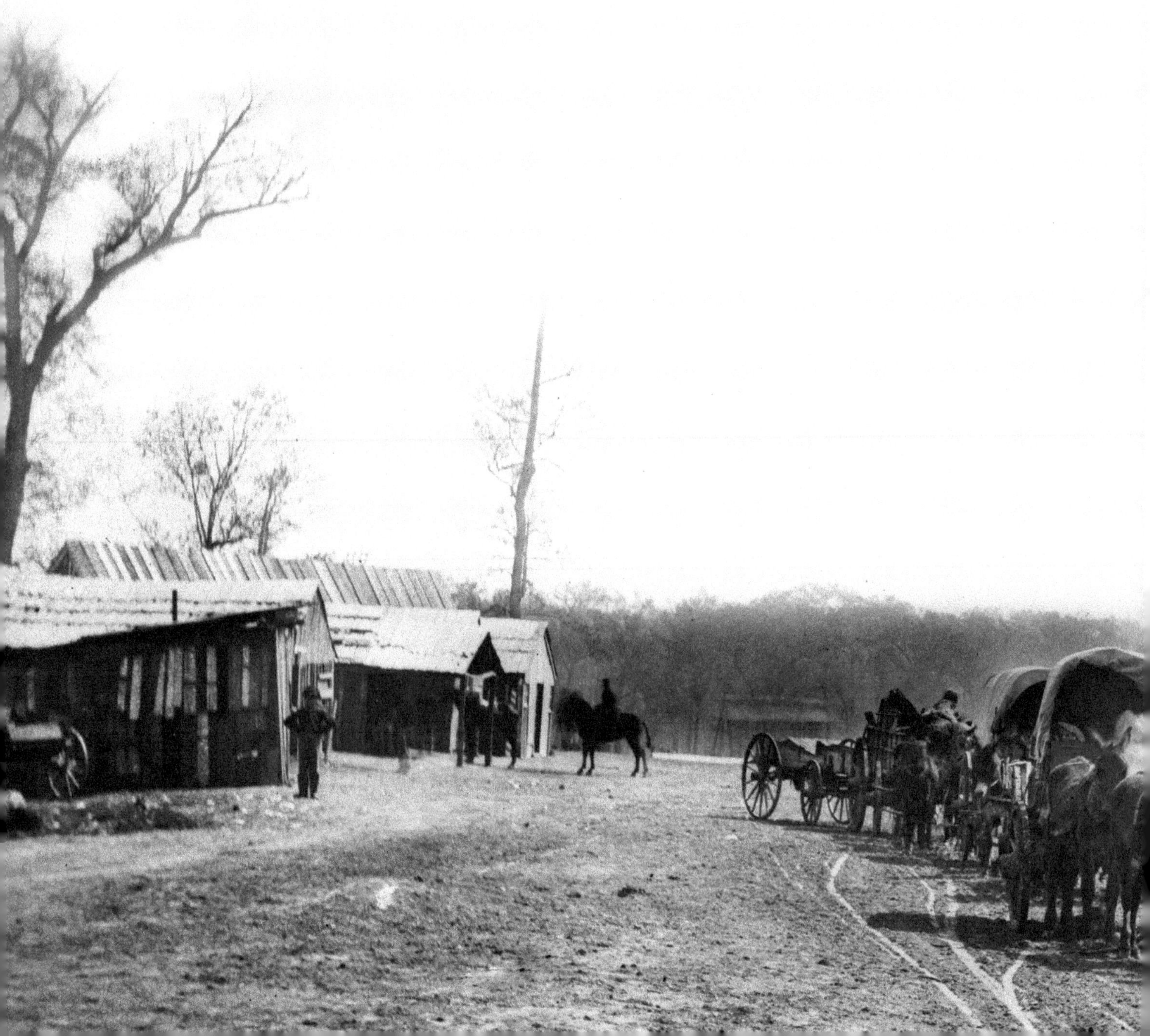

HISTORIC PHOTOS OF
MISSISSIPPI

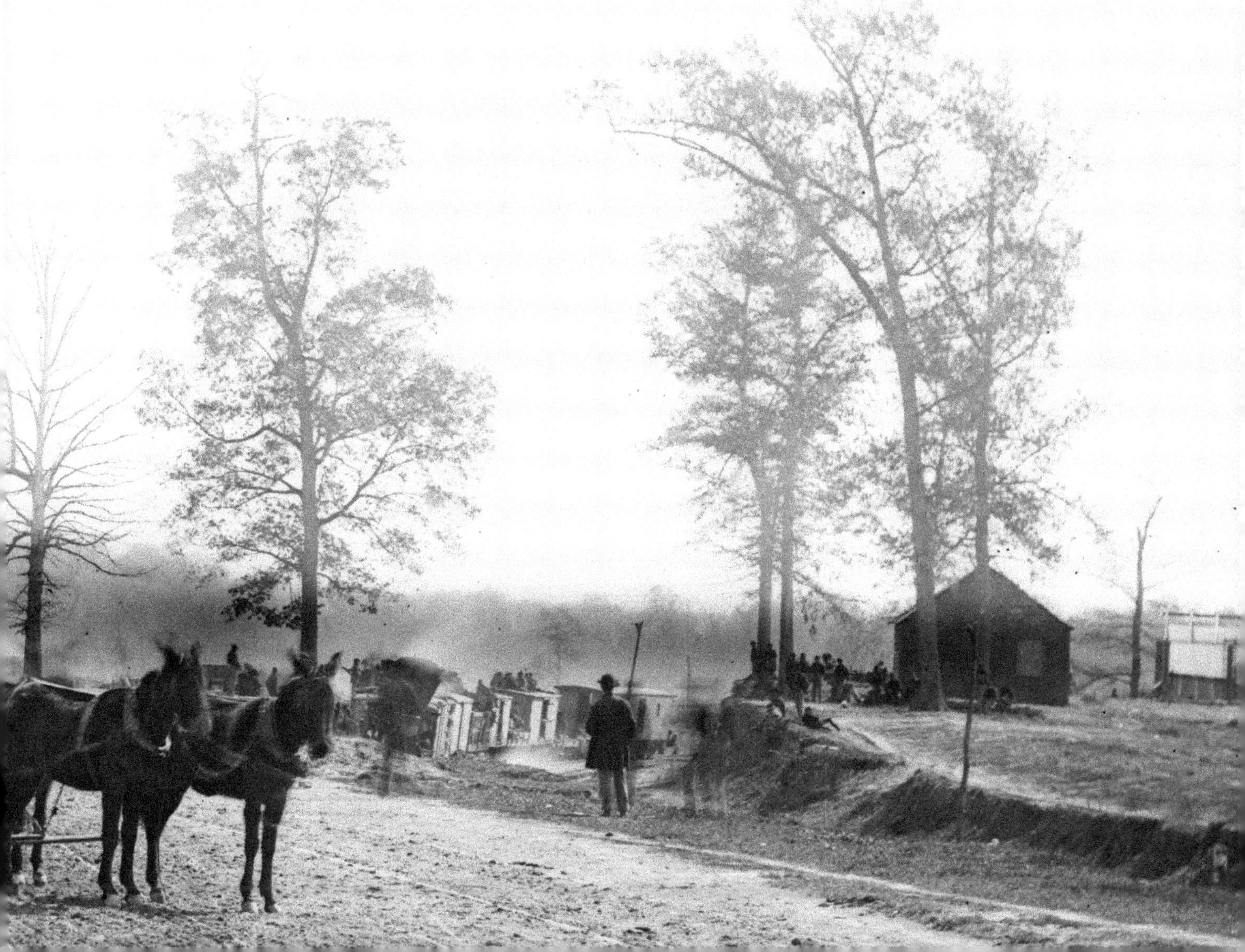

Turner Publishing Company
www.turnerpublishing.com

Historic Photos of Mississippi

Library of Congress Control Number: 2009921342

ISBN-13: 978-1-59652-528-3

Printed in the United States of America

ISBN 978-1-68442-084-1(hc)

Contents

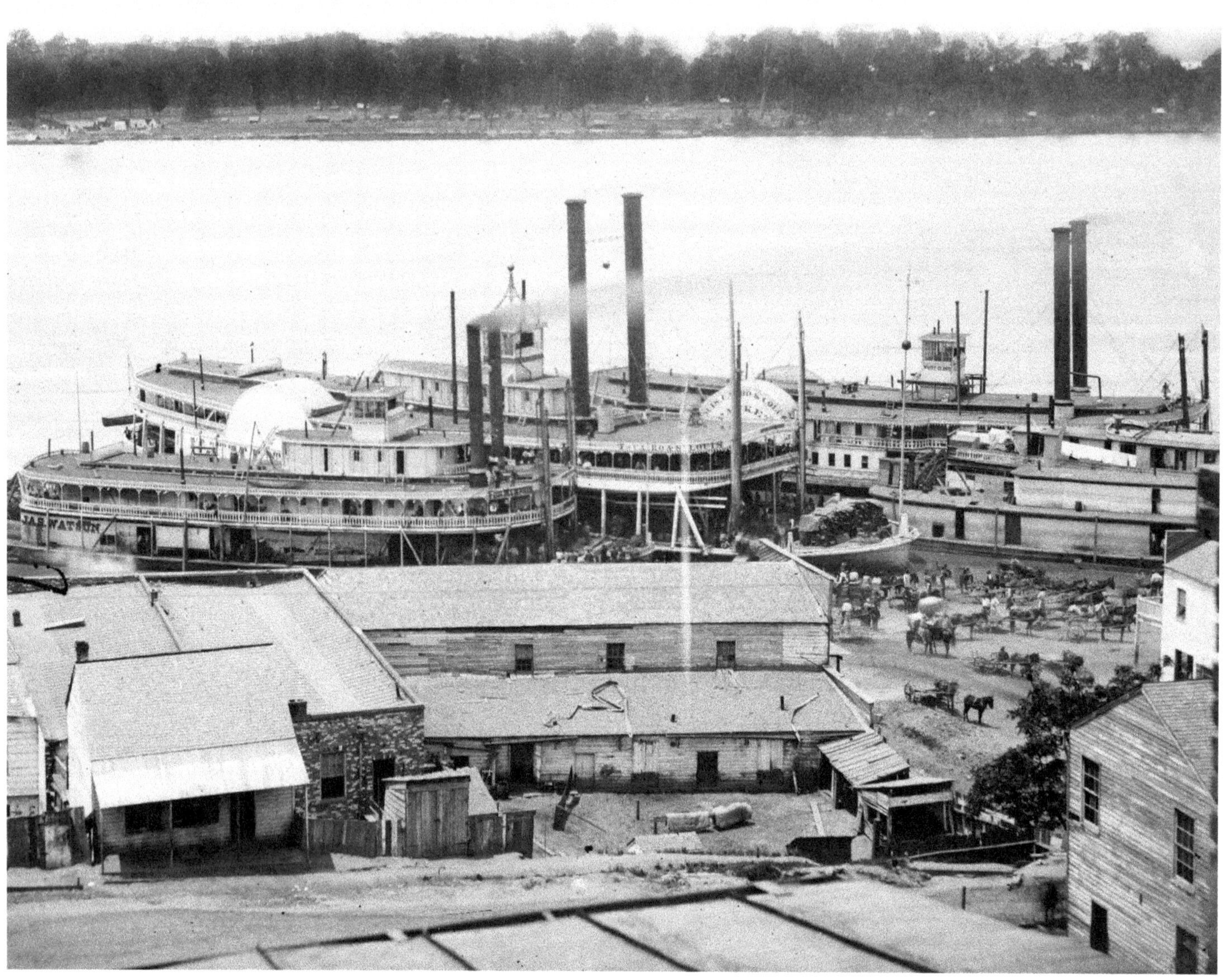

Old Man River, the majestic Mississippi, flows on in February 1864, unconcerned with the flurry of war-related activities on the levee. Steamboats are lined up awaiting the next load as mules and men prepare for the next destination.

Acknowledgments

This volume, *Historic Photos of Mississippi,* is the result of the cooperation and efforts of many individuals and organizations. It is with great thanks that we acknowledge the valuable contribution of the following for their generous support:

Lauderdale County Mississippi History and Archives
Library of Congress
Mississippi Department of Archives and History
Moore's Boler's Inn Private Collection

We would also like to thank the following individuals for valuable contributions and assistance in making this work possible:

Lauderdale County History and Archives Director Ward Calhoun, and his staff, Leslie Joyner and Janet Bunker, worked tirelessly to locate unusual and significant photos for the book. In addition, I must thank Margaret Remy, owner of Quick Prints Photography Shop, and professional photographer Keith Jacoby, both of Meridian, for their valuable assistance.

Most important was the support of my husband and family, especially my daughter-in-law, Kelly McKee, an English instructor at Meridian Community College, who spent hours providing the necessary edits needed to allow the manuscript to flow as smoothly as the Old Man River—namesake of our great state of Mississippi.

The goal in publishing this work is to provide broader access to this set of extraordinary photographs, as well as to inspire, provide perspective, and evoke insight that might assist citizens as they work to plan the state's future. In addition, the book seeks to preserve the past with adequate respect and reverence.

With the exception of touching up imperfections that have accrued with the passage of time and cropping where necessary, no changes have been made. The focus and clarity of many images is limited by the technology and the ability of the photographer at the time they were taken.

Preface

William Faulkner, one of Mississippi's most famous novelists, once said, "To understand the world, you must first understand a place like Mississippi." Another Mississippi writer, Willie Morris, explained it this way: "Physically beautiful in the most fundamental and indwelling way, [in that] it never leaves you." A recent Mississippi advertisement said, "Mississippi. Feels like coming home." All of these sentiments are true, but they miss the sweet essence of the state and the strong spirit of the people. There is no other place like Mississippi, where the people think with their hearts and love with their souls.

History tells of the Choctaw and other tribes who once walked the land, followed by an influx of settlers who traveled by wagon to follow their dreams into the new frontier called Mississippi. To work the land, African peoples were brought to the rich and fertile ground as the property of plantation owners eager to make the land prosper. Slavery was the darkest period in Mississippi history, and the Civil War which ended it was bloody, brutal, and bitter. Natchez, the oldest settlement on the Mississippi and which had once been home to more than 500 millionaires, was largely spared the ravages of the war, but other places were not so fortunate. The capital city of Jackson, for one, was burned to the ground.

The war ended in overwhelming defeat for the South, and on its heels Mississippians weathered postwar Reconstruction, with its beaten lands and broken hearts. Losing the Civil War was not anticipated. Many Southern warriors did not come home, and without their return, those who remained were left with little more than blood-soaked memories. Nor were the emancipated people prepared for freedom. Where were they to go? What were they to do? Many returned home to live near their former owners. Some worked as tenant farmers and hired themselves out to do the same work as before the war. Together, Mississippians put their shoulders to the plow and pulled out of a desperate time.

The golden age for Mississippians (the years 1899 to 1920) brought new hope and prosperity with exciting innovations and new opportunities. Railroads continued to crisscross the state providing good jobs. Mississippians once again enjoyed the arts, music, education, and a better life. Industry grew and the land flowed with milk and honey.

Too soon the winds of war returned. Soldiers left their Mississippi homes to fight World War I, joining the war effort at Camp Shelby and heading overseas to the trenches of Europe. Ten years after the war ended, the Great Depression spread a black cloud across the United States. In Mississippi, the flood of 1927 brought hard times in advance. Once again, Mississippians worked together to sustain themselves through the calamity. The Works Progress Administration and other federal programs provided make-work jobs and many Mississippians subsisted on wild game, turnip greens, and whatever they could gather.

World War II took Mississippi soldiers overseas again, and industry kicked in to supply our armies throughout the world. Mississippi women learned skills traditionally performed by men. They filled positions in the defense industry and munitions factories, holding jobs as welders, pipe fitters, and boilermakers. Camp Shelby became the largest training camp for the army in the United States. With victory at hand and the depression a fading memory, a new era promised new hope. The civil rights movement of the 1950s and 1960s encouraged that hope, helping to bring an end to the era of segregation.

As the future dawned, Mississippians could look back on a wealth of accomplishments in the Magnolia State. The first nuclear submarine built in the South was built here. The first can of condensed milk was created here. Celebrities born here include Jim Henson, creator of the Muppets; legends of music Jimmy Buffett, Bo Diddley, B.B. King, Muddy Waters, Conway Twitty, Jimmie Rodgers, and of course Elvis Presley; and actors Morgan Freeman and Ray Walston. Literary icons Tennessee Williams, Eudora Welty, and William Faulkner were Mississippians. The Dentzel Carousel in Meridian is a National Historic Landmark and tours of the antebellum homes of Natchez delight visitors to this day. The Old Spanish Fort in Pascagoula is the oldest structure west of St. Augustine, Florida, and Natchez is the oldest town on the Mississippi River. Oliver Pollock, buried near Pinckneyville, is credited as the inventor of the dollar ($) sign, and Barq's Root Beer was invented by Edward Barq of Biloxi. Of geographical interest, Jackson sits 2,900 feet directly above an extinct volcano, the only city in the United States so placed. And especially important to catfish aficionados everywhere, Mississippi produces more farm-raised catfish than any other place in the world.

Mark Twain once had one of his characters say that muddy Mississippi water is "wholesomer to drink than the clear water of the Ohio." If the sediment settles in the pitcher, he said, what you want to do is "to keep it stirred up."

We Mississippians tend to agree.

—Anne B. McKee

A lone soldier gazes into the distance from the banks of Chickasaw Bayou in February 1864. The bayou betrays no sign of the recent carnage. Following the engagement here, when Union forces commanded by Ulysses Grant were repulsed at Vicksburg by Confederate troops under the command of General John C. Pemberton, Grant chose to besiege the city. After 47 days, with supplies depleted and no sign of reinforcements, Pemberton's garrison finally surrendered on July 4, 1863, yielding Vicksburg to Union control. Eighty years would elapse before the citizens of Vicksburg would again celebrate July 4 as Independence Day.

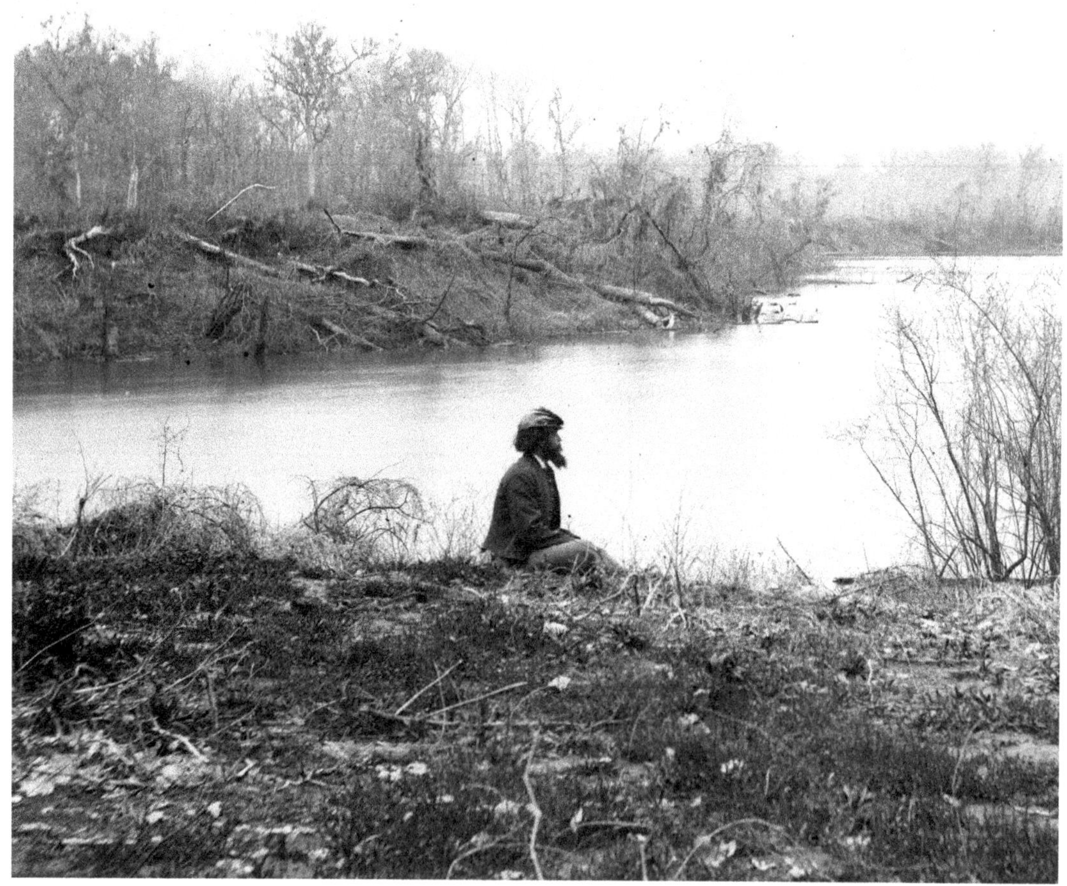

Civil War and Survival

(1860–1899)

"When Will This Cruel War Be Over?" In 1863, the lyrics to this haunting tune resounded throughout the state as women and children struggled to stay alive while their men were gone to war.

Mississippi had become the second state to secede from the Union on January 9, 1861, joining six other cotton states to form the Confederate States of America in February. The decisive step was made with great fanfare, at first, as young men volunteered in droves at mustering points, but the seriousness of the act soon became apparent as the bloody war was brought to the very doorsteps of Mississippi families.

From the time of statehood in 1817 to the eve of the Civil War in 1860, Mississippi became the most dynamic and largest cotton-producing state in America. Population numbers surged until, by 1860, there were more than 790,000 Mississippians—353,901 whites and 436,631 slaves, with cotton production recorded at 535.1 million pounds in 1859.

The signing of treaties between the United States and the Choctaw and Chickasaw nations had opened land for settlers. Mississippi became known as the western frontier, and Mississippi heroes like Sam Dale guided hundreds of Eastern families to the state, hopeful of building better, more prosperous lives in the state's wilderness of untapped forests and bottomlands.

Toward the latter 1850s, the railroads promised prosperity, but ultimately their importance brought ruin as Union troops poured into the state wreaking havoc on the South's infrastructure during the Civil War. In 1862 the Battle of Shiloh gave Union forces control of the Tennessee River and opened the way to attack Corinth, a railroad center vital to the South. The siege of Vicksburg in 1863 gave control of the Mississippi River to the Union and prompted General William Tecumseh Sherman's devastating campaign through the state, which included the burning of Jackson.

By war's end, 59,000 Mississippians were dead or wounded. Those who survived still had one another, the river, the blue skies, and the rich soil. The war ended life as Mississippians had known it, but it also ushered in a future that, following Reconstruction and with the turn of the century, would yield prosperity.

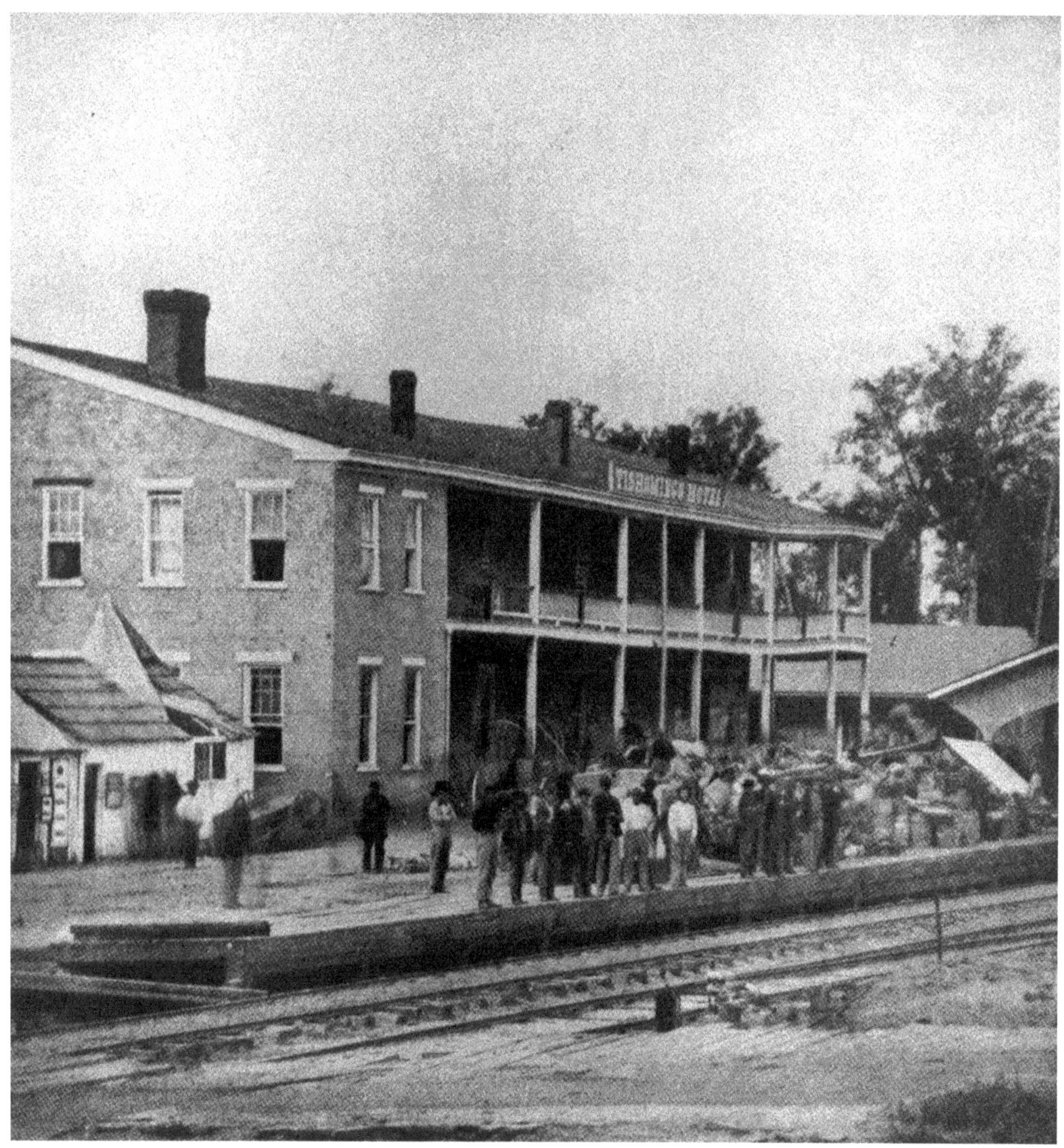

The train station at Corinth, Mississippi, in 1862, at the height of the Civil War. The location of Corinth in Alcorn County, with its junction of two railroads, made it strategically important to the Confederacy, and it had fallen to Union occupation in the spring of 1862. On October 3-4, 1862, Confederate forces commanded by generals Earl Van Dorn and Sterling Price attempted to retake the town, but early successes led to overconfidence and ill-conceived planning, ultimately ending in a Union victory.

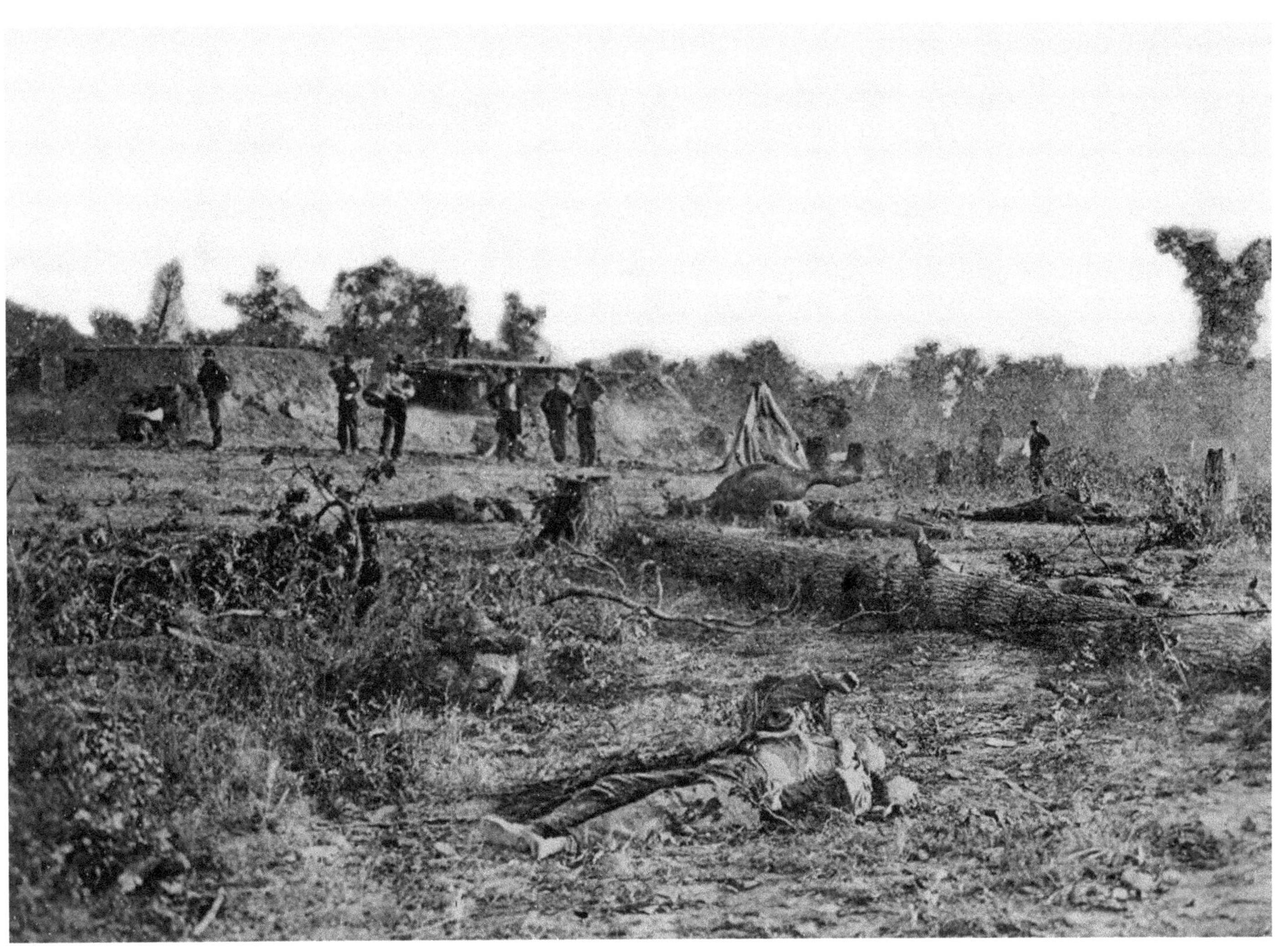

Federal determination to hold two major railroads at Corinth resulted in a fierce battle and a Union victory on October 3-4, 1862. Seen in this photograph the morning after the attack are Confederate dead and Union troops surveying the aftermath of the conflict.

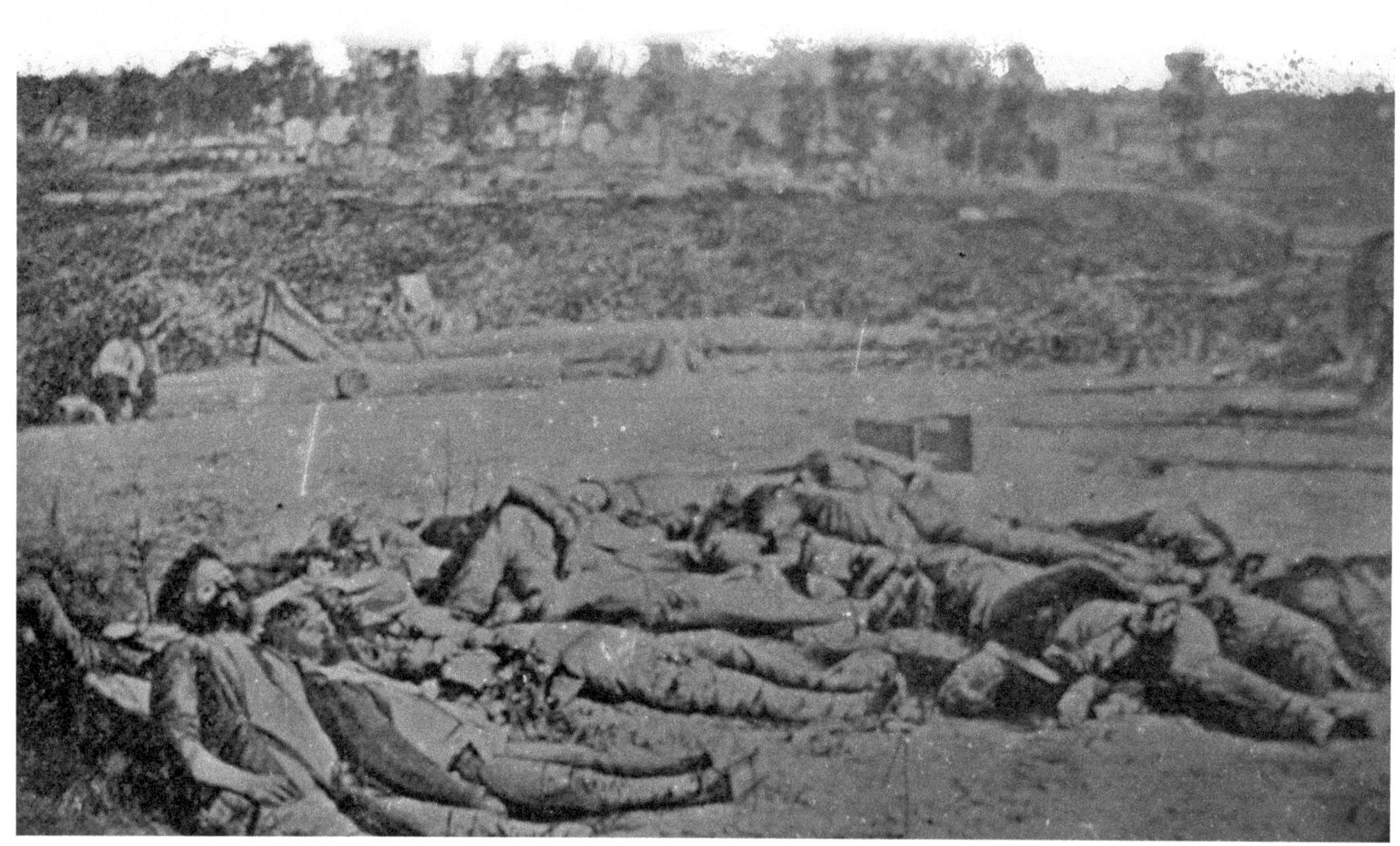

Aftermath of the battle at Corinth, along Battery Robinette, the morning after the Union victory of October 3-4, 1862. A valiant effort was made by Confederates to rescue the town, named for the city in Greece when founded in 1853, from Union control.

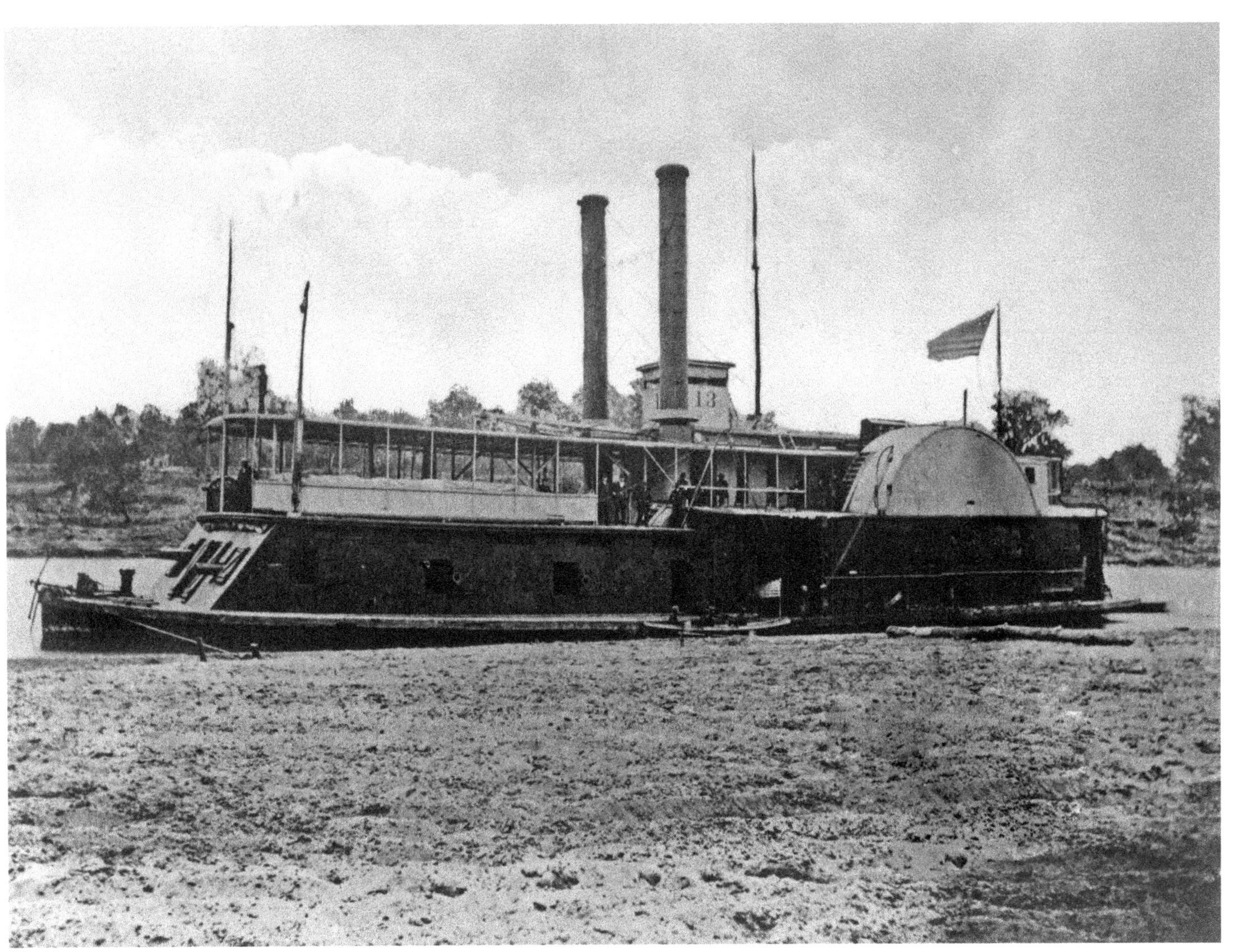

This U.S. Navy tin-clad side-wheeler was used during the Civil War to patrol navigable waterways with the goal of preventing the South from trading with other countries. In July 1863, the steamer headed an expedition up the Little Red River, a tributary of the Black River, capturing quantities of Confederate government provisions. The armored vessel also transported Union troops and Confederate prisoners of war.

The battlefield of Chickasaw Bayou, in Warren County, was the scene of a fierce struggle on December 26-29, 1862, the opening salvo of the Vicksburg campaign. Union major general William T. Sherman and Confederate lieutenant general John C. Pemberton commanded their respective troops in the swamps near Walnut Hills, where the Union defenses were ultimately repulsed. Sherman then withdrew, giving the Confederacy a victory.

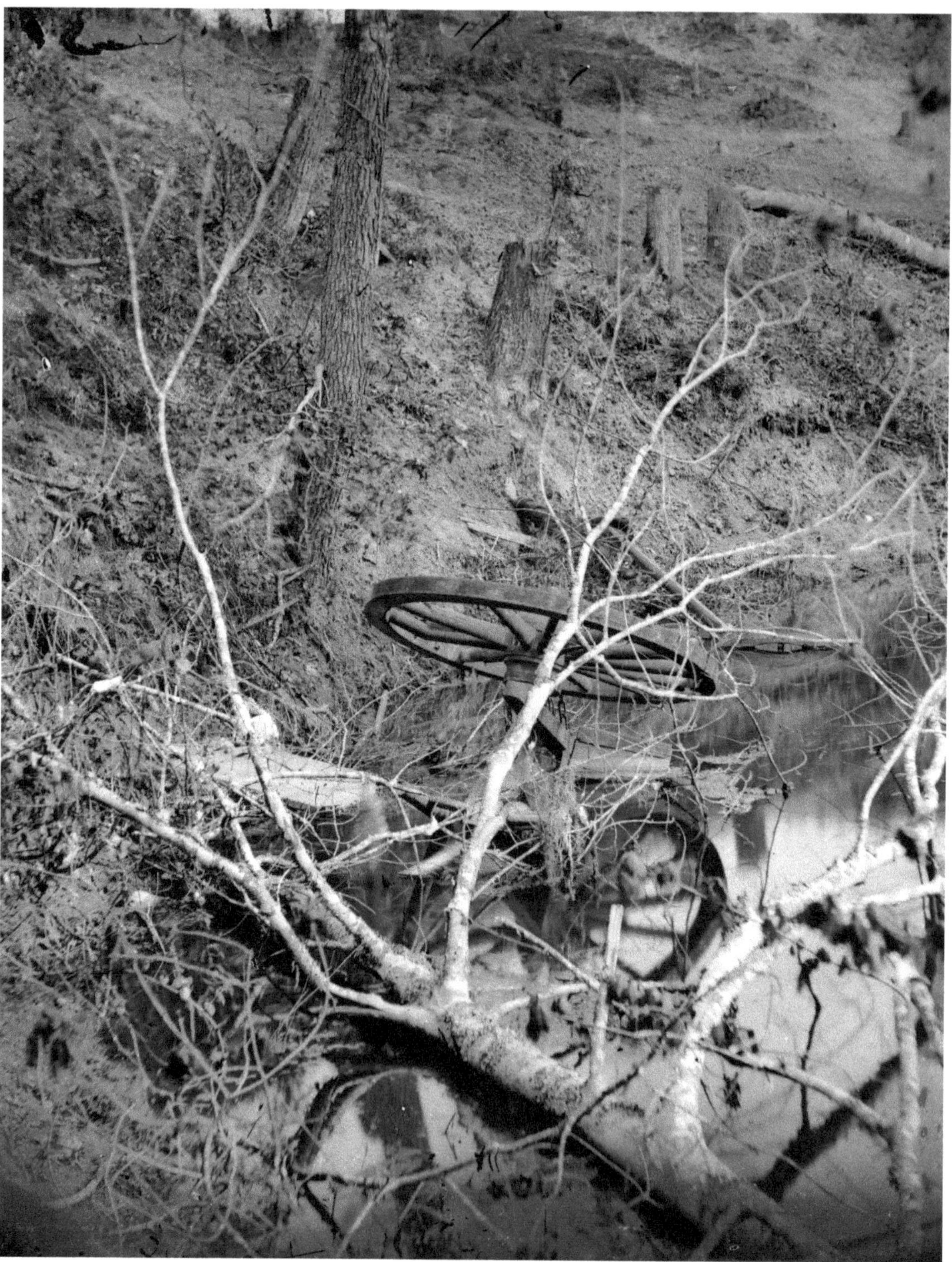

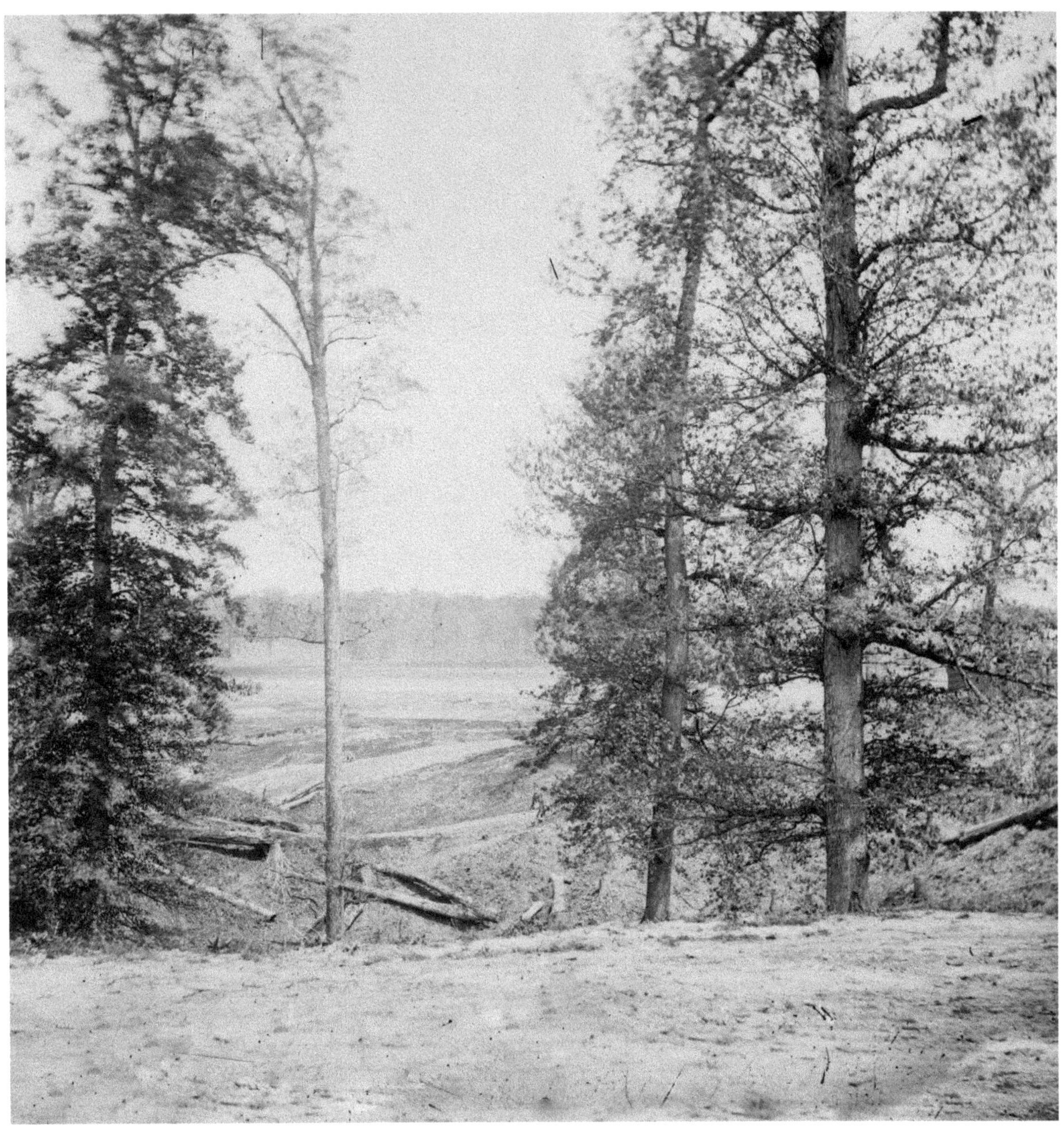

The Battle of Big Black River Bridge or Big Black, of May 17, 1863, was waged as part of the Vicksburg campaign and resulted in a Union victory. Confederate forces, confused and panicked, withdrew across the Big Black on two bridges, setting fire to the bridges to prevent Union pursuit.

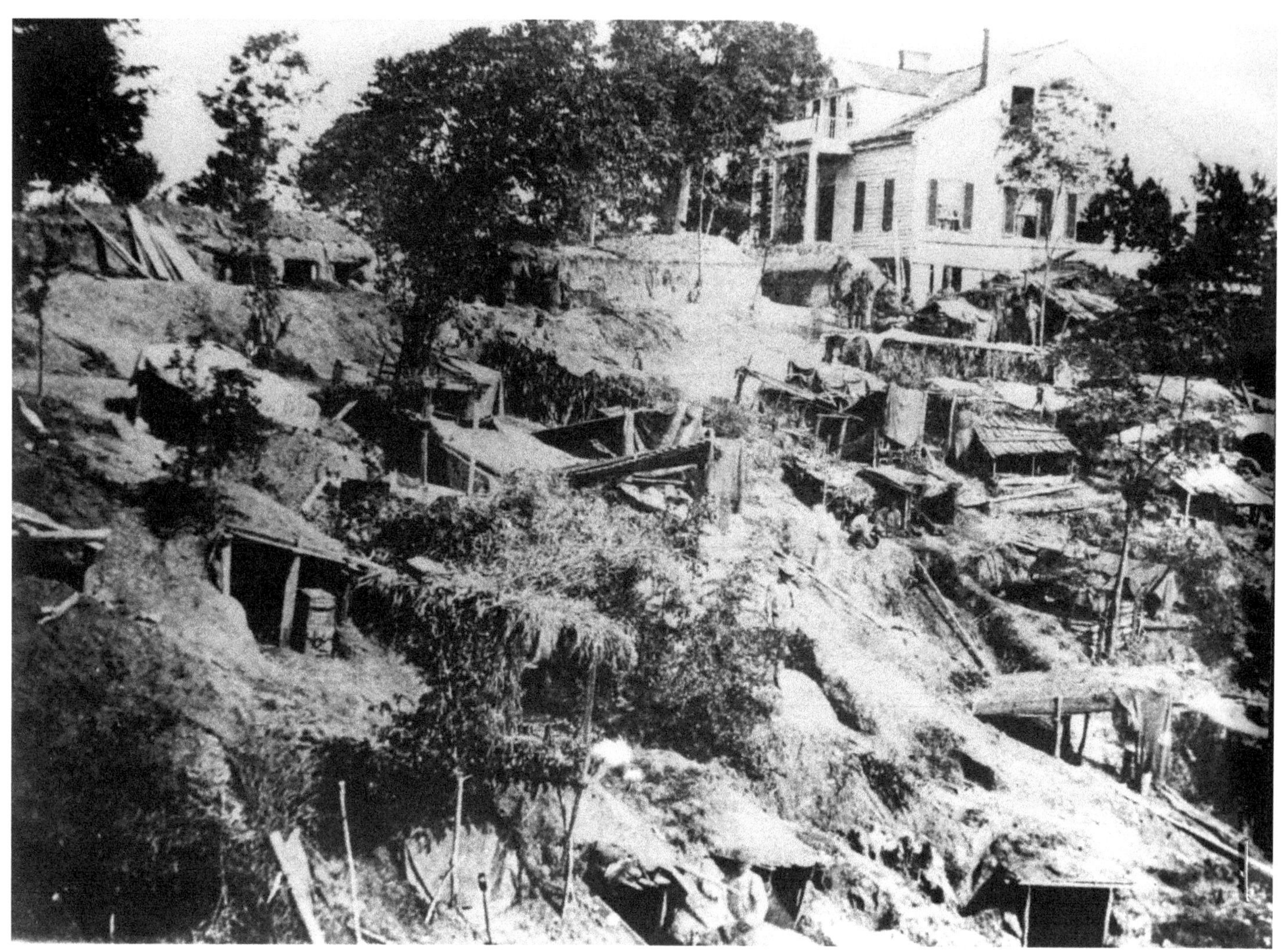

The war has ravaged the environs of this antebellum home. The scene depicts the siege of Vicksburg and how one lovely home survived. Caves have been dug and makeshift shelters erected, clear evidence of the plight of locals during the bombardment by Union forces.

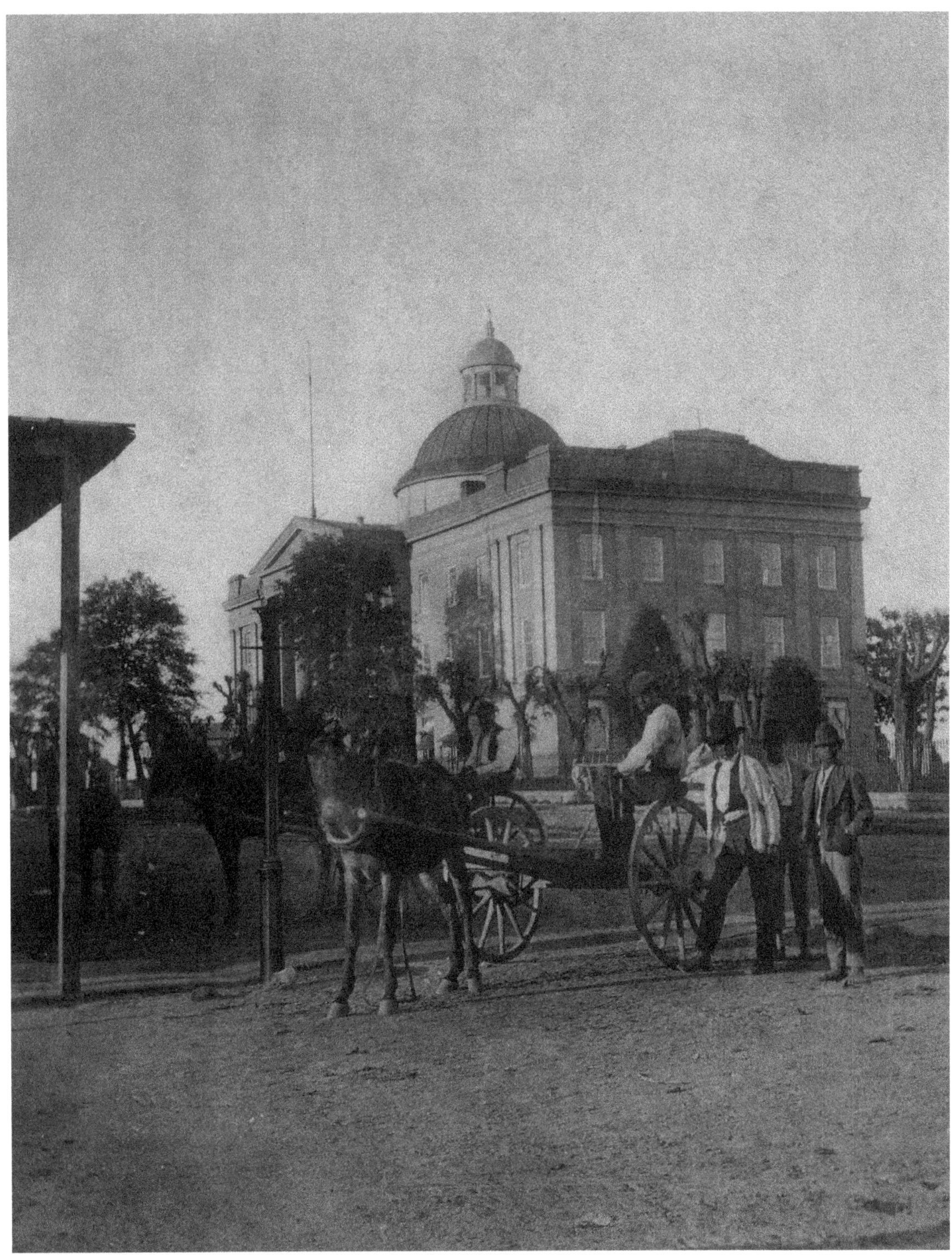

Goings-on at the corner of Pearl and State streets in Jackson. The old state capitol with its dome rises in the background. When Mississippi became a territory in 1798, Natchez served as its first capital. Following statehood in 1817, Jackson, on the Pearl River, became the capital city.

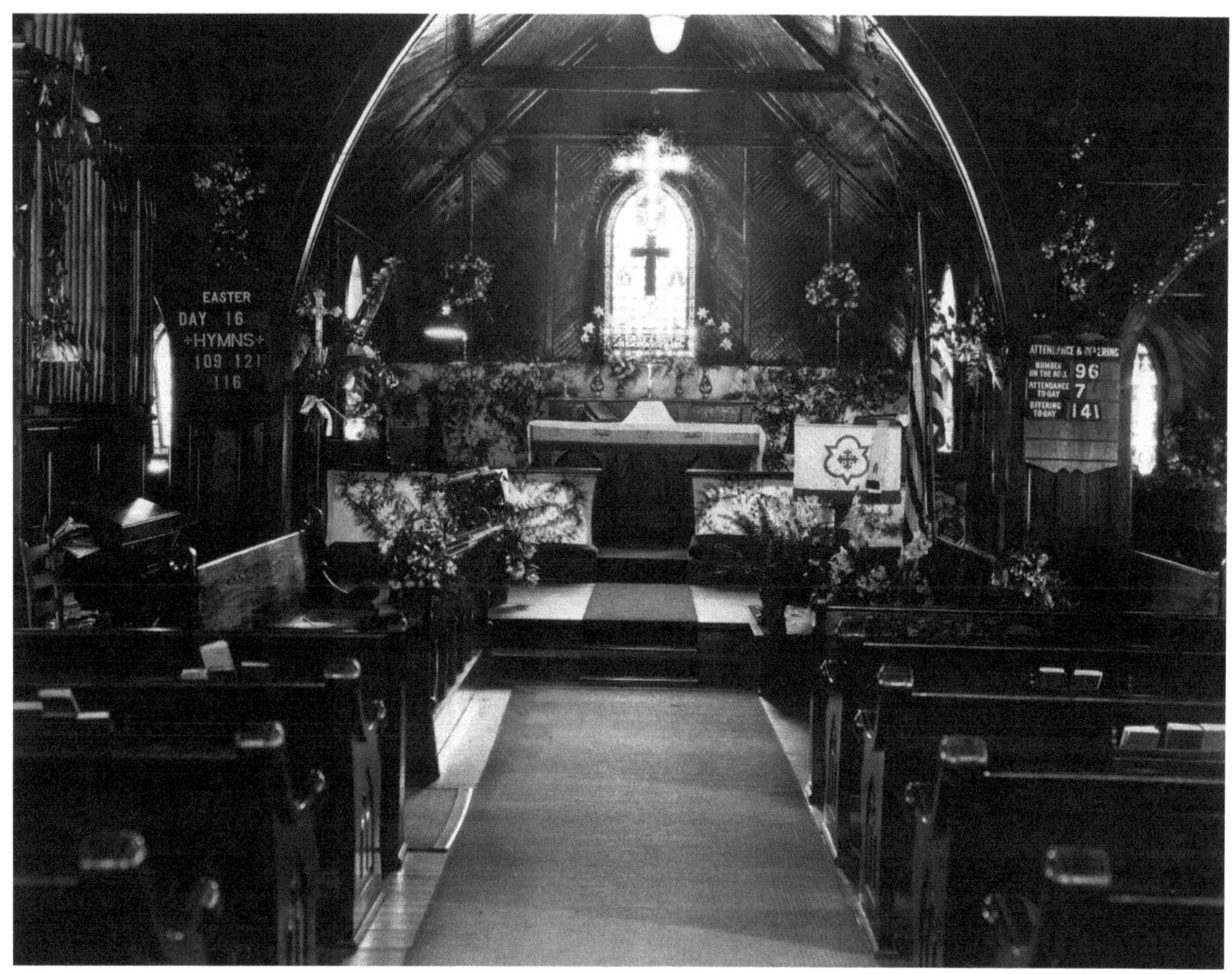

Interior view of a church in Jackson, facing the altar and pulpit, with carved wooden pews, hymnbooks, stained-glass windows, Christian icons, announcement board, flowers, and other features. The ornate beauty of the church is impressive and the sanctuary of peace it offered vital, especially during a time of war. According to the boards, Easter was being celebrated. Of 96 members, 7 had attended the most recent gathering, contributing $1.41 to the offering plate.

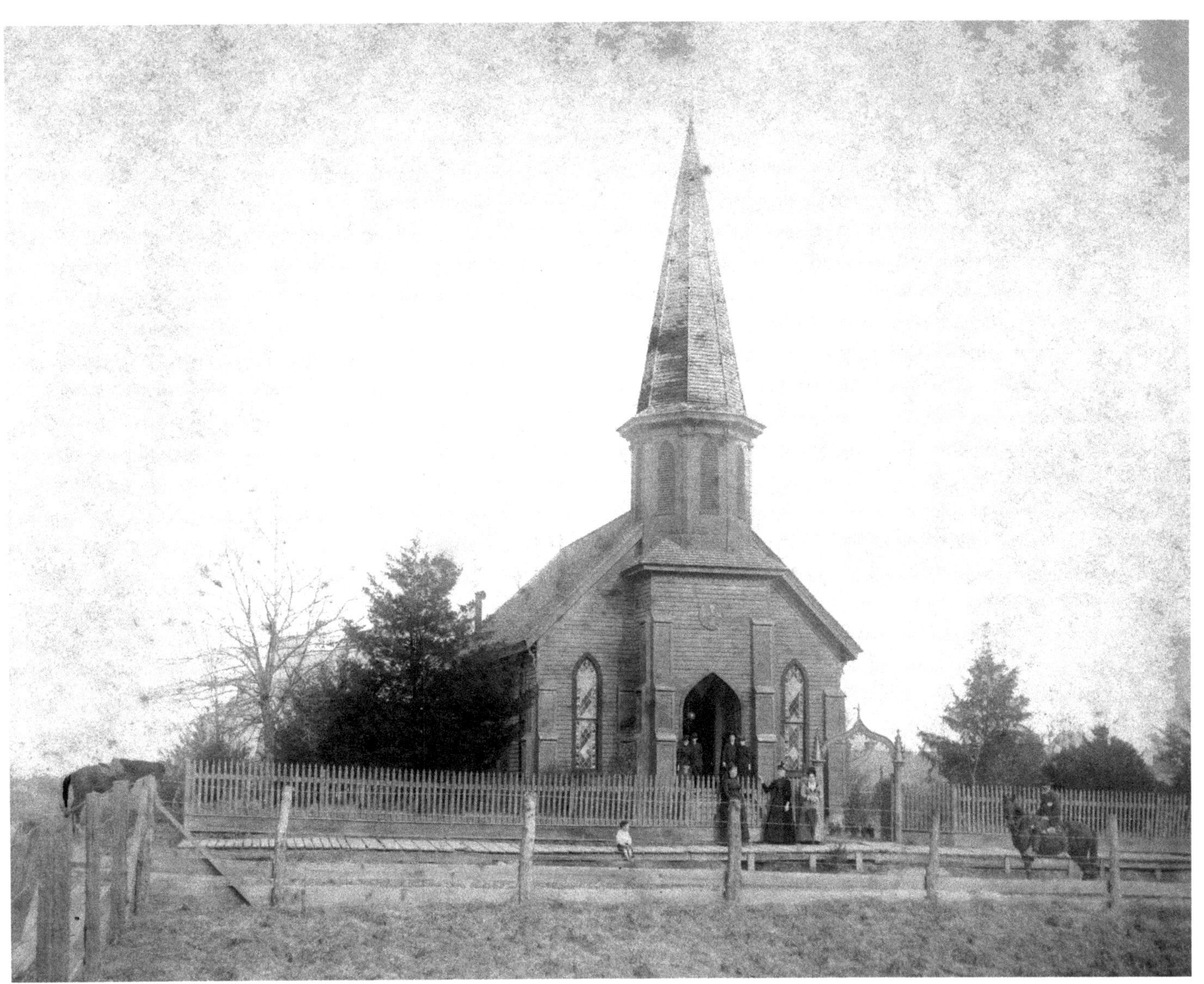

This clapboard church in Jackson, photographed in 1870, features an octagonal belfry, spire, stained-glass windows, and a Tudor arched entrance. A wooden sidewalk and picket fence front the structure, where a group of locals pose for the camera.

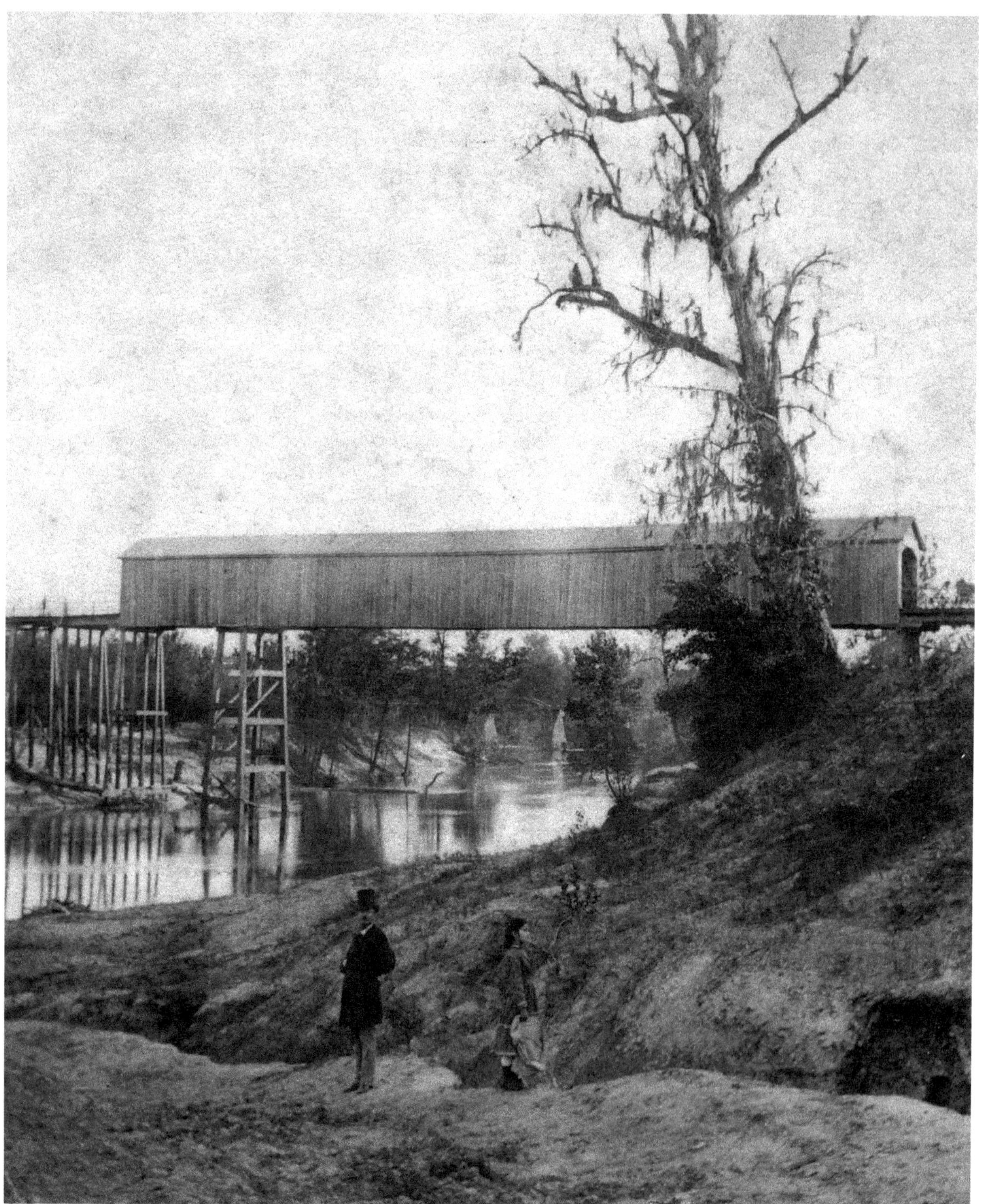

A covered bridge over the Pearl River at Jackson, with Spanish moss clinging to the tree at right. The Pearl River got its name by being an early site of French pearl fisheries. The bridge was used to corral prisoners of war during the Civil War.

The Pearl River prison bridge collapsed after the war, a 5-dollar fine for "driving faster than a walk" notwithstanding. Seen here is the wreckage, some of it submerged beneath the waters.

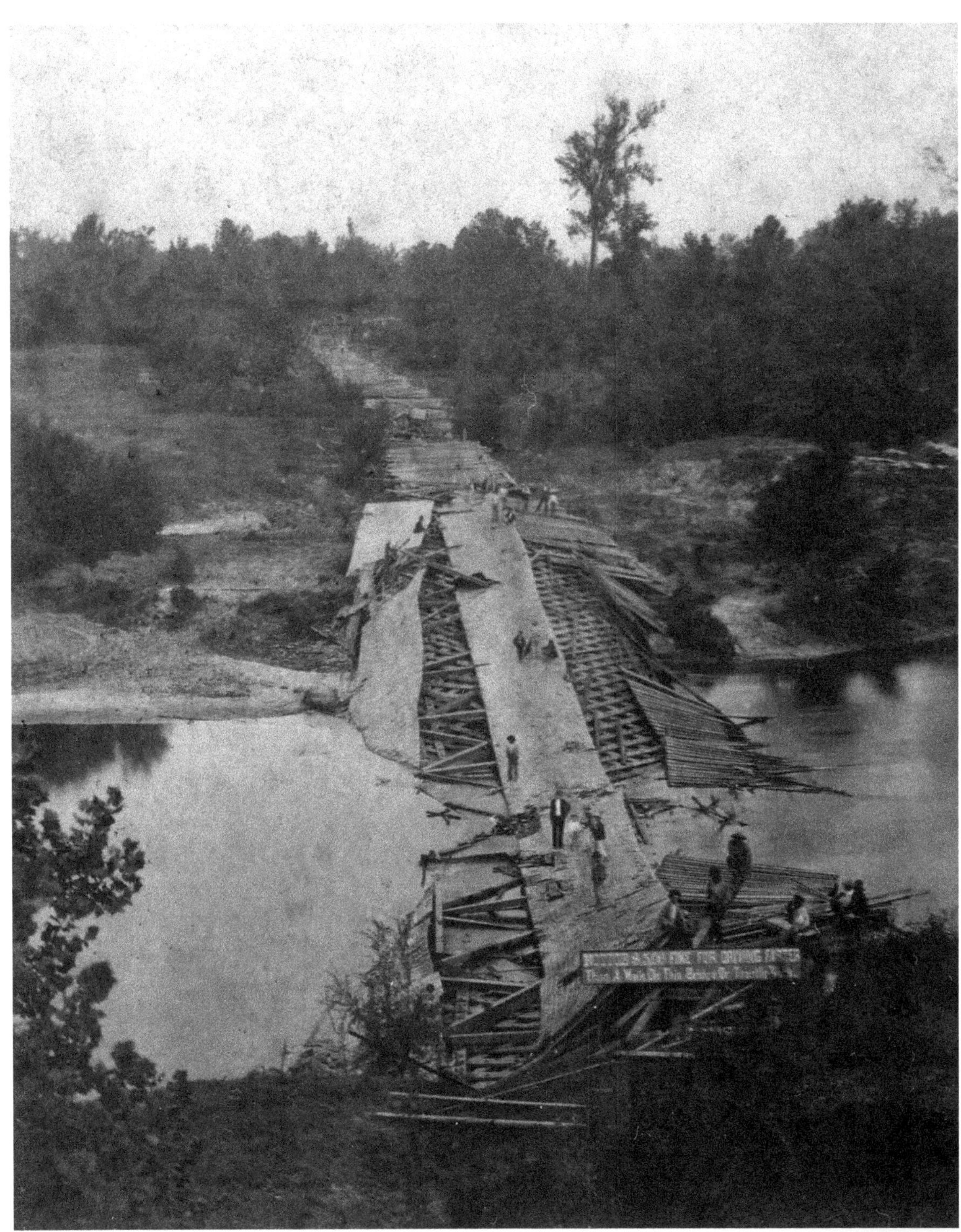

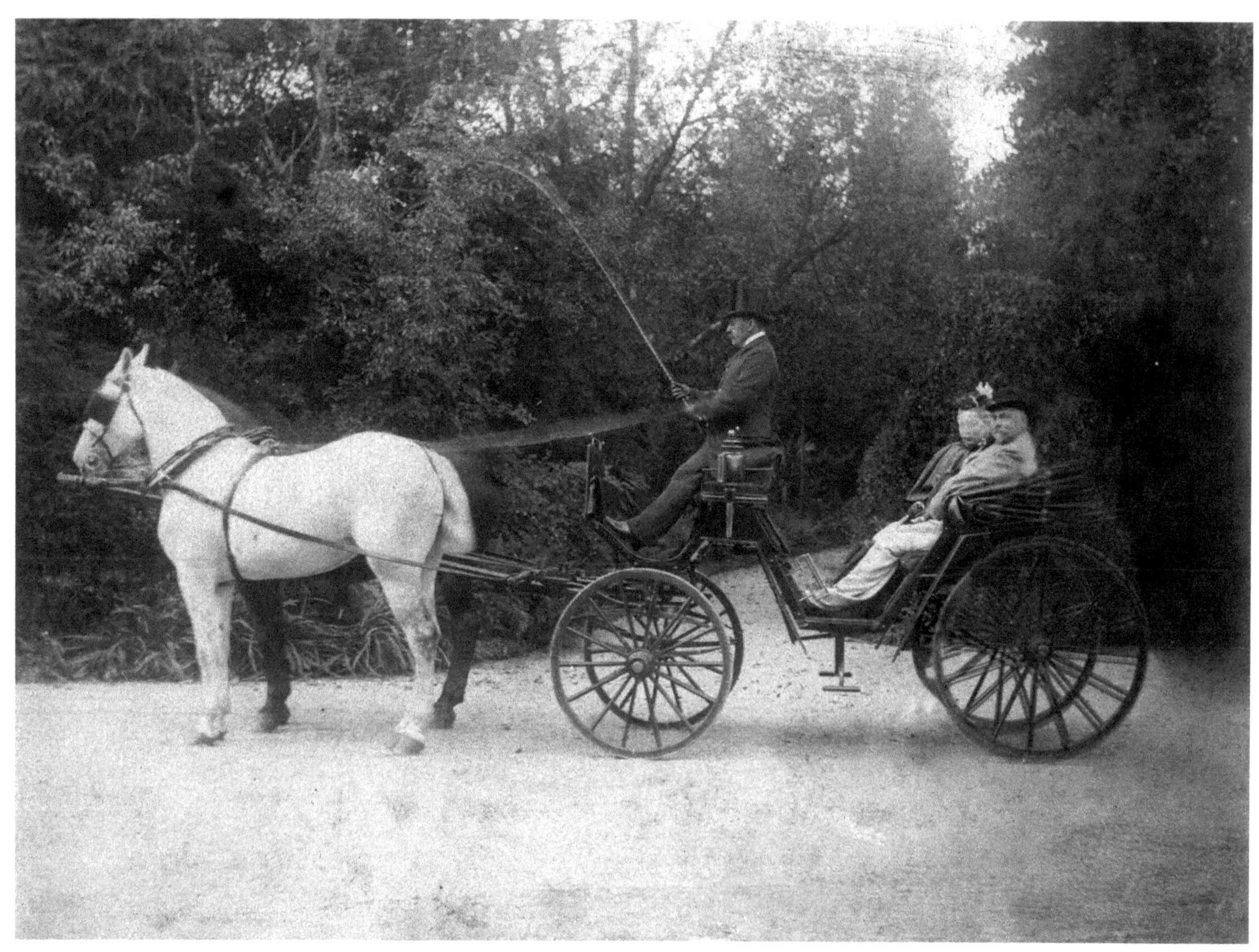

Well-heeled citizens of Jackson and their driver interrupt their outing for a photograph around 1870.

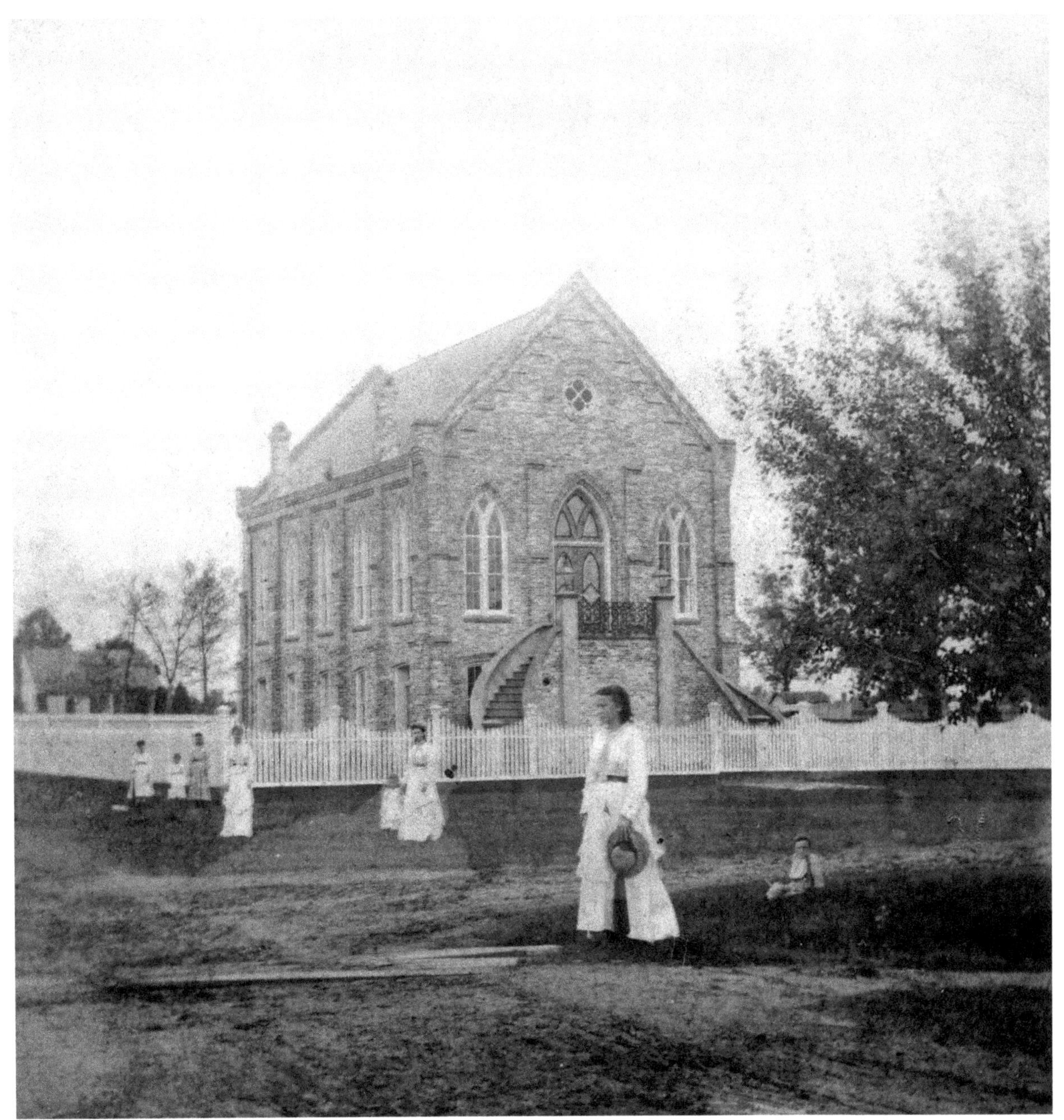

Women and children of the community dressed in their Sunday best pose in front of this two-story brick church in Jackson around 1870. To prevent blurring, camera technology of the era generally required subjects to remain motionless.

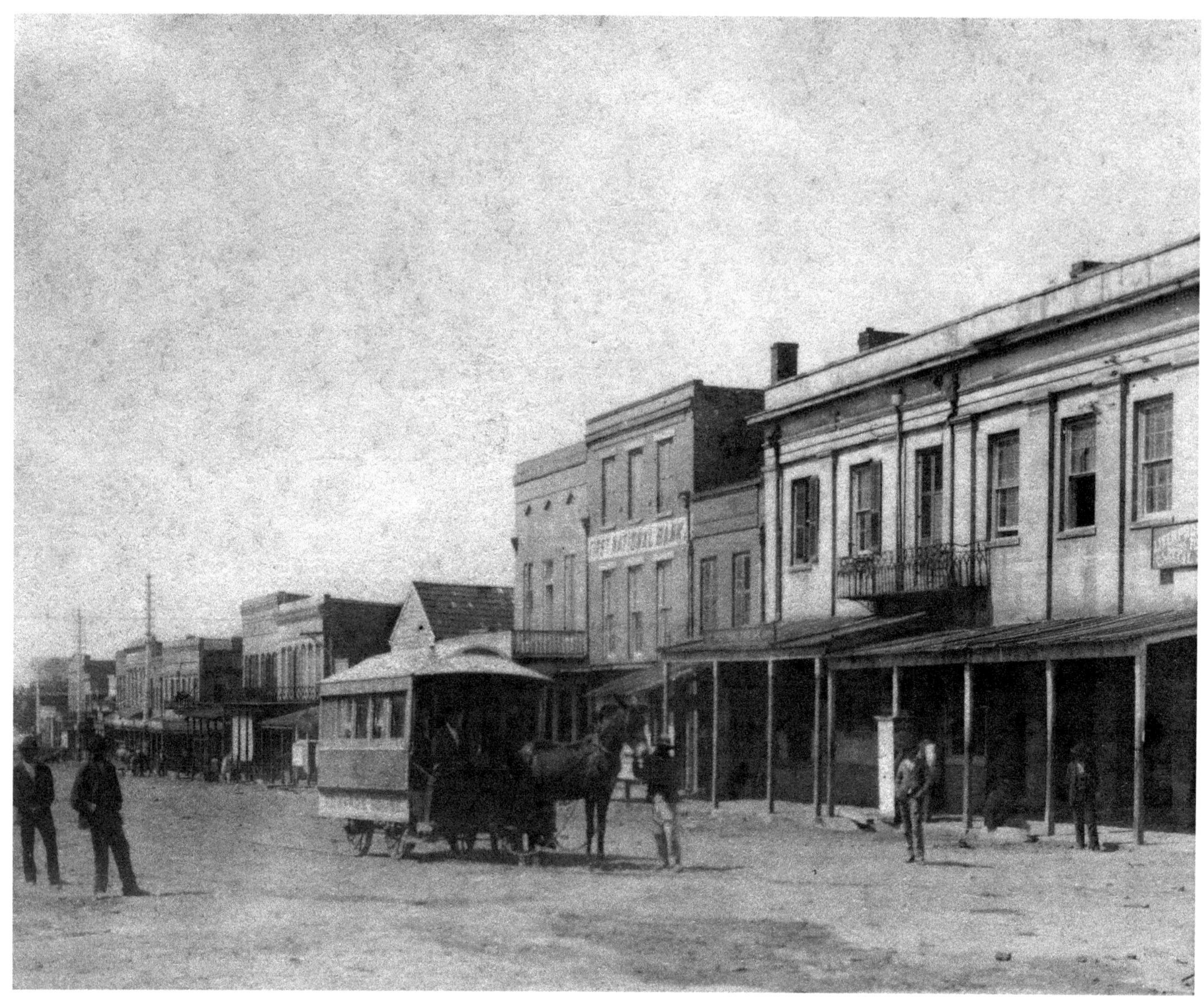

An 1870s view of Capital Street in Jackson, where a mule-drawn streetcar plies the business district, with the First National Bank visible to the right of the vehicle.

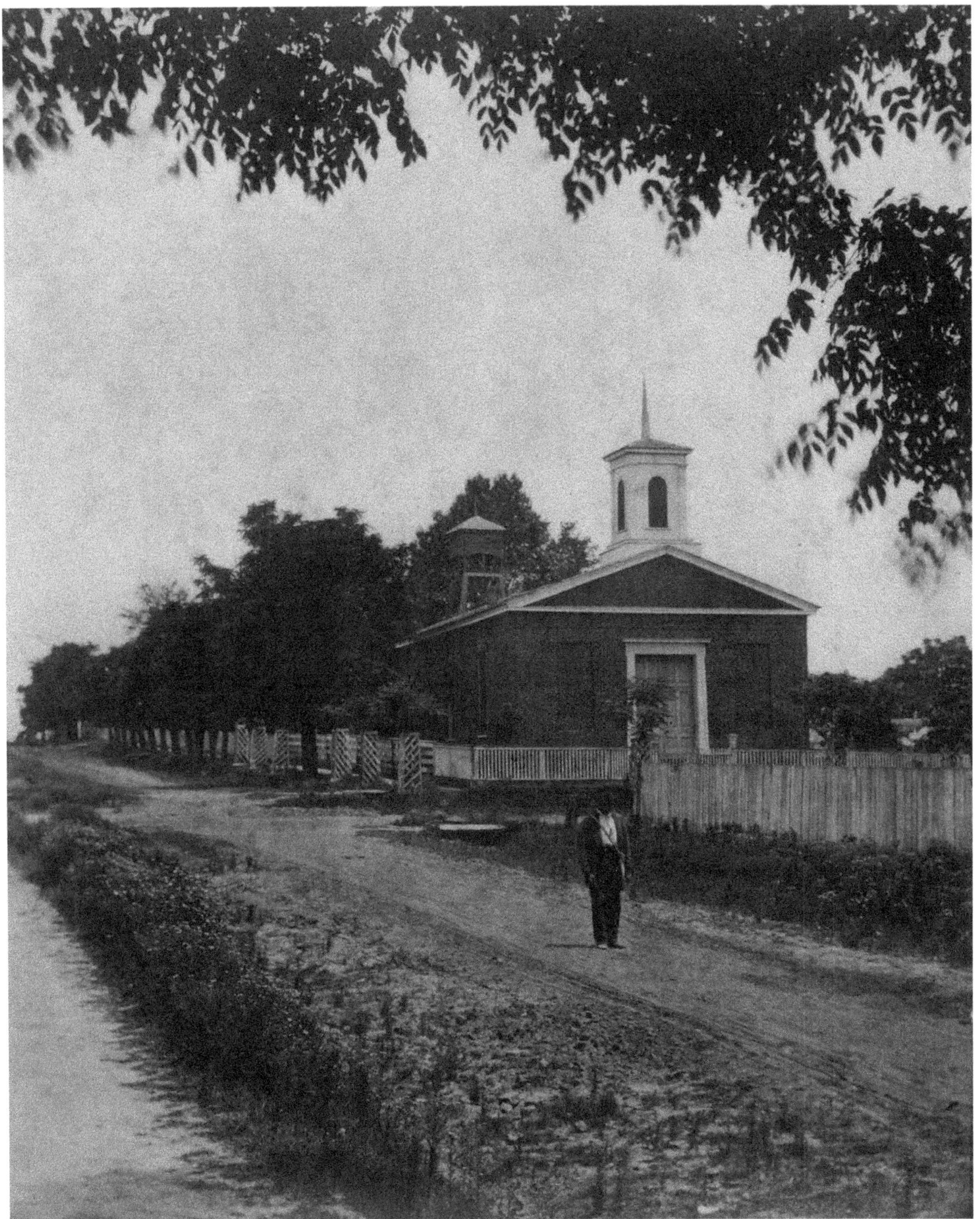

First Christian Church stood at the corner of Mississippi Street and North President Street in Jackson. Latticework enclosures protect saplings alongside the church from damage by careless horses.

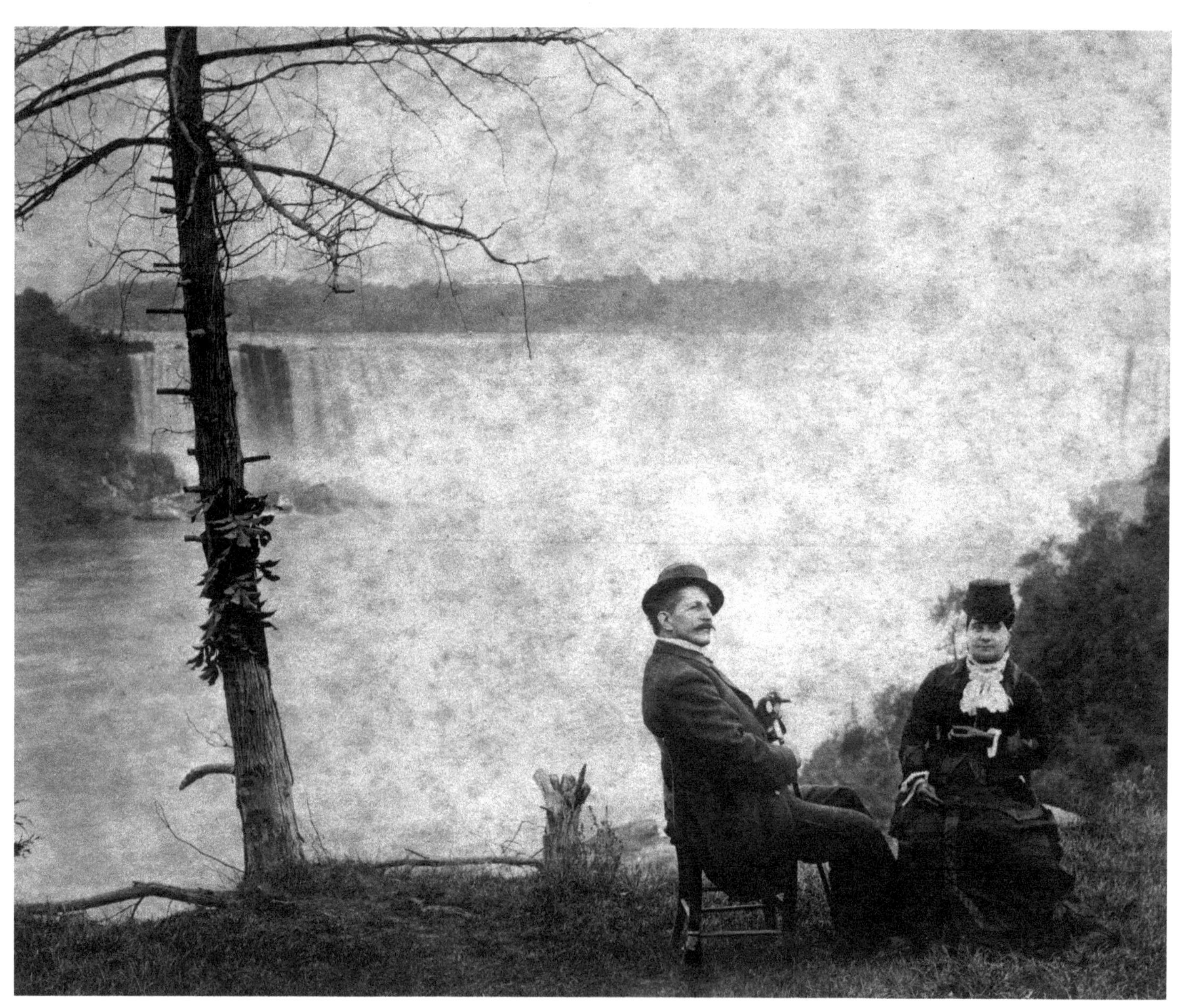

Jackson photographer Elisaeus von Seutter and Mrs. Von Seutter enjoy the vistas created by a large waterfall on September 10, 1880.

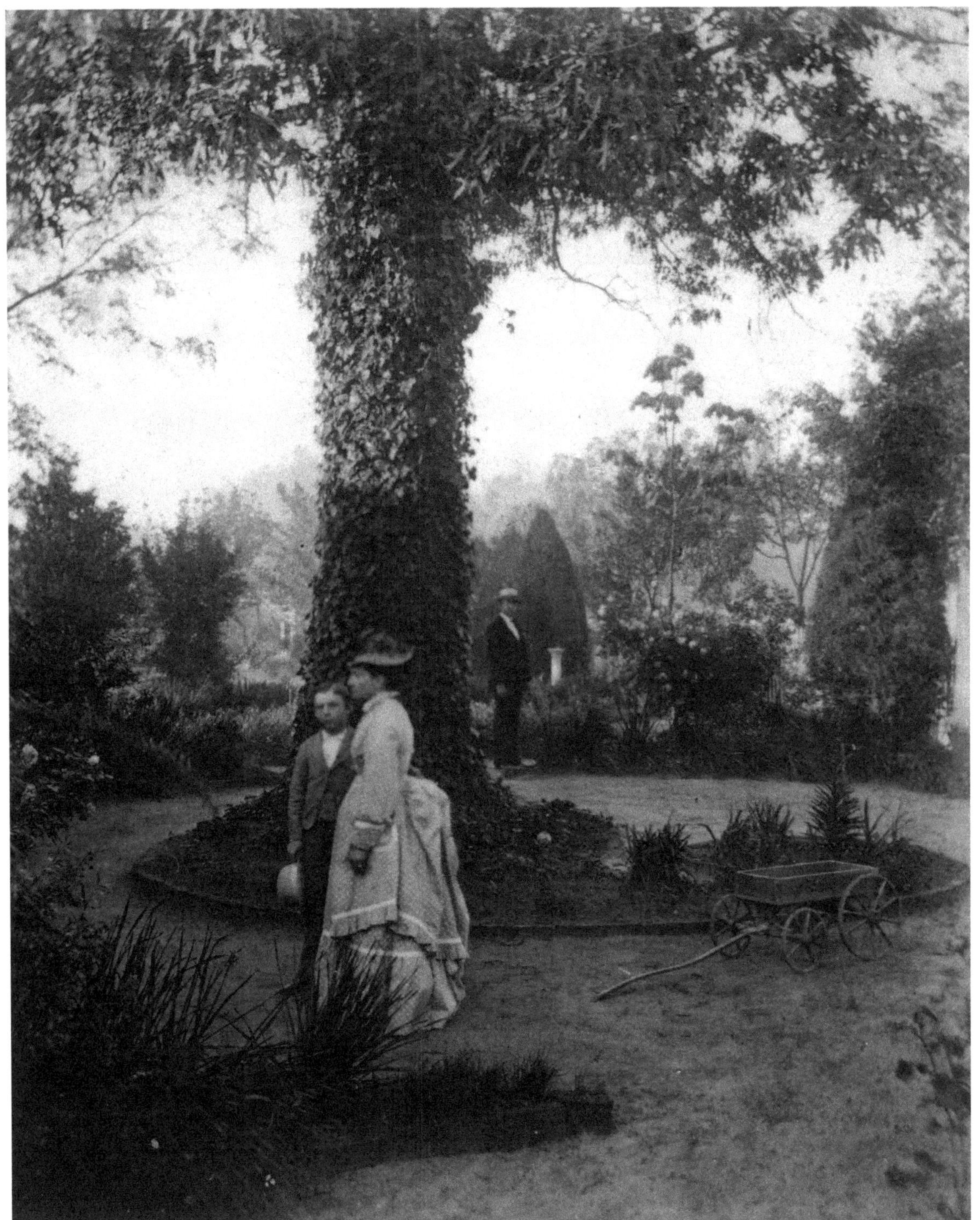

A picture-perfect view of the garden surrounding the home of Elisaeus von Seutter, who conducted business in Jackson during the mid to late 1800s. Locals enjoy the garden, where roses are blooming and ivy has covered a large oak tree.

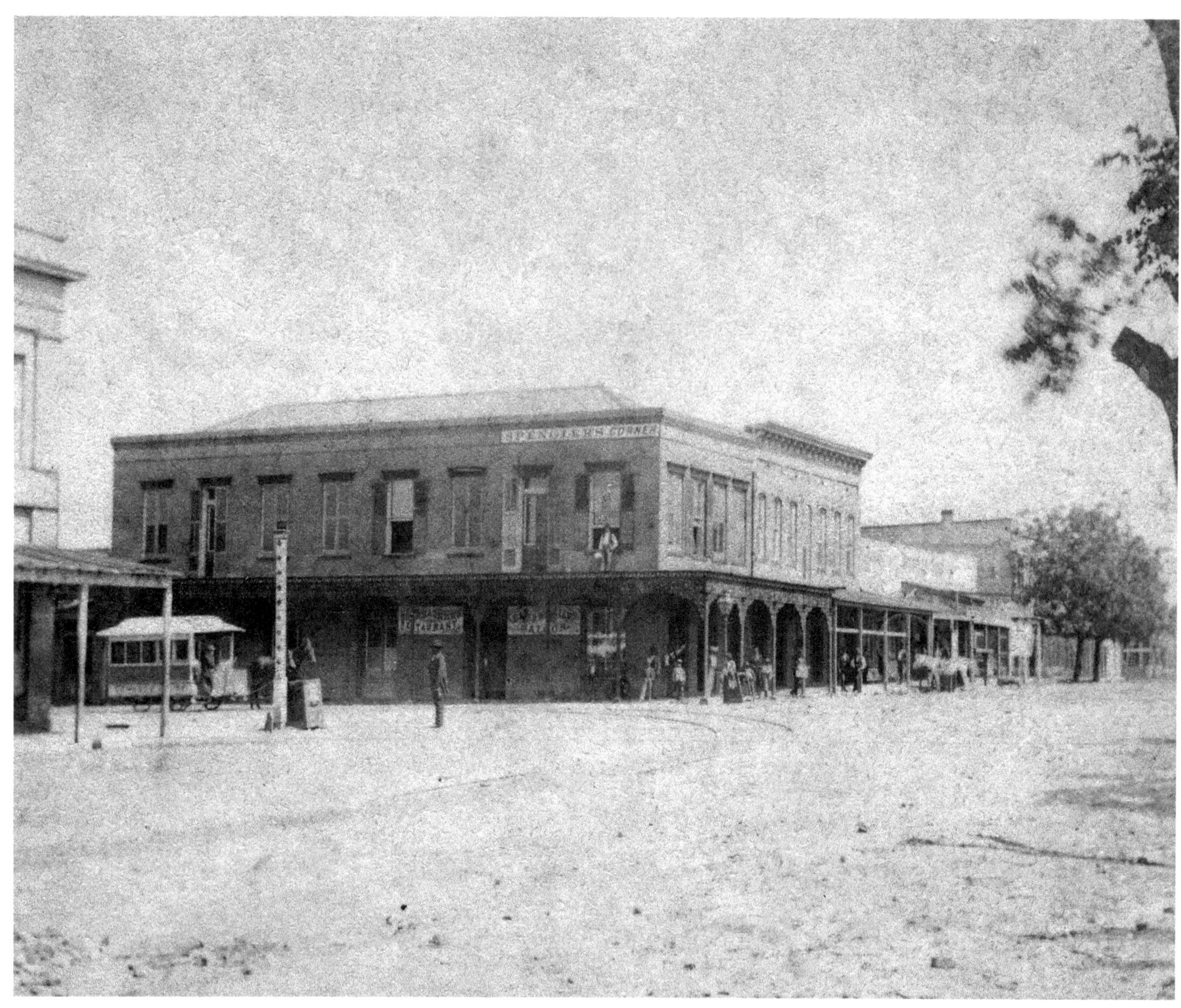

Spengler's Corner, at the northwest corner of State and Capital streets in Jackson. The Spengler brothers had opened a machine shop on State Street in 1858, lending their name to the corner.

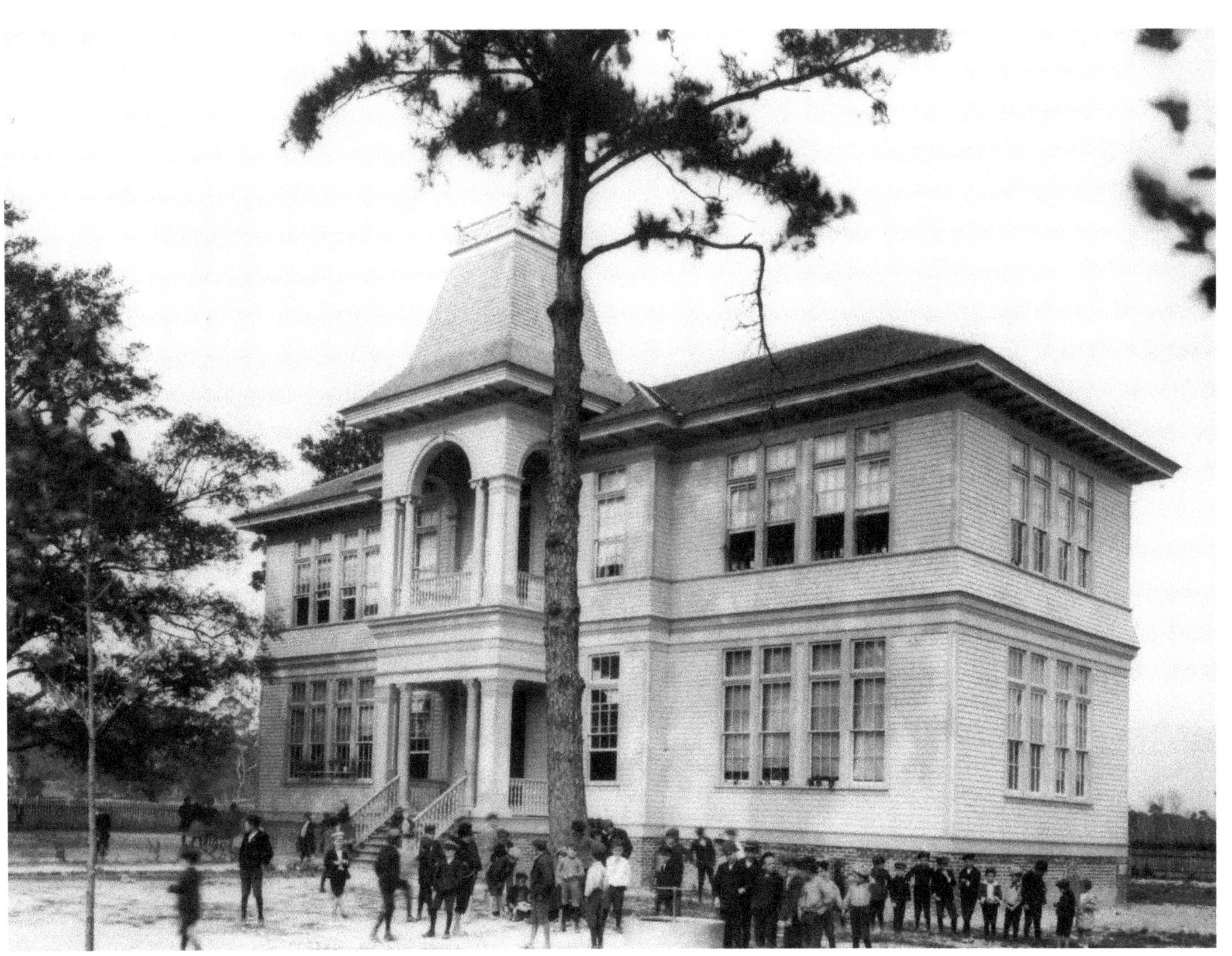

Between the years 1880 and 1910, the number of educational facilities in Mississippi increased rapidly. This two-story school, located at Biloxi in Harrison County, shows a large number of students milling about on the school grounds.

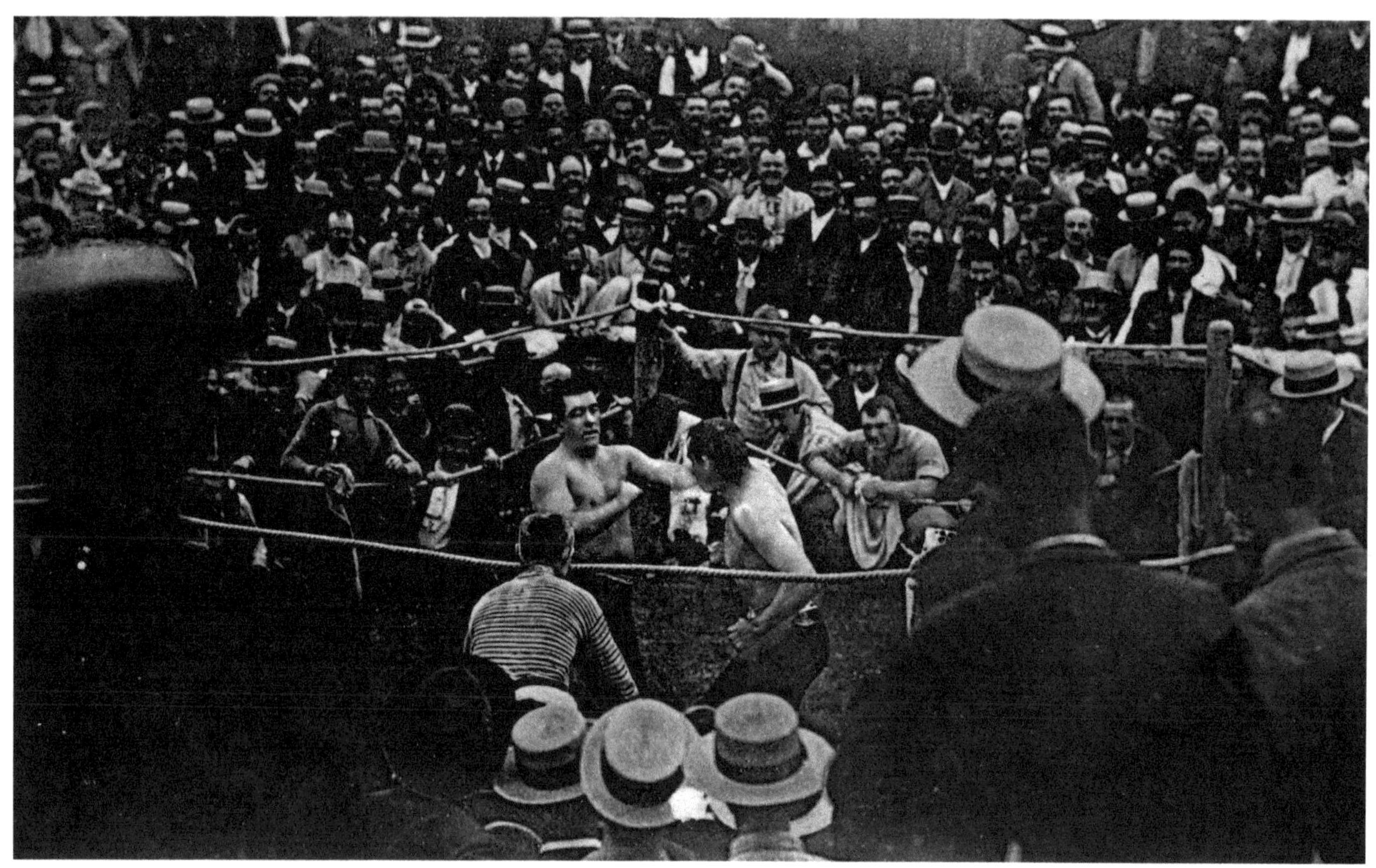

On July 8, 1889, sports history was made in the small sawmill community of Richburg in Lamar County. This was the site chosen for the last professional bare-knuckle championship boxing match in America, between heavyweight champion John L. Sullivan and the challenger, Jake Kilrain. Sullivan refused to sit between rounds, saying it was pointless: "I got to get right up again, ain't I?" After 75 rounds, Sullivan was declared the victor. The boxer became America's first national sports celebrity and the first athlete to earn more than a million dollars.

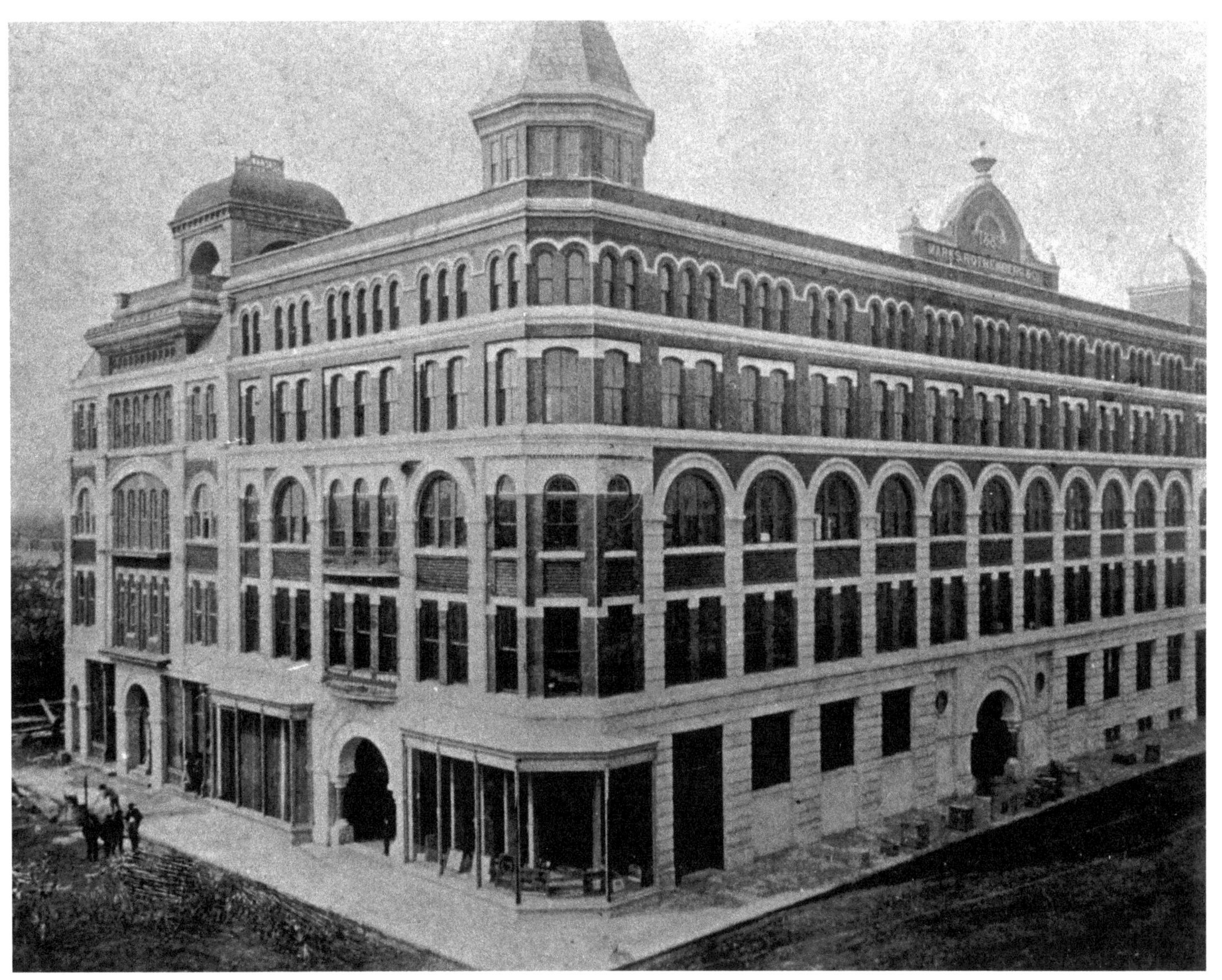

Meridian, in Lauderdale County, experienced a boom in the aftermath of the Civil War and enjoyed a golden age around the turn of the century. Between 1890 and 1930, Meridian was the largest city in Mississippi and a merchandising center. Marks Rothenberg, which did business in the impressive department store shown here, was a leading retailer.

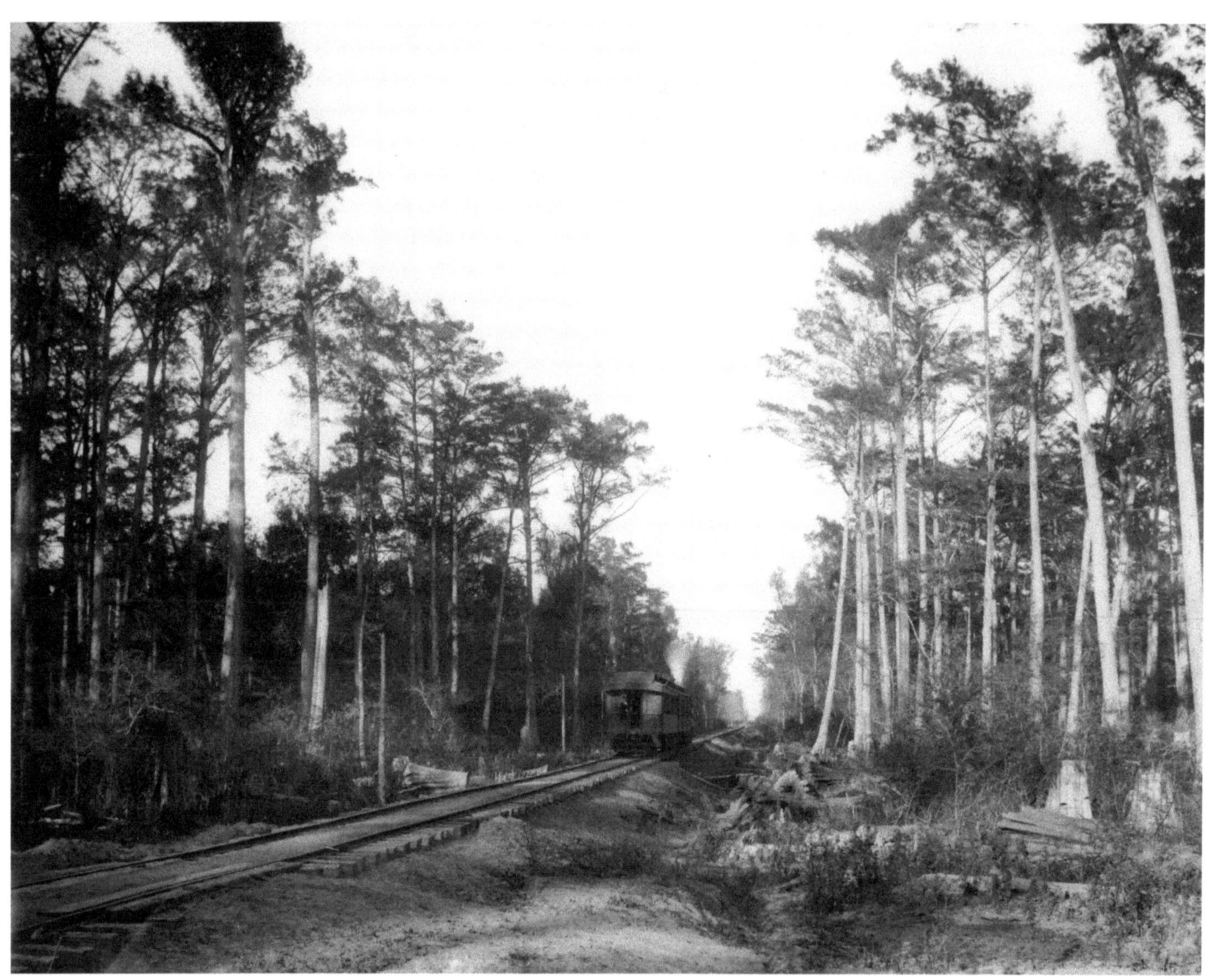

An early vintage passenger train steams through an old-grove Mississippi cypress forest, as a lone passenger gazes at the tranquil beauty of the receding scenery from the platform of the observation car. The cypress has long been admired for its majestic stature and longevity.

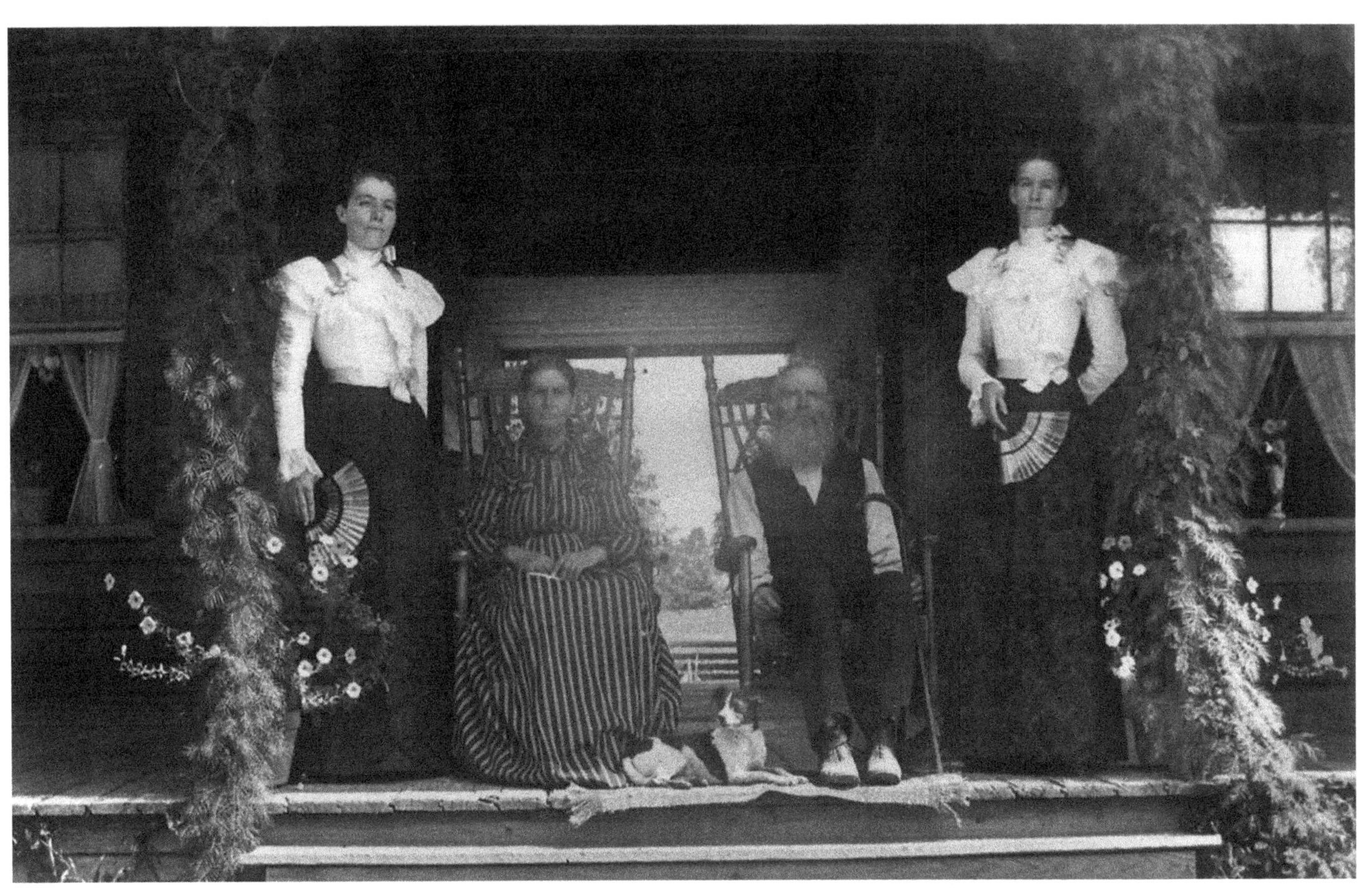

The lovely Kittrell sisters stand for a family portrait beside Mom and Dad on the front porch of their east central Mississippi home in 1889. To each side are potted petunias and what appears to be the red-flowering cypress vine, both annuals still popular among gardeners today.

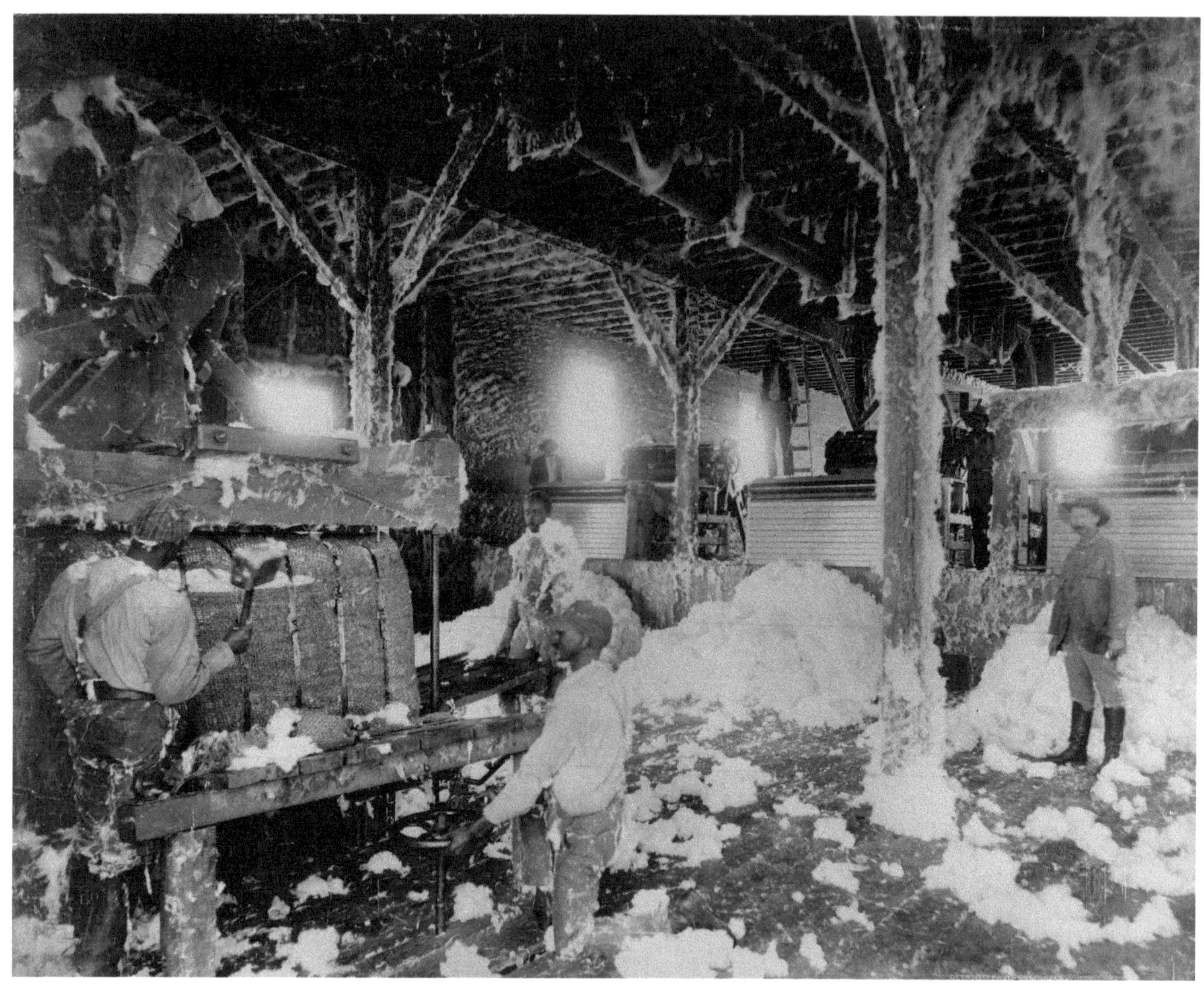

Workers in the Bolivar County town of Dahomey refine cotton in 1890 using a cotton gin. Cotton remained a mainstay of agriculture in the state long after the Civil War ended, aided by labor-saving devices like the gin. With cotton fibers clinging to everything in this image, state fair goers may derive a much greater appreciation for a state fair favorite—cotton candy—so aptly named.

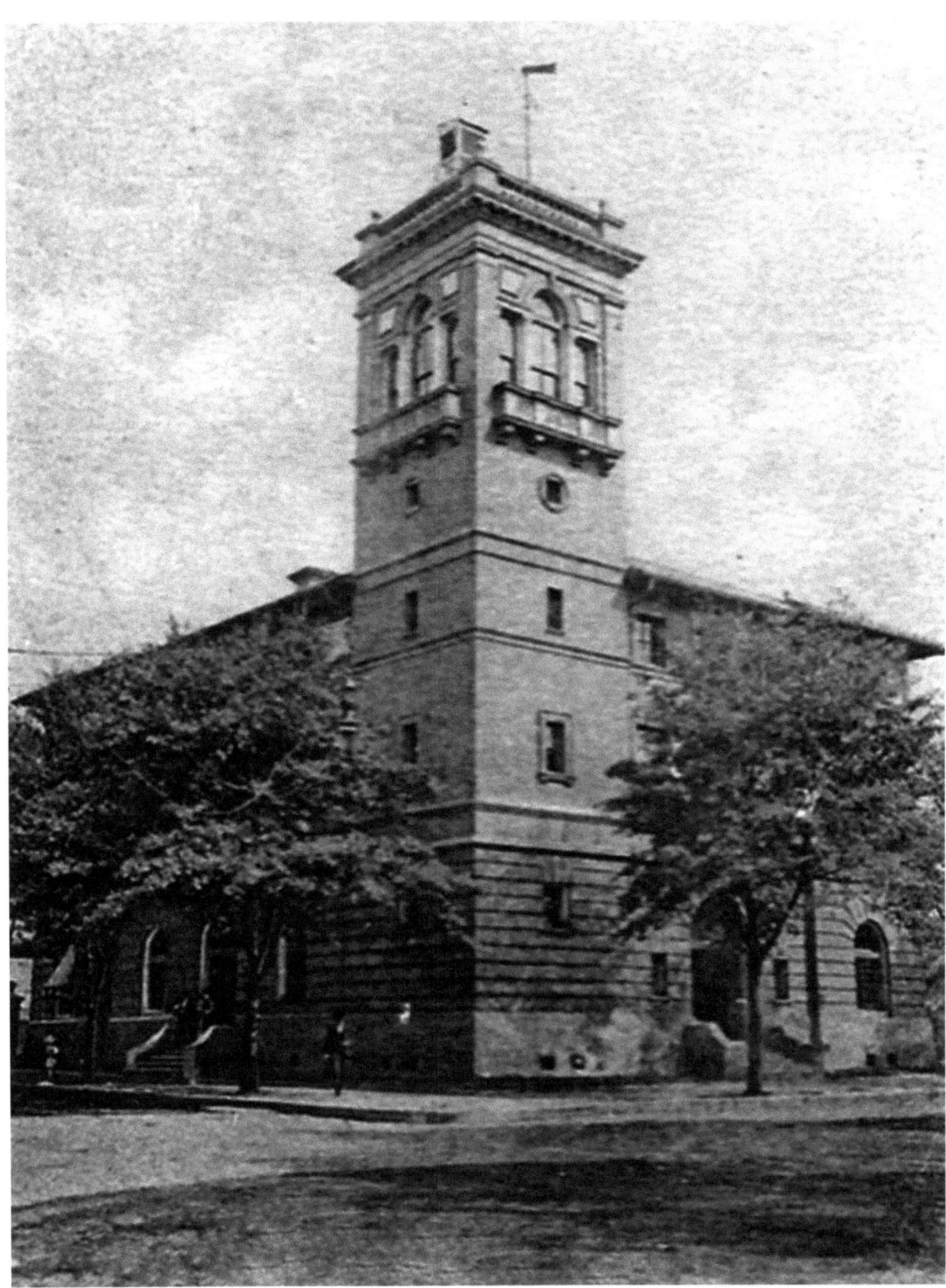

The Federal Building and Post Office at Meridian opened December 30, 1897.

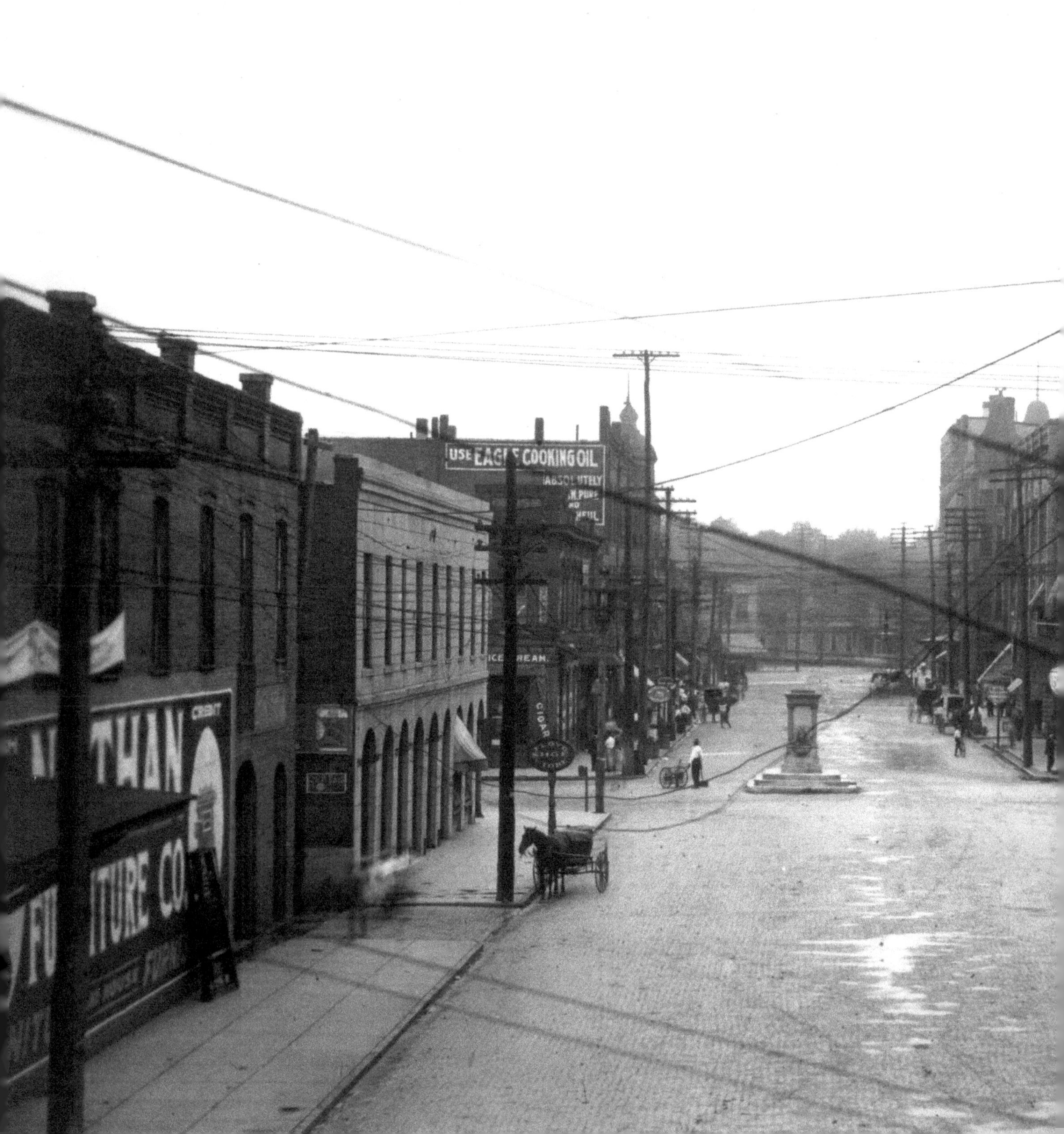
USE EAGLE COOKING OIL
ICE CREAM
CIGAR
CREDIT
ITURE CO.

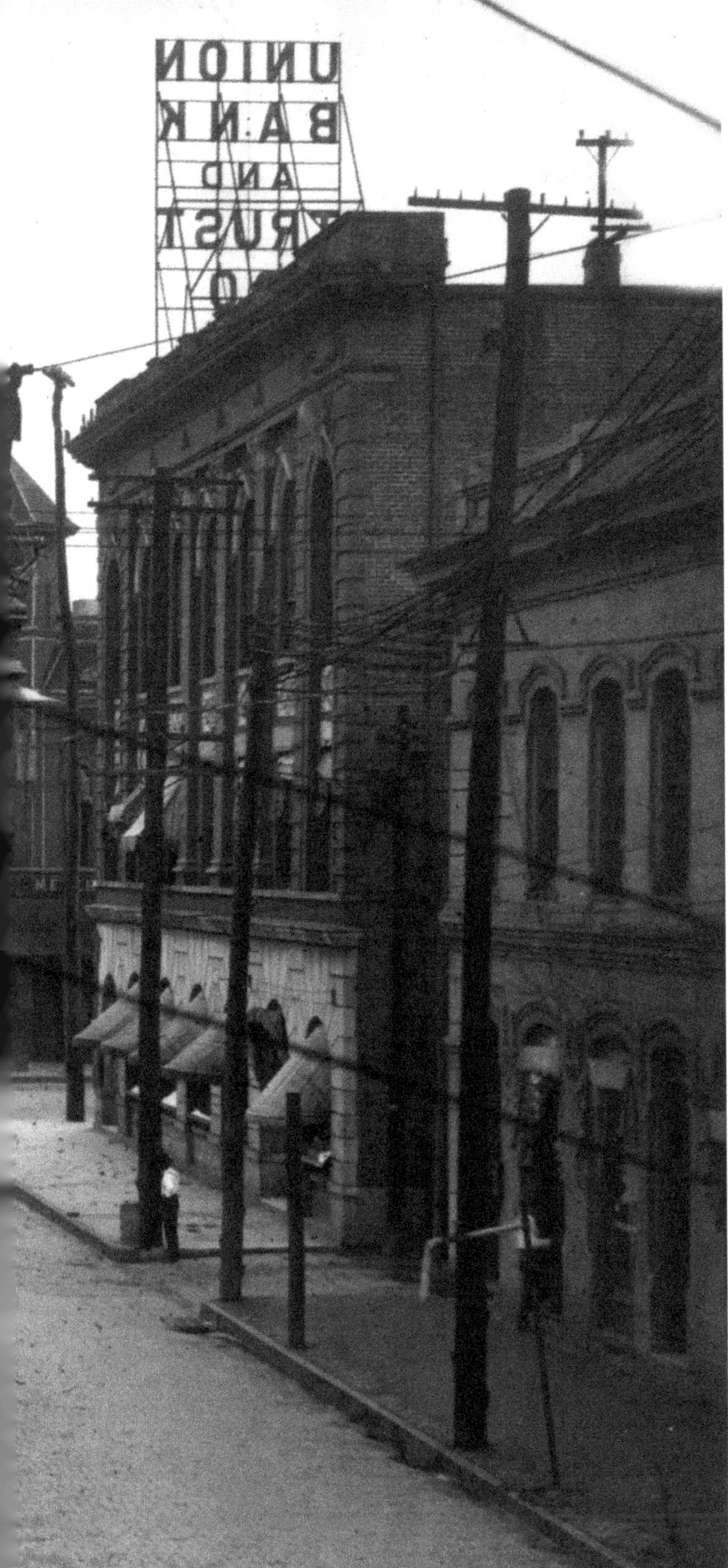

Downtown Meridian early on a morning in the late 1800s. An artesian well adorns the center of the street as a street sweeper pushes his cart and broom. Electricity was a new reality for the east central Mississippi city, and power lines are visible everywhere crisscrossing and dangling from power poles to buildings.

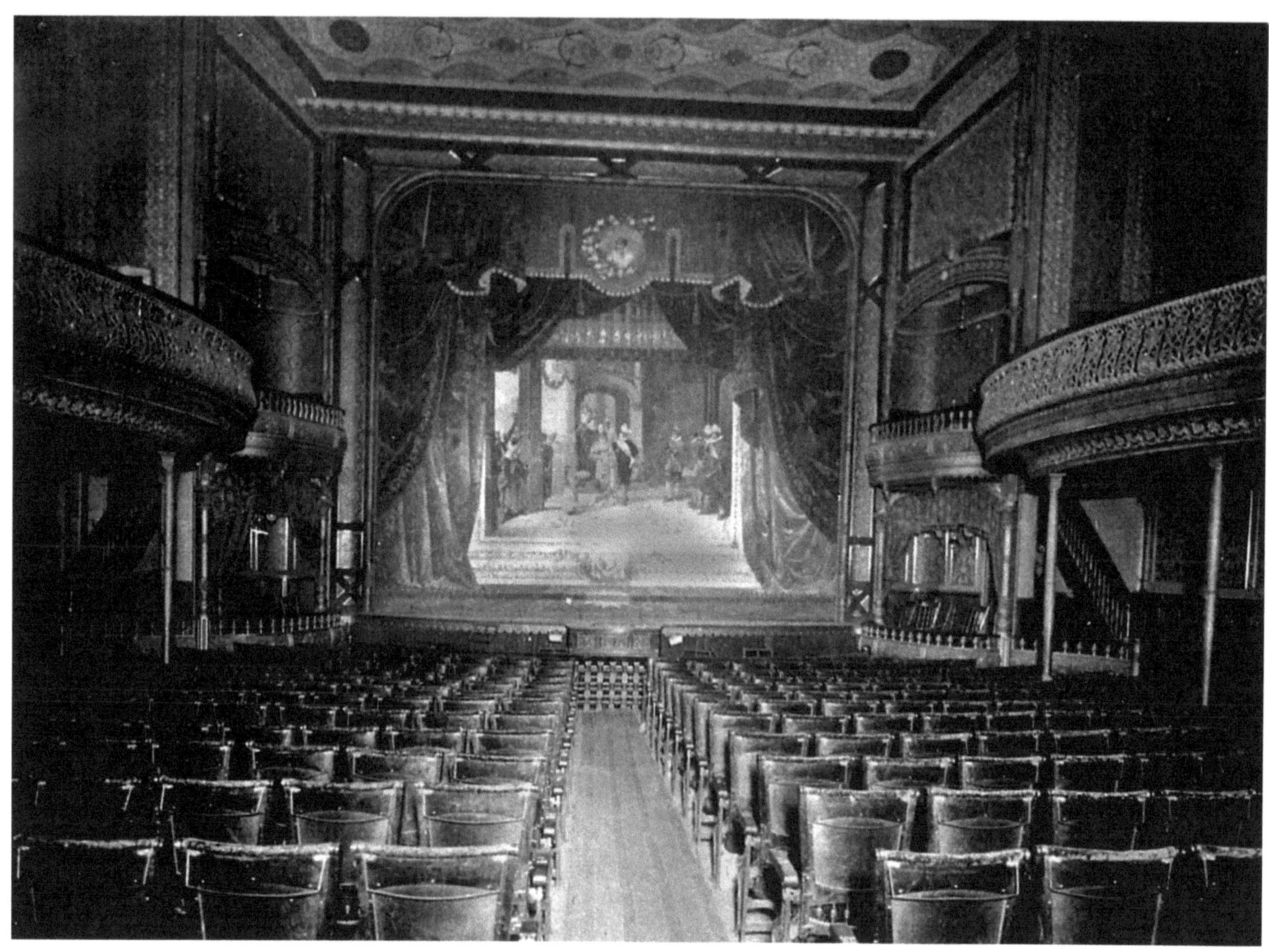

The original 1890 stage of the Grand Opera House in Meridian. At 30 feet wide by 50 feet deep, the stage could accommodate the largest, most lavish shows from New York. Under the 35-foot-high arched proscenium was an ornate painted border, which featured the famous "Lady." The Lady eventually became the symbol of the Opera House.

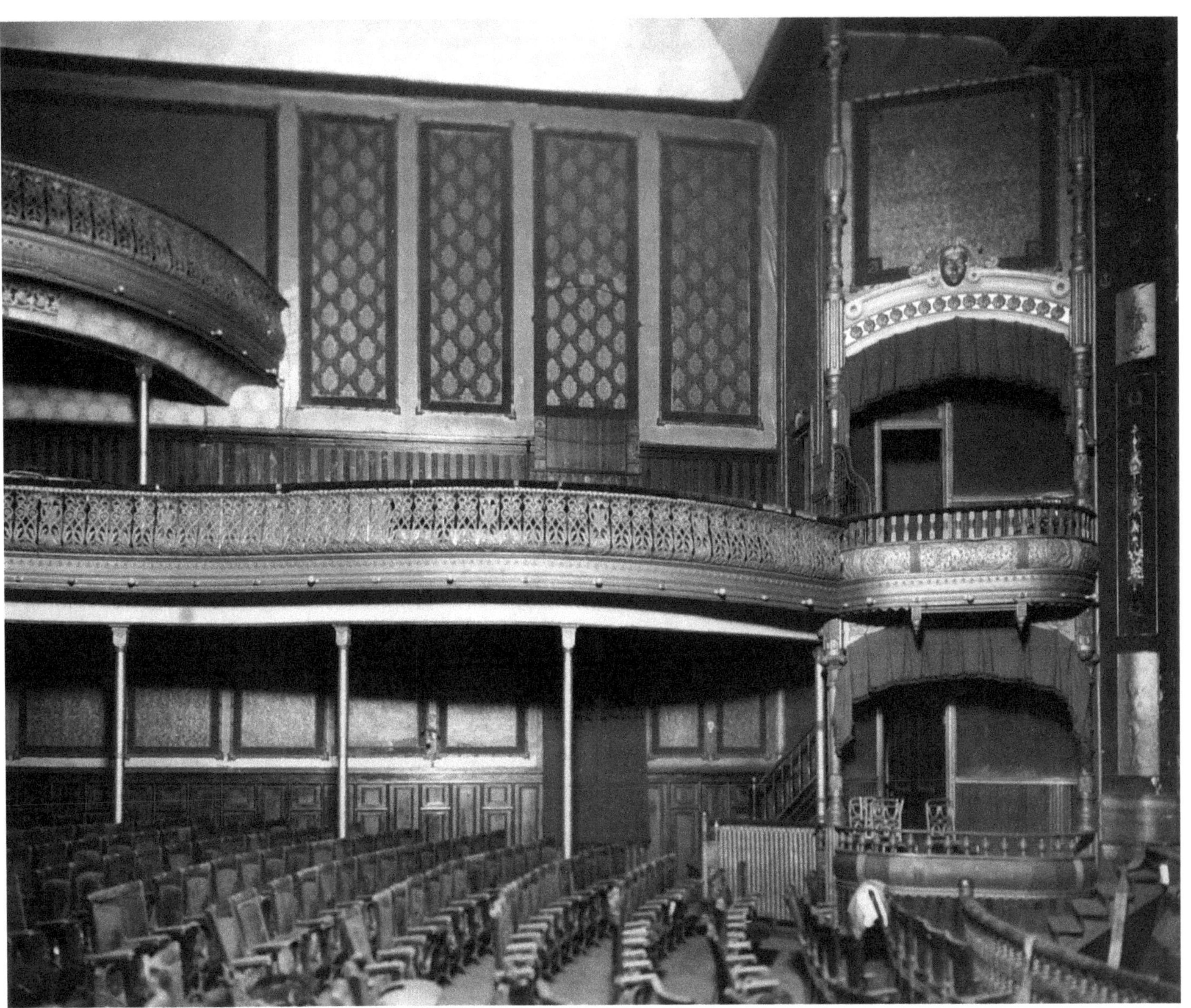

The Grand Opera House was a center for the arts of east central Mississippi. Its inaugural performance was held December 17, 1890, with the impressive opening act of Johann Strauss's *The Gypsy Baron*. The firm J. B. McElfatrick of New York designed the interior. McElfatrick designed more than 200 theaters across the United States, including the Metropolitan Opera House of Philadelphia.

Wagonloads of cotton and other freight are hauled to the levee at Vicksburg, for river transport north and south on the Misissippi River. The *Falls City,* in the foreground, and other steamboats are anchored wharfside awaiting cargo.

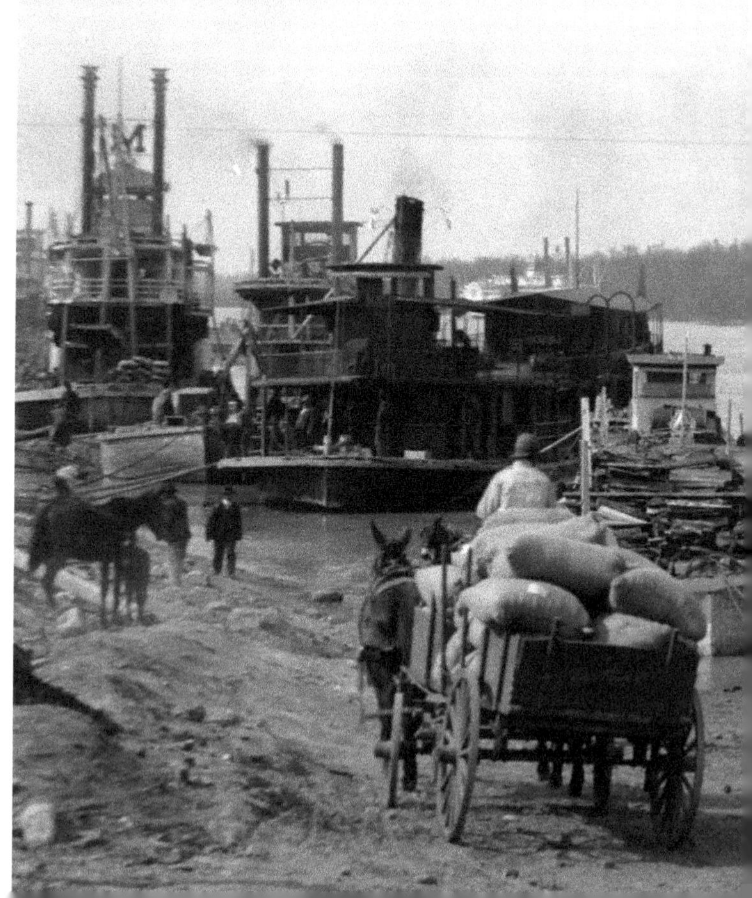

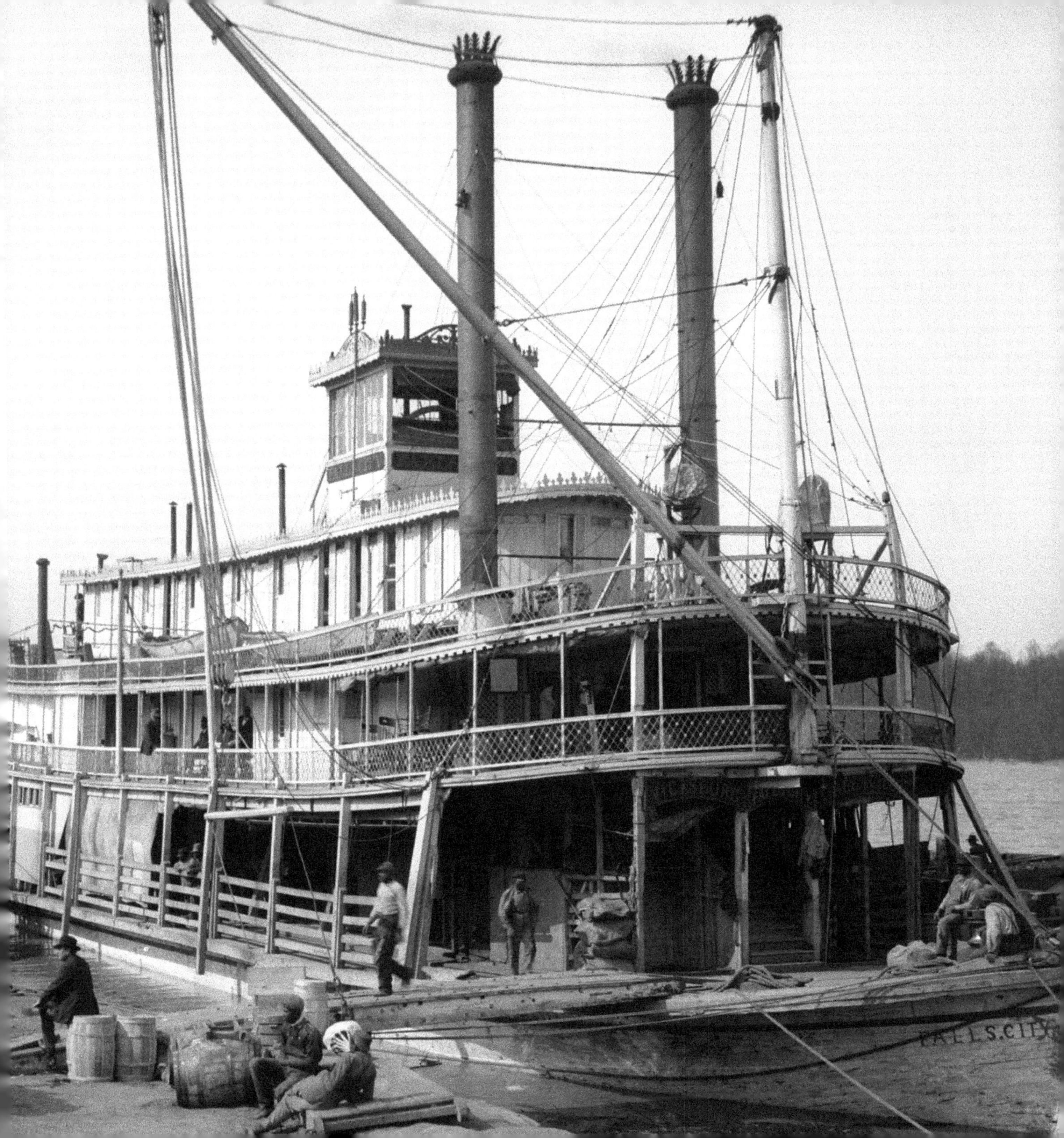
FALLS.CITY

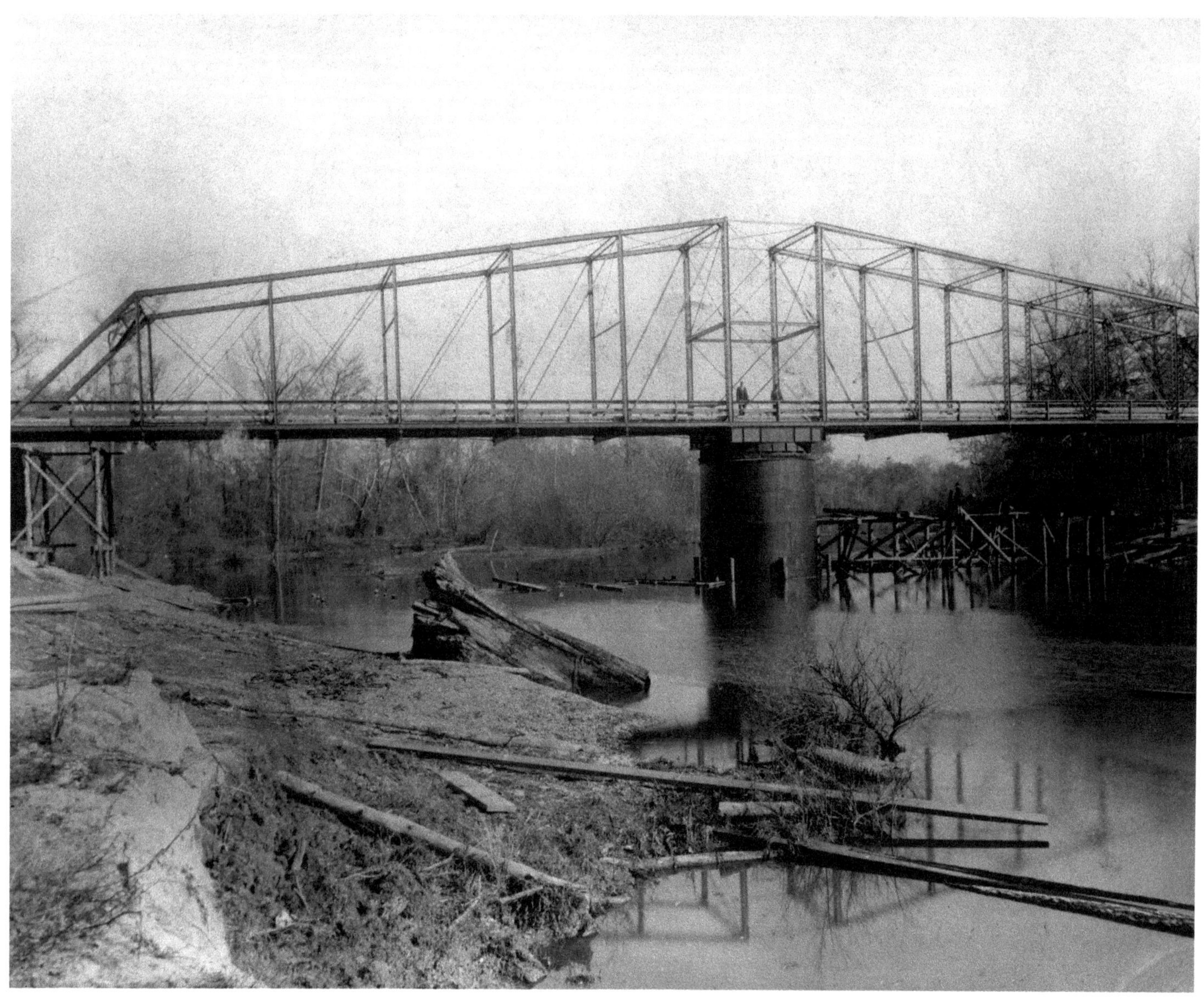

The Old Amory-Bigbee Bridge, in Monroe County, soon after completion in 1899. The swing bridge spanned the Tombigbee River, part of a regional transportation network of bridges built between 1880 and World War II that relied on techniques devised for bridges built to span the Mississippi River.

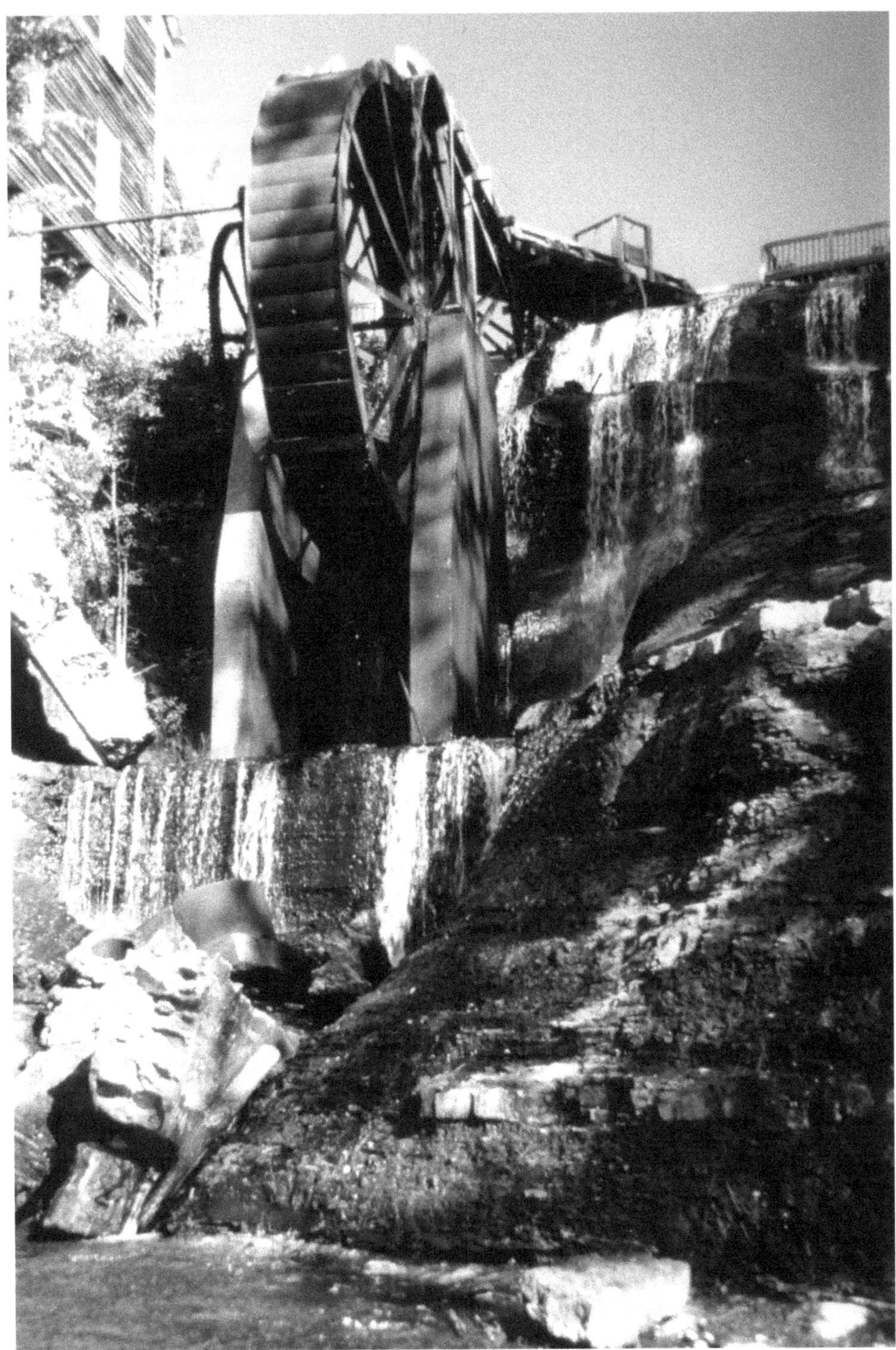

Beautiful Dunn's Falls, a 65-foot waterfall shown here in the late 1800s, was once used as the power source for a gristmill. The falls is located on the Chunky River at Enterprise, in Clarke County. John B. Stetson learned the trade of hat-making here, honing the skill that would make his brand famous.

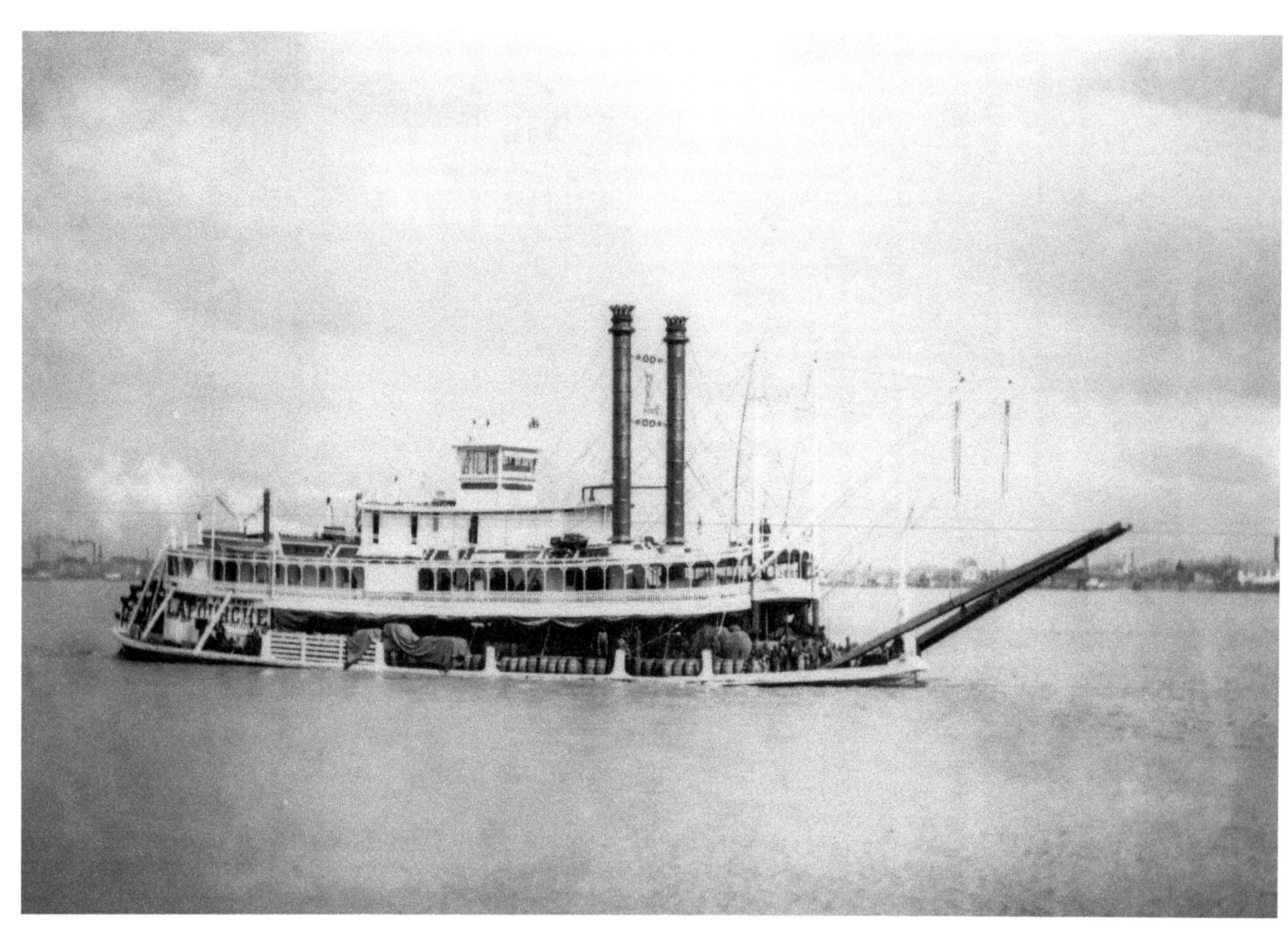

Laden with freight, the stern-wheeler *Lafourche* plies the mighty Mississippi River in 1898.

The Joy of the Golden Age

(1900–1919)

Mississippi novelist Eudora Welty said, "The excursion is the same when you go looking for your sorrow as when you go looking for your joy." Mississippi had seen the sorrow, and by 1900 it was time for joy. Some have said that Mississippi rode the rails to progress, which is partly true. The railroads were overwhelmingly important to Mississippi's recovery following the Civil War. Just as important, however, were timber and cotton.

As the state blossomed economically, socially, and culturally, Mississippi entered its golden age of prosperity. The trend would steadily continue until the Great Depression. Between 1890 and 1900, the miracle of electricity had modernized the state, and individual towns installed sewer systems, paved roads, and sidewalks. New industry in the form of foundries, factories, machine shops, and all categories of merchandising also began to flourish.

With the new flow of money, the supply of services and goods rose, which prompted the opening of additional banks throughout the state, and with the rise in the quality of goods that were readily available to citizens, civic improvements were on the increase. Parks and theaters opened, followed by educational institutions for blacks and whites through public schools and higher education. By the 1900s, as the Mississippi public school system organized schoolhouses across the state, education was an opportunity not just for the children of the wealthy, but for the children of the average worker.

With music, drama, athletics, education, entertainment, and jobs that permitted Mississippians to enjoy more than just the necessities of life, citizens of the state would enjoy a lengthy run of good times. The literary world in particular would benefit. The playwright Tennessee Williams, born in Columbus in 1911, would rise to prominence with *Cat on a Hot Tin Roof* and *The Glass Menagerie.*

In 1918, World War I would require the service of Americans everywhere, and more than a few of them came through Camp Shelby at Hattiesburg.

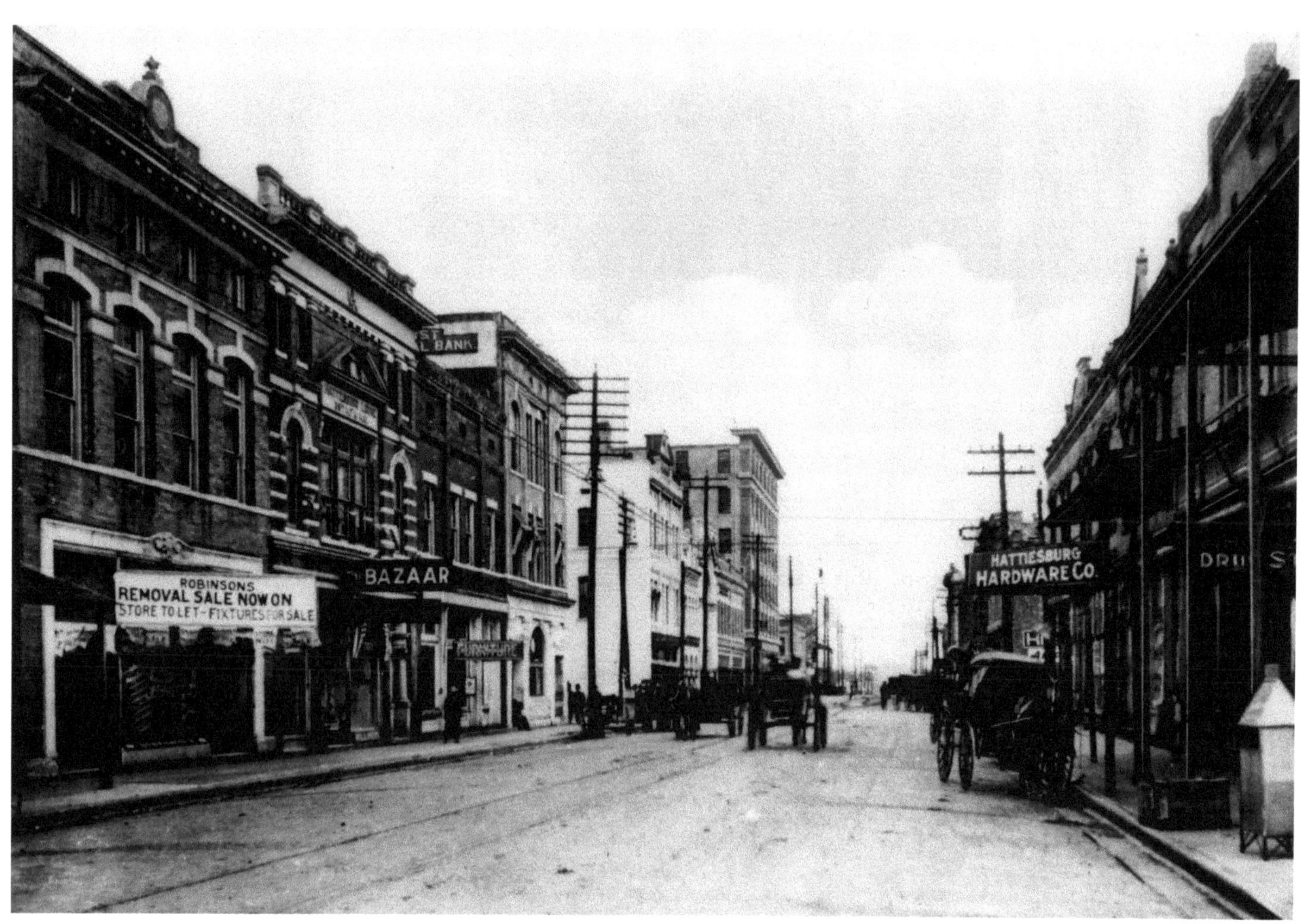

Main Street in Hattiesburg, in Forrest County, as it appeared during the early 1900s. The town was incorporated in 1884 when the Southern Railway system was built from Meridian to New Orleans, passing through the hamlet known originally as Twin Forks and later as Gordonville. Captain William H. Hardy, a local pioneer lumberman, civil engineer, and early settler, contributed the final name of Hattiesburg in honor of his wife, Hattie.

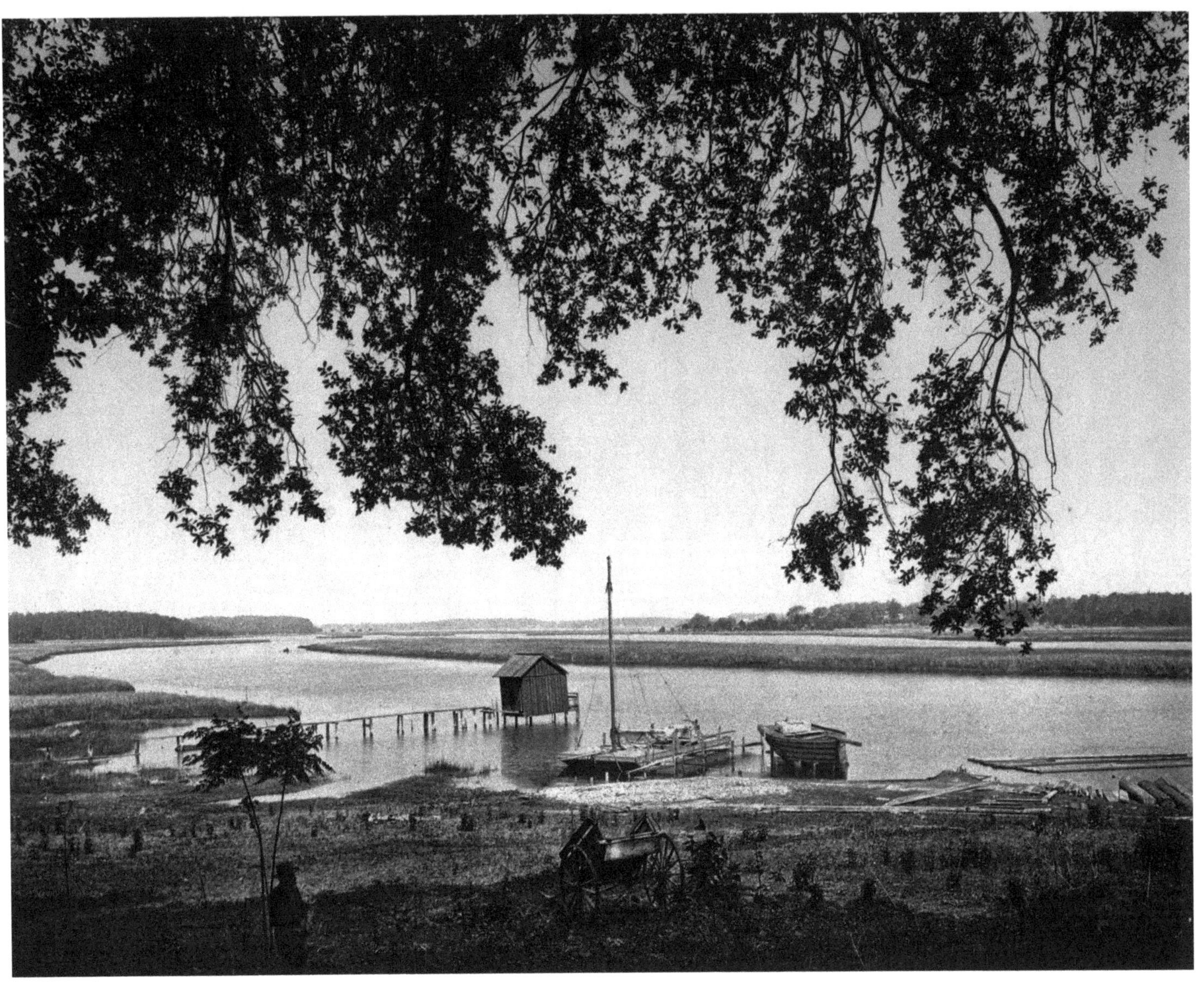

The site of Old Fort Bayou, at Ocean Springs in Jackson County, as it appeared in 1901. Mineral springs were discovered in the 1850s and a sanatorium was built. Ocean Springs was founded as Fort Maurepas by the French in 1699, to discourage the Spanish from encroaching on French territories in the new world.

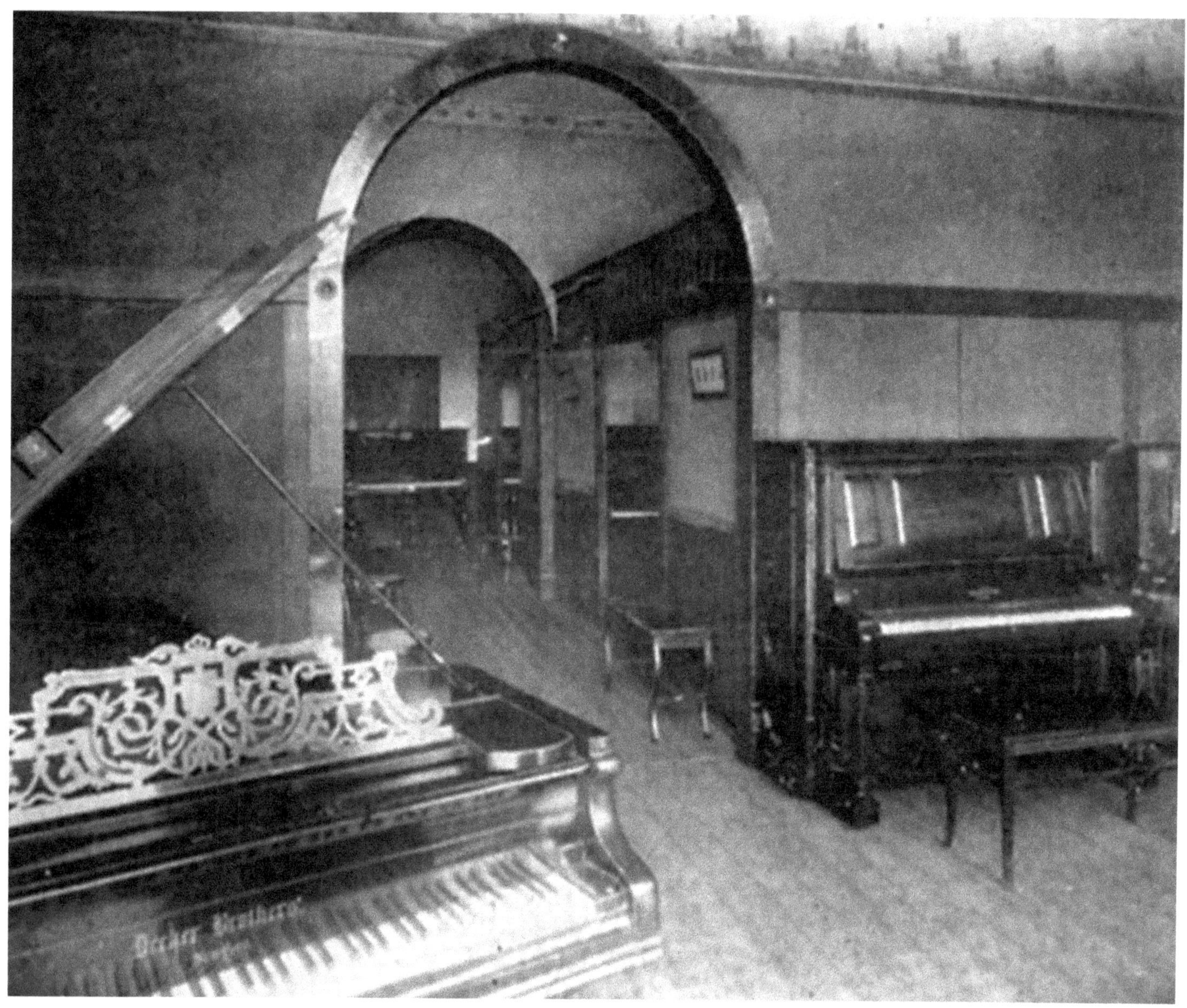

The study of music was of exceptional importance during the golden age of Mississippi, and piano parlors were very popular. This parlor was photographed in the early 1900s in Meridian.

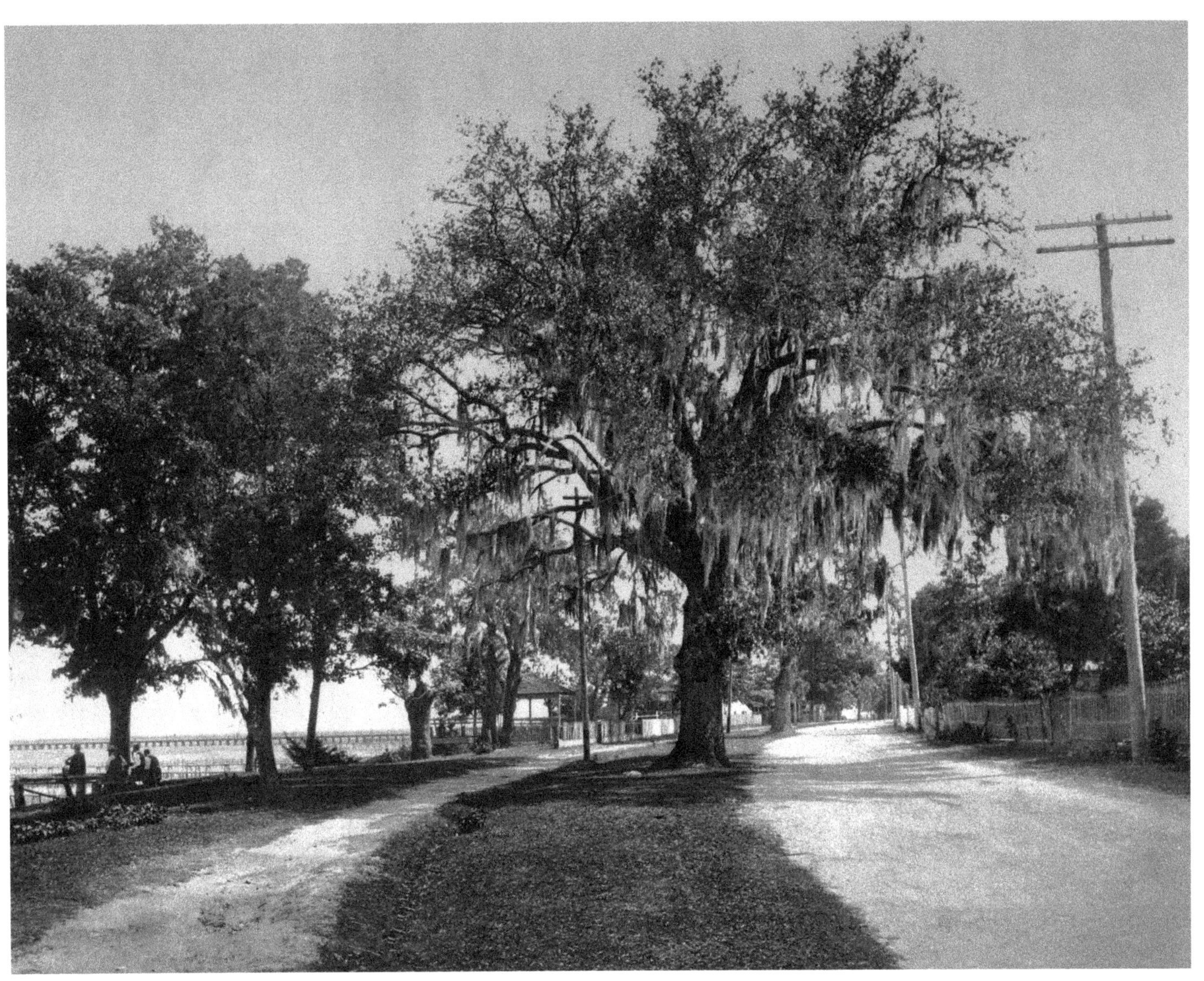

An early 1900s view of the charming beachside at Bay St. Louis in Hancock County. Locals gaze toward the bay, accessible by a long pier visible in the distance. The town was named for King Louis IX of France.

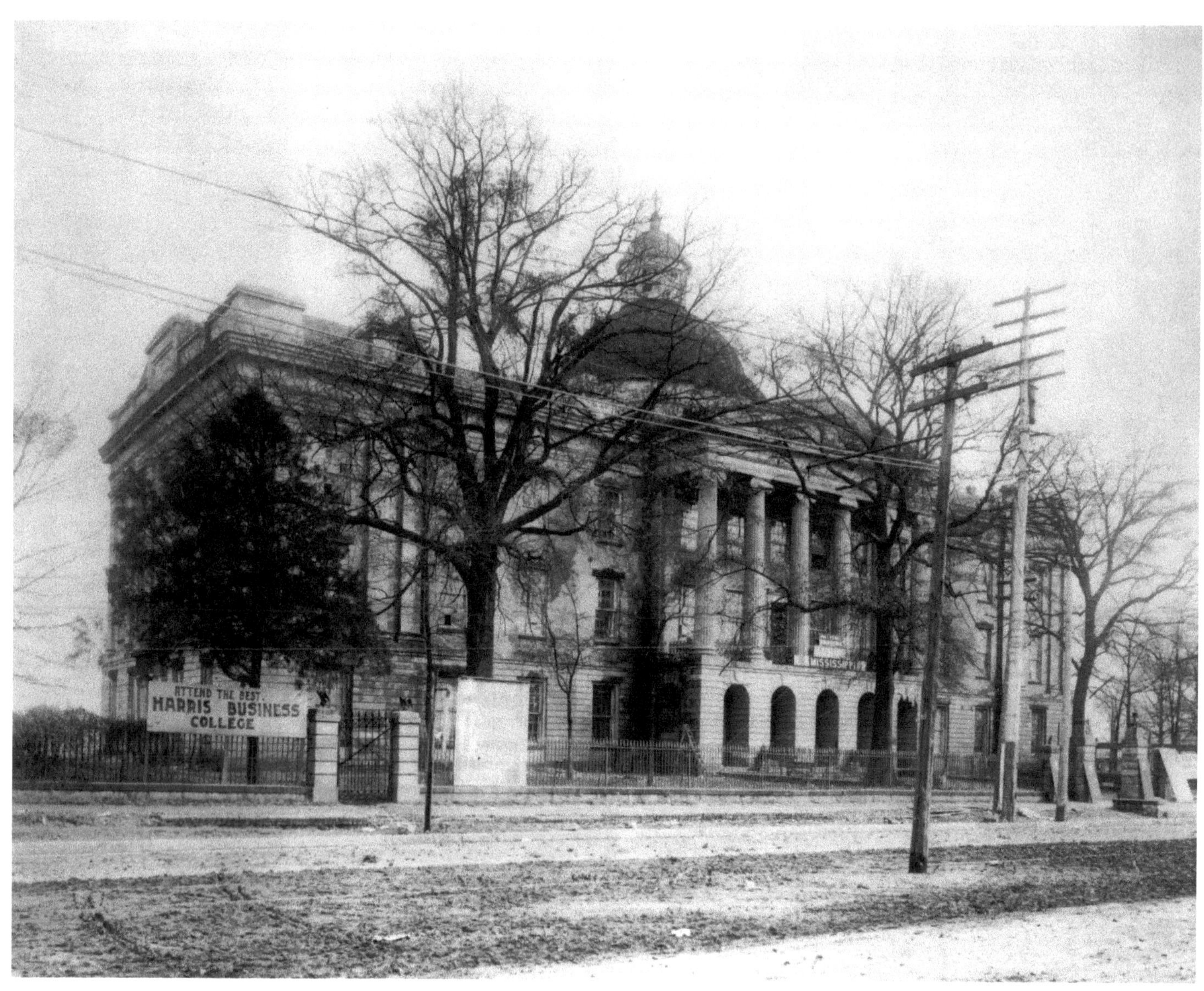

The Old Capitol at Jackson, in Hinds County. Jackson remains the state capital and is named for the seventh president of the United States, Andrew Jackson. The Old Capitol served as the home of the Mississippi state legislature from 1839 to 1903.

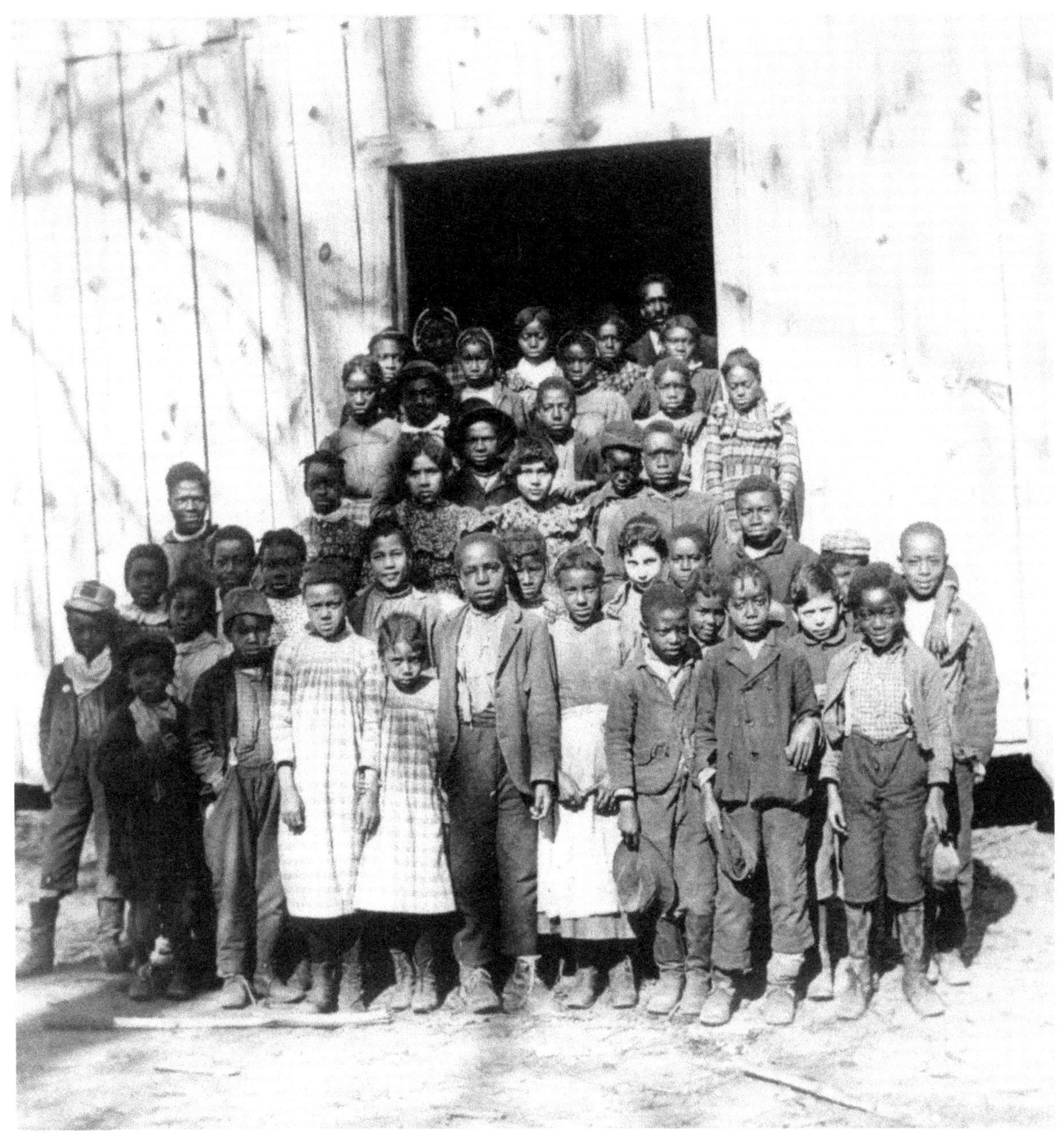

Class photo day at the Sykes Chapel School, an early African-American school. These early 1900s students have filed out of the building for the group portrait.

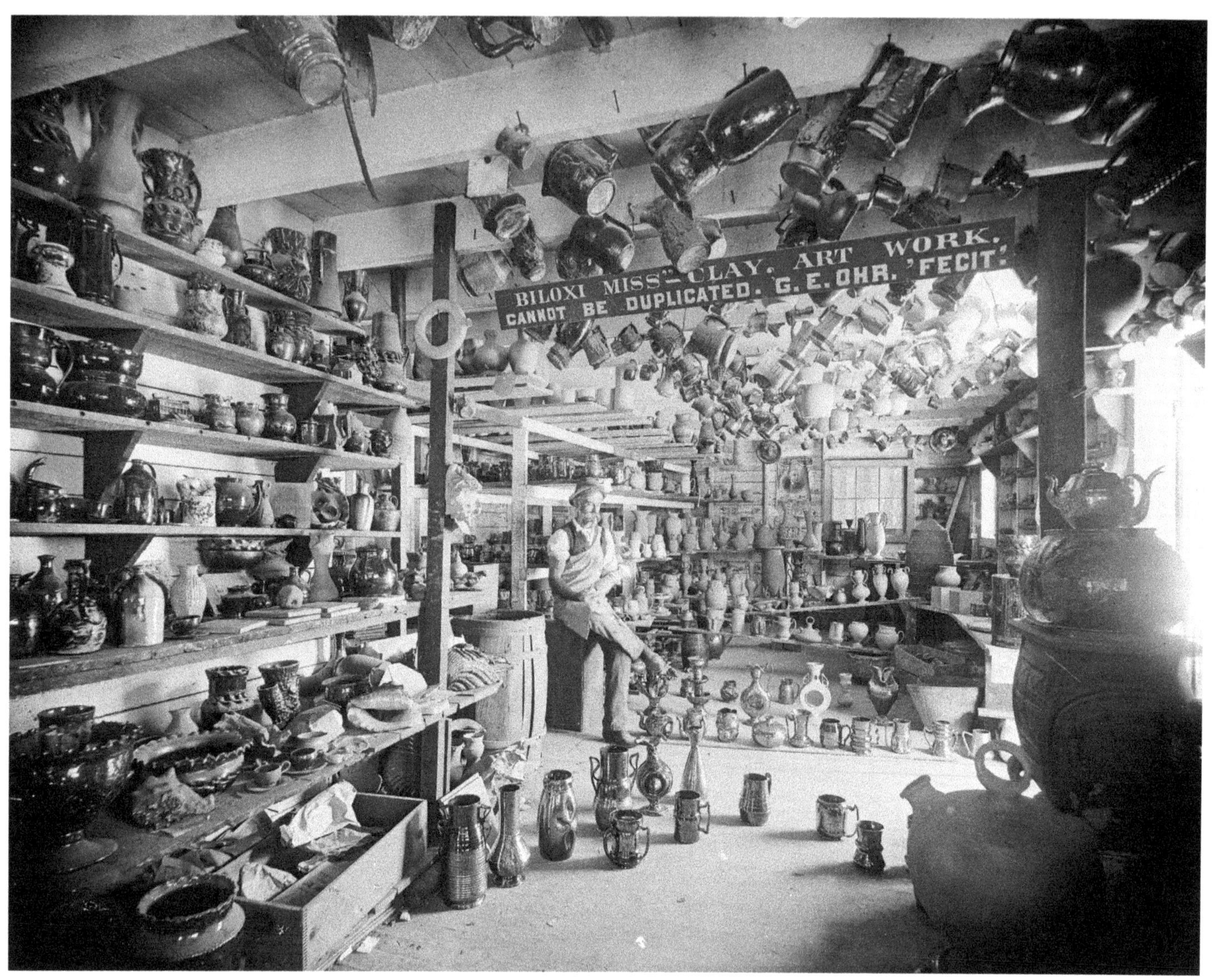

George Ohr is shown here in 1901 at his pottery shop in Biloxi. Examples of his work fill the studio. Ohr's works were one-of-a-kind, as unique as his one-of-a-kind handlebar moustache.

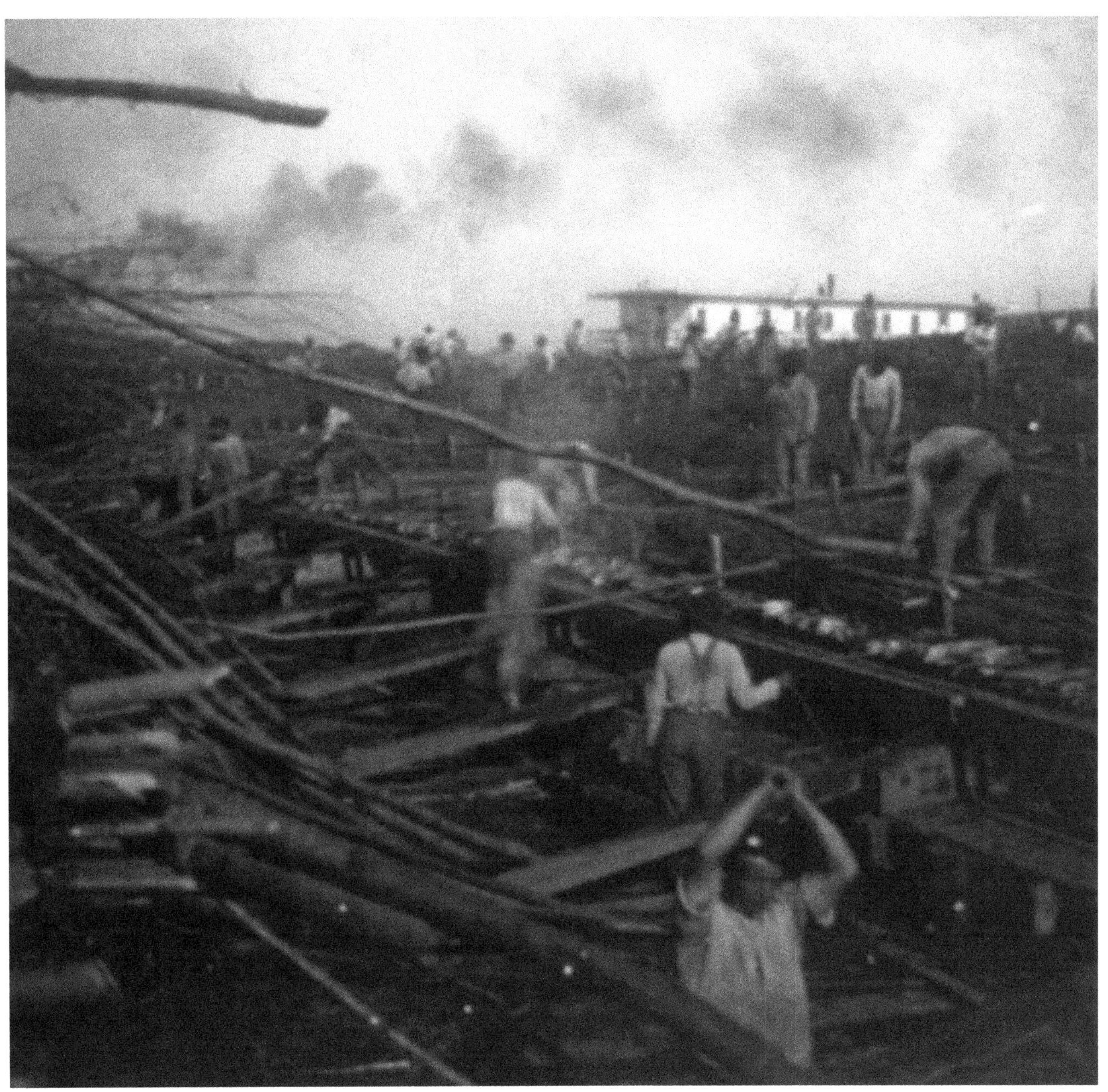

Men at work in the Mississippi River Delta are building a jetty mat in the early 1900s. The area, named Southwest Pass, was the main shipping channel, developed by the French as early as 1699. Jetty mats were a kind of dry dock for boats, makeshift and temporary.

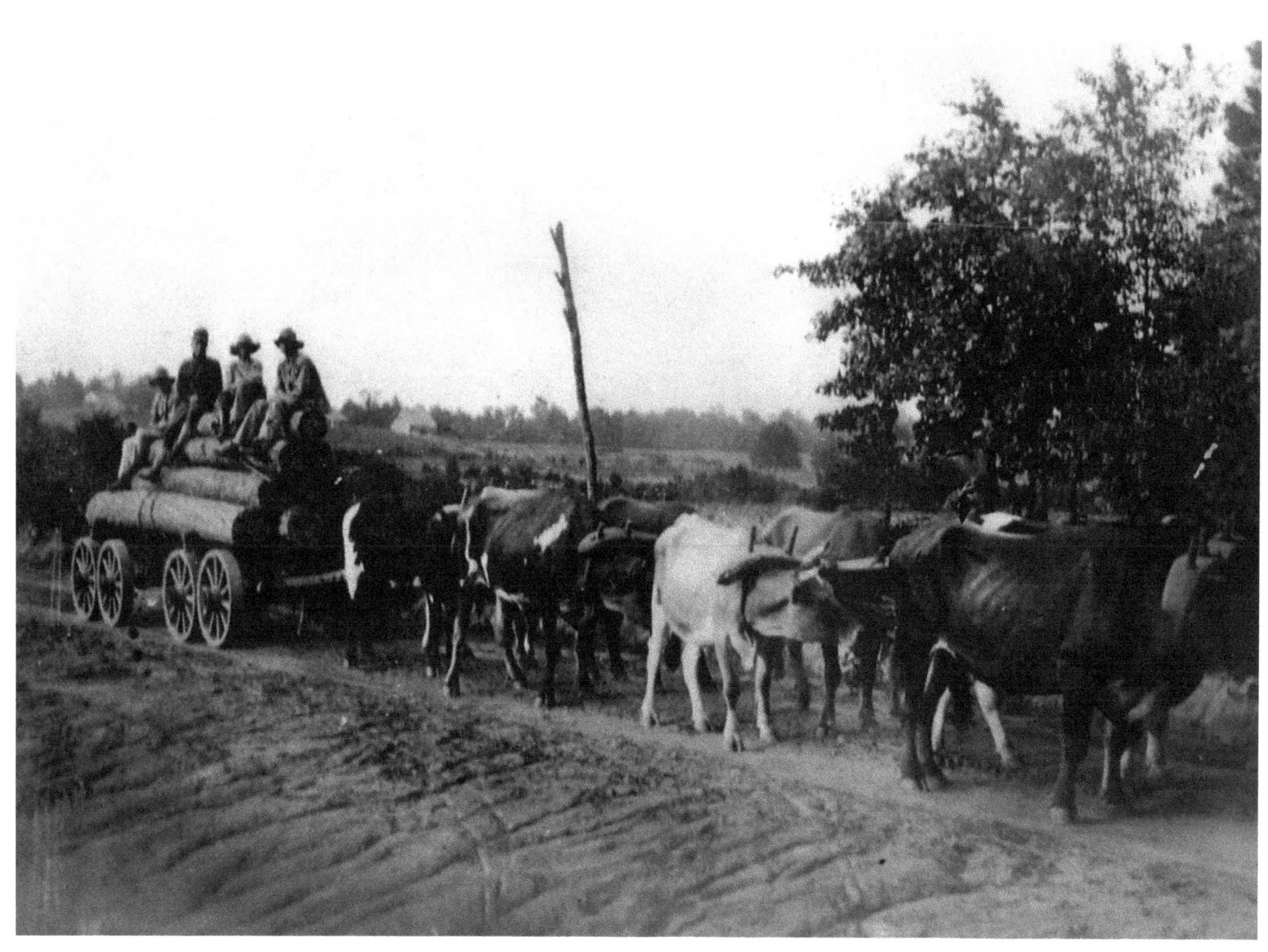

Four lumberjacks end their long day of cutting and loading timber as they sit upon a sturdy wagon pulled by oxen. The lumber business in Mississippi provided a paycheck and a way of life for many.

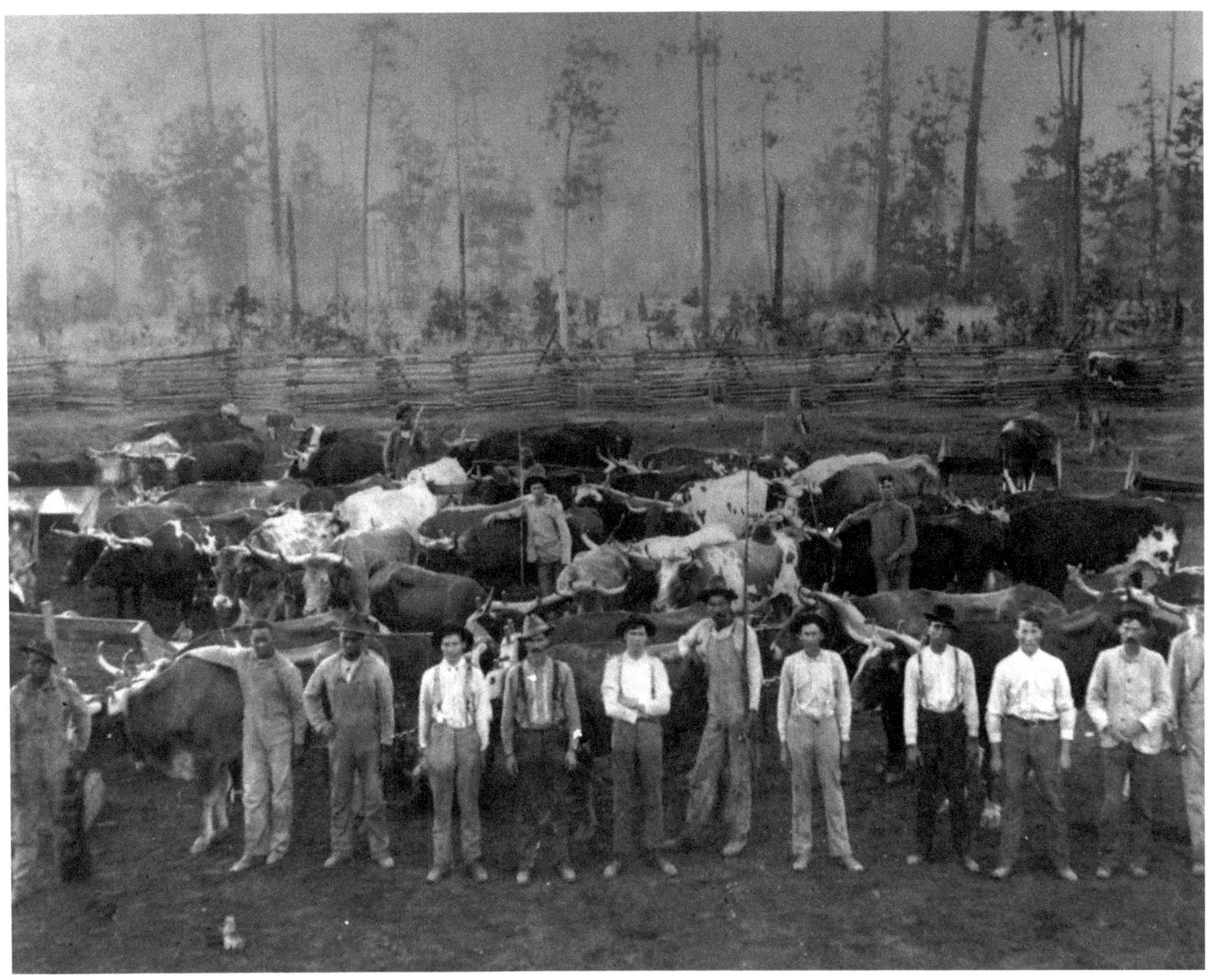

This magnificent herd of longhorn cattle is being tended by the hard-working cowhands lined up here. Oxen were essential to the logging business in the early 1900s.

Following Spread: A 1910 panorama of Jackson, with the Old Capitol visible in the background. The early 1900s brought a new vitality to the state of Mississippi, including the capital city.

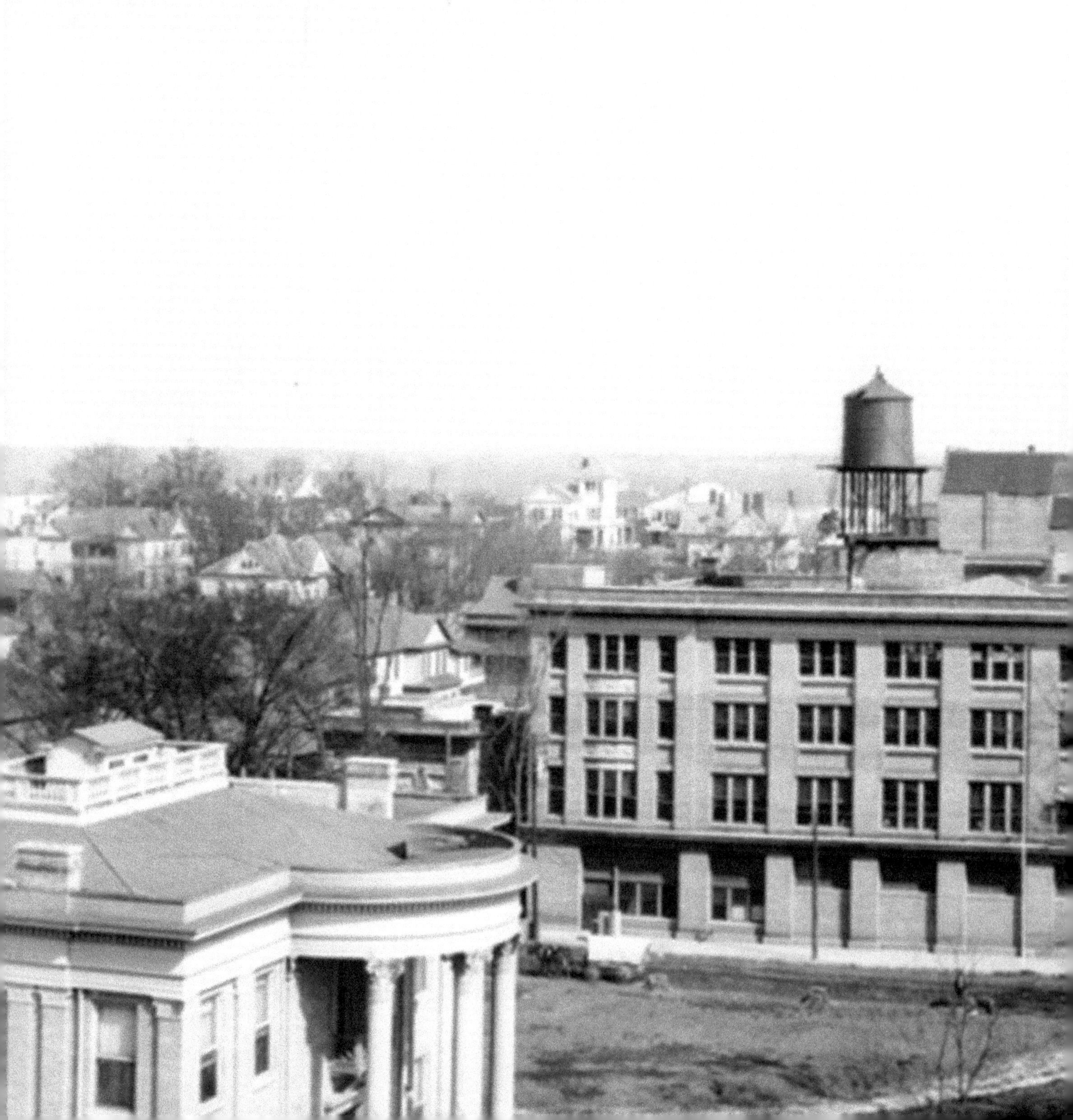

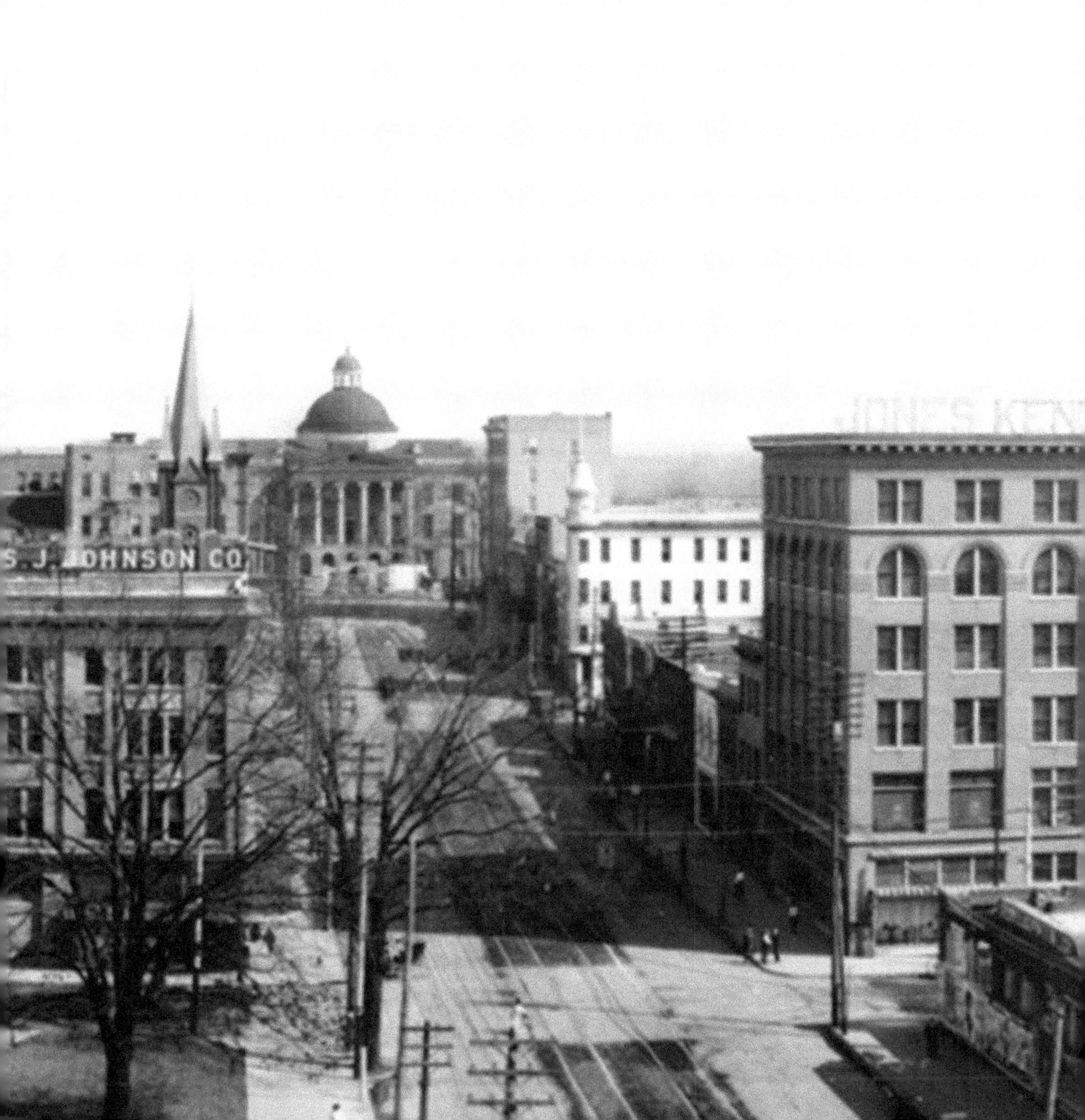
S. J. JOHNSON CO
JONES KEN

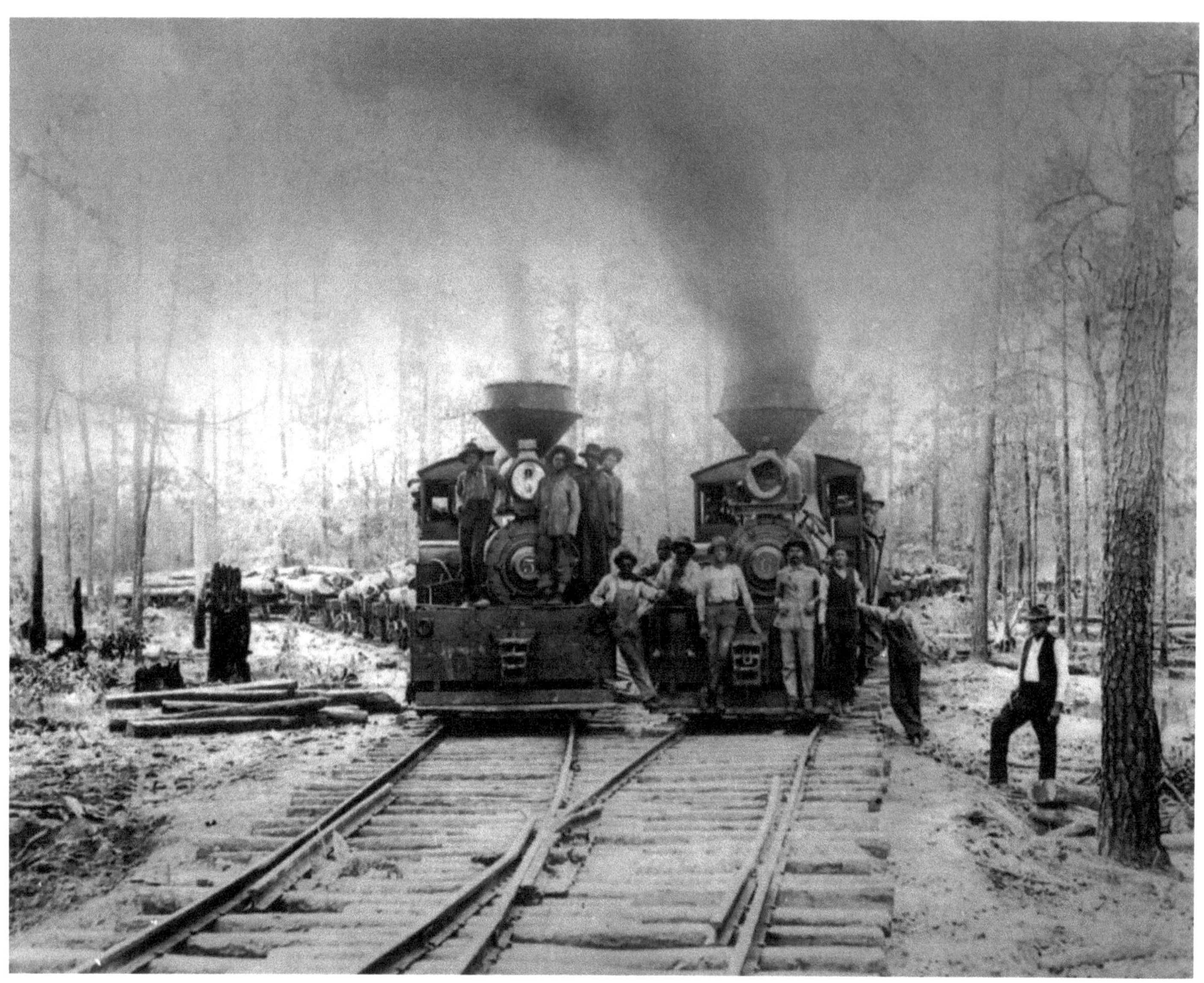

Steam engines pair up in Wayne County to haul pine logs from the forests of east central Mississippi in 1905. The lumber and lumber transport businesses flourished during the late 1800s, as logging became the main industry of the area. These loggers are shown at Robinson Lumber Company.

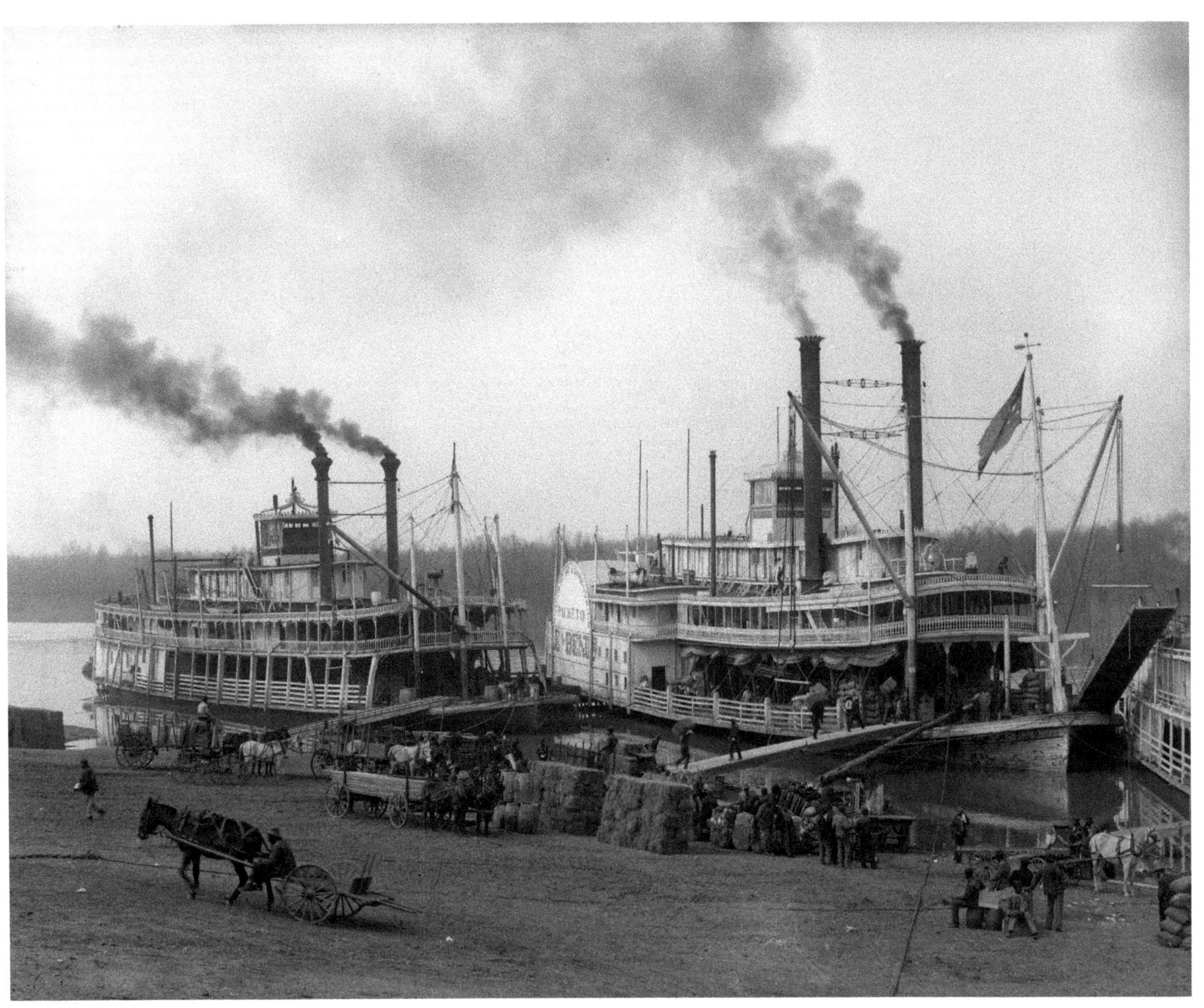

Between 1900 and 1906, the mighty Mississippi continued as a brisk river-transport opportunity. Shown here are the stern-wheeler *Belle of Calhoun* and (at right) the side-wheeler *Belle of the Bends,* of the Vicksburg and Greenville Packet Company.

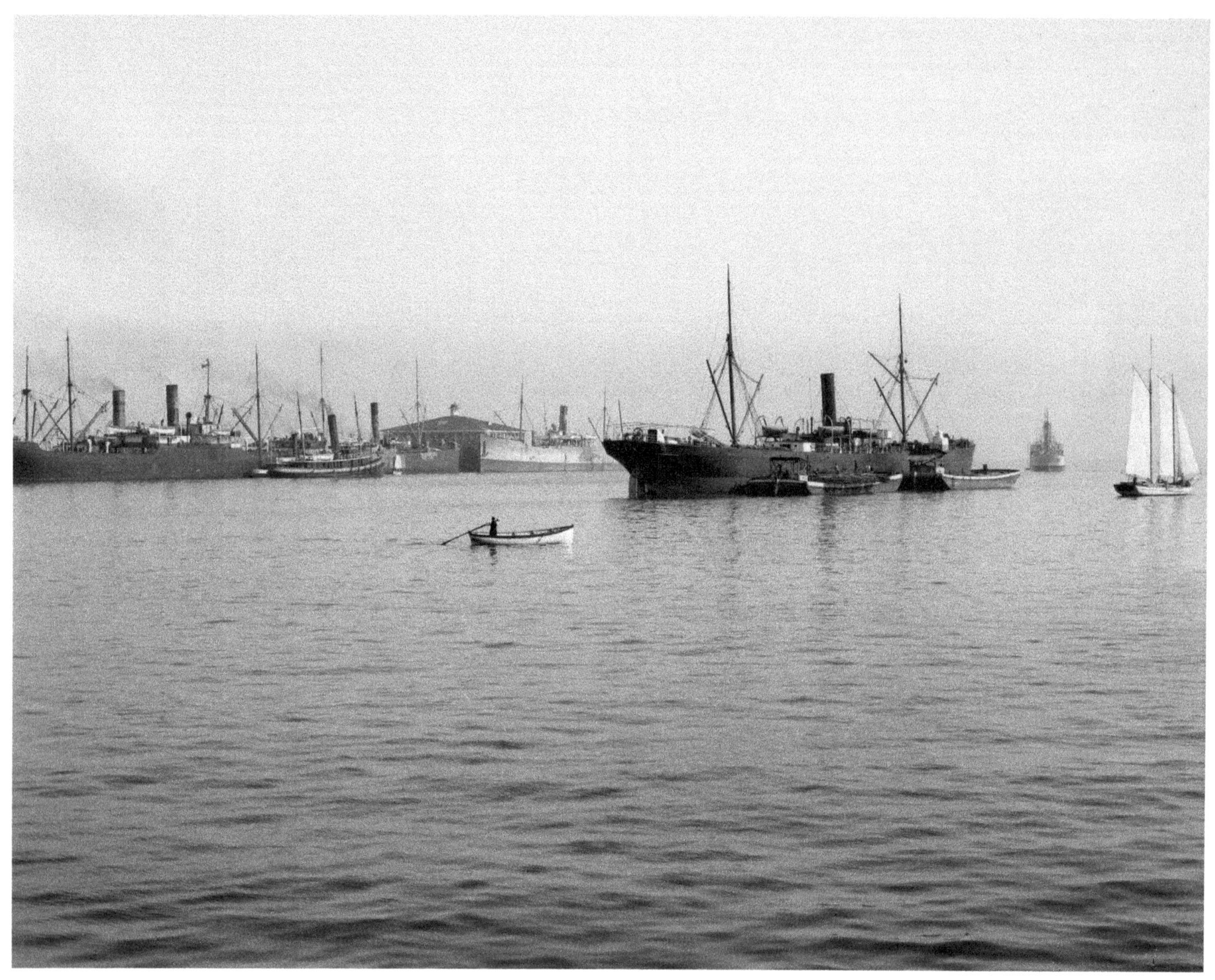

The Harbor at Gulfport, in Harrison County, as it appeared in the early 1900s. In view are fishing boats, sailboats, freightliners, and a boat dock in the distance.

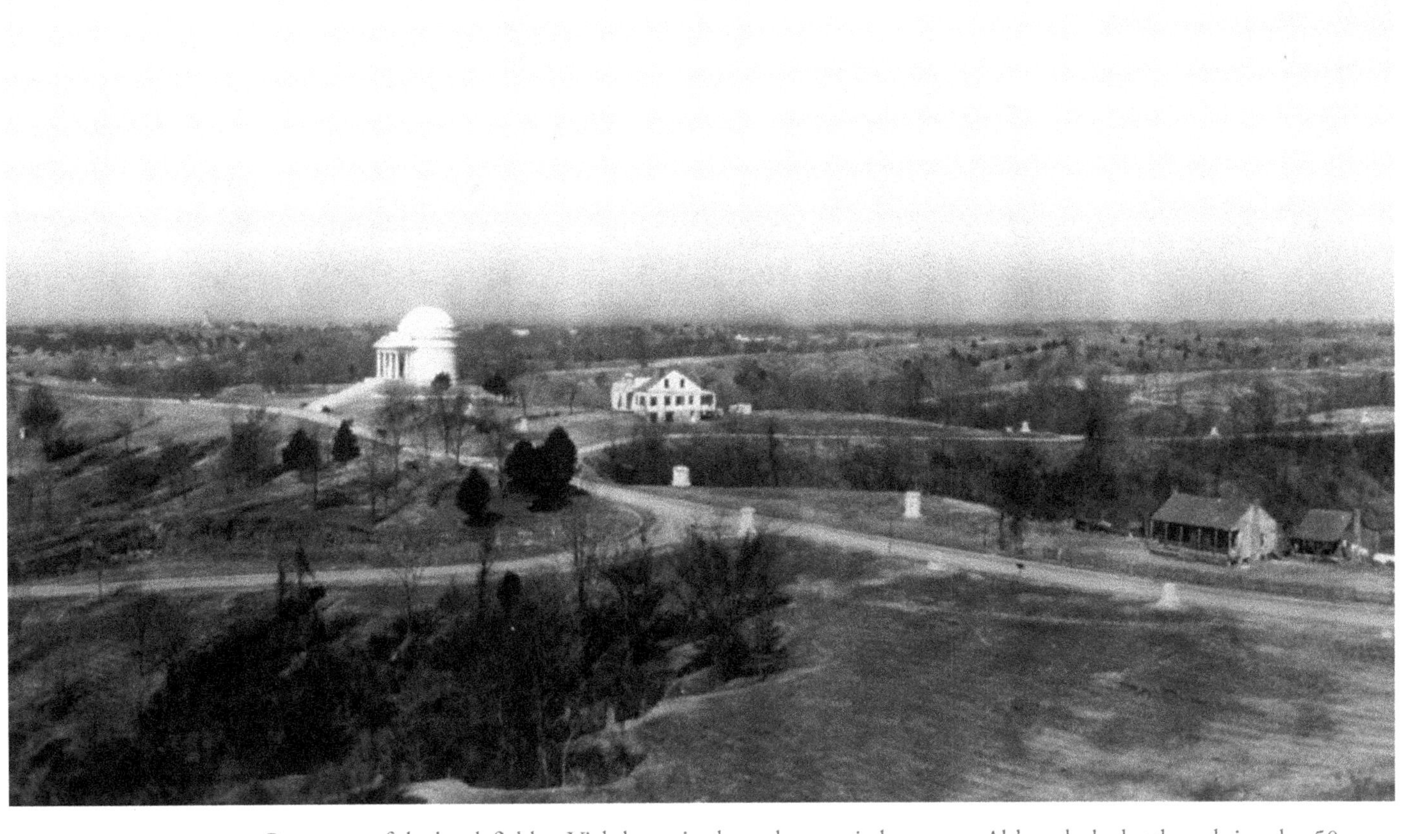

Panorama of the battlefield at Vicksburg, in the early twentieth century. Although the battle and siege lay 50 years in the past, the landscape is still barren. Prominent among the many monuments to fallen heroes is the Illinois State Memorial, the domed structure at left. Modeled on the Roman Pantheon, it was dedicated in 1906. Forty-seven steps lead to it, one step for each day of the Vicksburg siege.

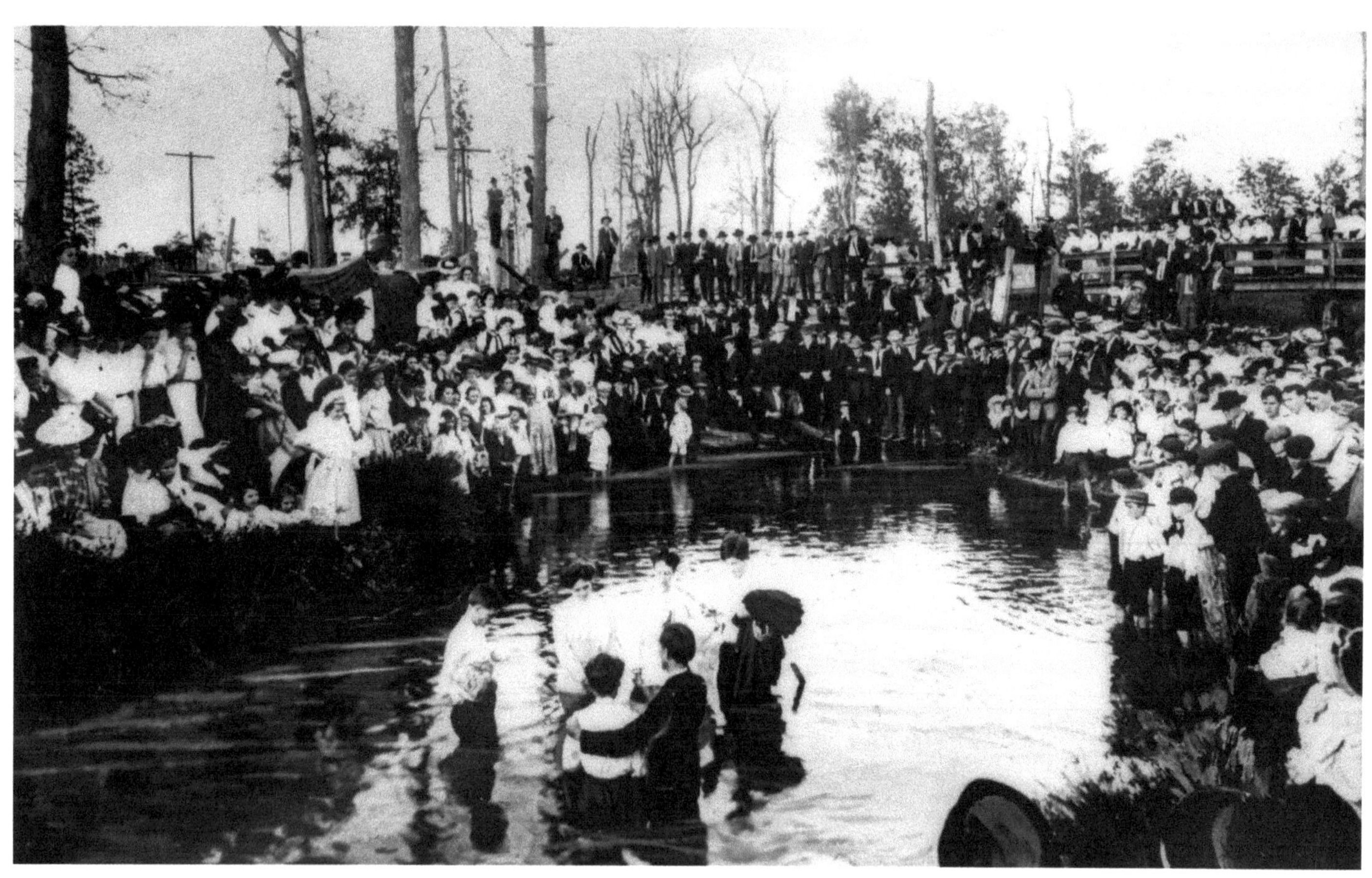

"Shall we gather at the river?" The Emanuel Baptist Church at Hattiesburg holds a baptismal service in 1910, immersing converts in a local body of water.

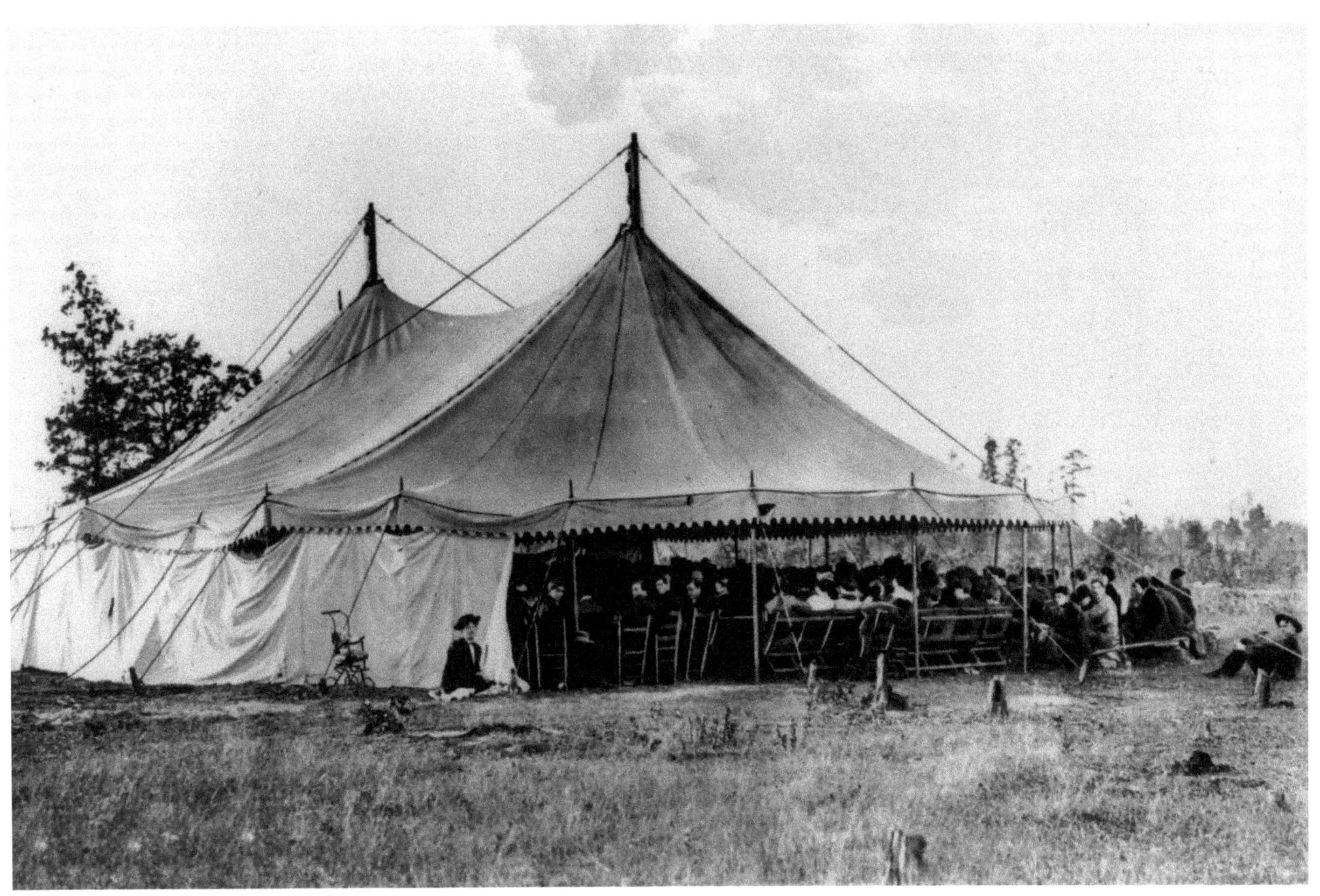

The beginnings of the Emanuel Baptist Church in Hattiesburg. Early churches were often organized following evangelistic revivals held at camp meetings where large tents were filled to capacity.

Following Spread: Millsaps College, located in Jackson and shown here in 1910, was founded in 1889 by Confederate veteran Major Reuben Webster Millsaps with a donation of $50,000 and land. Major Millsaps and his wife are interred near the center of campus. Notable alumni include TV's *Tonight Show* host Johnny Carson, author Ellen Gilchrist, and General Louis H. Wilson, a decorated war veteran who served as Commandant of the Marine Corps.

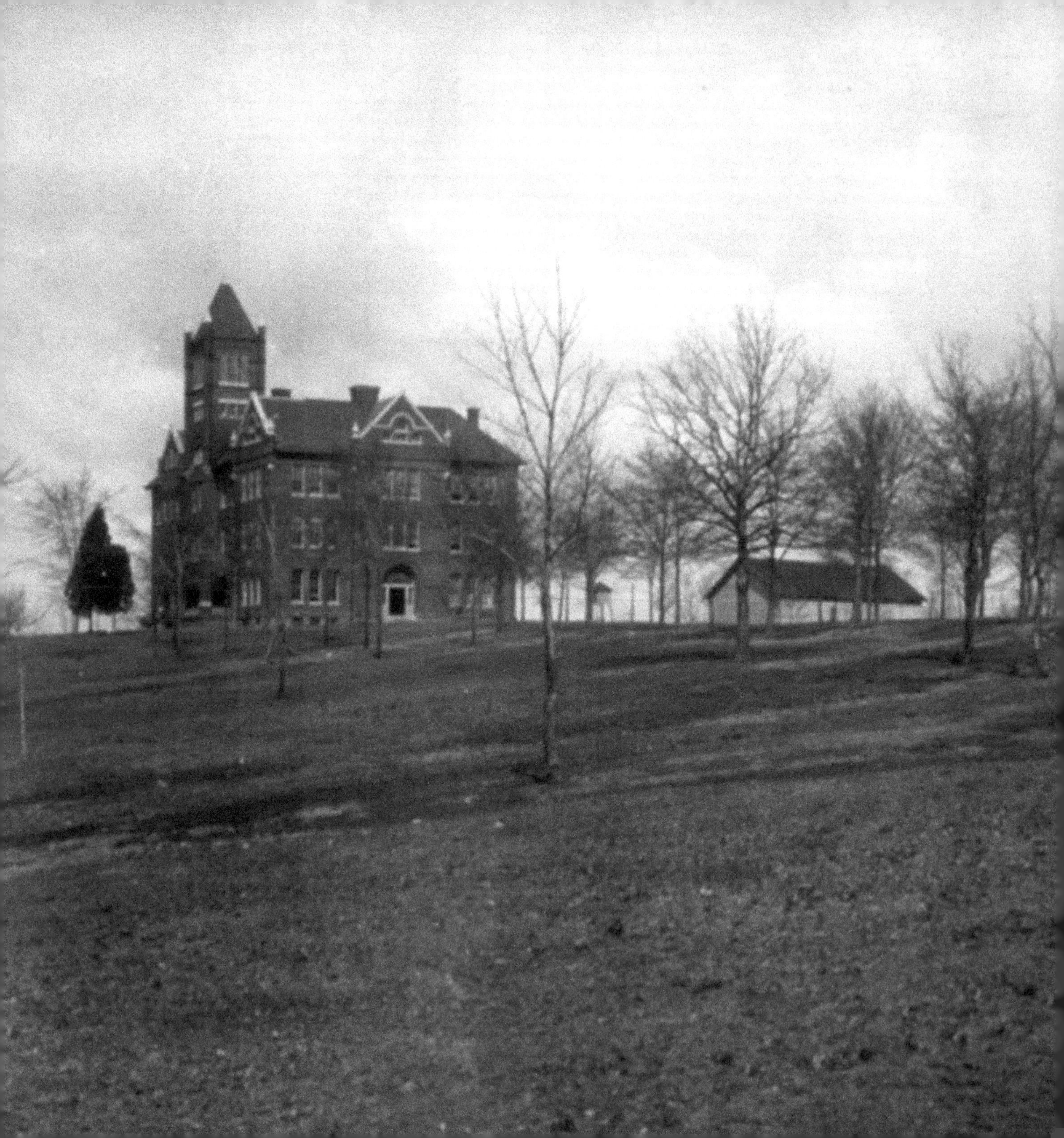

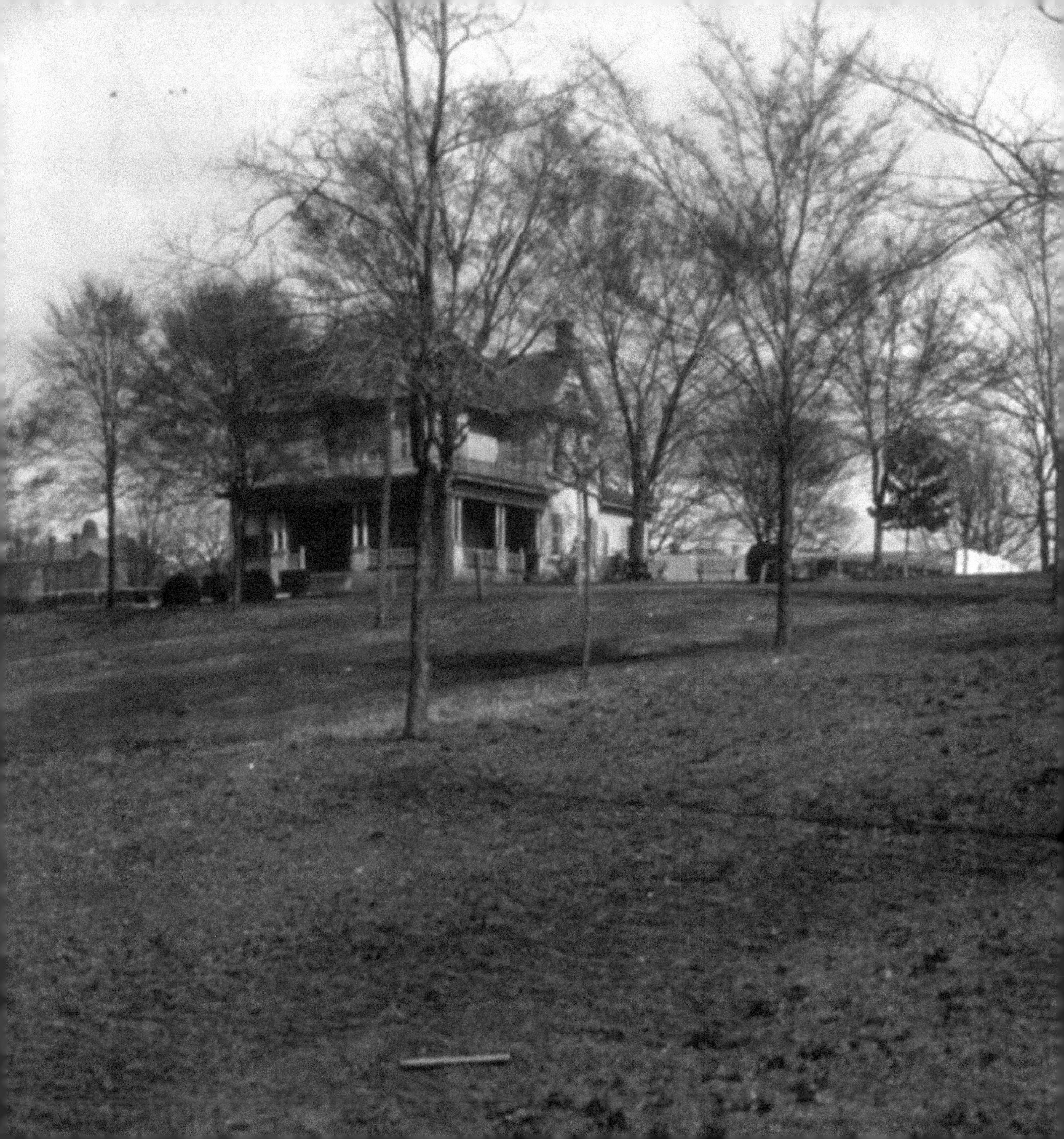

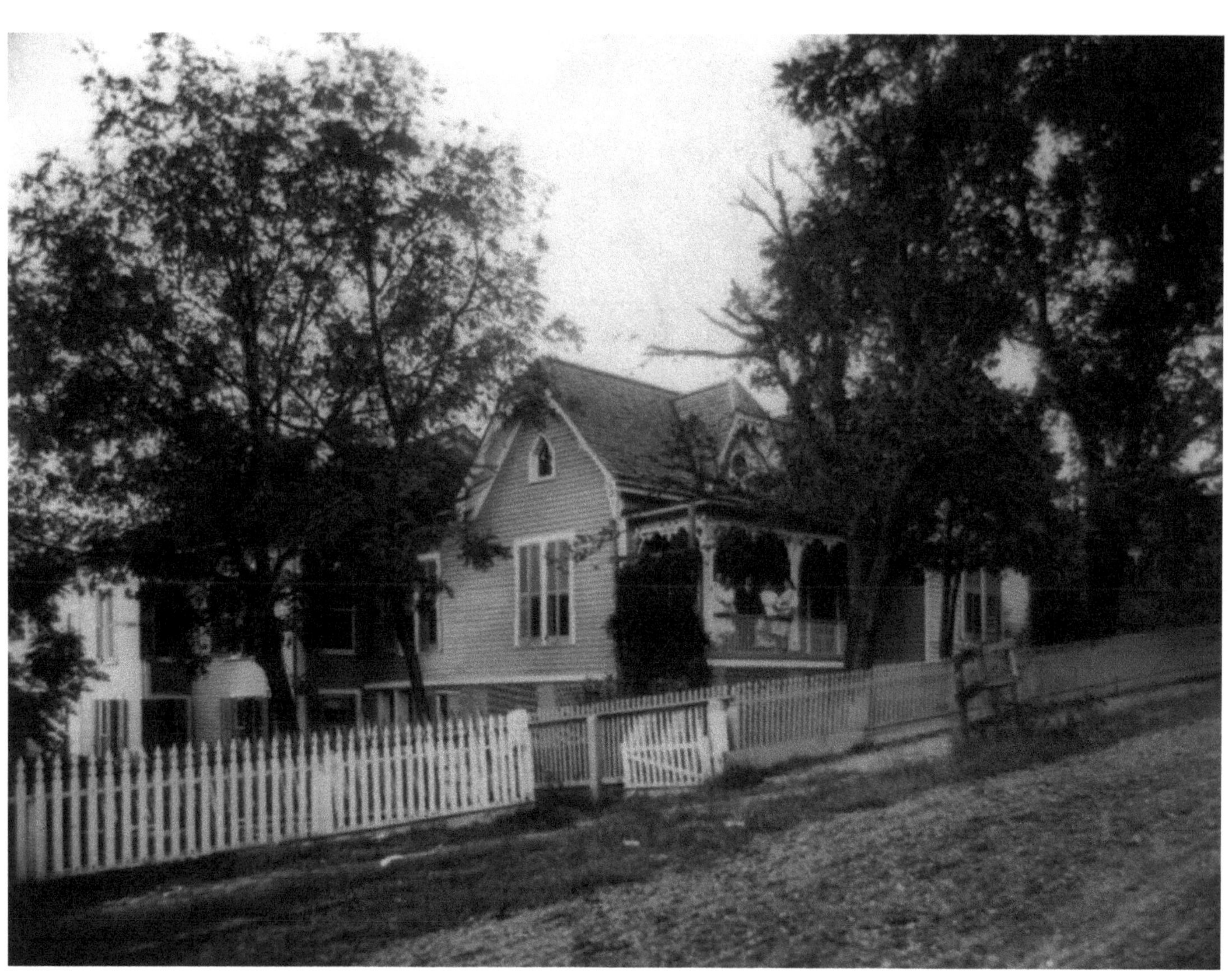

The home of John Sharp Williams, in Yazoo City, as it appeared in 1908. Williams represented Mississippi in the U.S. House of Representatives from 1893 to 1909 and the U.S. Senate from 1911 to 1923.

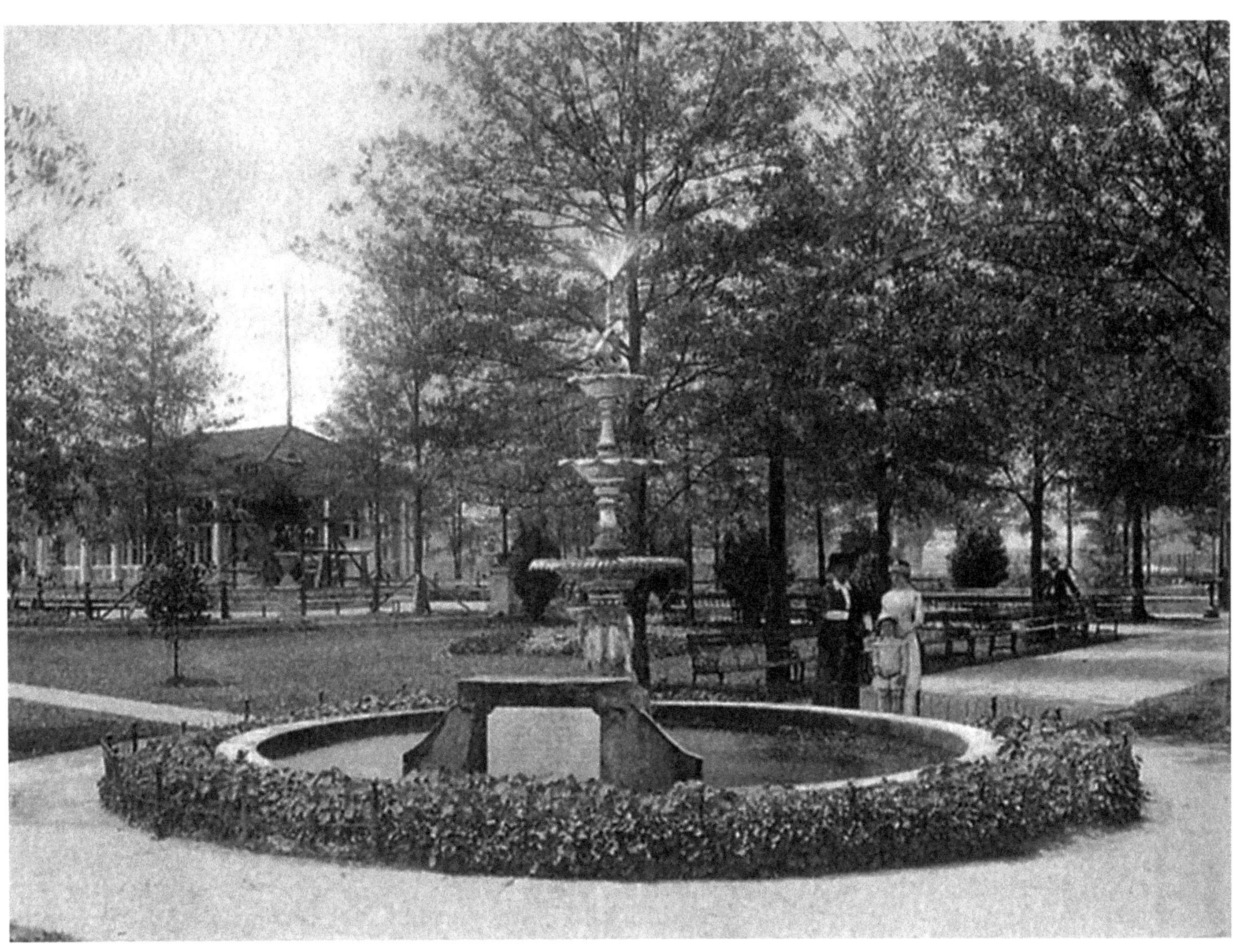

The lovely Highland Park in Meridian on a Sunday afternoon in June, to which the city advertised street railway service, concerts, open-air silent movies, a bandstand, and a dance pavilion. Visitors pose for a photograph at this park fountain in 1909. The park was Meridian's most popular recreational area during the first half of the twentieth century.

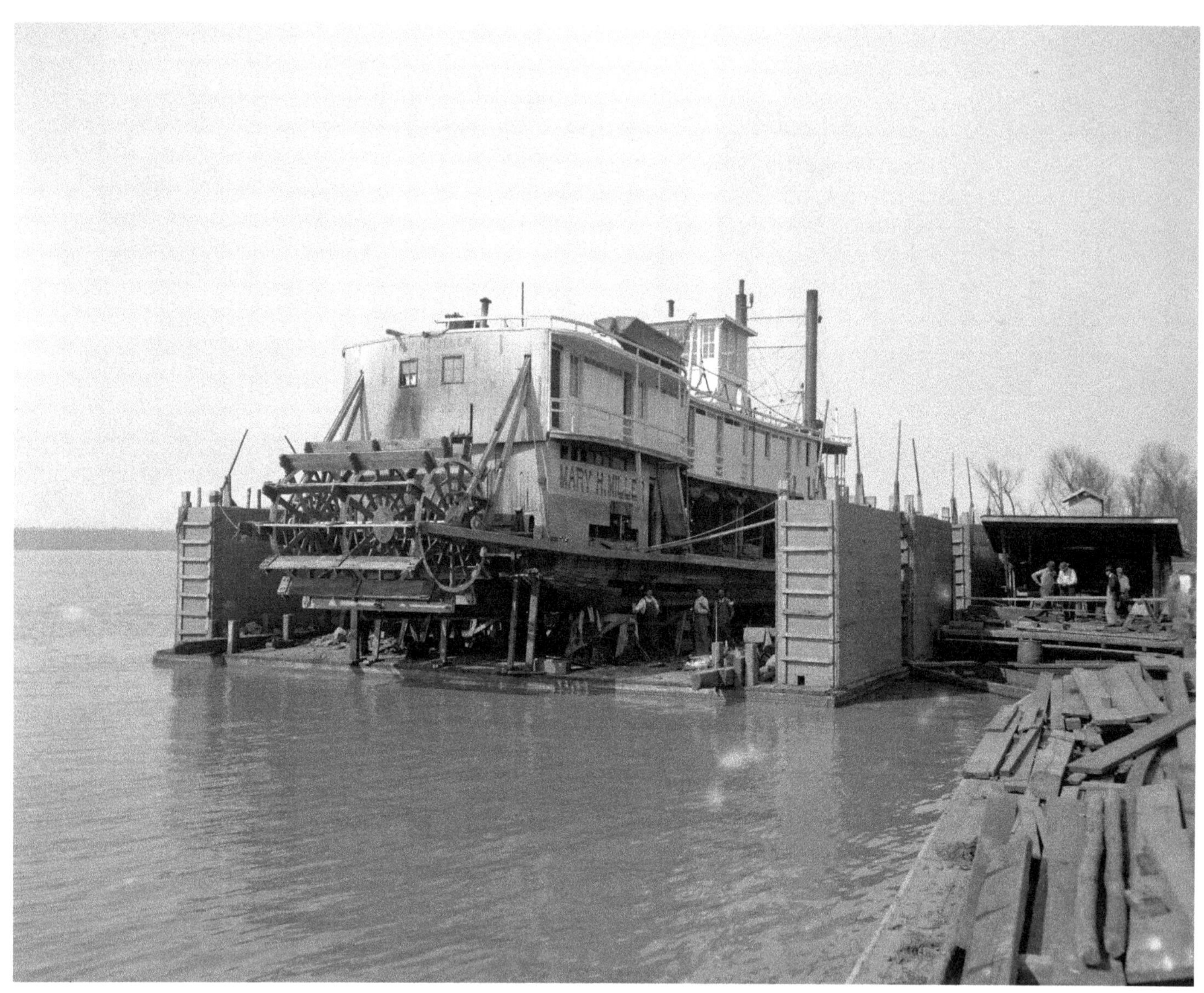

This 1910 image shows a Mississippi River floating dry dock, loaded with the stern-wheeler *Mary H. Miller,* which is undergoing repairs.

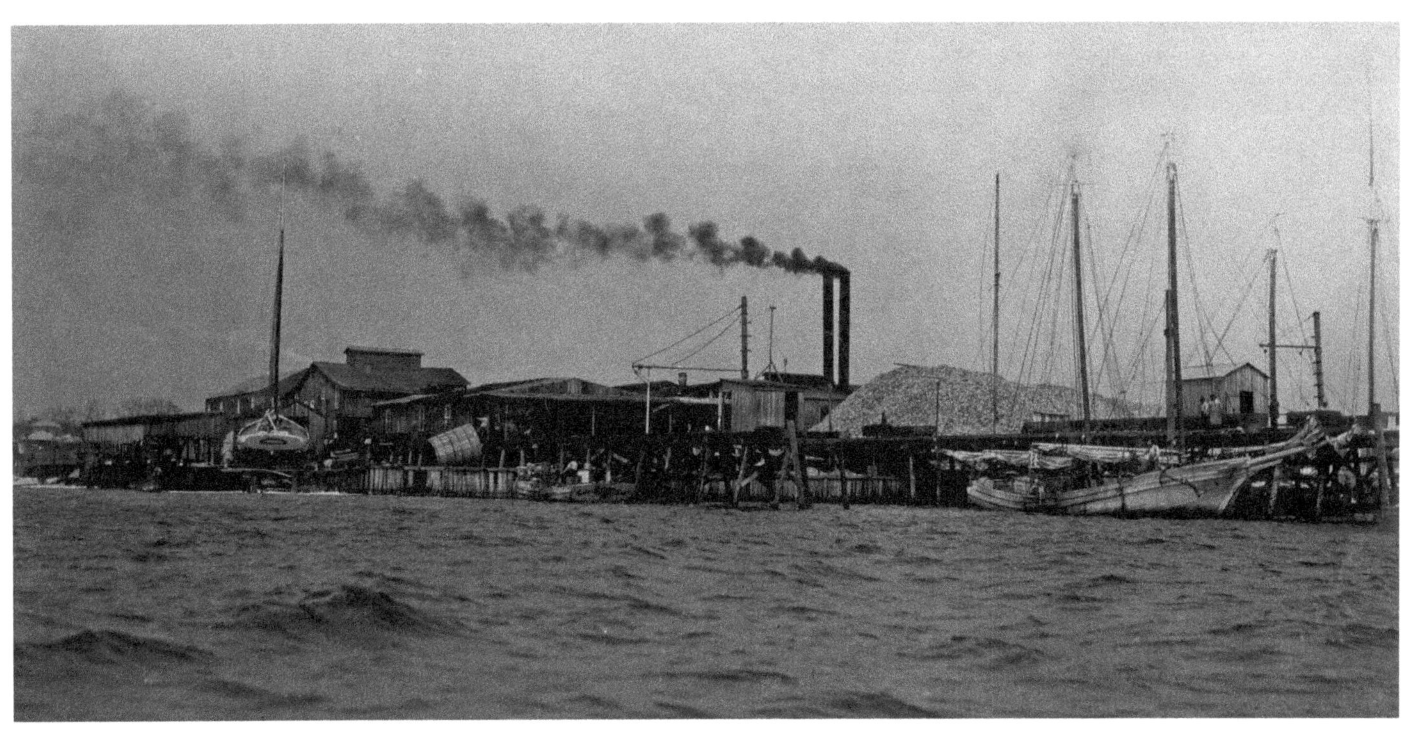

Work is under way in February 1911 at the Pass Packing Company, in the town of Pass Christian. The rippling waters of the Gulf of Mexico are visible in the foreground. Pass Packing Company was a cannery specializing in the shucking and canning of oysters.

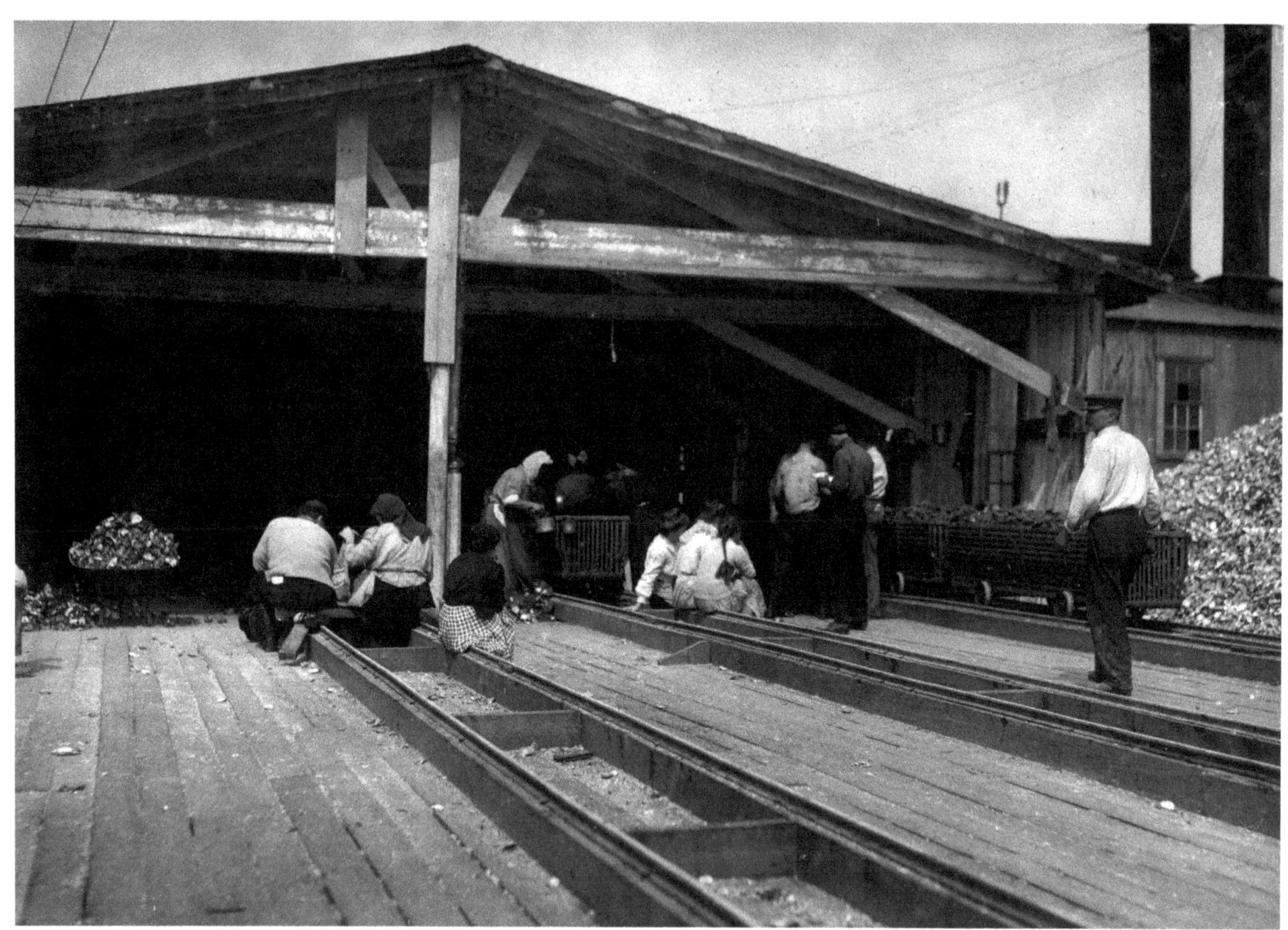

Another day at the Pass Packing Company in February 1911. Discarded oyster shells and a system of tracks and track carts for moving the product from point to point are visible at right.

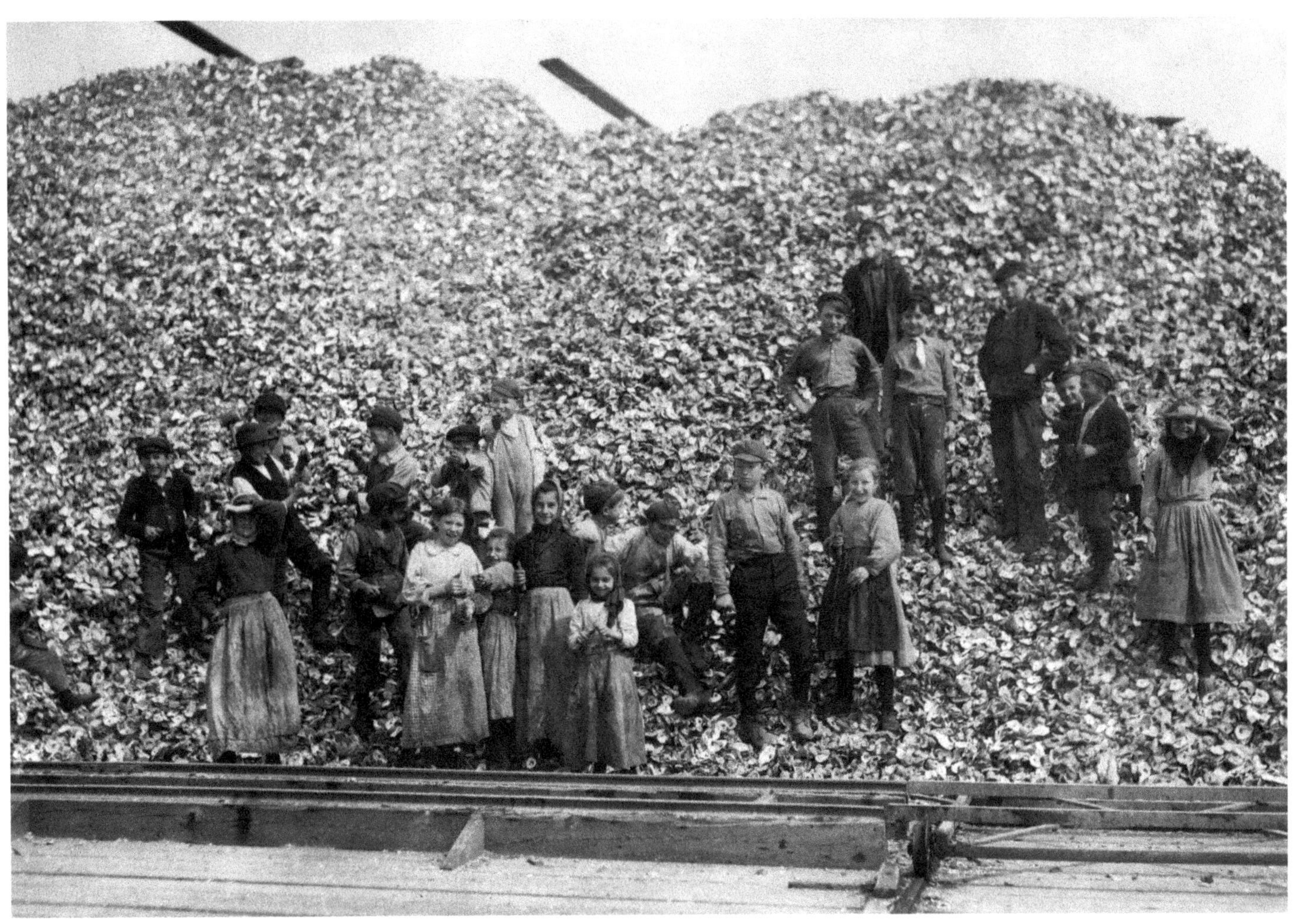

The well-known photographer Lewis Wickes Hine recorded these children at the Pass Packing Company, employed at the cannery as oyster shuckers in 1911. During the 1910s, Hine was a freelance photographer for *The Survey,* a leading social reform magazine, traveling nationwide to document child labor and its effects on the nation's youth. This image and several to follow provide a glimpse of some aspects of Mississippi society during this decade. These particular children are clearly wearing smiles, in spite of their challenging circumstances.

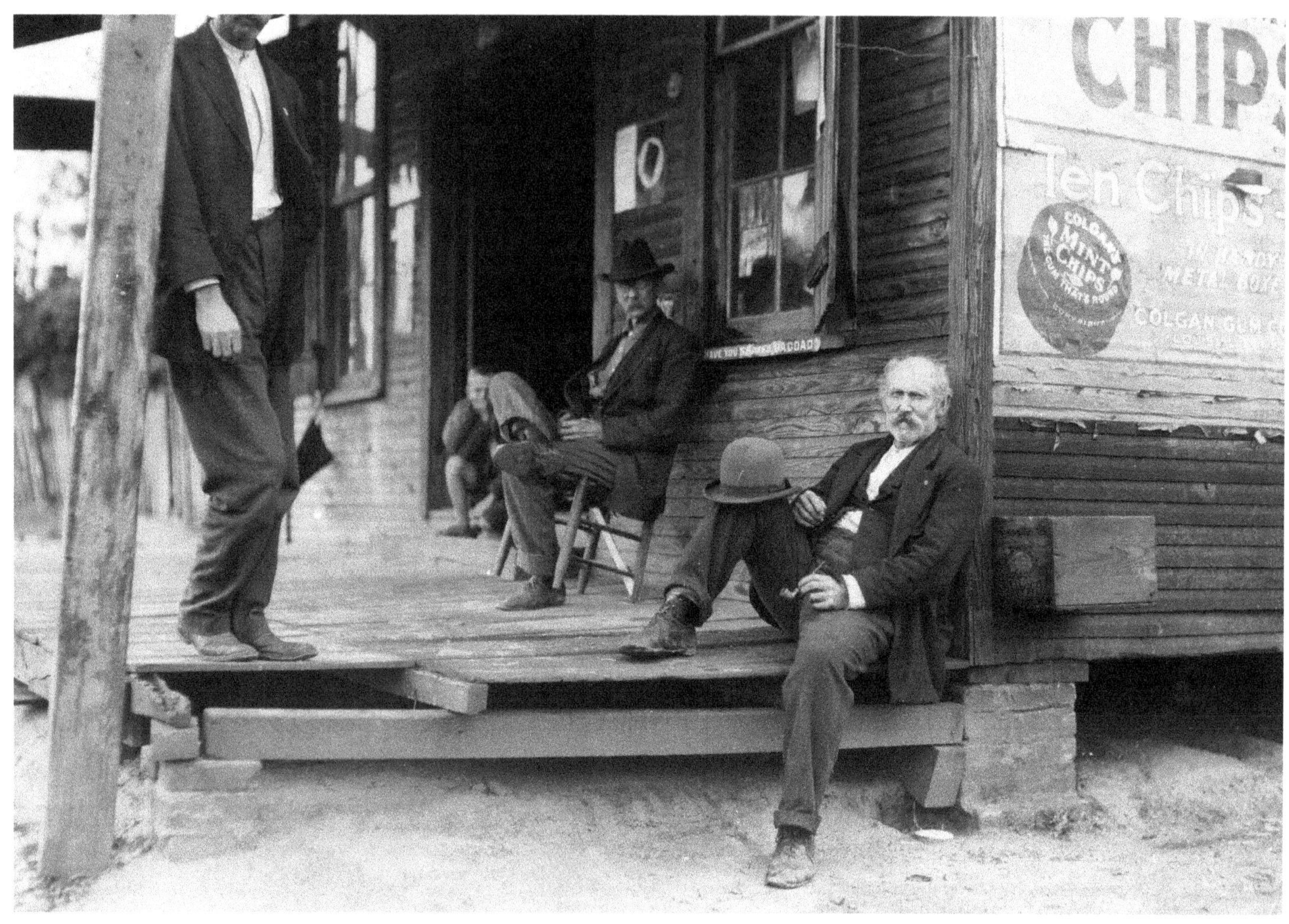

Lewis Hine recorded this image in 1911 at Meridian, titling it *The Dependent Widower*. The sign beneath the store window asks, "Have You Smoked Bagdad?"

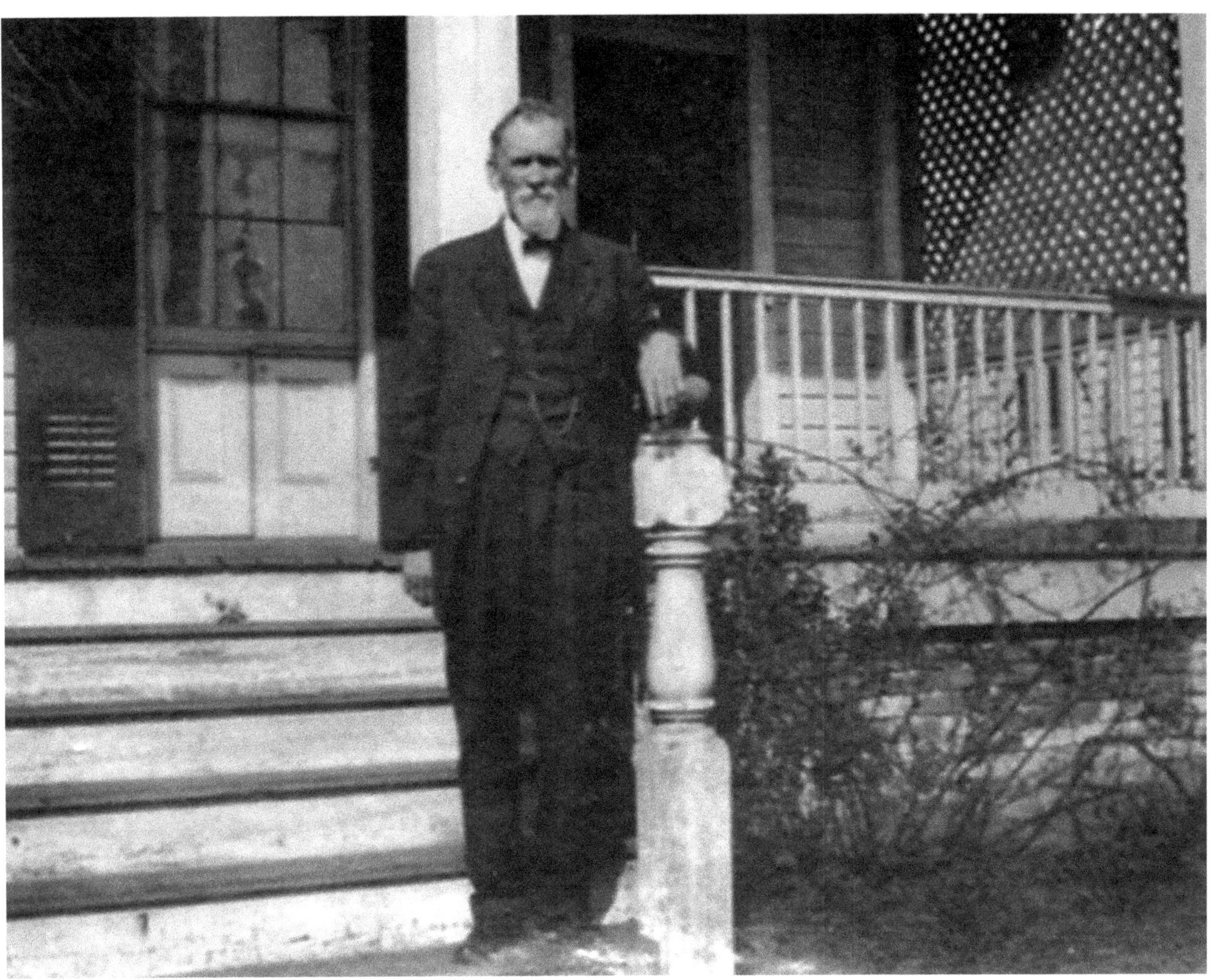

Mayor E. H. Dial, posing for a photograph in front of his home, served the city of Meridian for eight productive years during its golden age. His term in office included a massive street-paving and sidewalk-paving project, a $100,000 sewer system, and, in 1902, his preparation of the Code of Laws for the city, which was adopted by the Board of Councilmen.

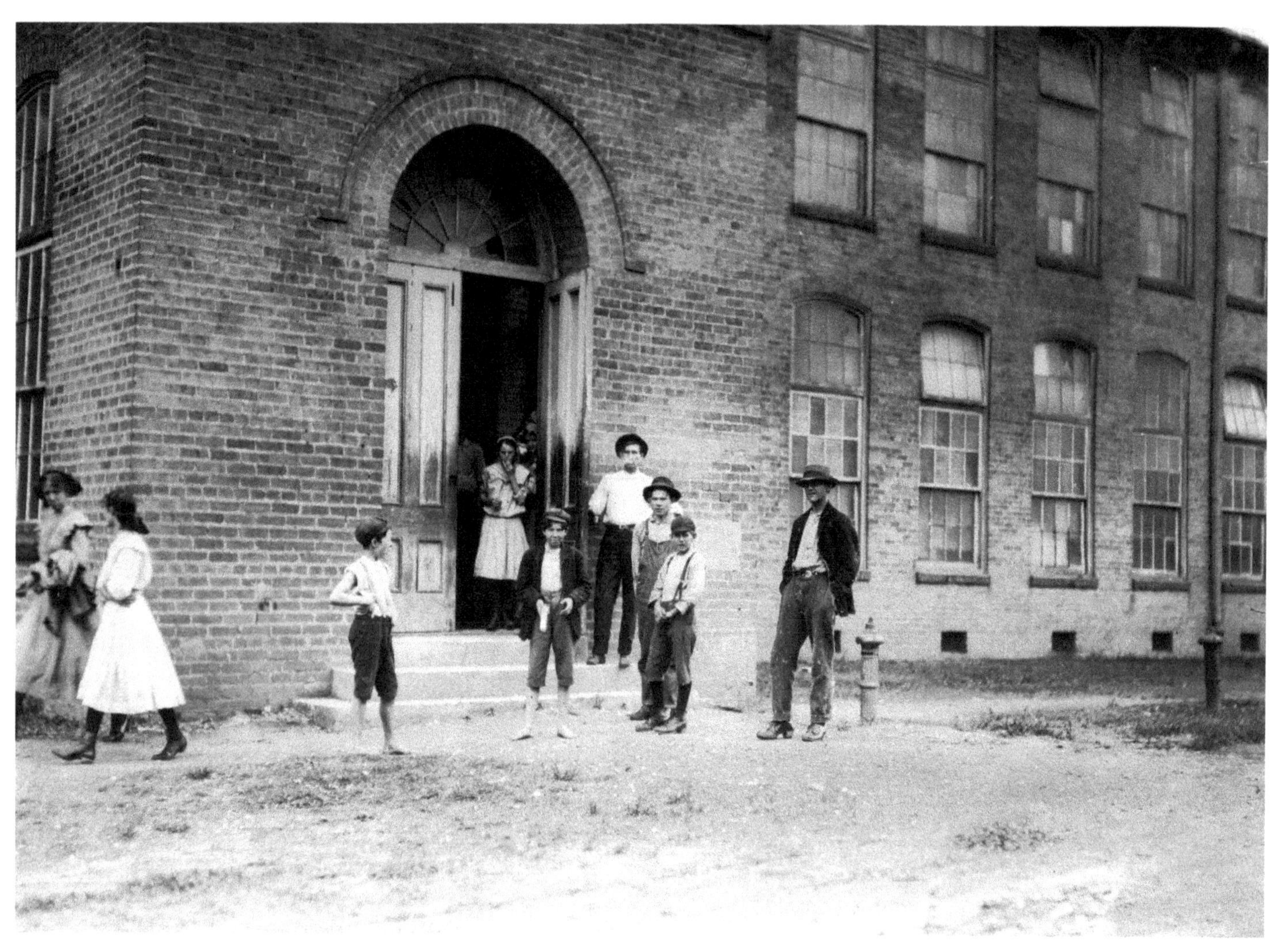

Workers break for the noon hour in May 1911 at McComb's Delta Cotton Mills, in Pike County.

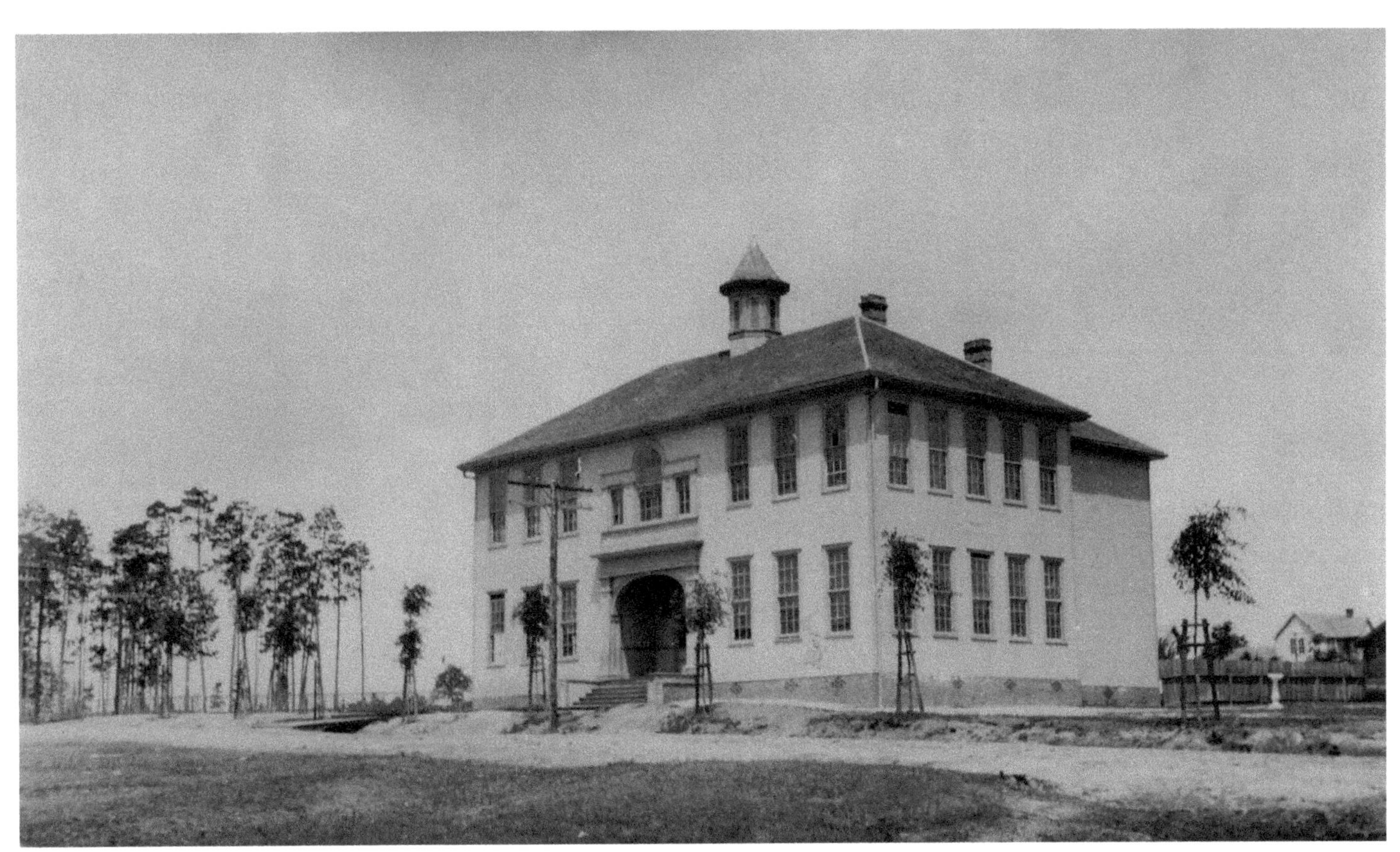

Shown here in May 1911, this two-story school at Laurel in Jones County served students who lived in the mill district. By 1900, 92 percent of textile mill workers lived in mill villages—owned by the companies that employed them—with houses for employees and their families, churches, a school, and the company store.

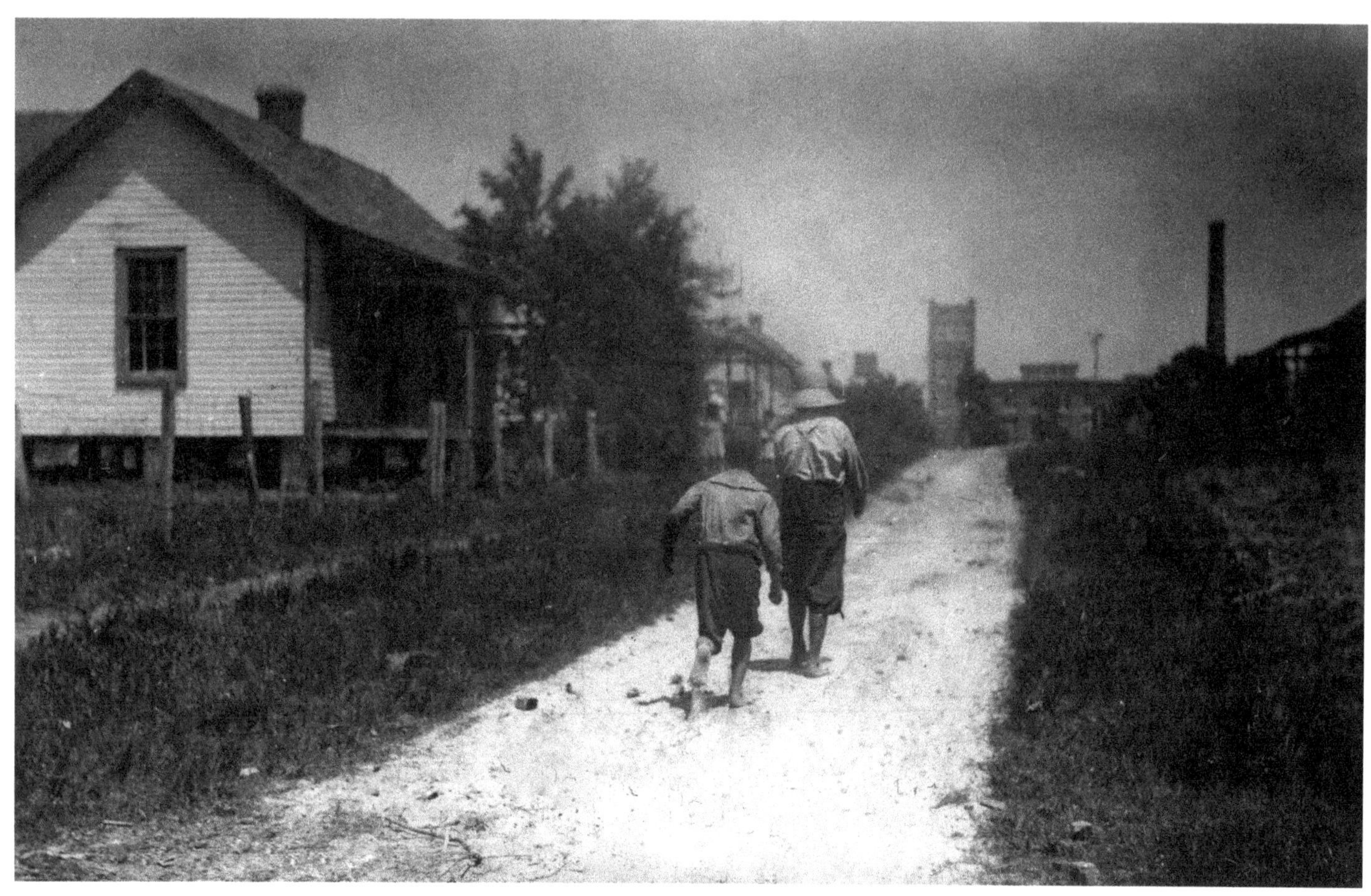

Two barefoot boys in Tupelo scramble up the dirt pathway toward the Cotton Mills company store in May 1911. To the left is a typical house for workers and their families, and in the distance rises the mill tower. Years later, in January 1935, rock 'n' roll legend Elvis Presley would be born in Tupelo.

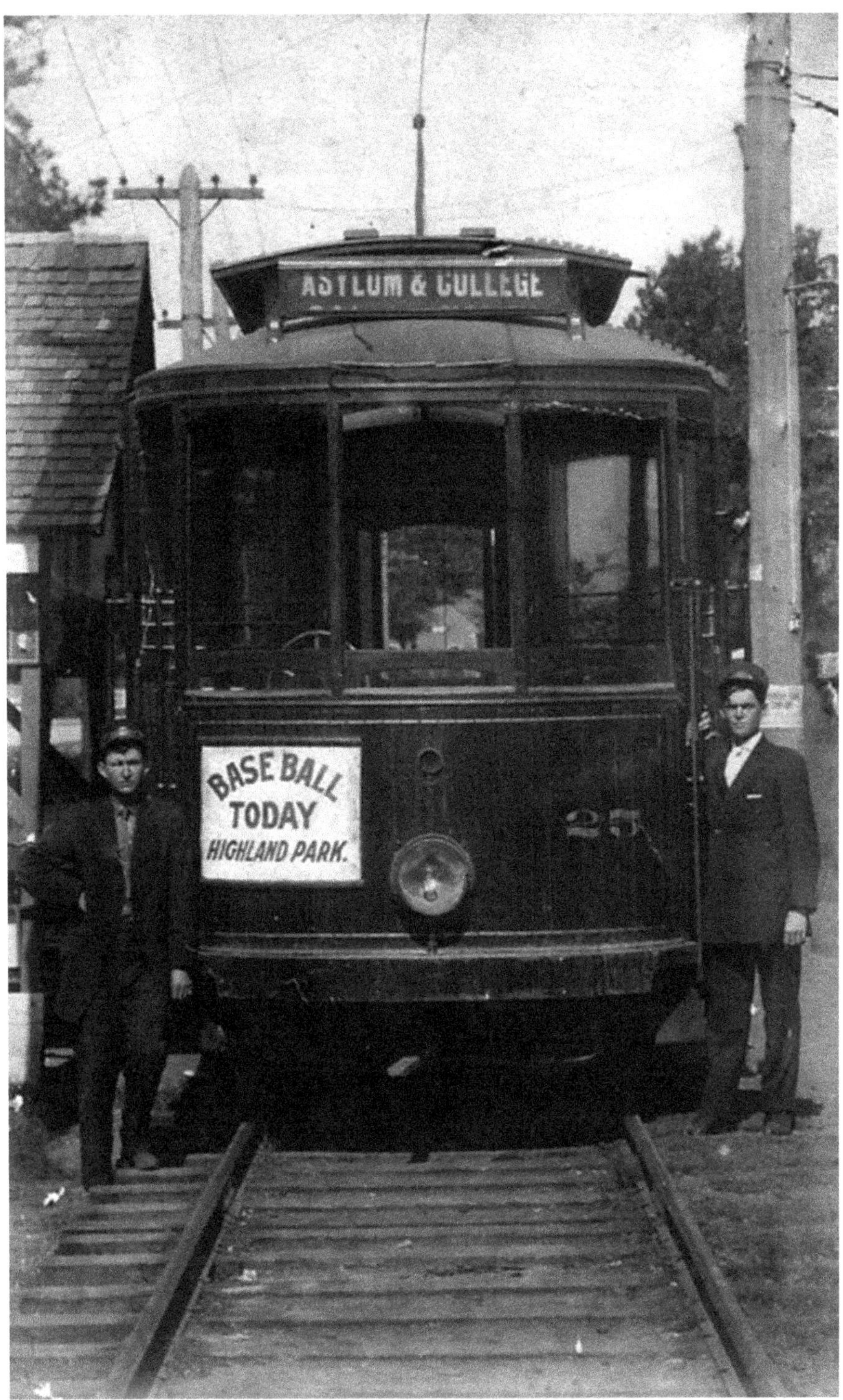

Jack Norworth's 1908 Tin Pan Alley tune "Take Me Out to the Ballgame" was inspired by a trolley sign much like this one in Meridian. The trolley ad announces, "Baseball Today: Highland Park," only a short streetcar ride and minutes away. The only double track running beyond downtown Meridian went to exciting Highland Park.

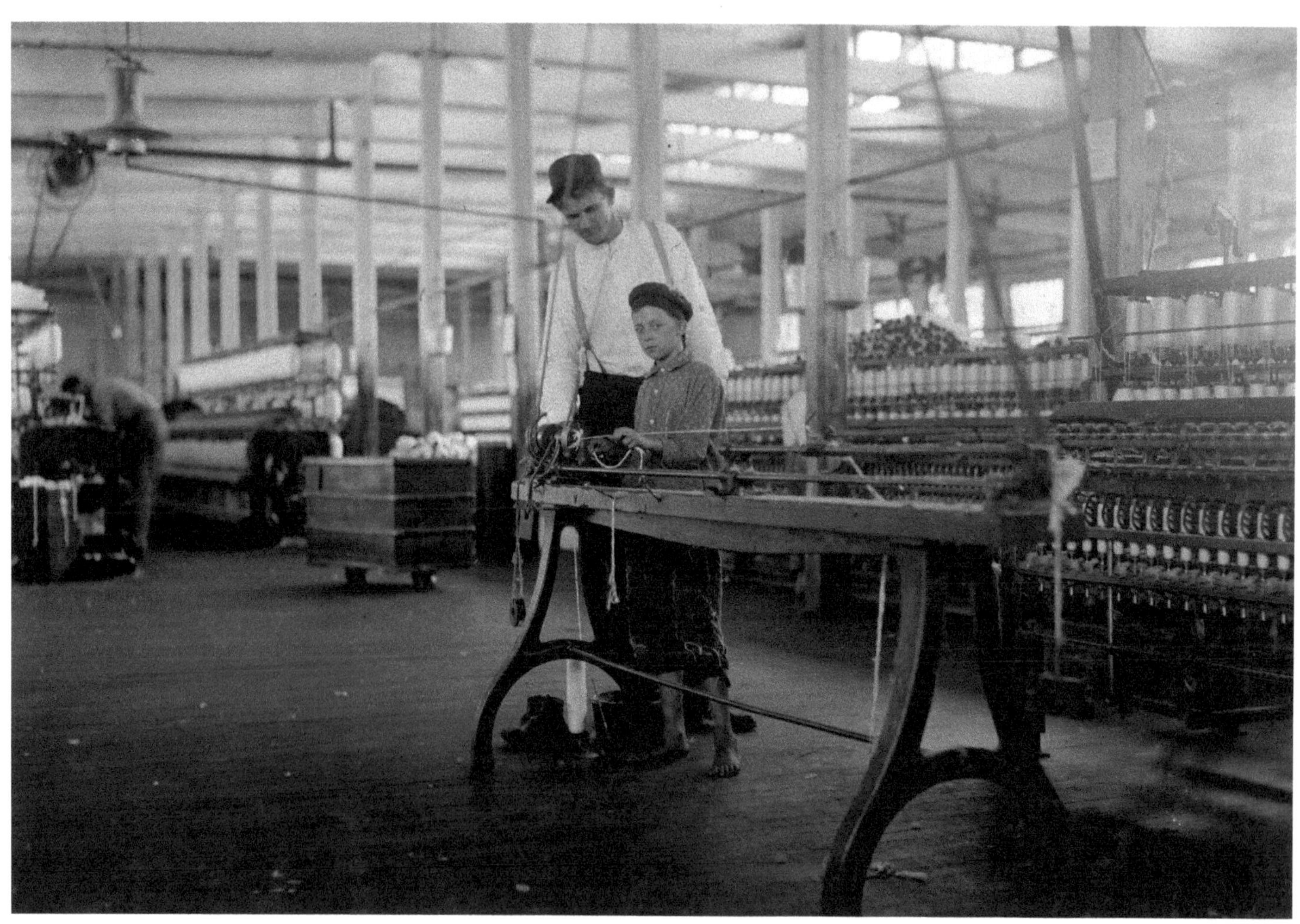

Lewis Hine recorded this young boy and an adult helper at work at the Yazoo City Yarn Mills, in Yazoo County, in May 1911. Yazoo City was founded in 1824 and burned twice—once when it was torched by Union forces during the Civil War, and accidentally in 1904 by a youngster playing with matches. The motivational speaker Zig Ziglar and Mississippi governor Haley Barbour both grew up in Yazoo City.

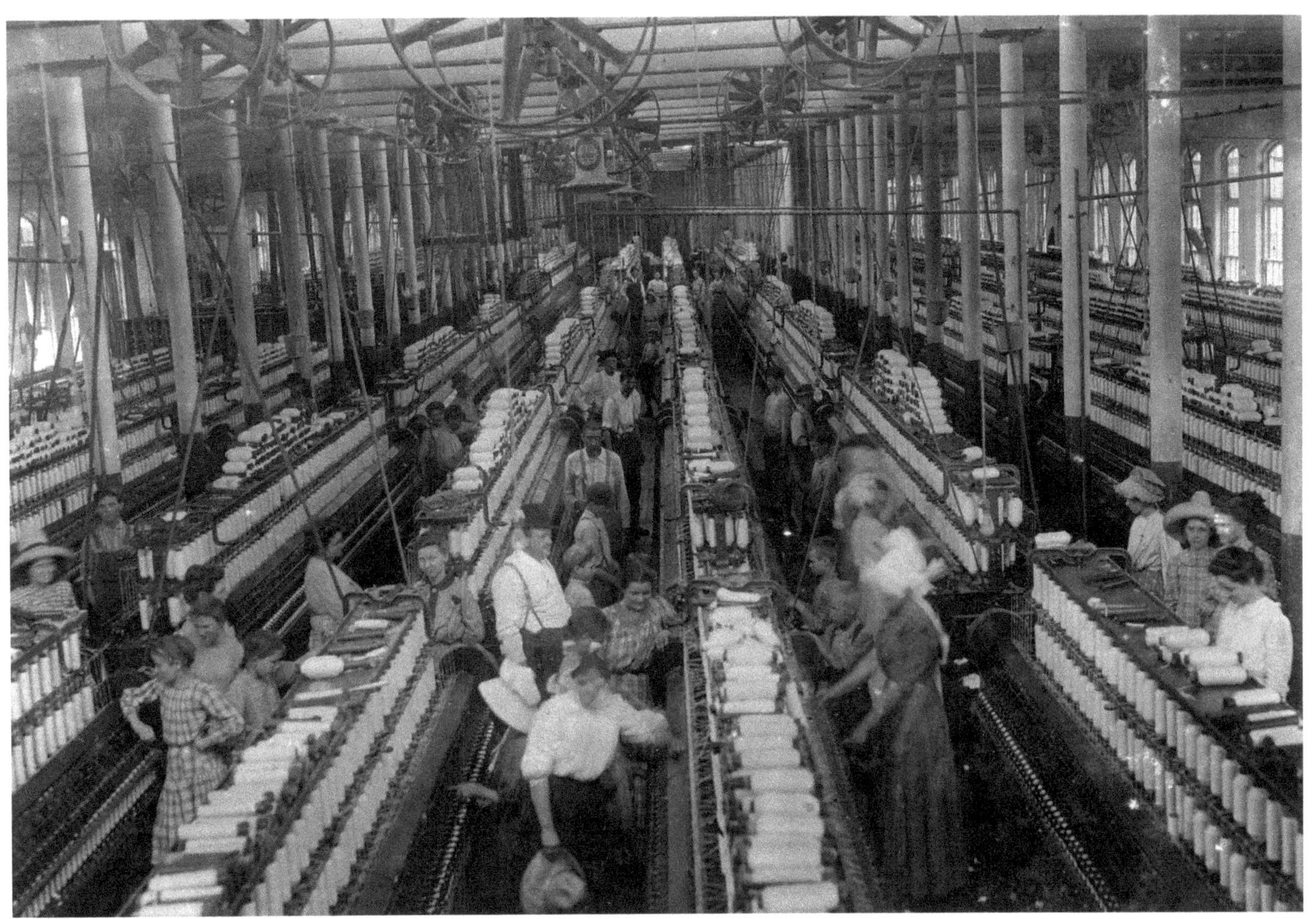

Lewis Hine photographed these workers, some of them children, inside the Magnolia Cotton Mills spinning room. Magnolia, in Pike County, was founded in 1856 by cotton planter Ansel Prewett, who hoped to take advantage of the approaching railroad then under construction. While serving as sheriff in the 1870s and escorting a prisoner along the same railroad, Prewett was killed by outlaws. The town itself would prosper as a popular destination for vacationing New Orleaneans.

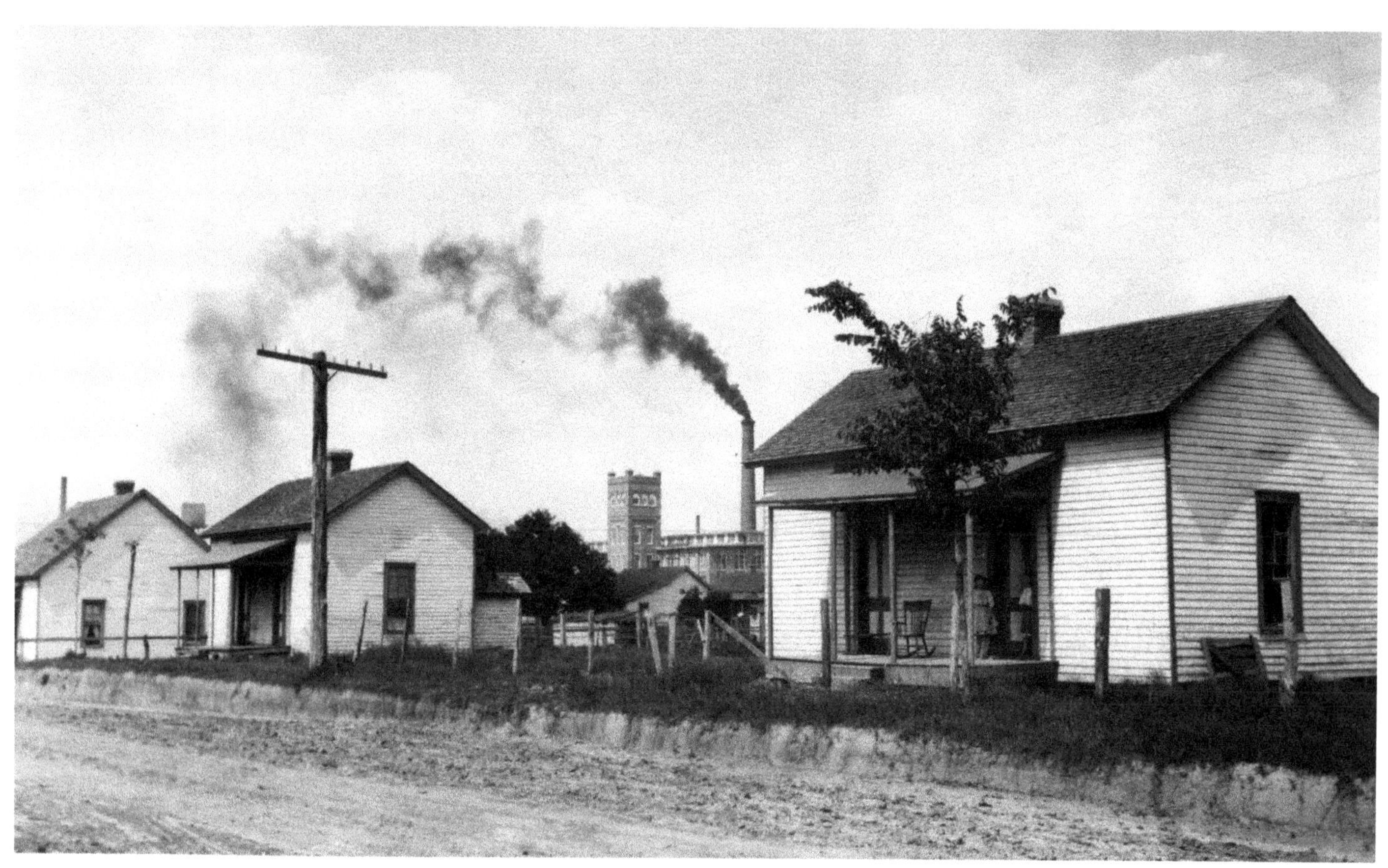

Lewis Hine noted in May 1911 that conditions in Tupelo were "rather good." Three houses for workers stand side by side, with the mill visible in the background. Known as Gum Pond before the Civil War and a battle that took place here, Tupelo is situated in the northeastern part of the state. A year before Elvis was born, Tupelo became the first city to get electric power through the newly created Tennessee Valley Authority.

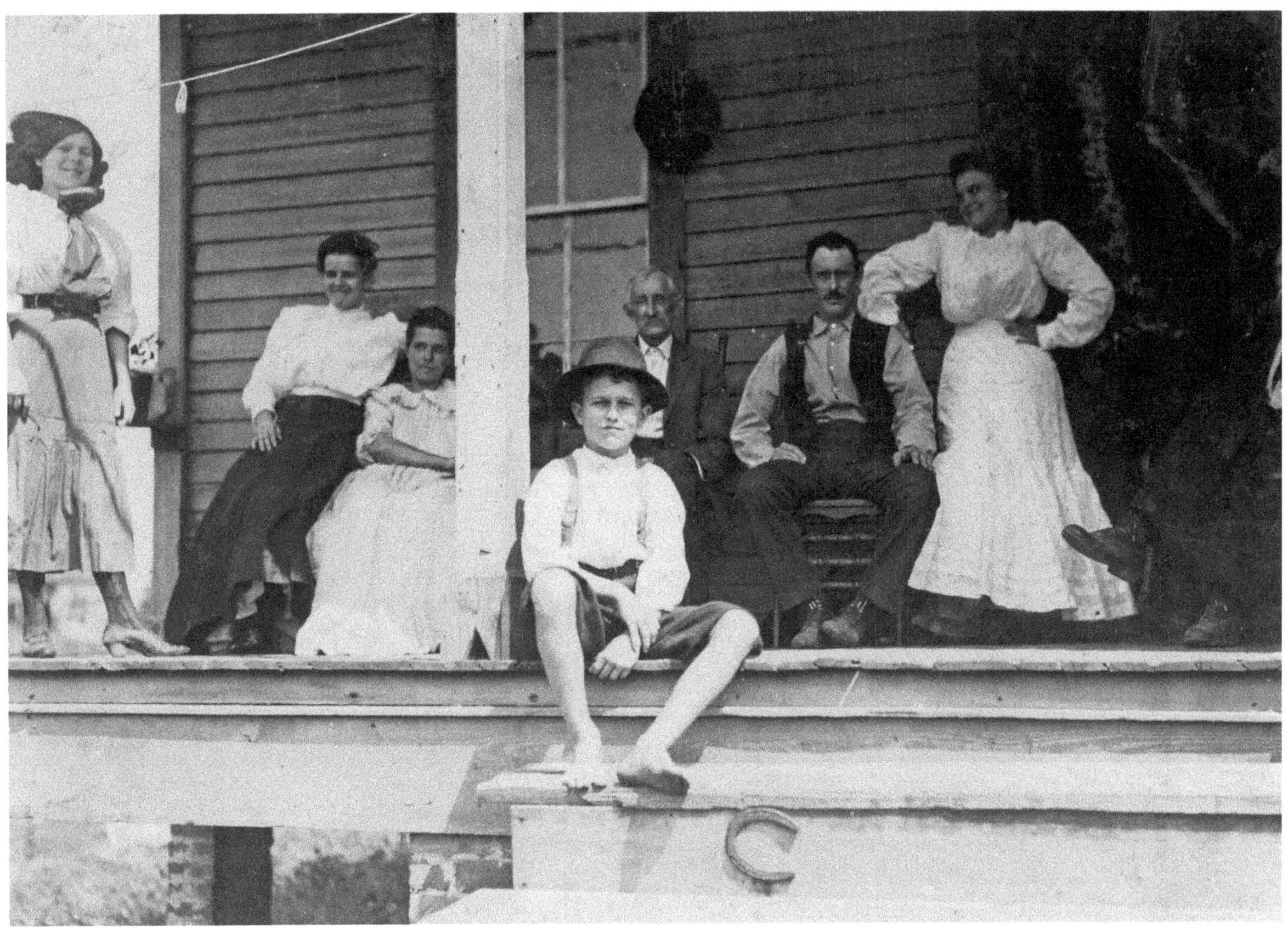

This mill family enjoys the front porch of their company-owned house in Magnolia, and they seem rather content, well fed, and nicely dressed. Hine indicates that all family members worked at the mill, including 13-year-old Wilbert Bennett, sitting on the porch steps.

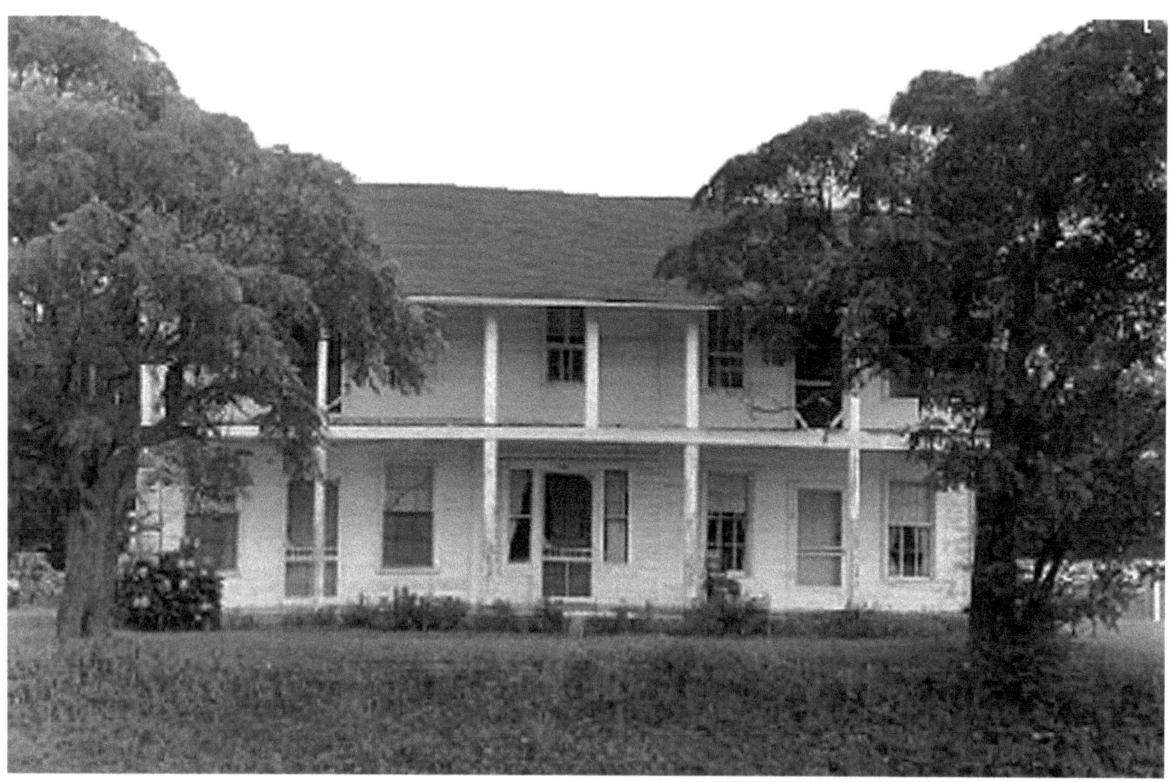

Constructed of virgin pine, Boler's Inn was built in 1856. It became a thriving stagecoach inn along an important road running from Montgomery, Alabama, to Jackson, Mississippi. Over the years the structure served as a hotel, saloon, residence, press for the Union Appeal newspaper, an additional location for the First Presbyterian Church, and a furrier. In February 1864, General William Tecumseh Sherman slashed through east central Mississippi, selecting Boler's Inn as a place to spend the night. To his credit, Sherman saved Boler's Inn and the town of Union, legend has it out of respect for its name, from the torch. The old inn still stands to this day.

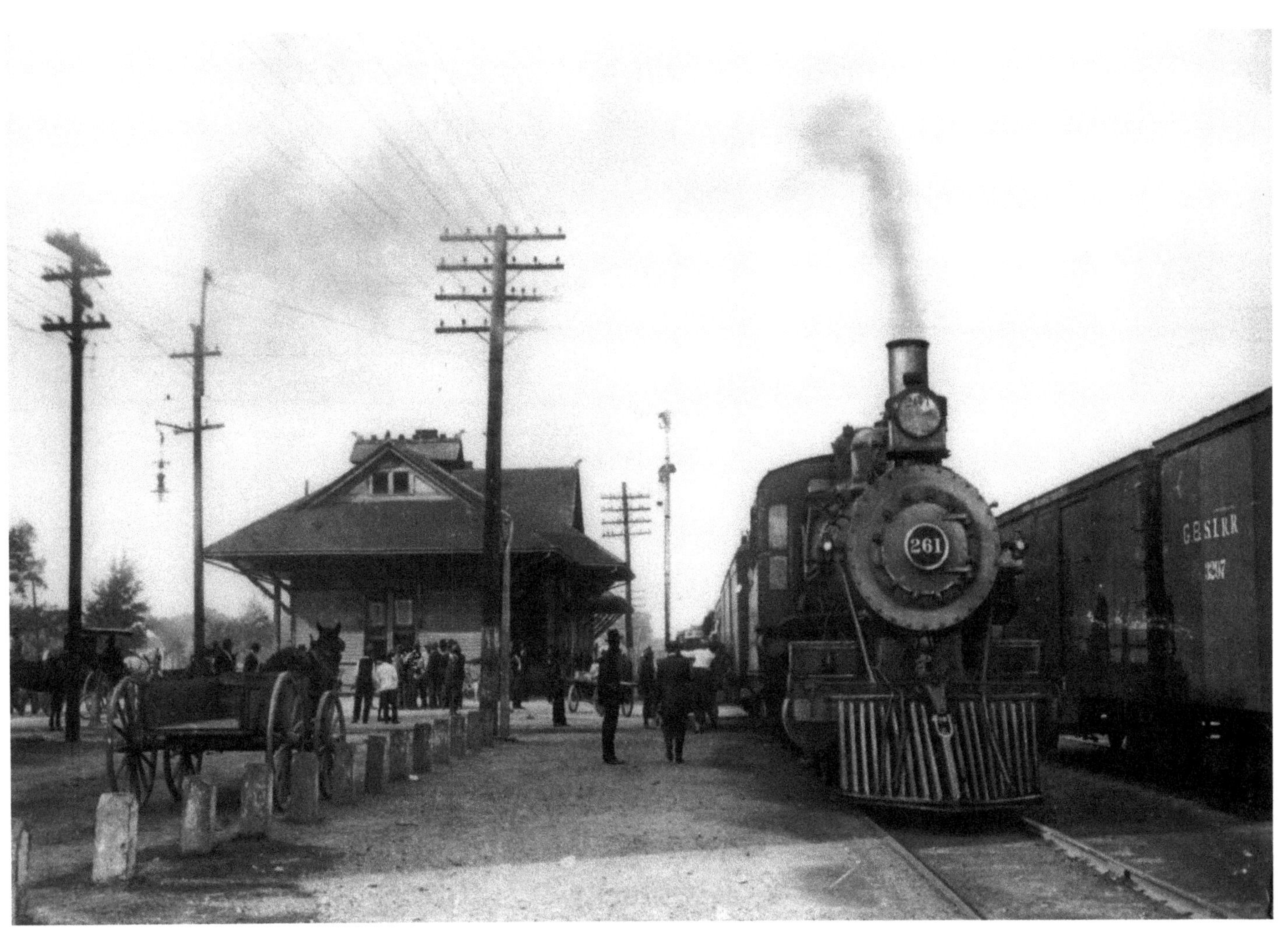

Engine no. 261 idles beside the depot at Biloxi. The railroads played an important role in the economic development of the entire state of Mississippi.

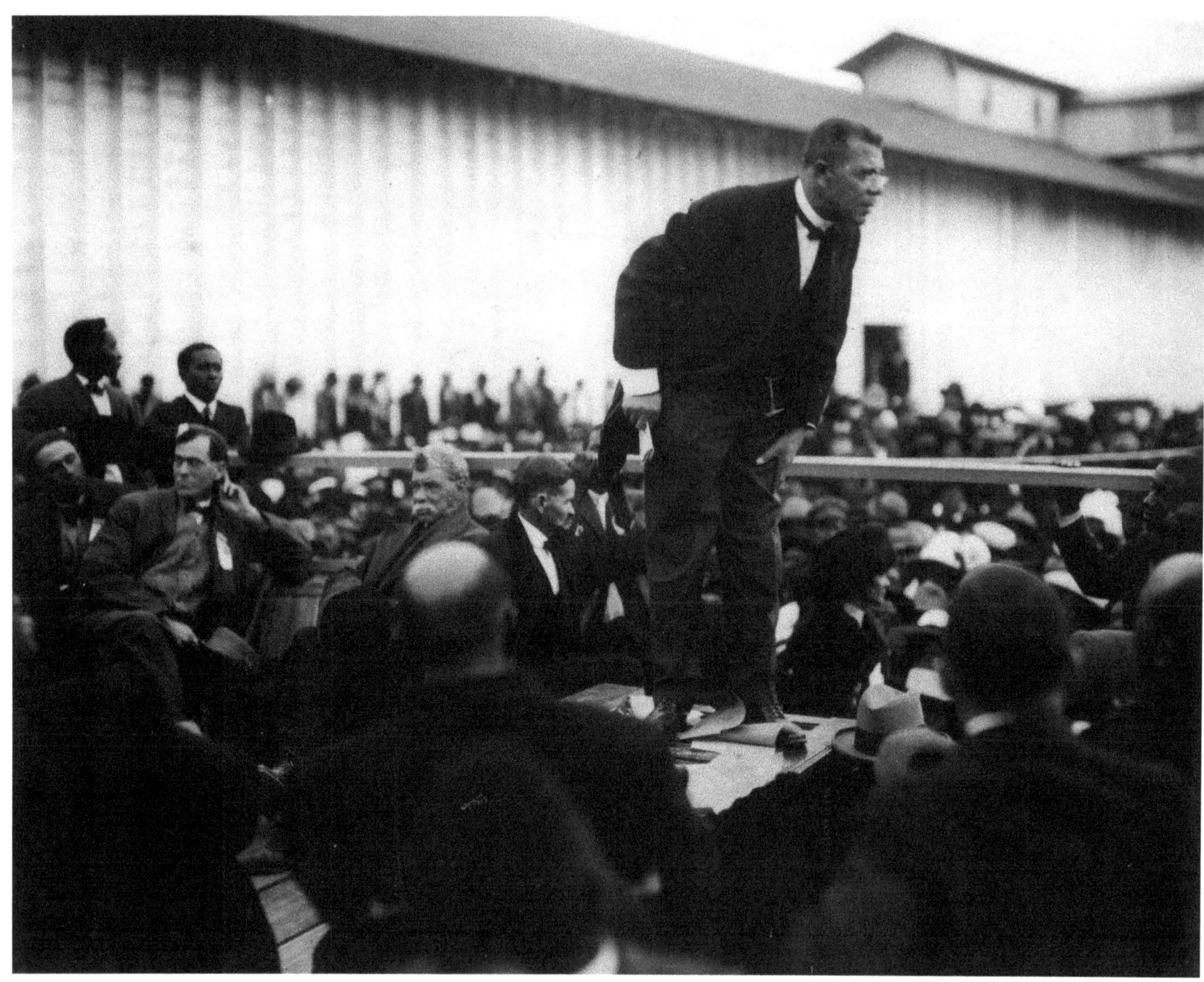

In 1912, Booker T. Washington, an educator, orator, author, and black leader, spoke at Mound Bayou, in Bolivar County, noteworthy for being founded by former slaves. The photograph suggests that Washington's speech was passionate and the audience attentive.

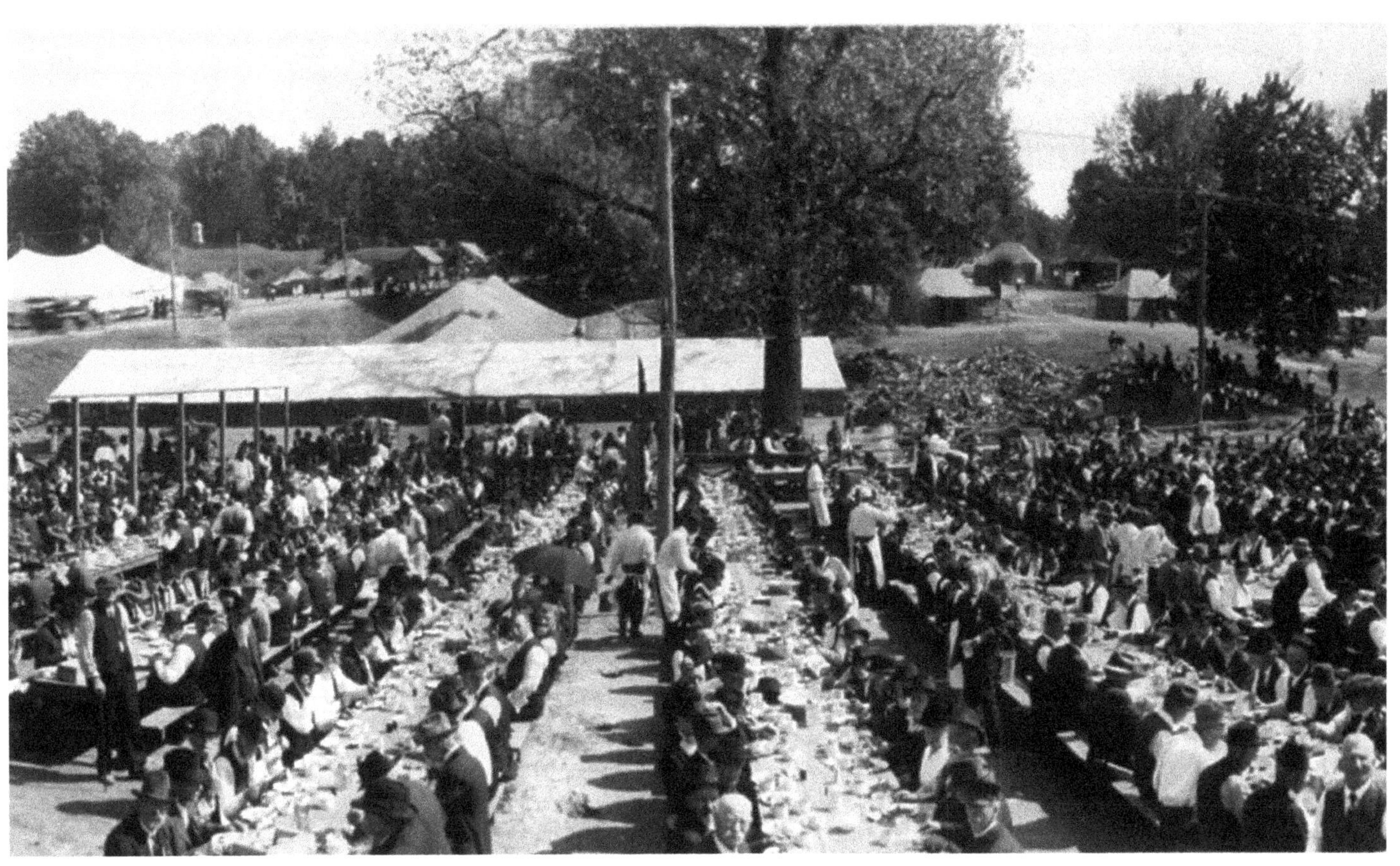

The National Memorial Reunion and Peace Jubilee in Vicksburg was well attended. The American Civil War Commemoration celebration was held October 16-19, 1917. More than 50 years after the war ended, the war veterans have aged, but their memories remain strong.

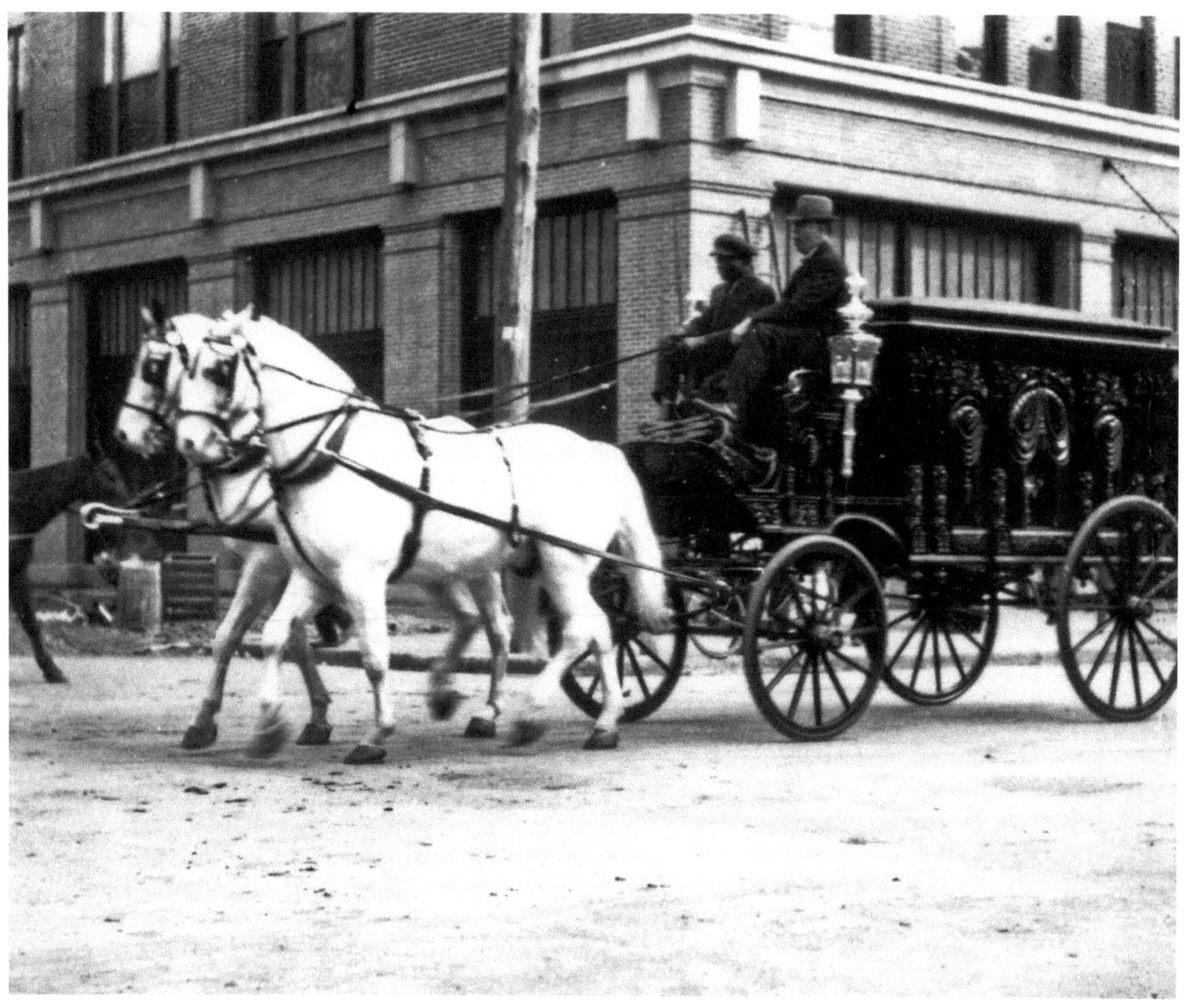

Queen Kelly Mitchell, queen of the Gypsies of North America, who died suddenly during childbirth, is laid to rest in February 1915, her funeral hearse drawn by a team of white horses. An estimated 20,000 people from all over America attended the funeral. The mahogany, glass-covered casket was taken to lovely Rose Hill Cemetery in Meridian. King Emil would later be buried next to his wife.

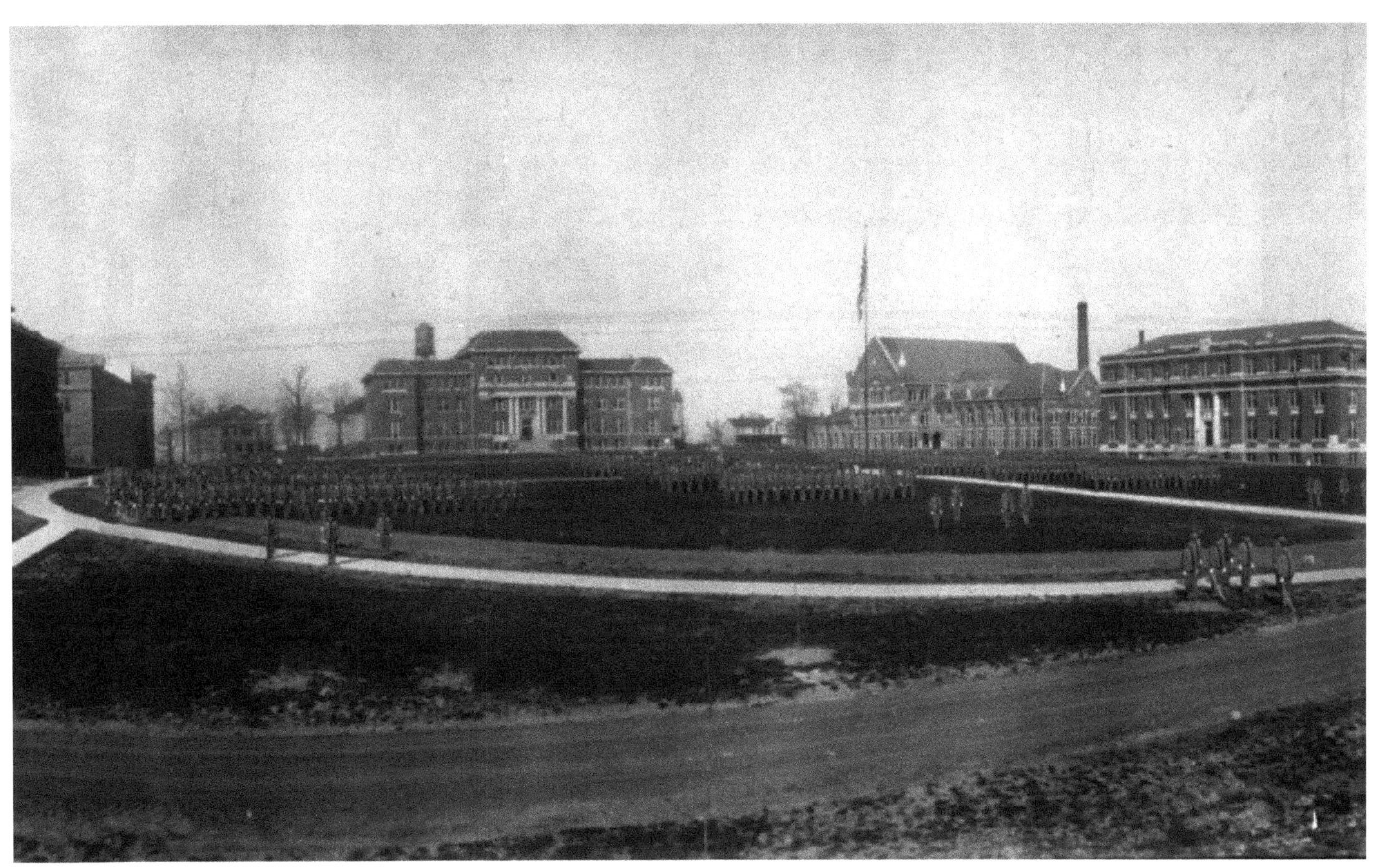

On March 15, 1914, at Mississippi A&M College, a regimental parade is in progress. The university began as the Agricultural and Mechanical College of the State of Mississippi, a land-grant institution made possible by the Morrill Act of 1862. In 1958, the university was renamed Mississippi State University.

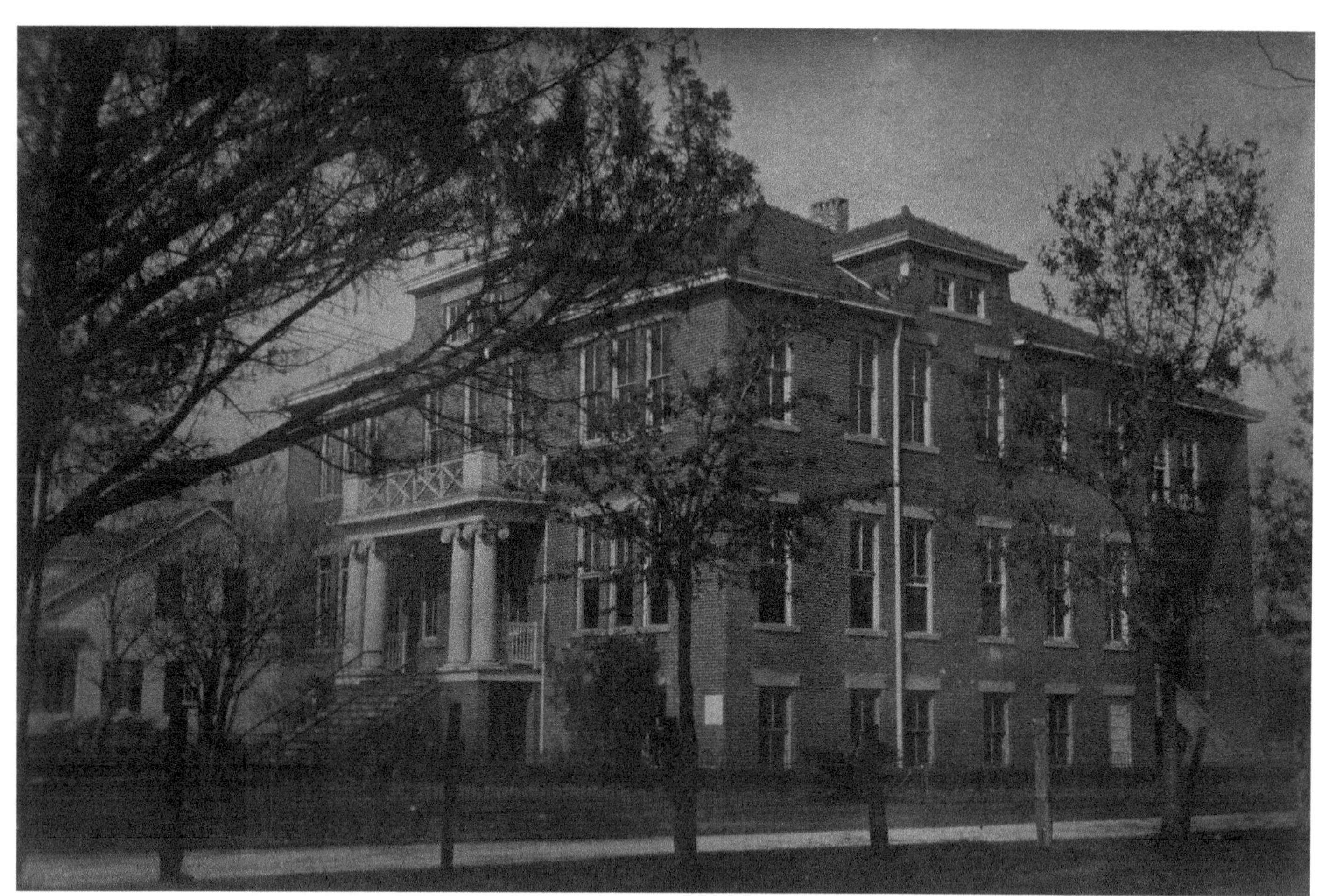

This three-story public school at Pass Christian was photographed in February 1916.

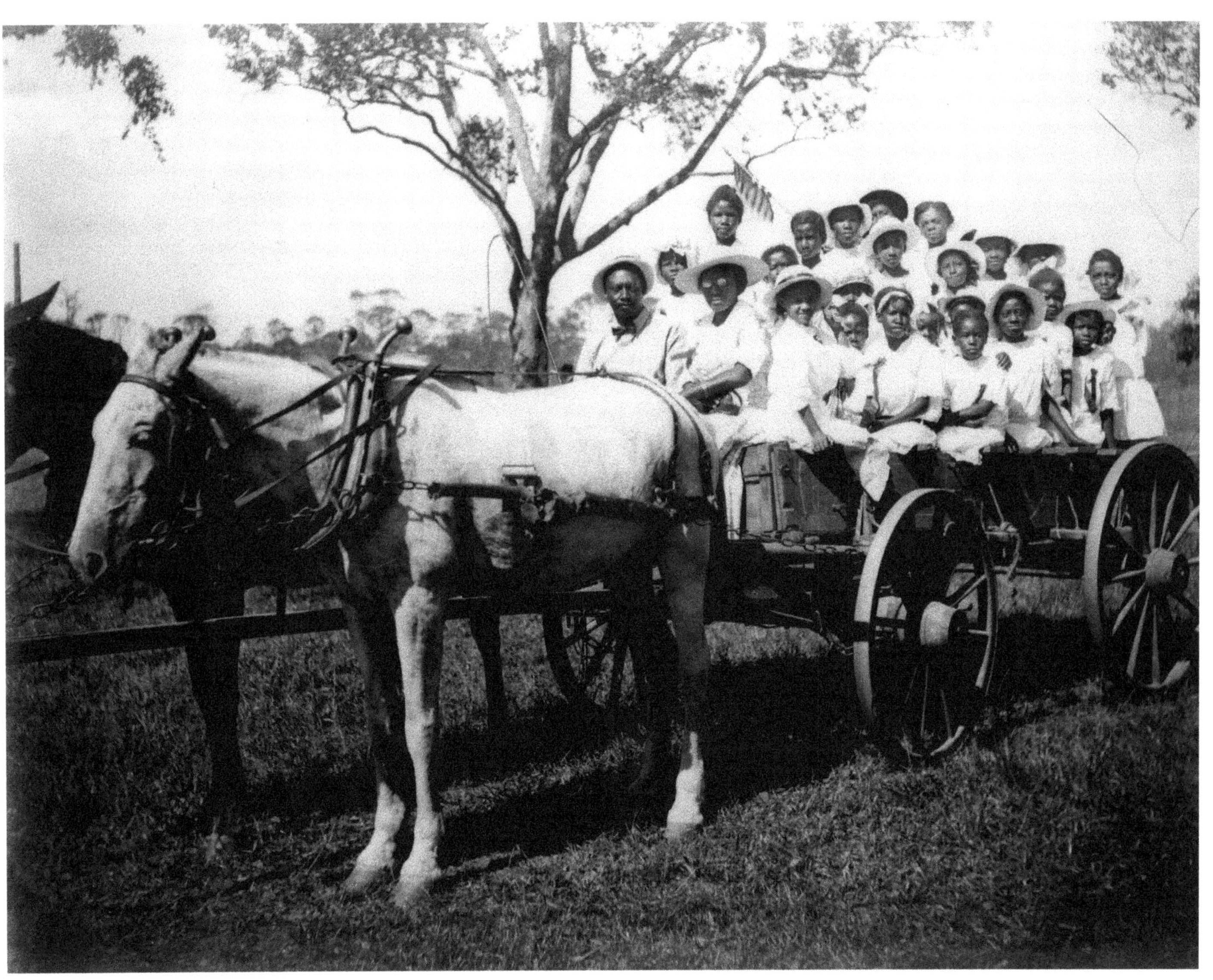

This patriotic group enjoys a Sunday afternoon outing in 1916, stopping their horse-drawn wagon to pose for a photograph. The couple at front and 22 youth all dressed in white suggests that they were members of a church class.

A pedestrian passes the impressive St. Joseph's Academy school for girls, at Bay St. Louis in Hancock County, in February 1916. The building was damaged in the great fire of November 16, 1907, but appears fully restored in this image. In 1965, the damage wrought by Hurricane Betsy would lead to the school's closing, and still later Hurricane Katrina would badly damage Our Lady Academy, the all-girls school that replaced it.

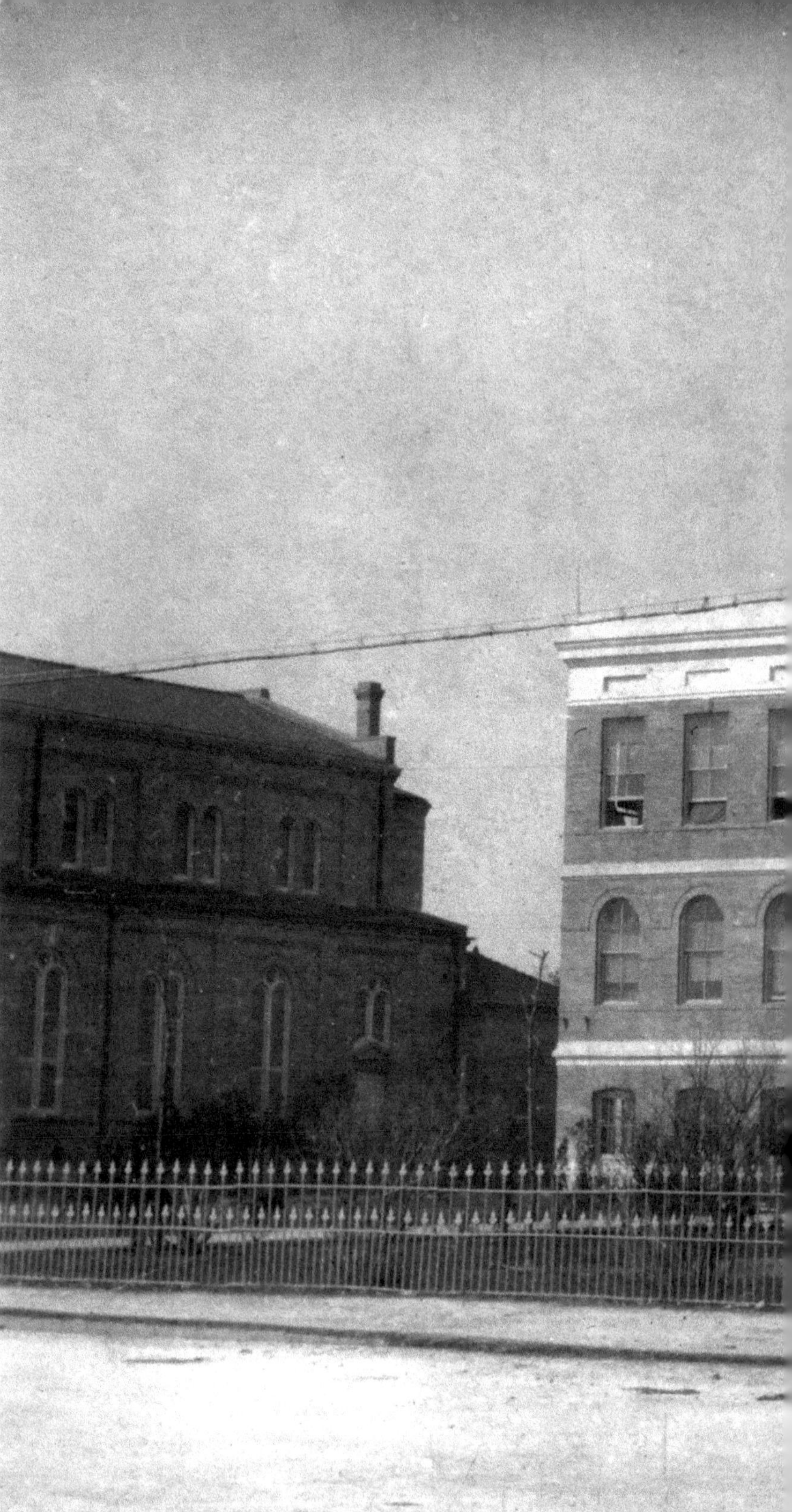

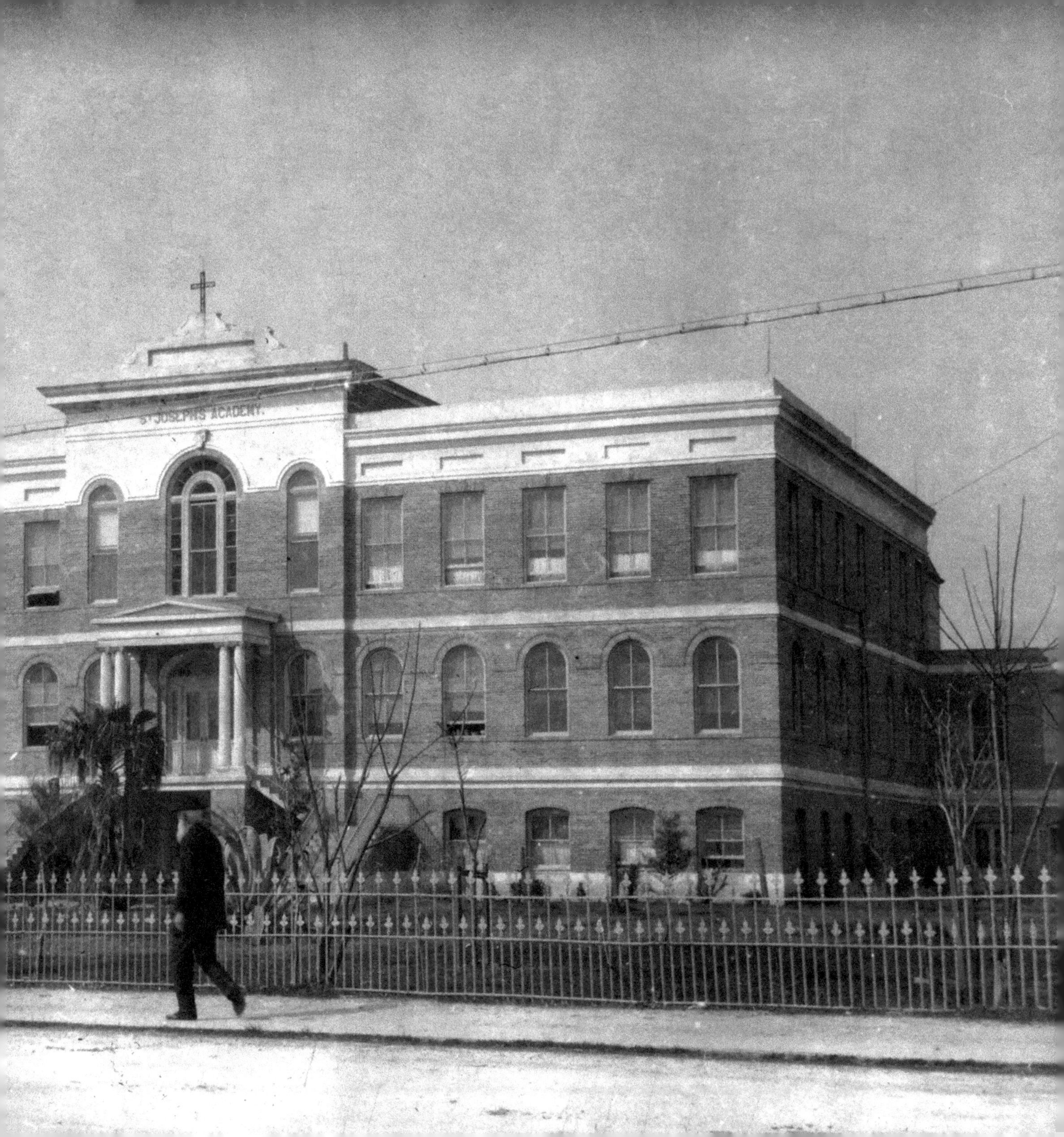
ST JOSEPHS ACADEMY.

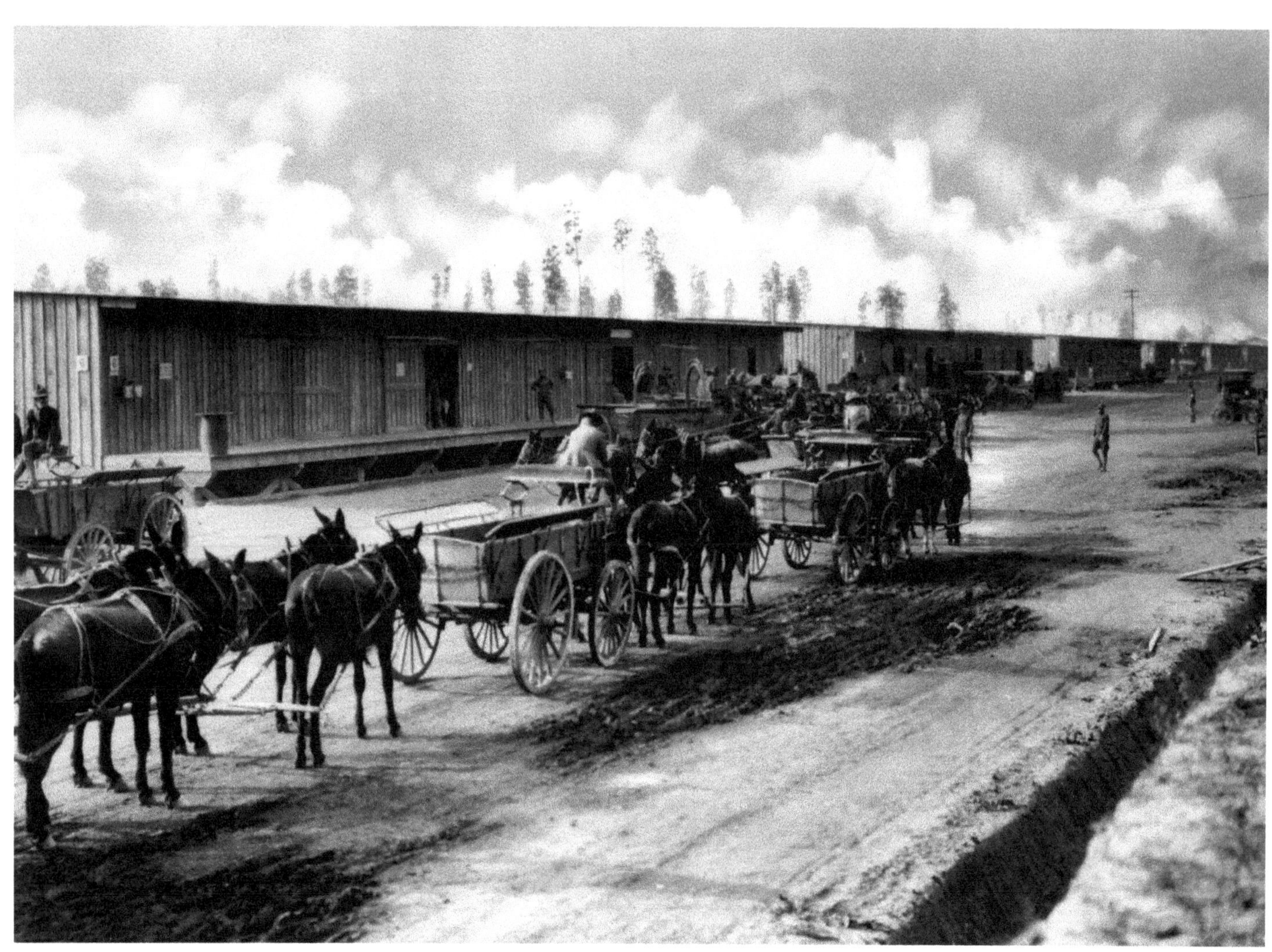

Warehouses with mules and spring wagons are shown at Camp Shelby military base in Hattiesburg in 1918. The military post was established in 1917 as part of the buildup for World War I.

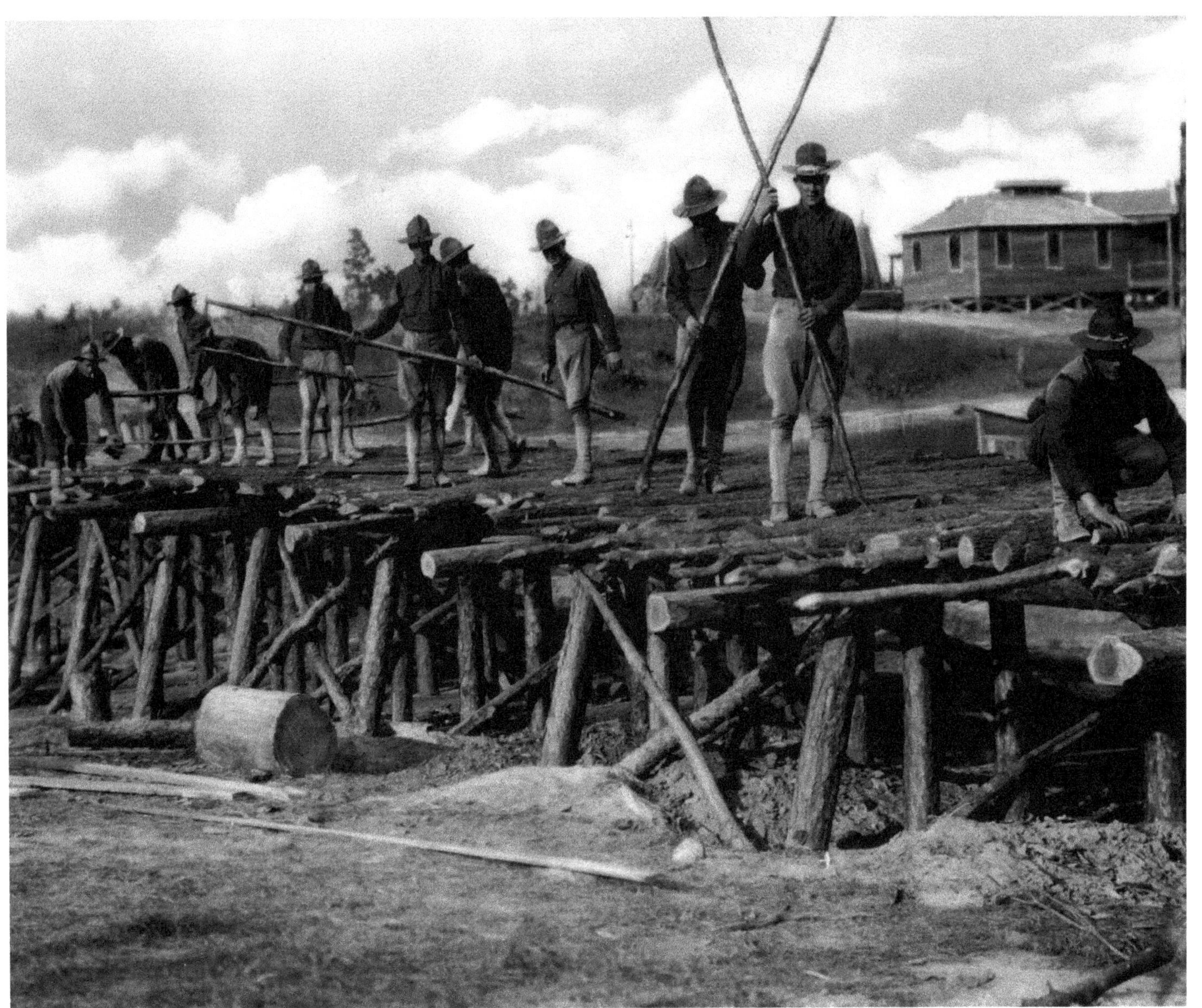

Soldiers are shown building a bridge in 1918. Camp Shelby played a vital role in the war effort during World War I.

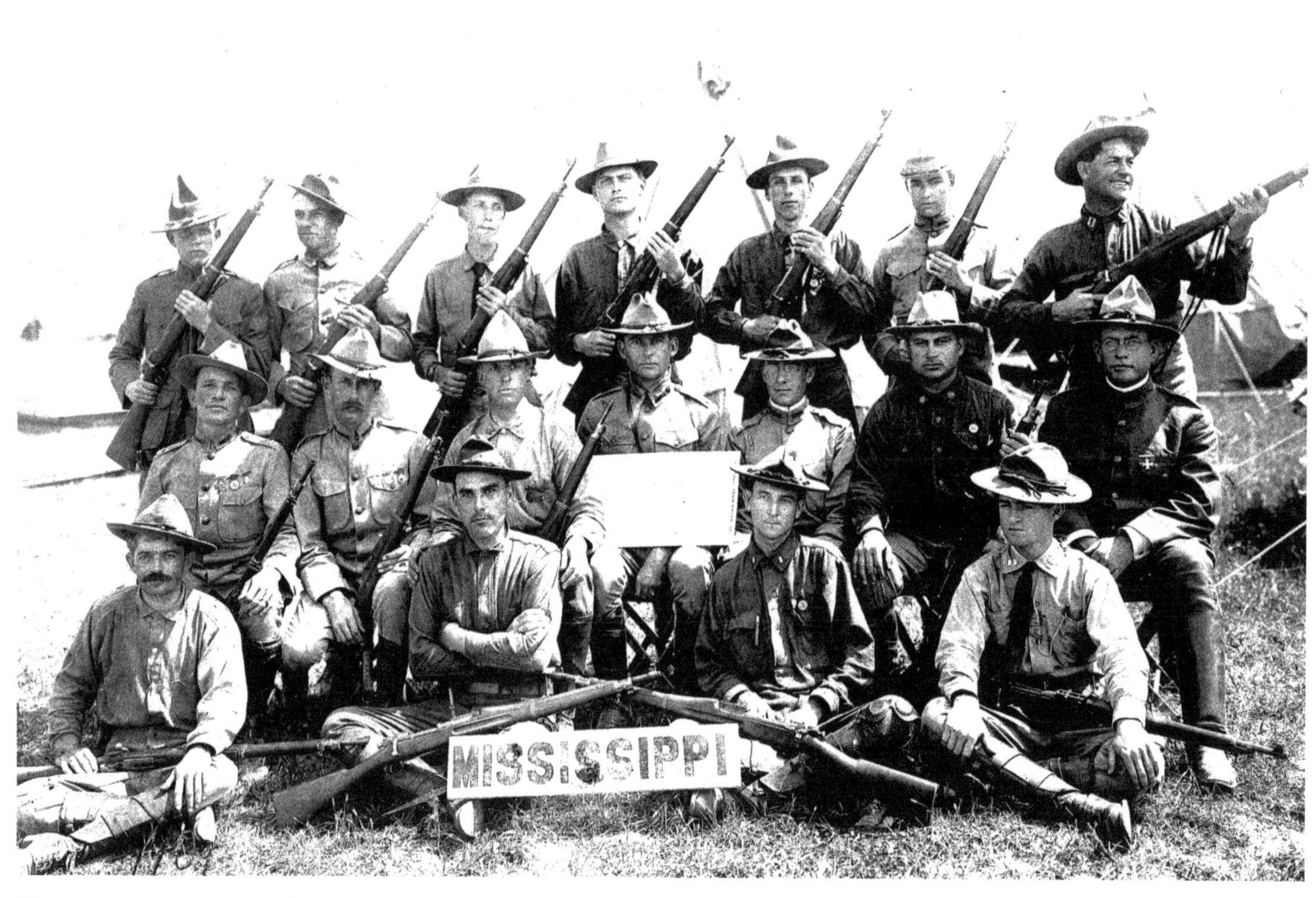

These young men, disciplined and courageous, are members of the World War I Mississippi Riflemen, known as Mississippi's oldest National Guard unit and the seventh-oldest infantry regiment in the United States Army. Its history predates statehood, back to June 1799. The unit accompanied General Pershing on the Mexican Expedition against Pancho Villa in 1916. During World War I, the unit was designated the 155th Infantry Regiment and fought with the 30th Division, and during World War II, they fought in the Pacific theater.

Depression Years and Singing the Blues

(1920–1939)

The Mississippi Delta is widely regarded as the birthplace of the blues, though the precise origins of blues music are unknown. The music came from many sources, notably through Negro spirituals sung by slaves working the fields and longing for a better life. Blues rose to prominence during the 1920s and the Great Depression, which seemed to come early to the state, hard hit by the great flood of 1927. In these years Delta blues legends Charley Patton and Robert Johnson made their best-known recordings. East central Mississippi reverberated with fiddles, banjos, and guitars as the people gathered to sing their hard times away. Singing schools became popular and groups sang the shape note music known as Sacred Harp. Also during the 1920s, Meridian native and railroad man Jimmie Rodgers, known as the Father of Country Music, rose to fame with his unique "blue yodels."

Many jobs ended during the economic downfall, and Mississippians remembered the lessons taught by their forebears of the inner strength needed simply to survive. The flood was followed by a severe drought in 1931, and the boll weevil devastated cotton crops throughout both decades. Hard times notwithstanding, enterprising entrepreneurs set up shop in the 1920s and 1930s, and despite the odds, many of them became successful. In Marion, Mississippi, a strawberry business started that blossomed as Marion Beauties, and in the 1920s a Meridian resident, Alvin Lowry, produced and sold "anti-snoring" devices. After 1932, Franklin Roosevelt's New Deal programs, including the Works Progress Administration, the Federal Emergency Relief Administration, and the Civilian Conservation Corps, brought government relief by creating jobs, including federal funding for art, literature, and music projects, sometimes criticized by Americans concerned about federal intermeddling.

Music had born its best fruit during hard times and independent of government, as did the literary arts. William Faulkner's *The Sound and the Fury* was published in 1929, followed by other major works during the 1930s. The darkness of the Great Depression would spread across the 1930s before the coming of war and a whisper of economic recovery was heard, but the words and the music continued on and on to lighten the load of weary Mississippians.

Civic leaders in east central Mississippi break ground for the latest project in the 1920s.

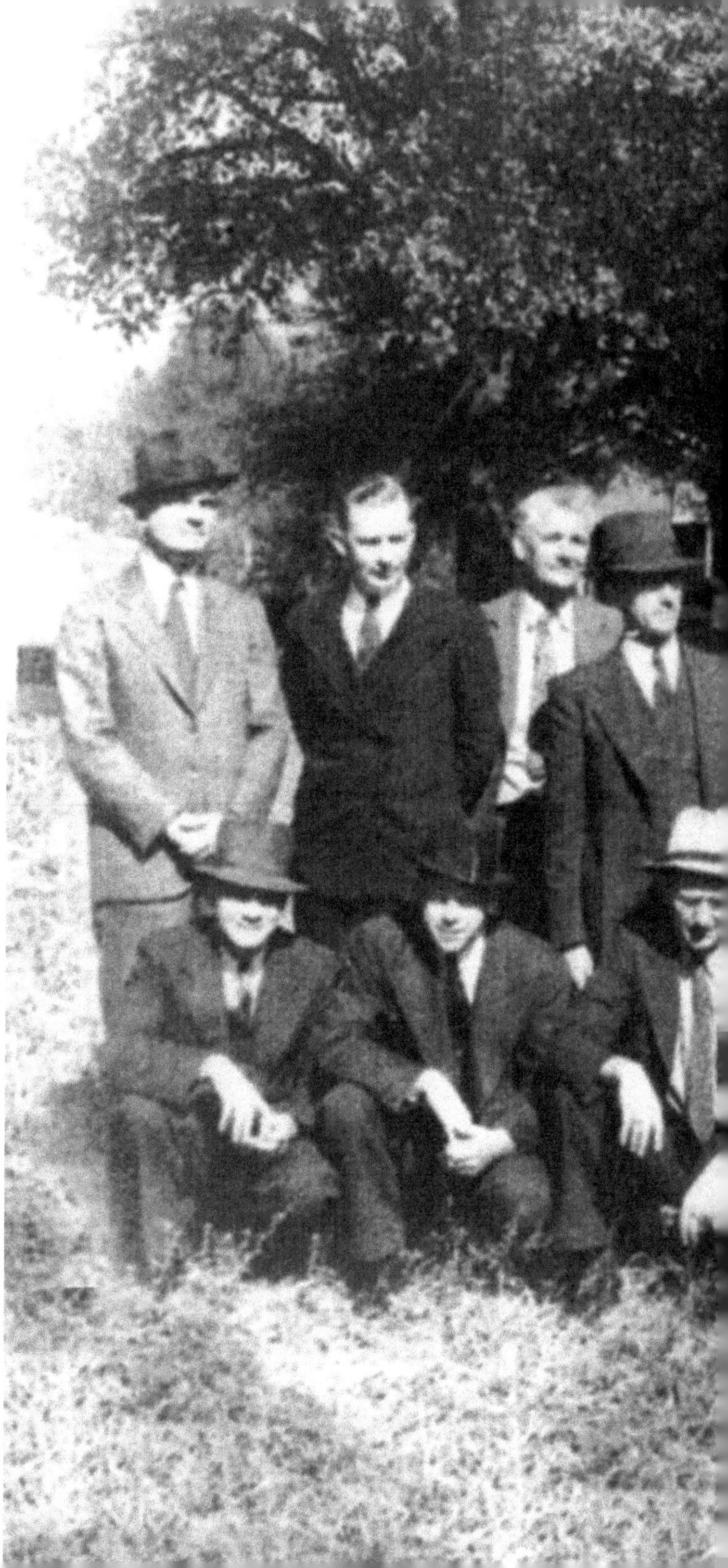

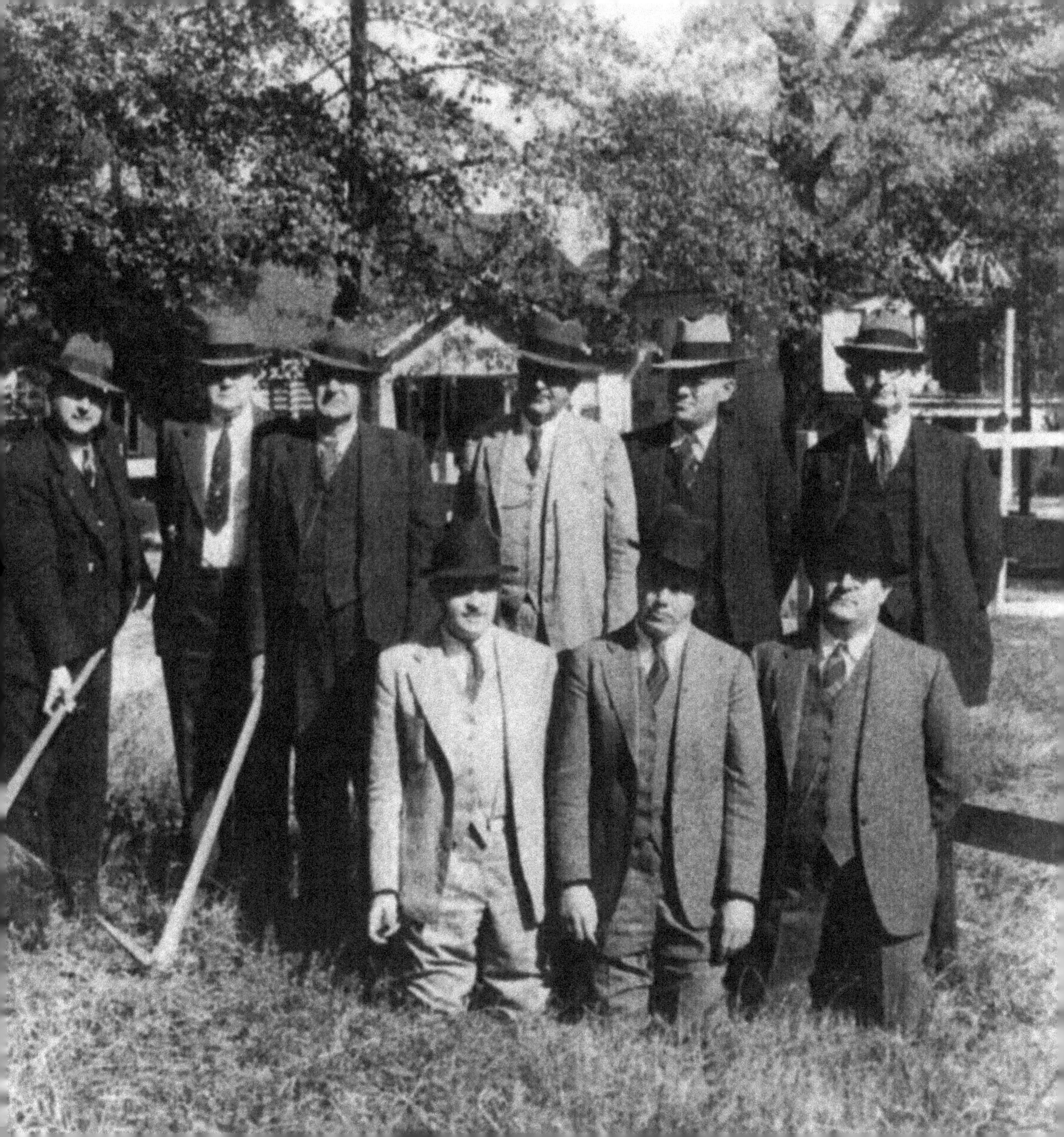

Built by local craftsmen in 1857, Stanton Hall at Natchez, in Adams County, remains one of America's largest antebellum mansions. Noted photographer Frances Benjamin Johnston recorded this image in the 1920s. In 1932, the Natchez Pilgrimage, an annual tour of the area's antebellum homes, would become a popular event that continues today.

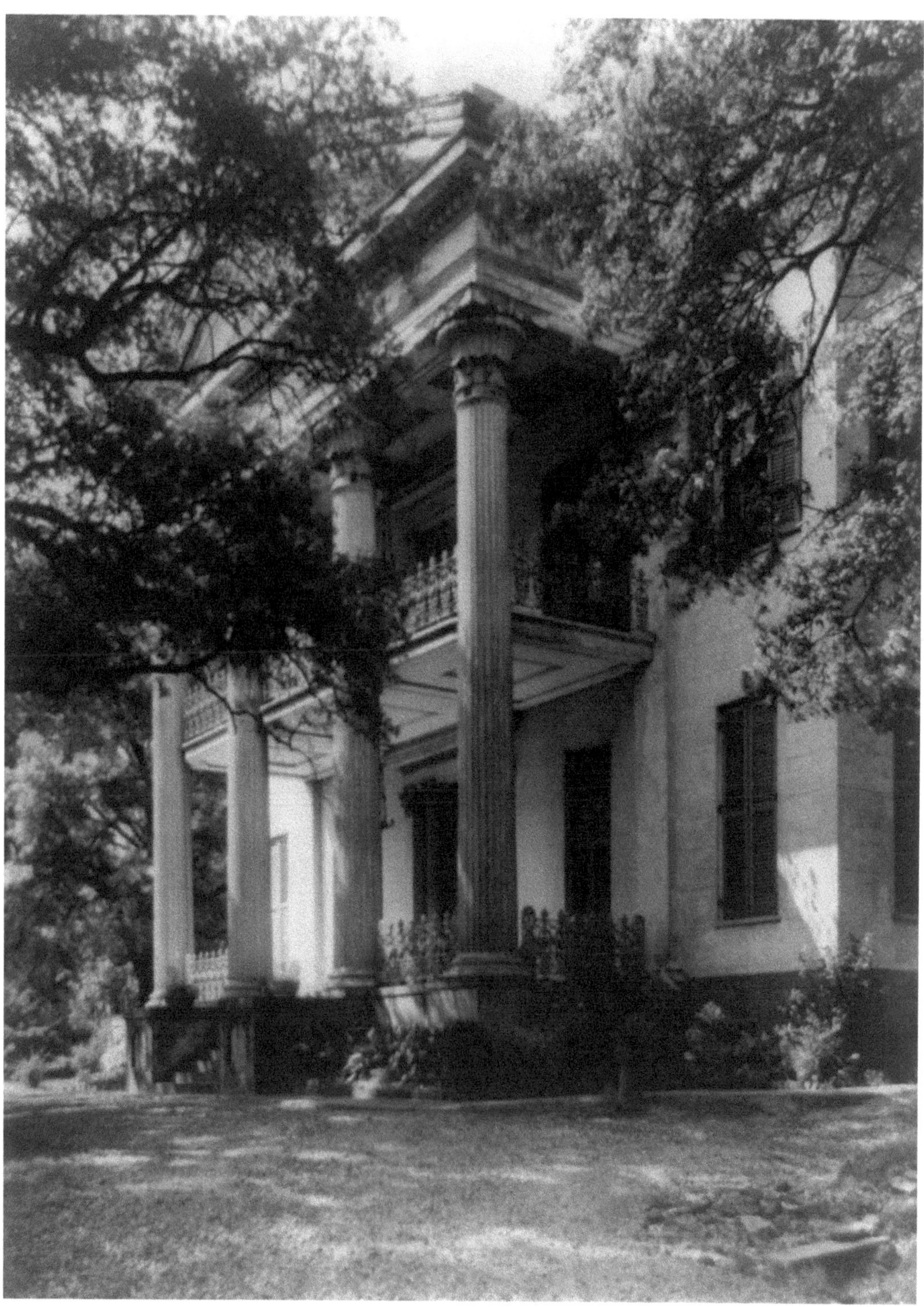

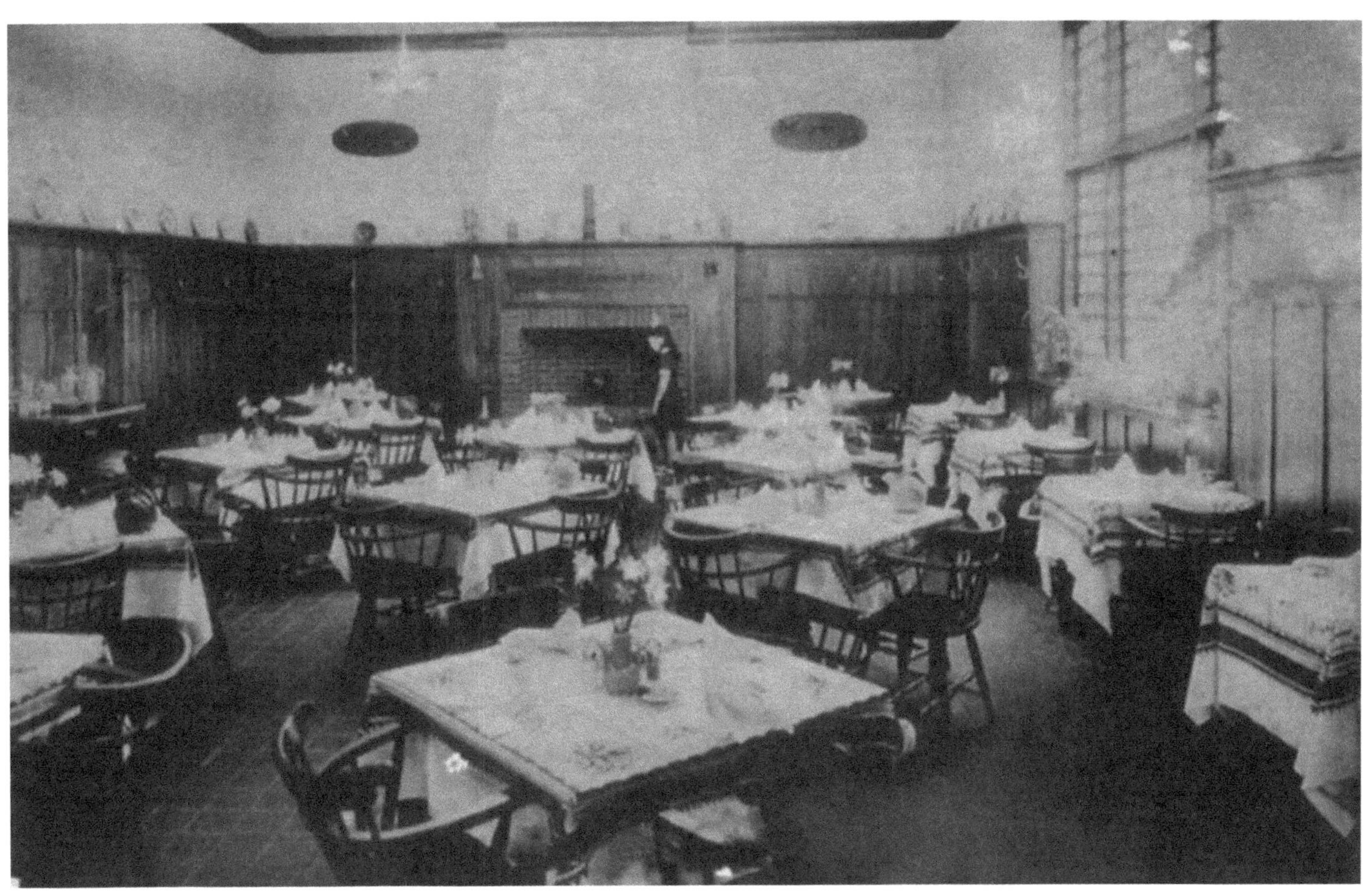

Inside Weidmann's Restaurant as it appeared in 1926. Felix Weidmann, a young Swiss immigrant from Zurich, worked his way to America in 1870 by serving as a cook on an ocean liner. He headed for Meridian and opened his first eating establishment the same year. The eatery is legendary throughout the South for its outstanding black-bottom pie, Southern hospitality, and gracious dining.

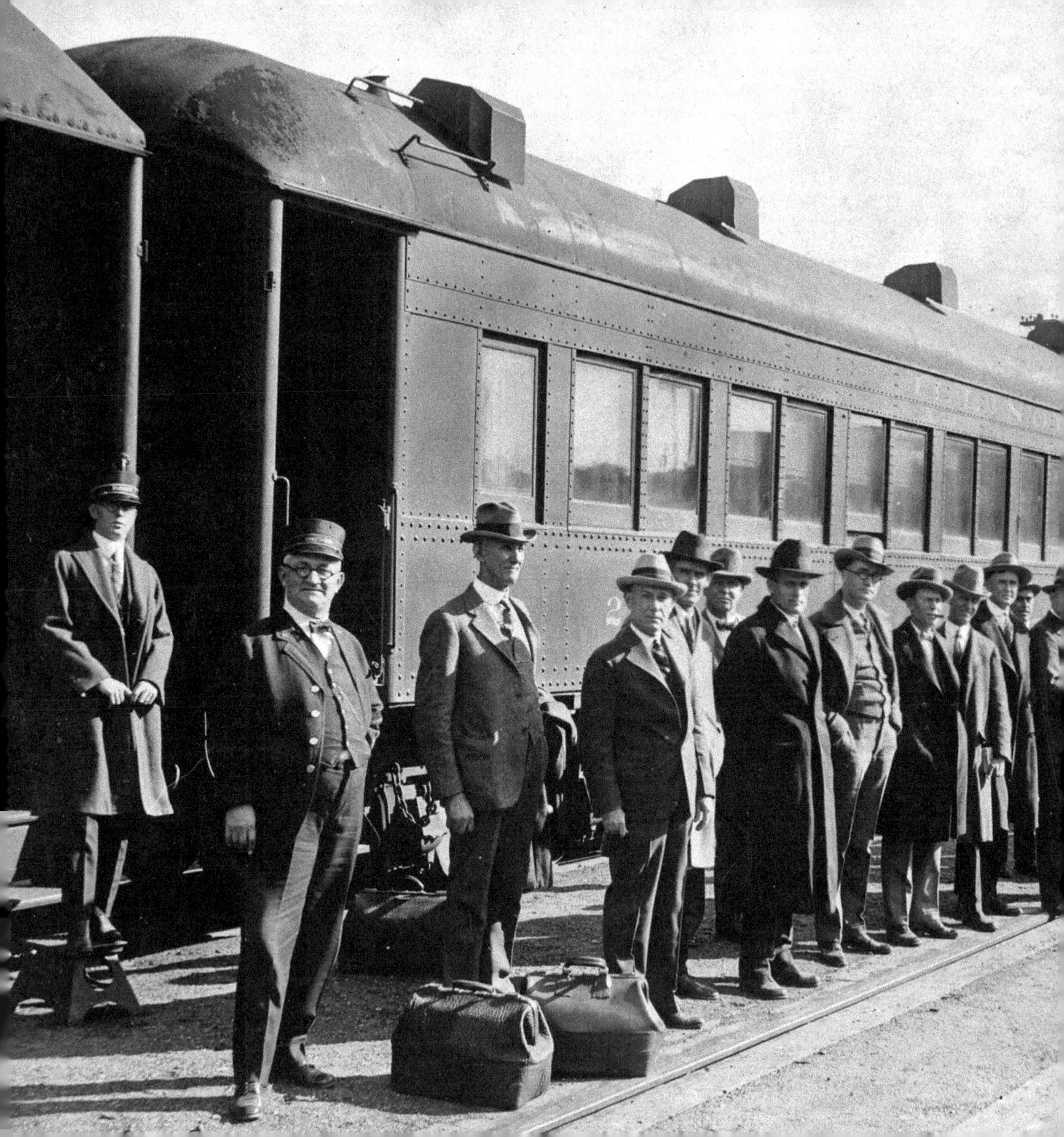

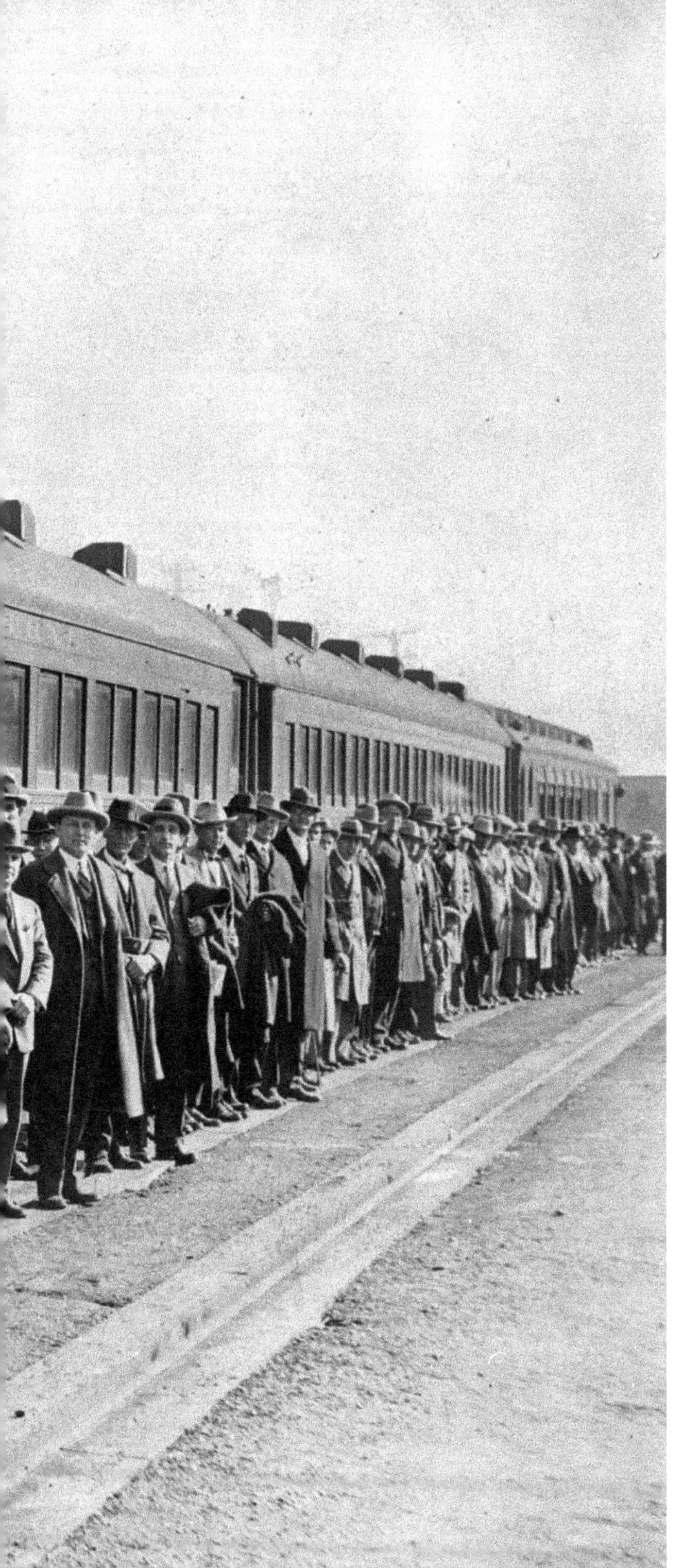

A special train idles at the depot at McComb, in Pike County, sometime around the 1920s. The train, sponsored by the McComb chamber of commerce, was carrying farmers and businessmen to the state agricultural college located at Starkville, to promote dairy development for Pike County.

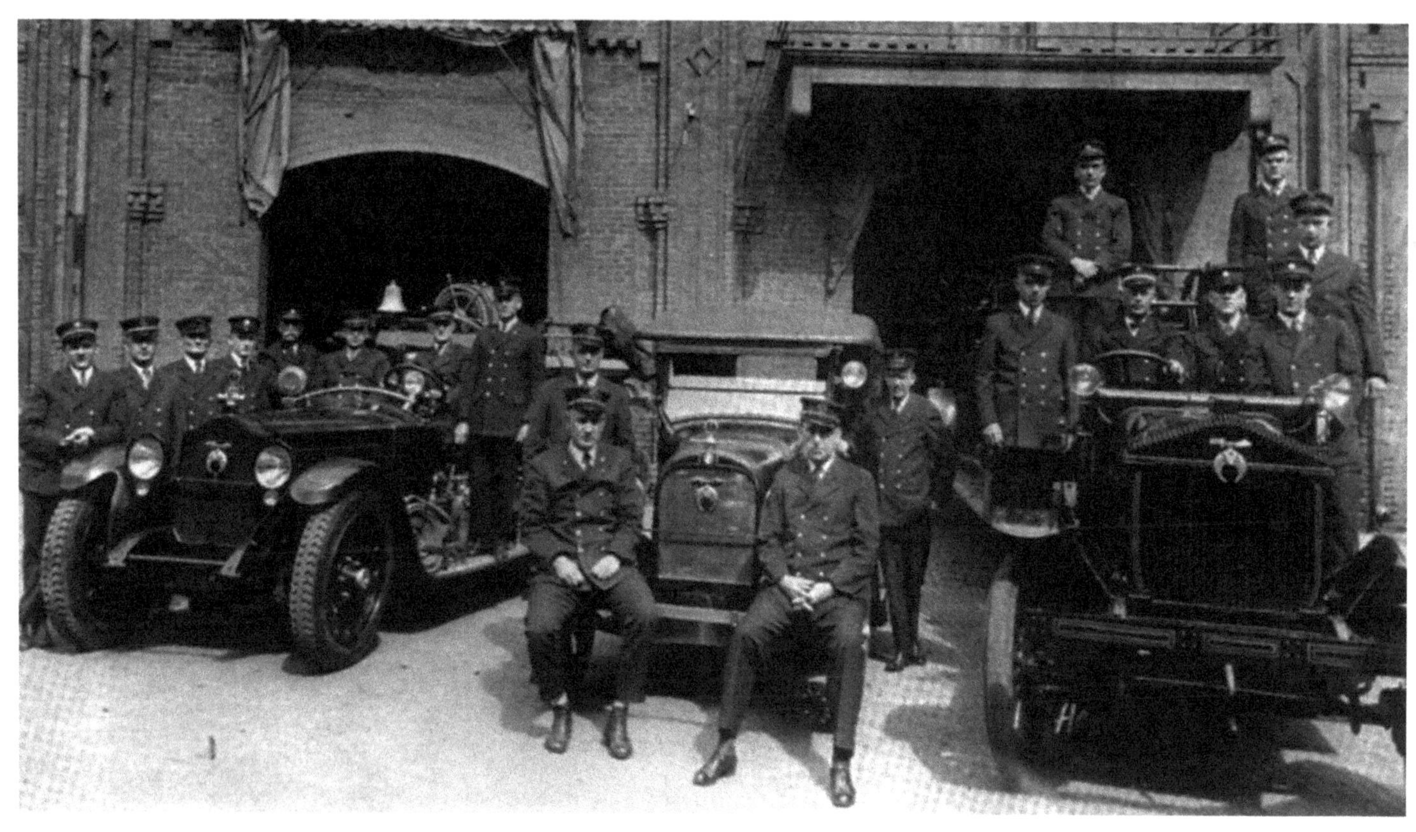

Between 1890 and 1930, Meridian was the largest city in Mississippi. Shown here is the Meridian fire department, smartly dressed with equipment gleaming, assembled for a group shot in 1920.

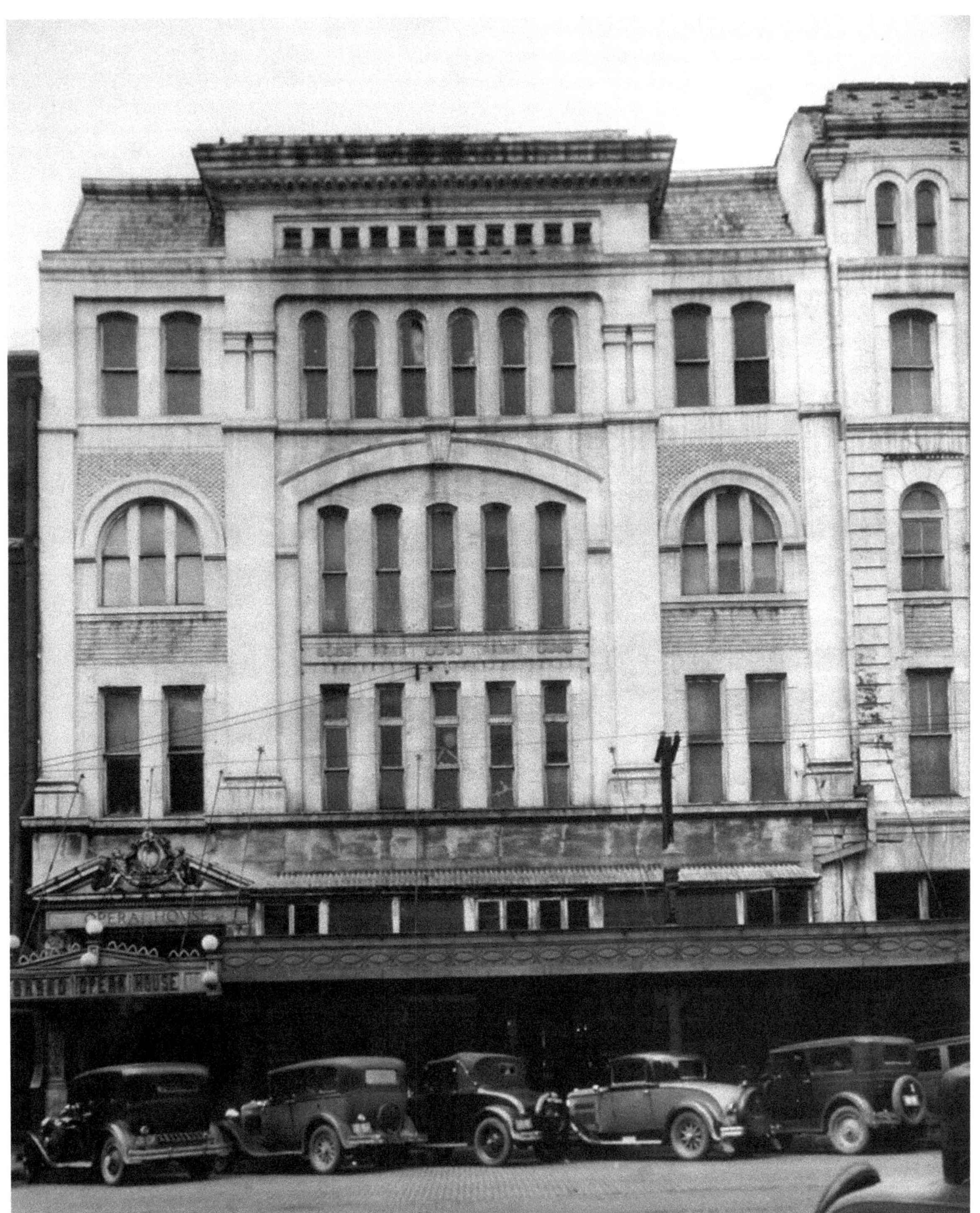

The Grand Opera House at Meridian originally opened in 1890. It was remodeled in 1902 and again in 1920, when it was converted in part to a movie theater. The lovely theater would succumb to neglect after 1927, but survived intact through the 1960s sheathed in metal siding. Today it stands restored to its original luster as the MSU Riley Center.

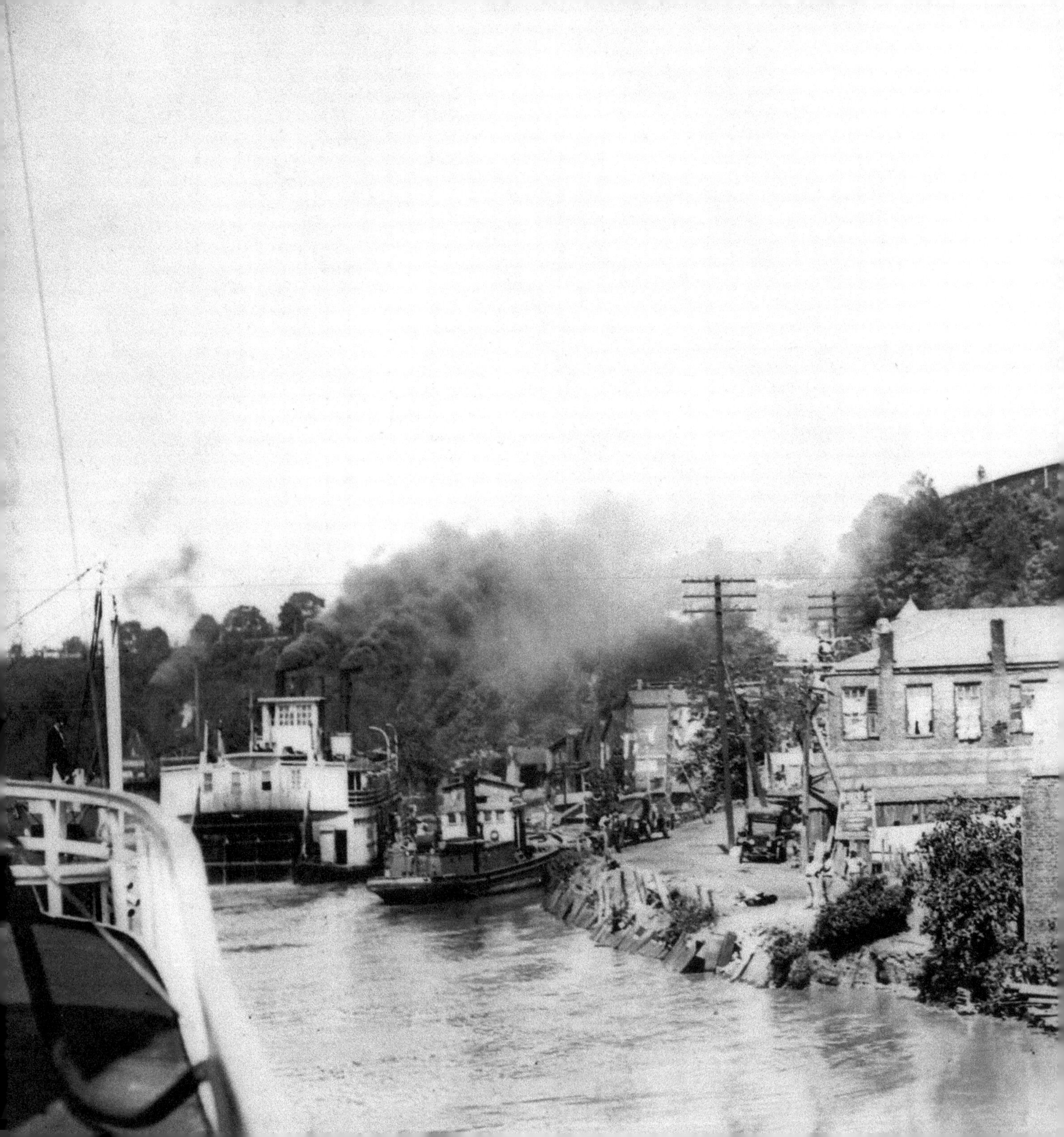

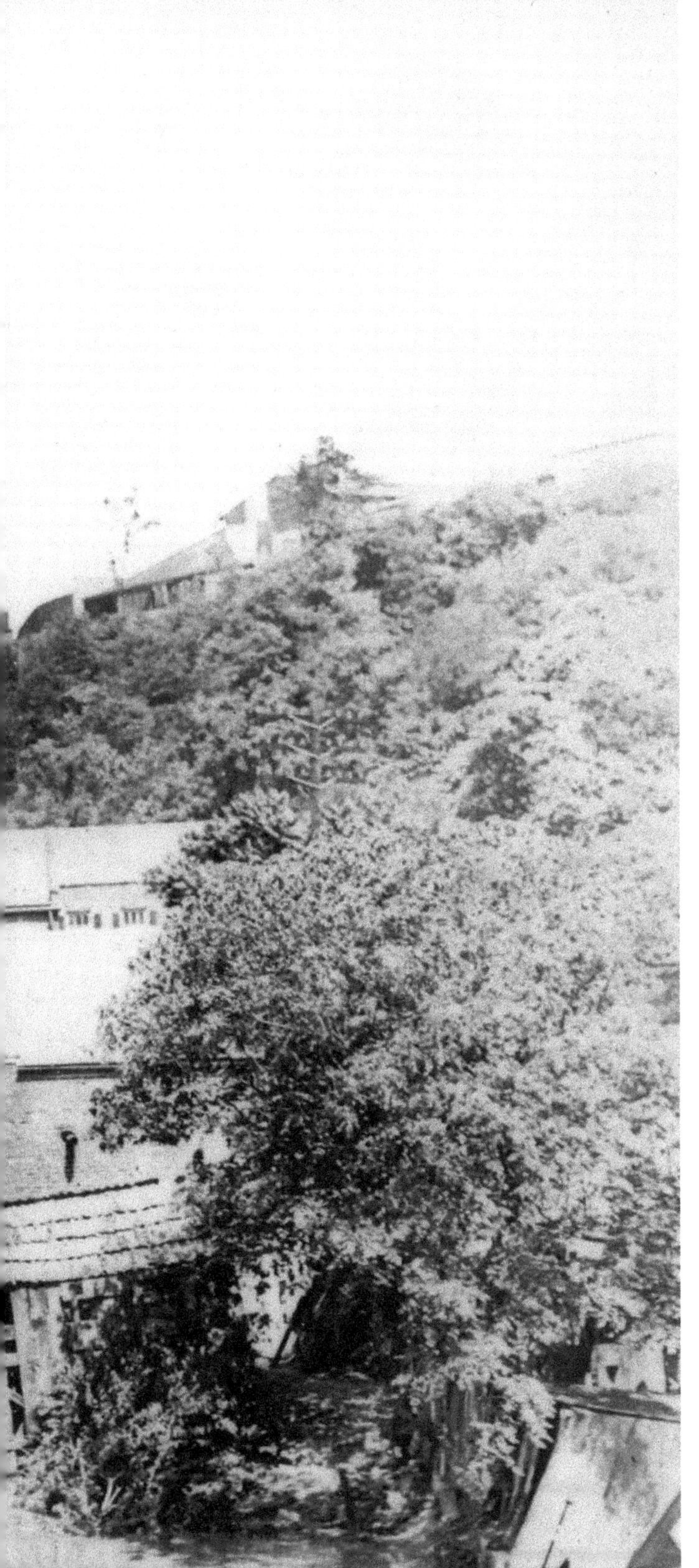

In 1927, the Mississippi River and tributaries flooded seven states, causing millions of dollars in damage, leaving thousands homeless, and killing hundreds of citizens. This image of the high waters was recorded at a ferry landing in Natchez.

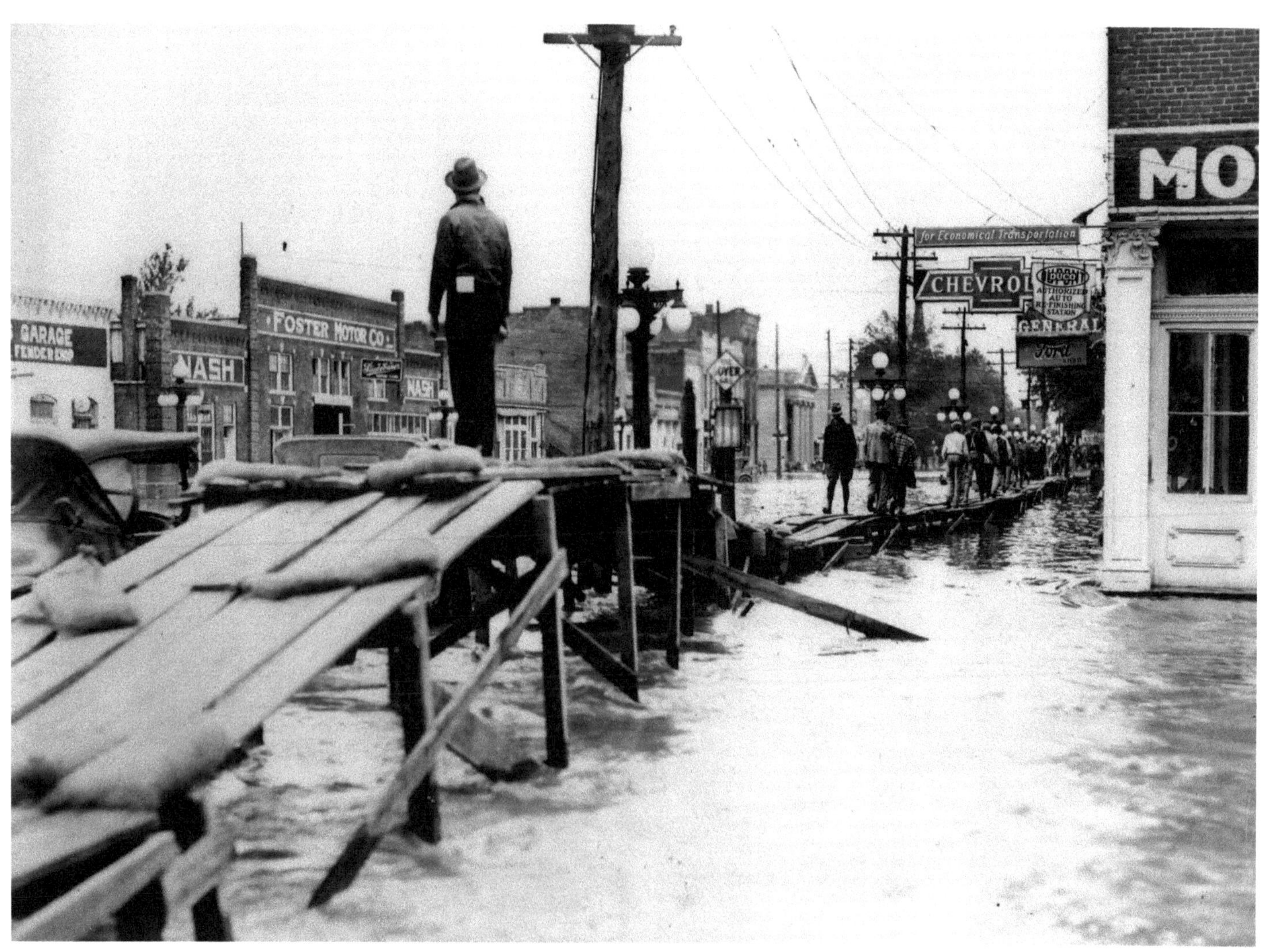

Citizens of Greenville make their way down a business street on an elevated plank walkway above floodwaters that have inundated businesses.

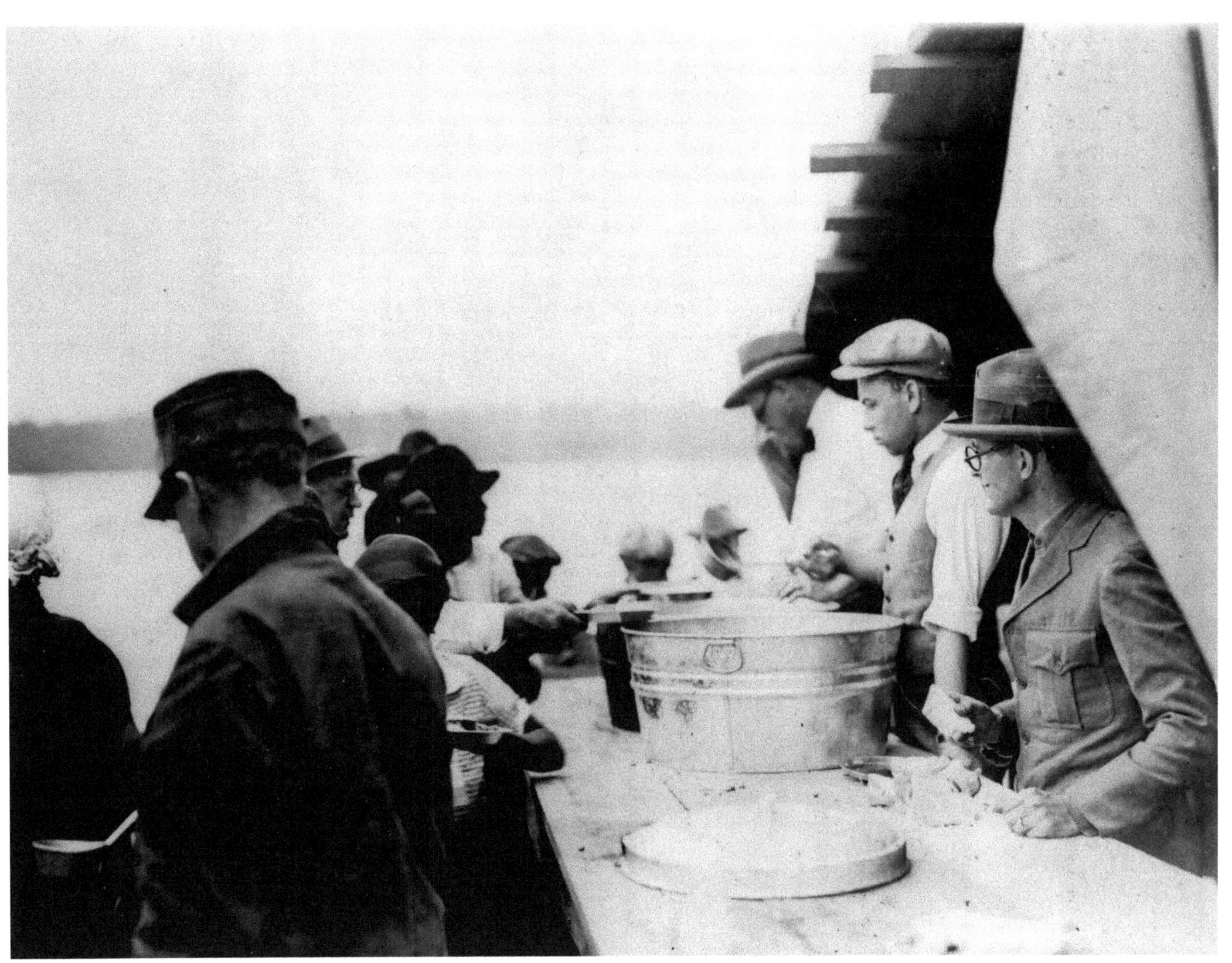

The great Mississippi River flood of 1927 brought everyday life in the Mississippi Delta to a halt. Shown here are refugees in a food line on the levee as food is dispensed.

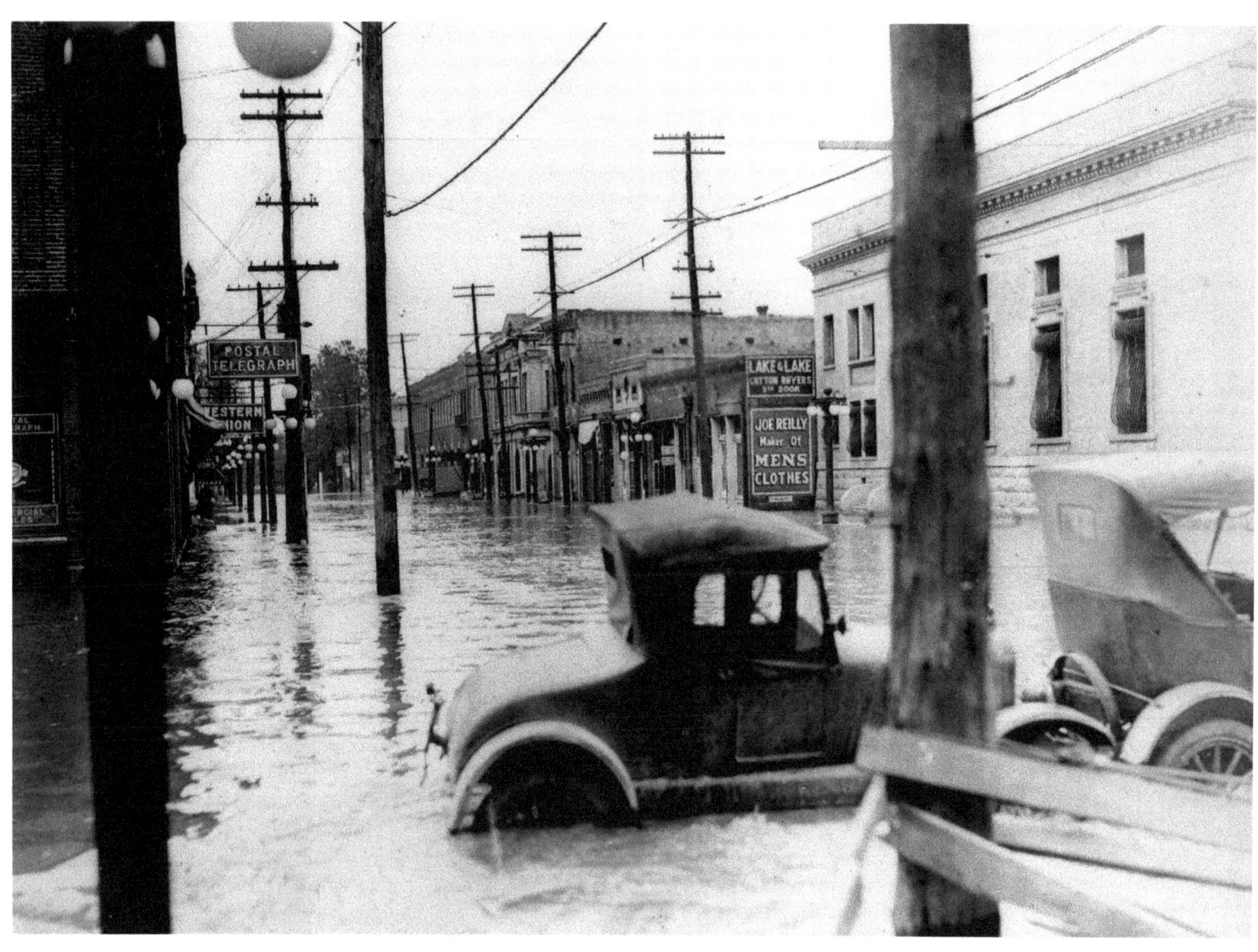

Greenville's Main Street and Poplar Street are shown in this view facing north during the great Mississippi River flood of 1927.

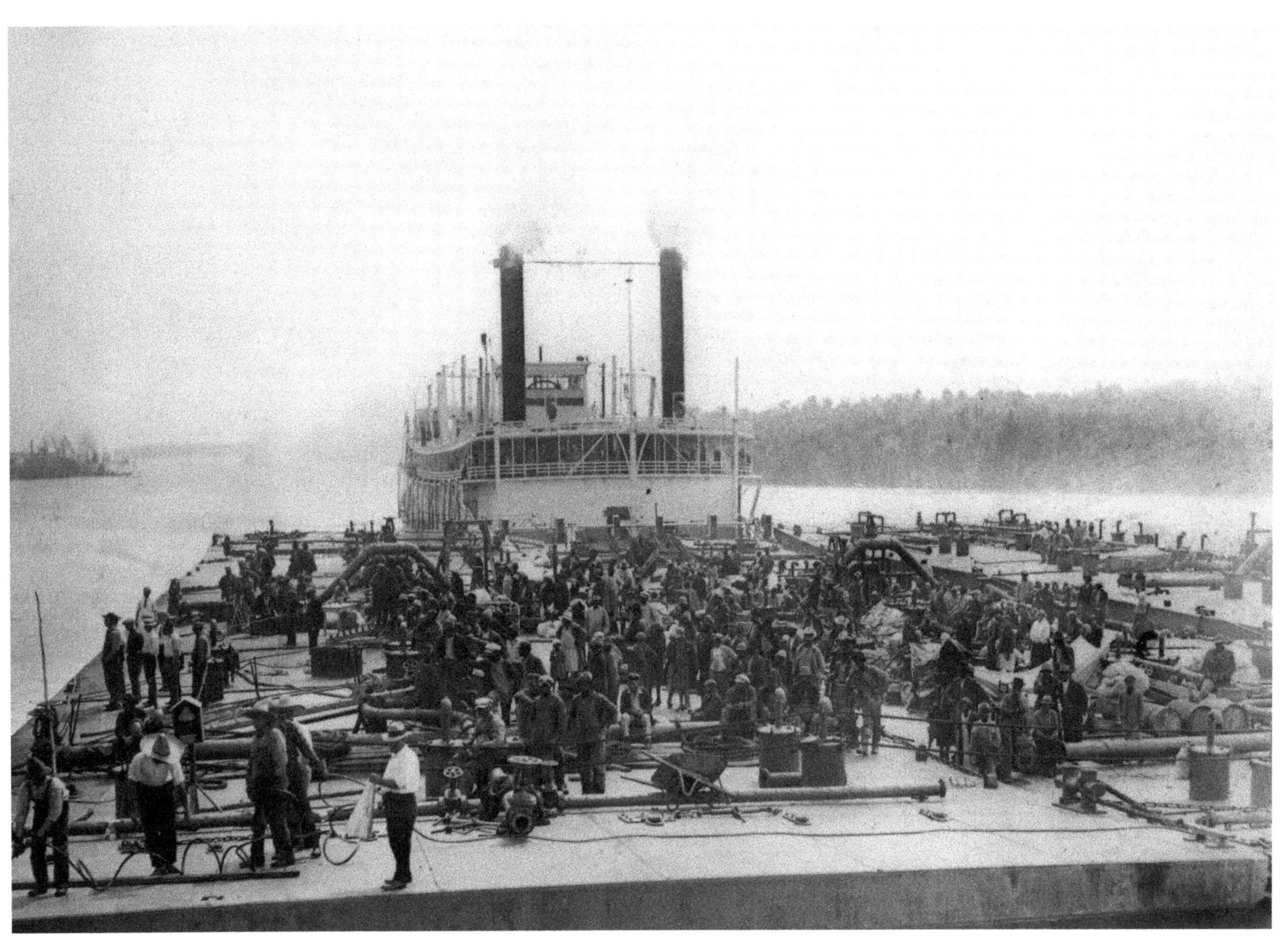

The *Sprague,* at the time the world's largest stern-wheeler towboat, is shown here on April 26, 1927, as it delivers more than 1,300 flood refugees to Vicksburg.

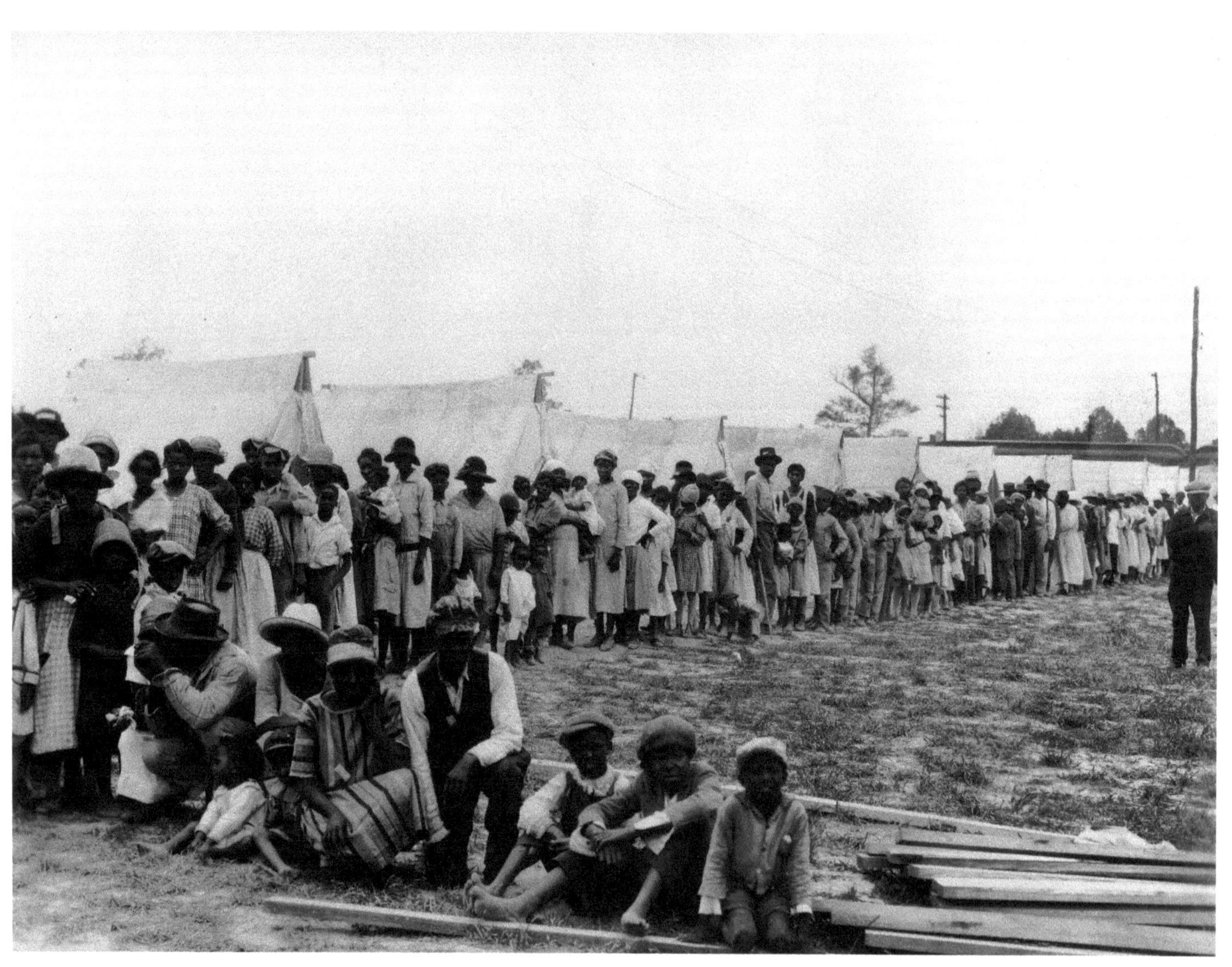

Flood refugees wait in line for food, water, clothing, and other essentials at the Birdsong Camp at Cleveland, in Bolivar County.

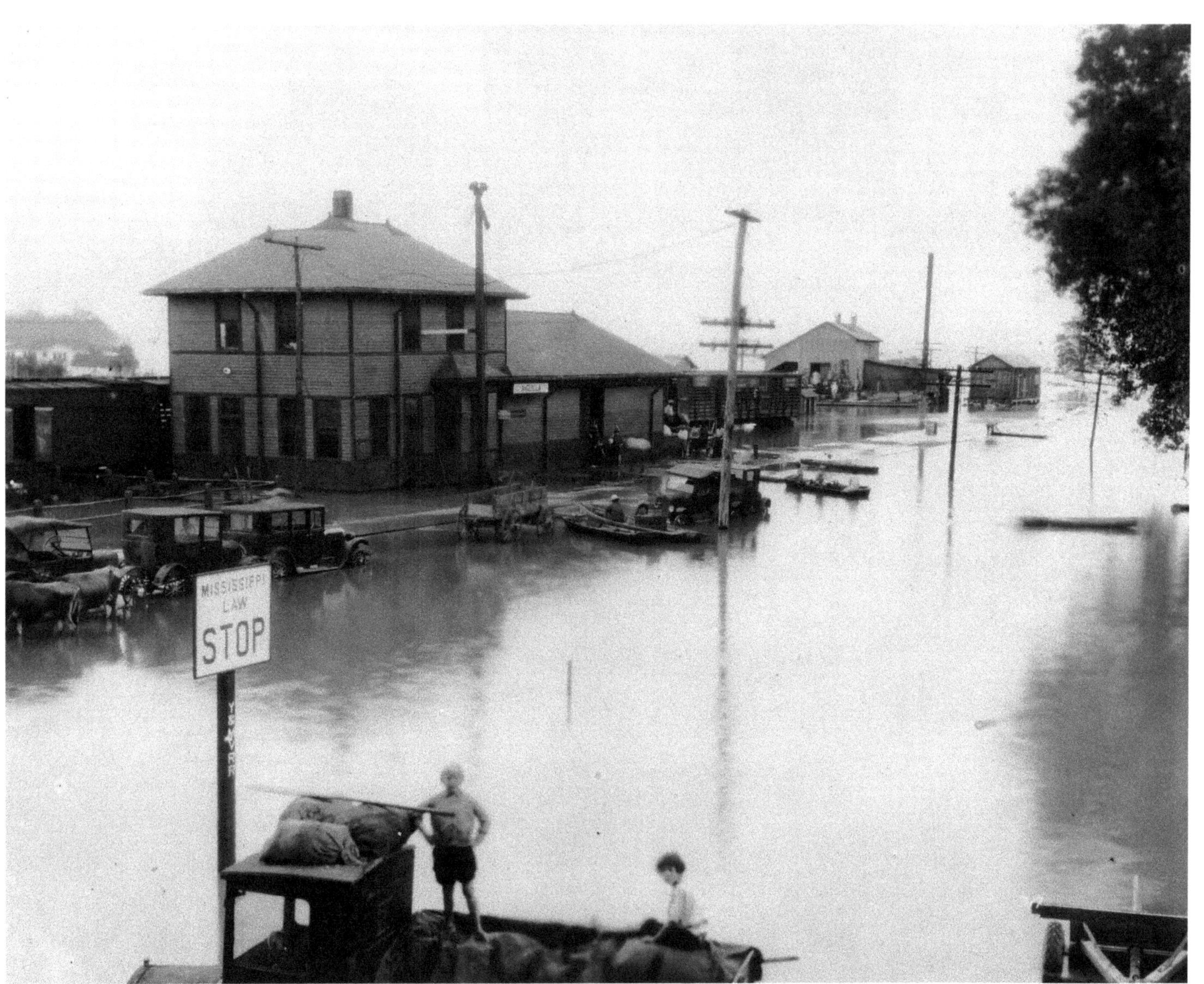

This image shows the flooding at the Yazoo and Mississippi Valley Railroad depot at Anguilla, in Sharkey County.

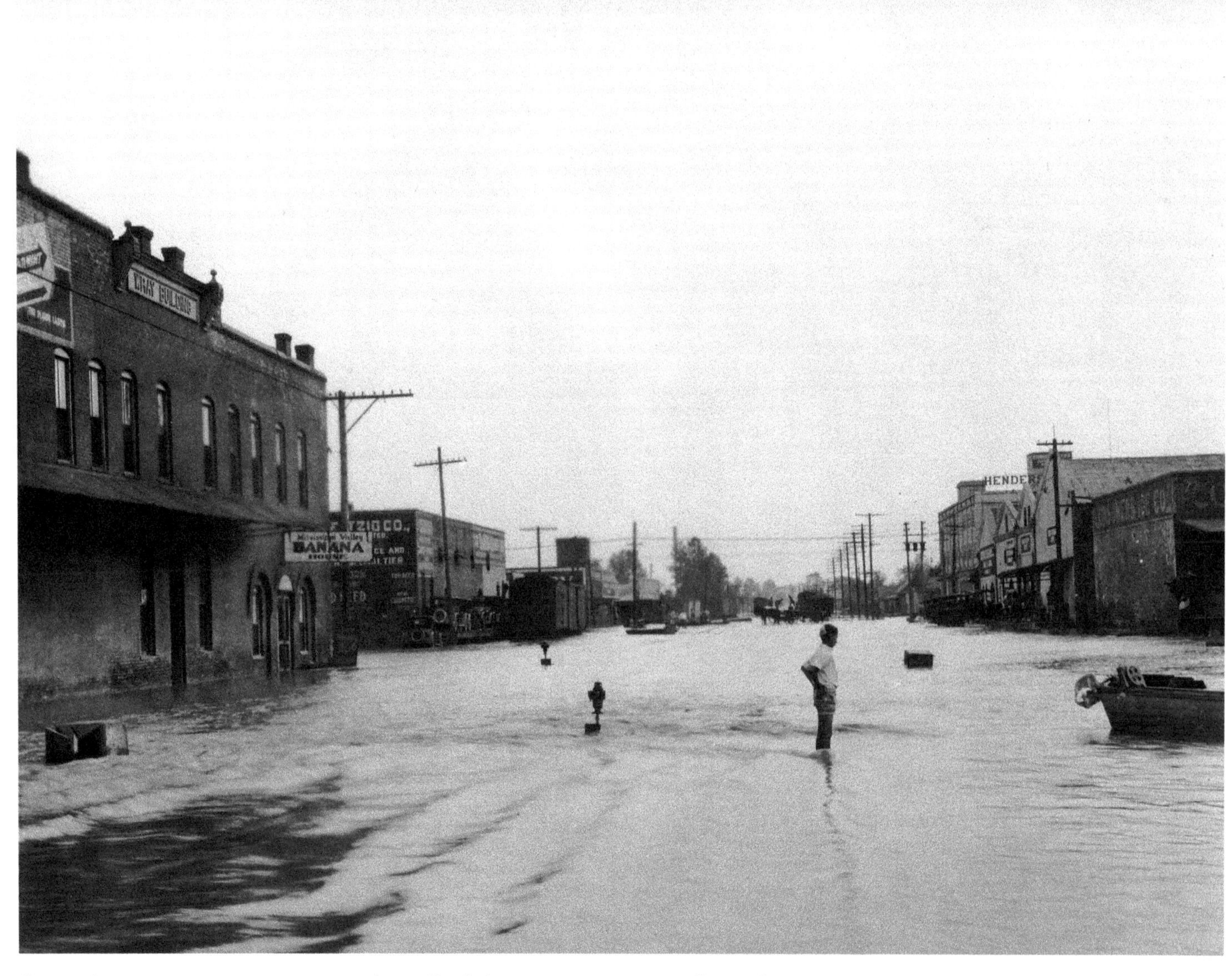

On April 30, 1927, one young man stands at a flooded intersection in Greenville. At the Mississippi Banana House on the left, where bananas are advertised at 30 cents a dozen, business is anything but brisk.

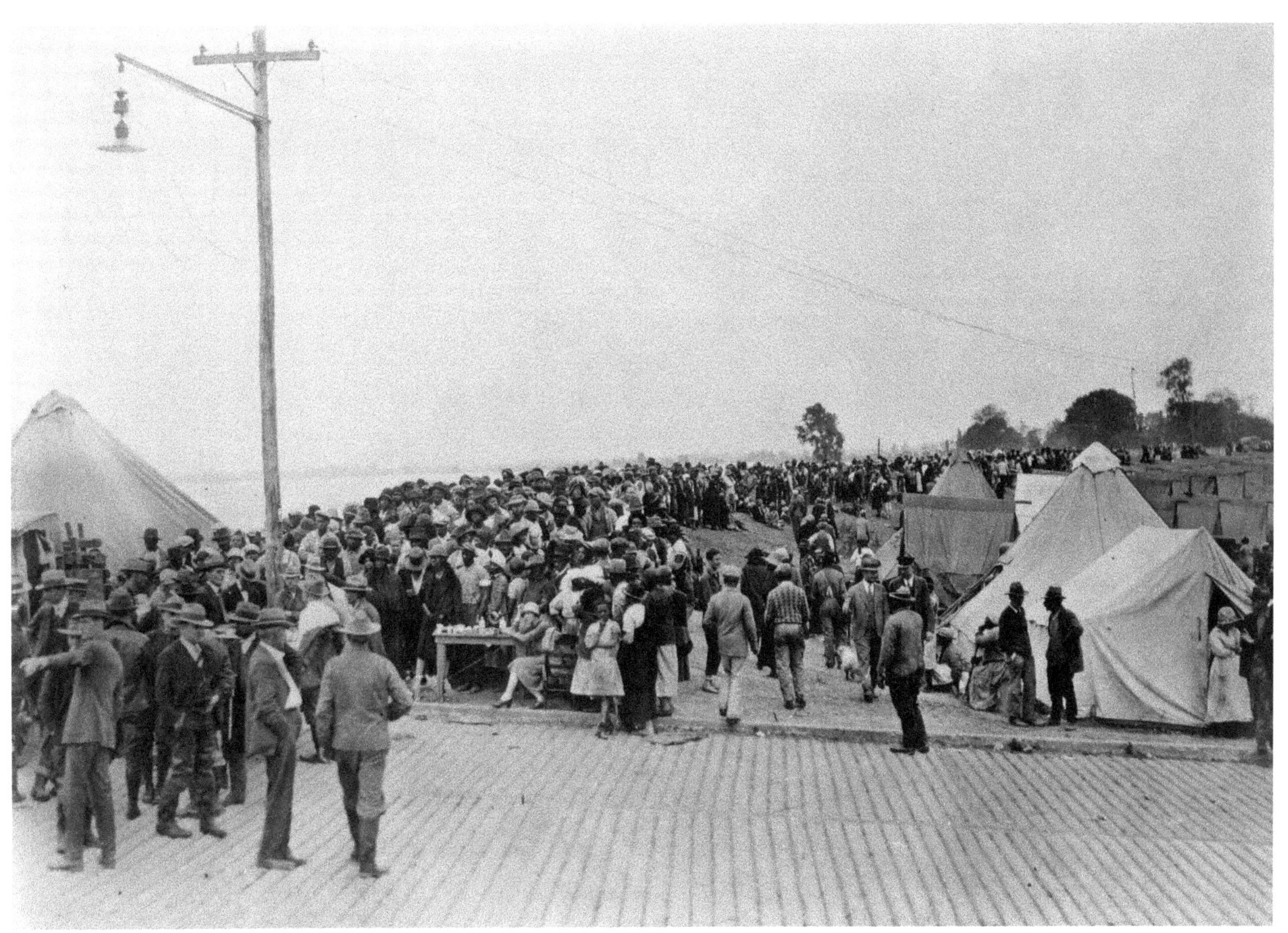

A large crowd has gathered in Greenville as the American Red Cross administers vaccinations during the flood of 1927.

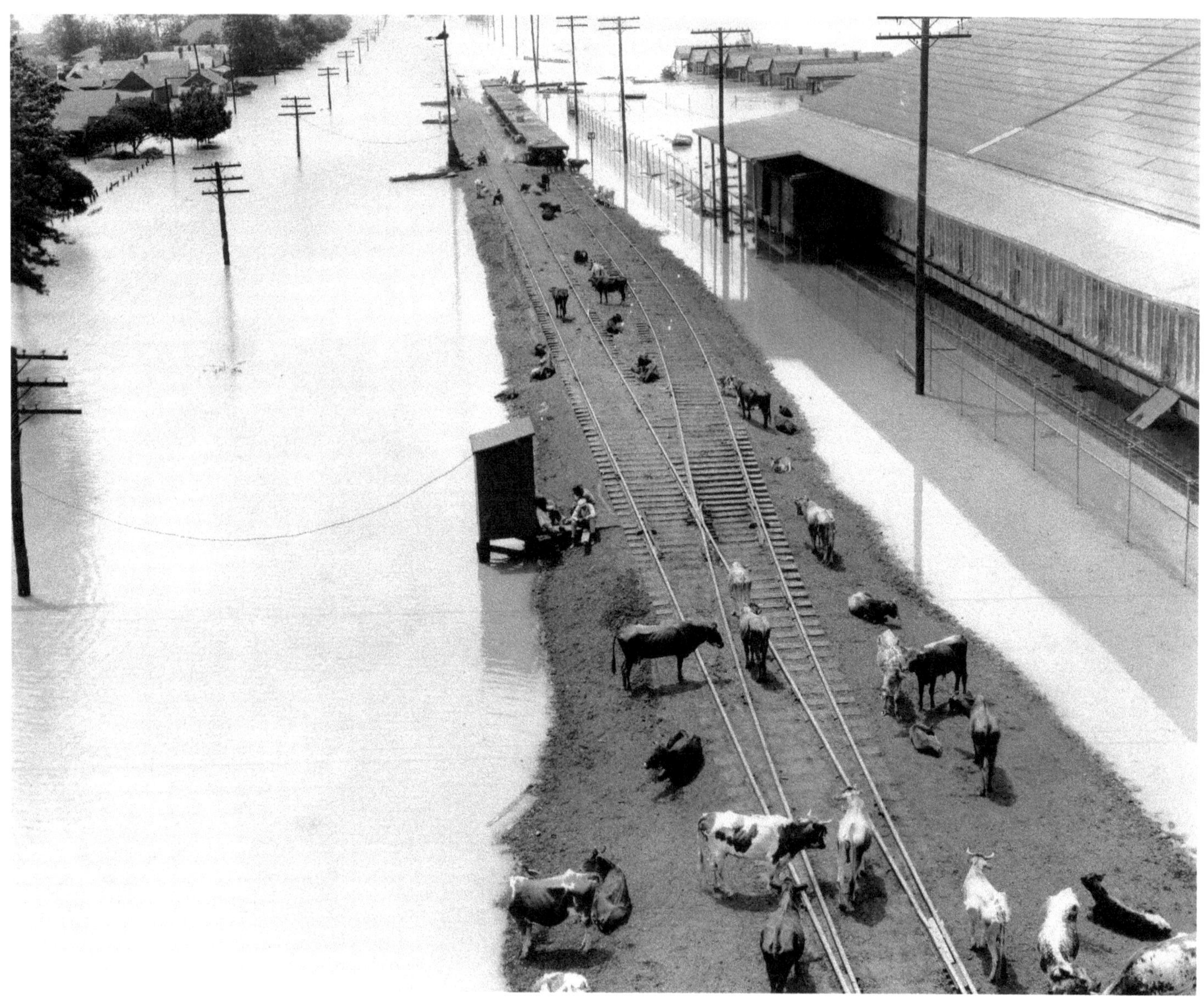

At Leland on April 30, 1927, citizens and livestock alike are stranded on a narrow strip of railroad track.

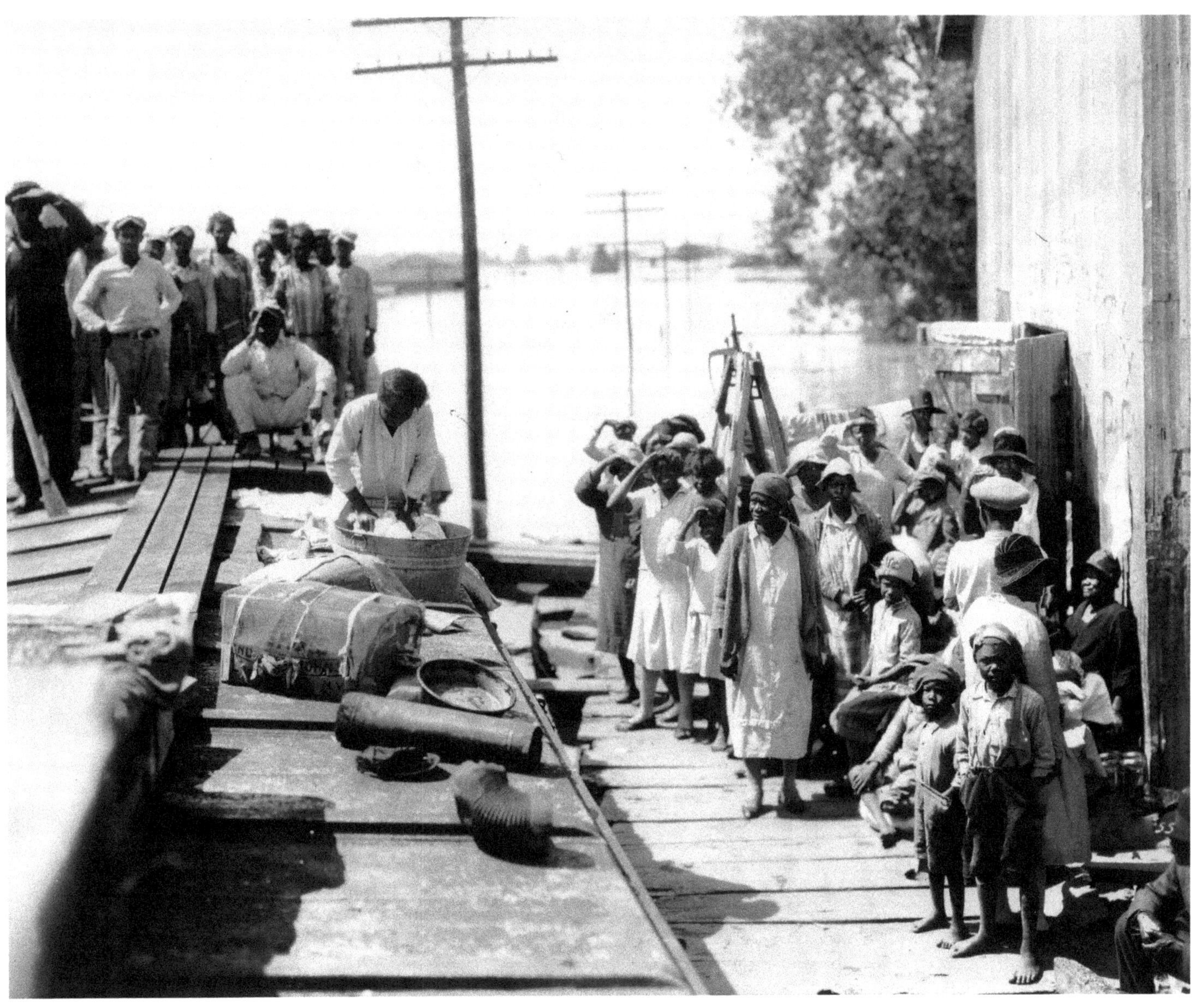

In Rolling Fork, on May 2, 1927, Mississippians affected by the flood stand on railcars and a loading dock, some of them observing one dauntless individual as she scrubs linens on a washboard.

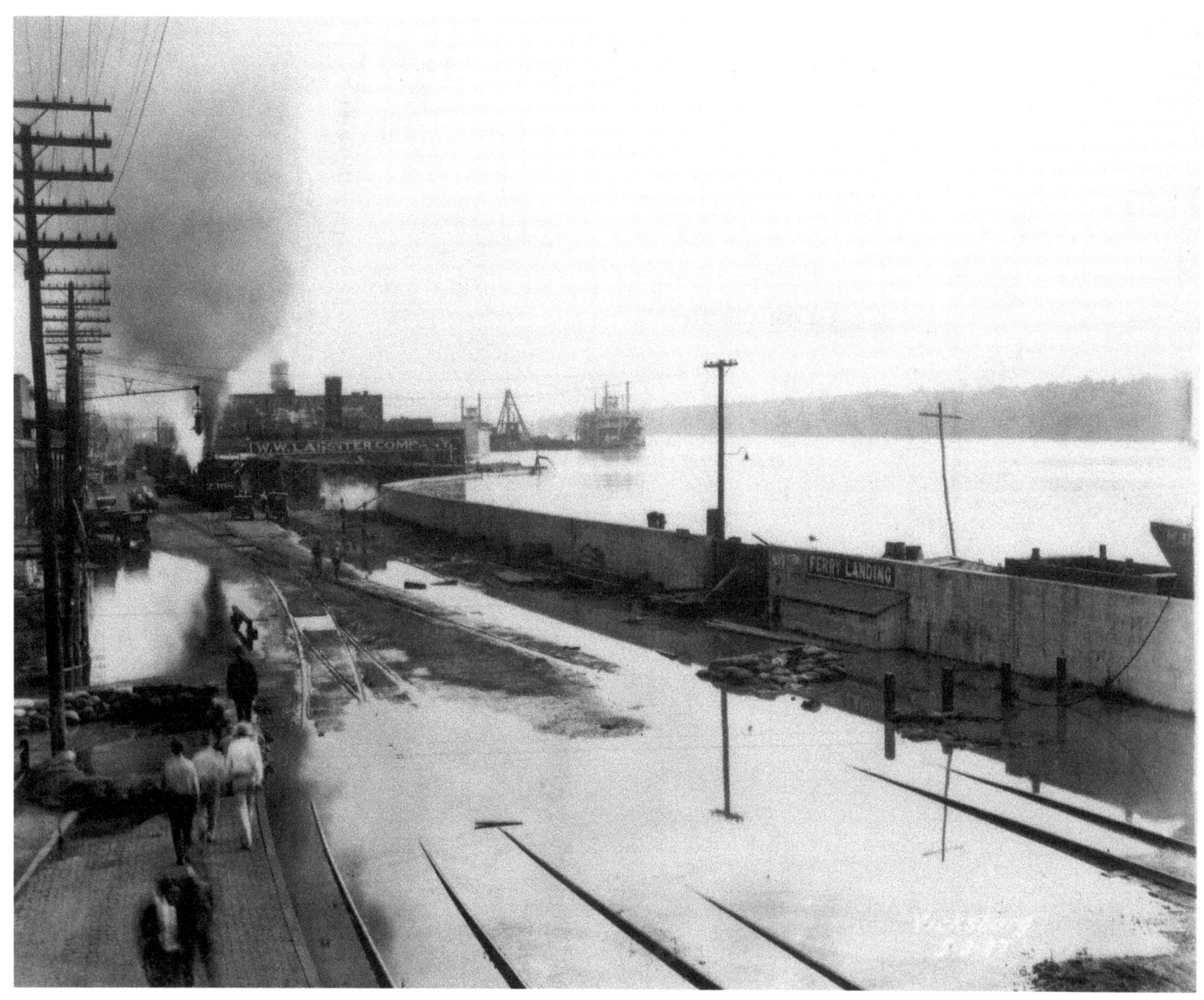

At Vicksburg along the Mississippi River, a riverside rail yard seems to be threatened with inundation should retaining walls crack.

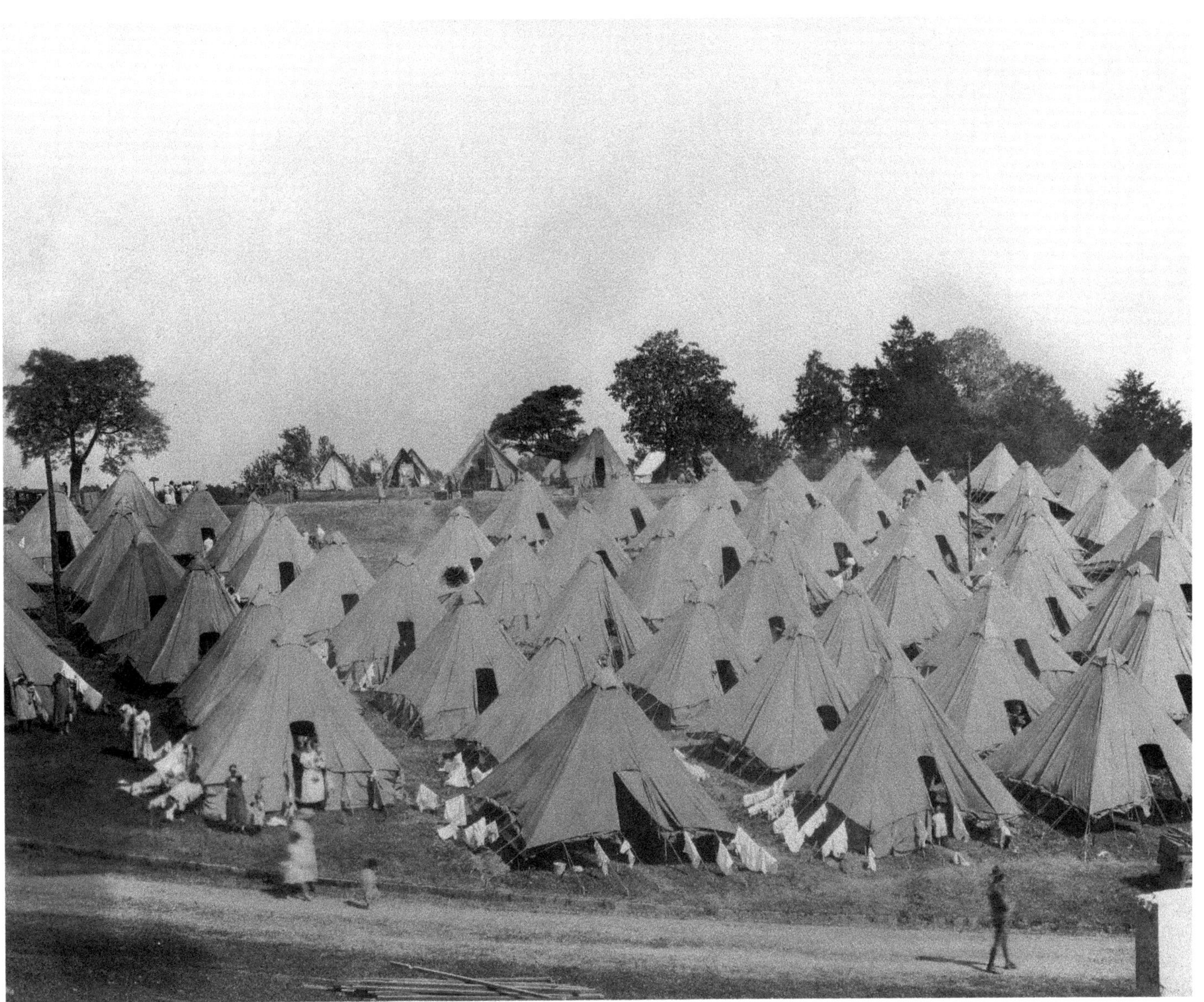

At Vicksburg, shown here on May 3, 1927, flood victims were resettled temporarily in a tent city, on or near the grounds of the national military park. A cannon and historical marker are visible along the treeline. Life goes on as refugees make use of tent ropes to dry laundry. With neighbor helping neighbor, the survival spirit of Mississippians was on full display in trying times.

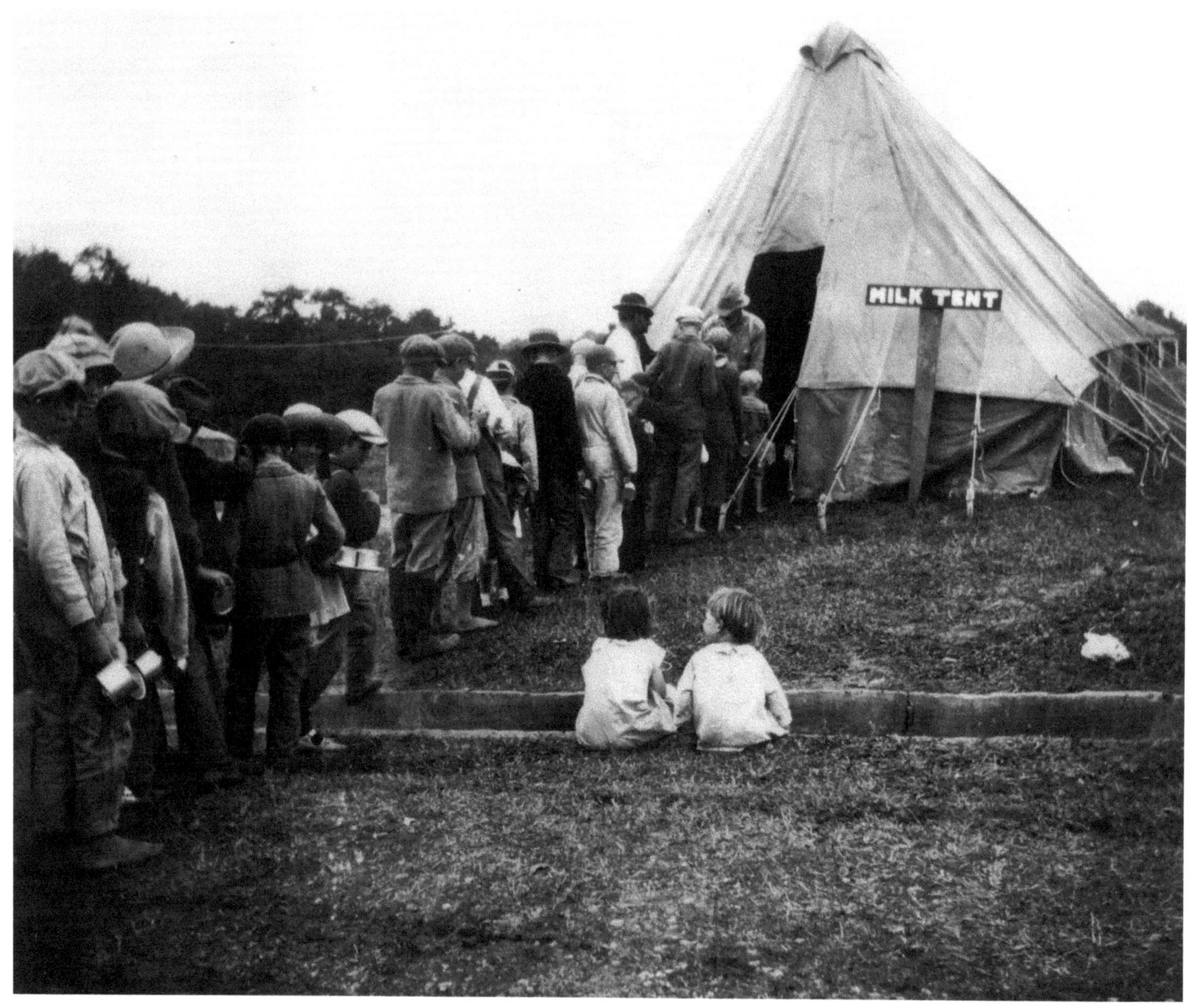

Children at the tent city in Vicksburg wait in line for milk in front of a survival tent during the flood of 1927.

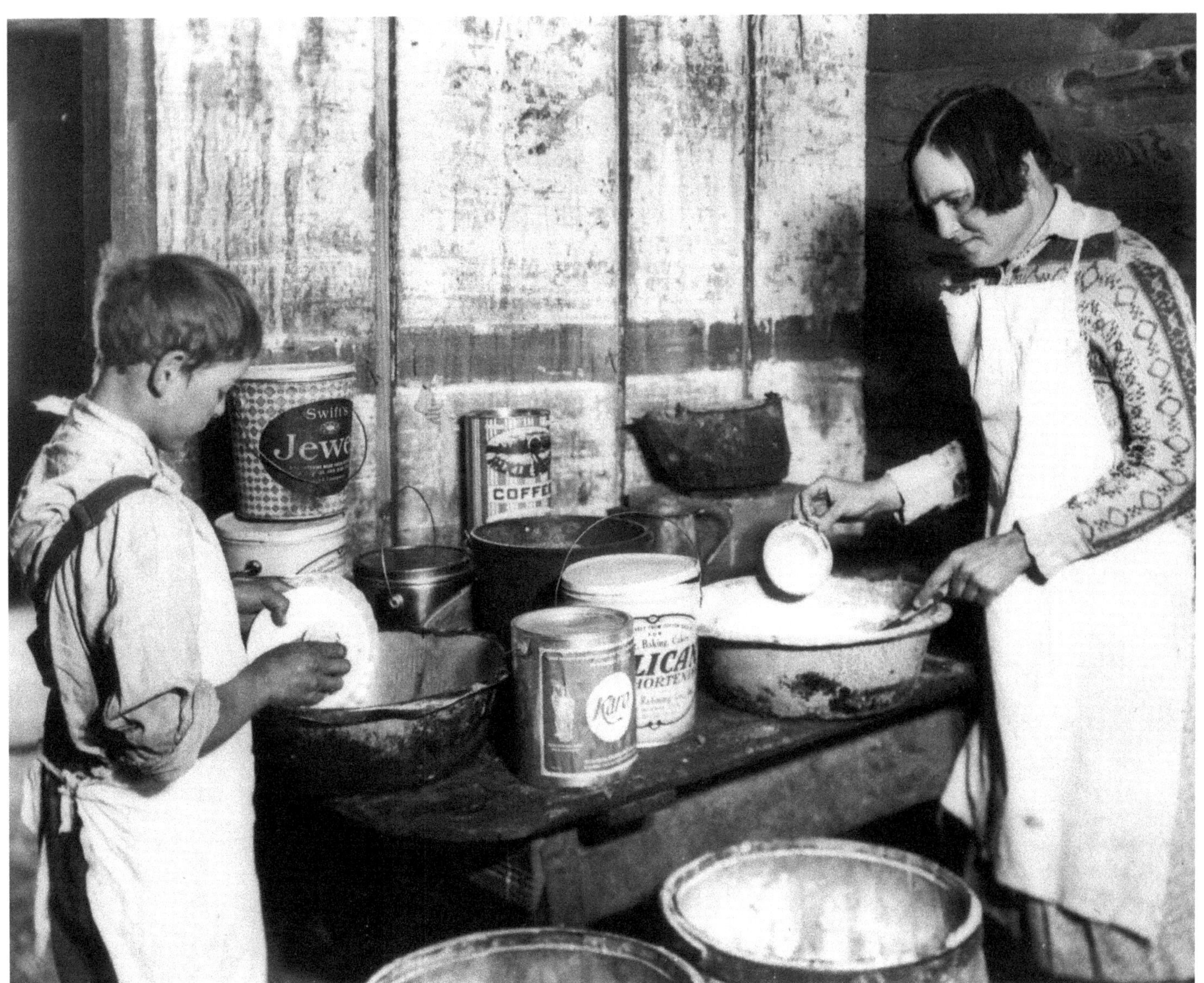

On the heels of the flood of 1927, a severe drought dealt Mississippians trouble in the early 1930s. The family of a tenant farmer works in their kitchen with disaster-relief food supplies provided by the Red Cross.

Mississippi schoolchildren at the Duncan consolidated country school eat lunches provided by the Red Cross during the drought of 1931.

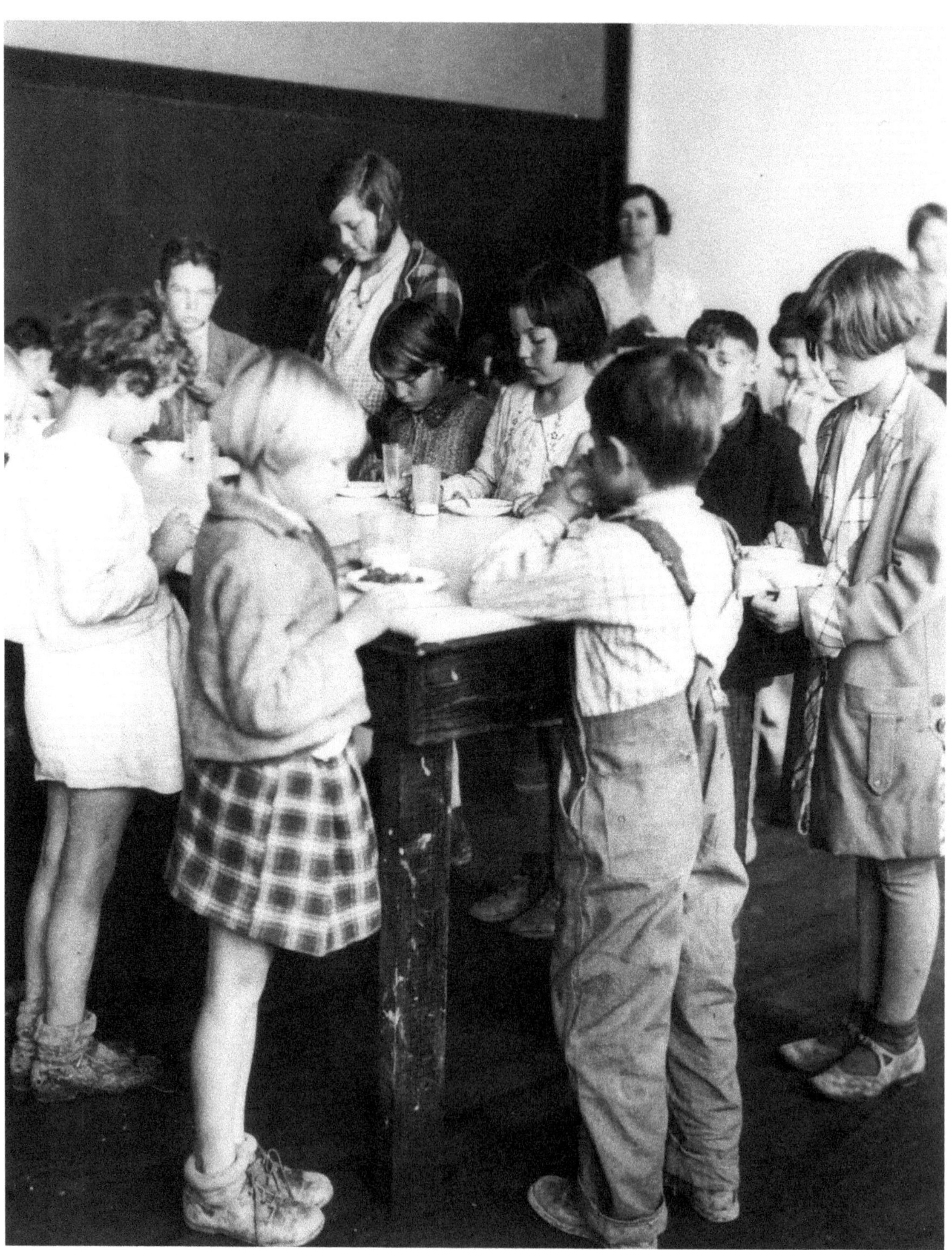

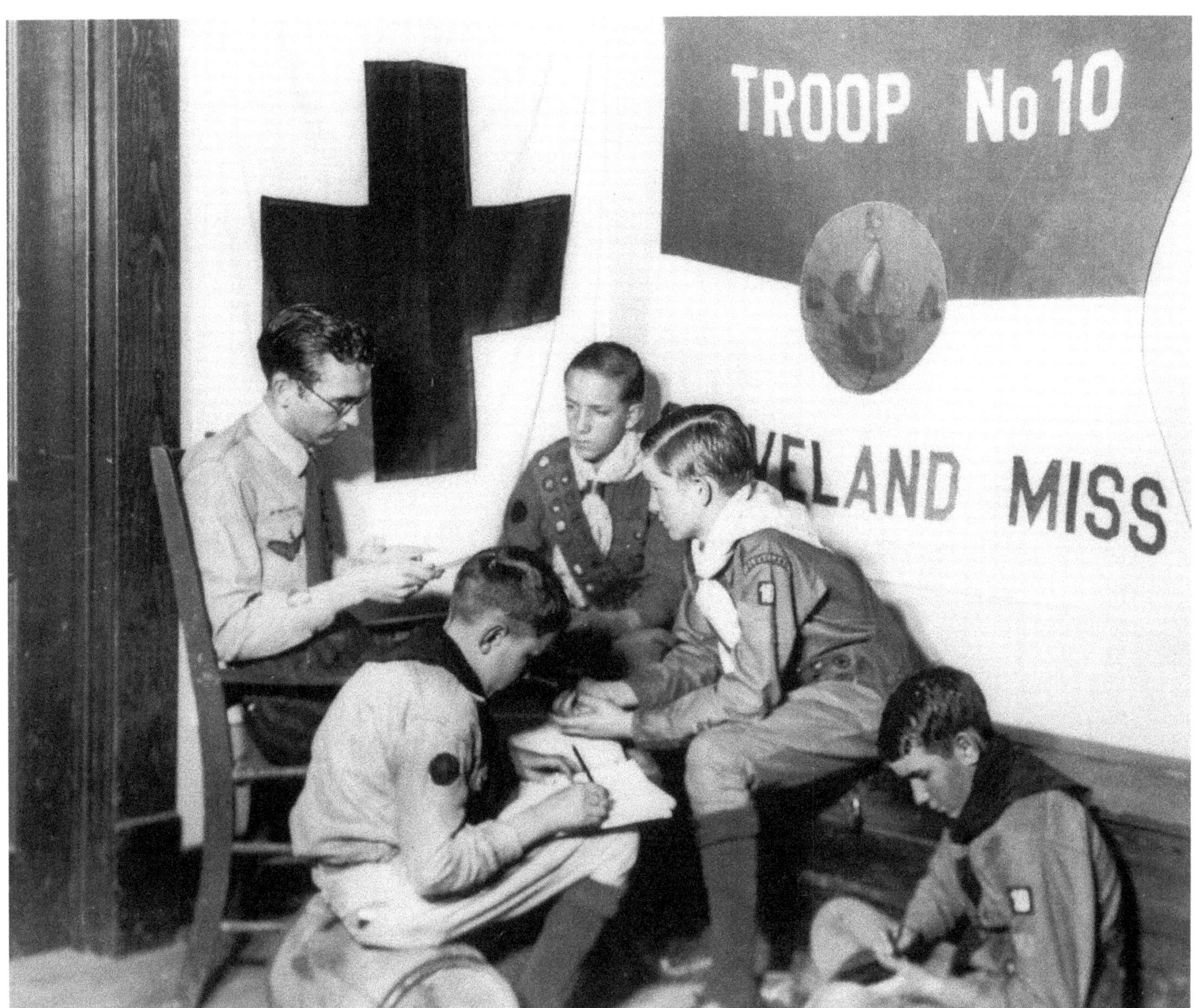

At Cleveland, in Bolivar County, Boy Scouts and their scoutmaster contribute valuable service to the Red Cross drought relief.

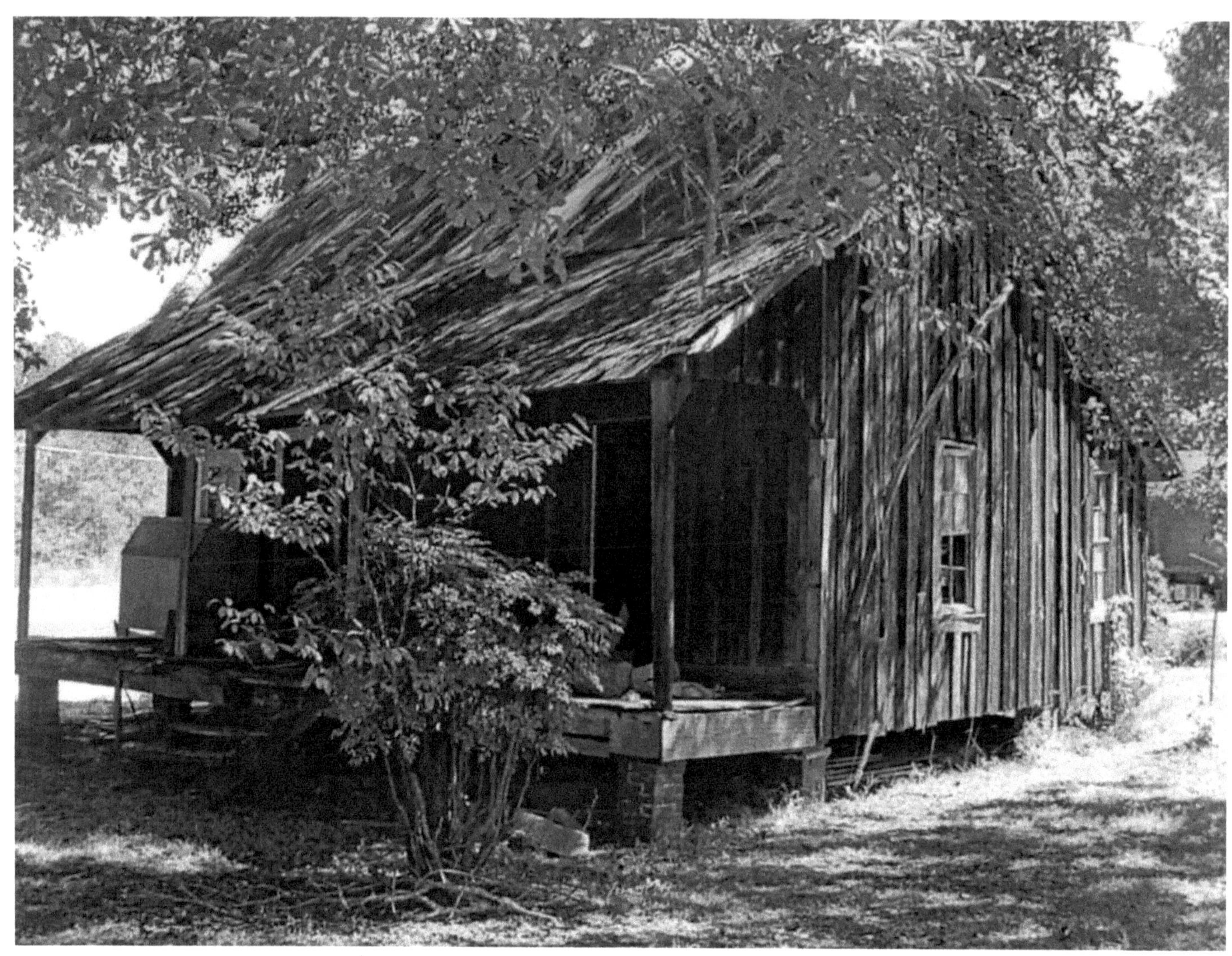

Isaac Pringle, a slave, left for the Civil War with Frank Pringle, a slave-owner, with the 24th Mississippi. Both returned from the war, whereupon Isaac began farming 80 acres of his own. He lived in this house and attended numerous Confederate soldier reunions, including the Walthal Camp of Confederate Veterans in 1933. Records indicate that he received a pension for serving in the Confederate Army.

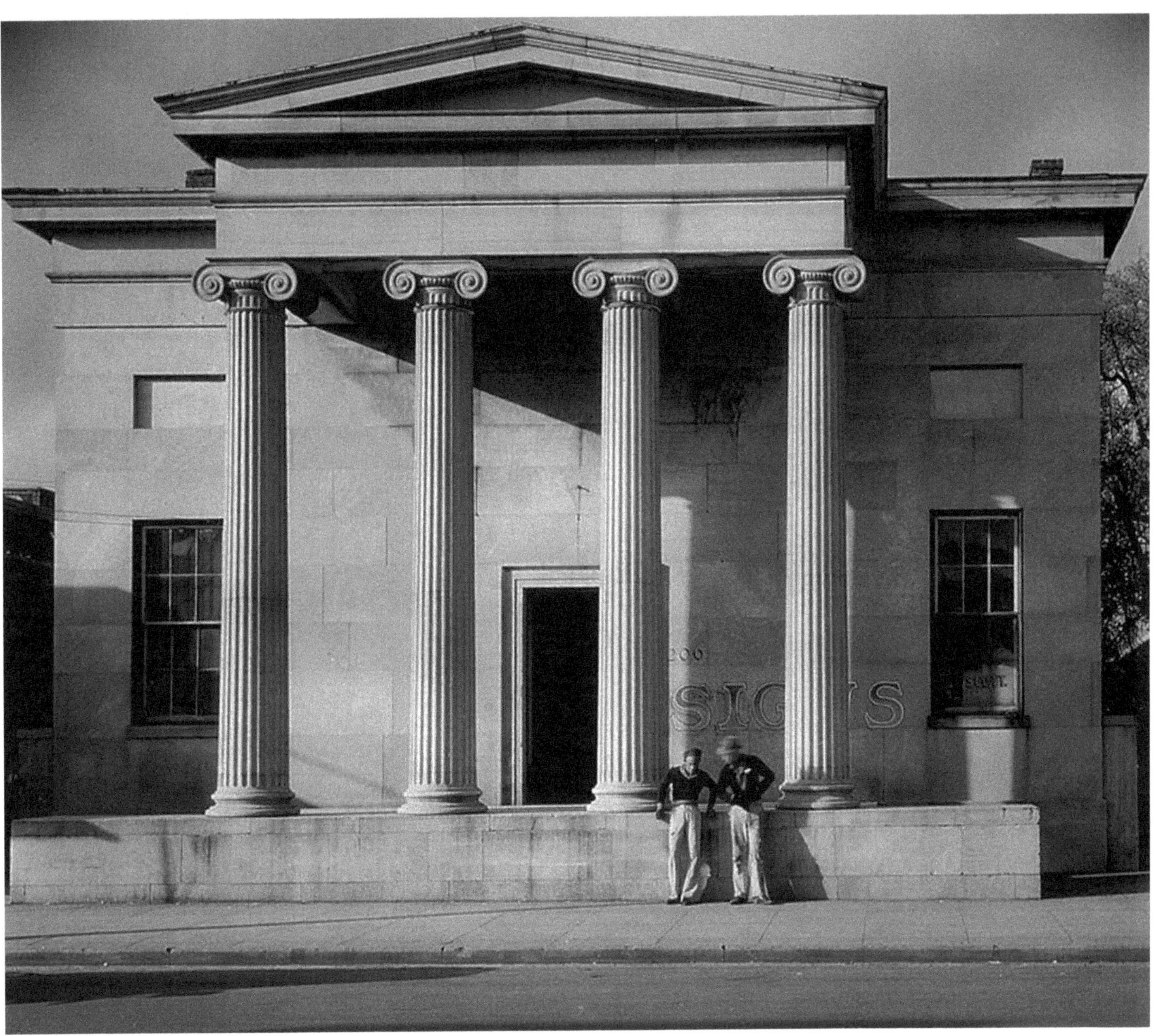

One of the outstanding historic buildings of Natchez is shown here in March 1935. The state of Mississippi proudly claims Natchez, founded in 1716, as one of its oldest cities. Natchez is the southern terminus of the Natchez Trace Parkway, which follows the original trace that linked Natchez to Nashville. Before the Civil War, Natchez boasted more millionaires per capita than any other city in the United States.

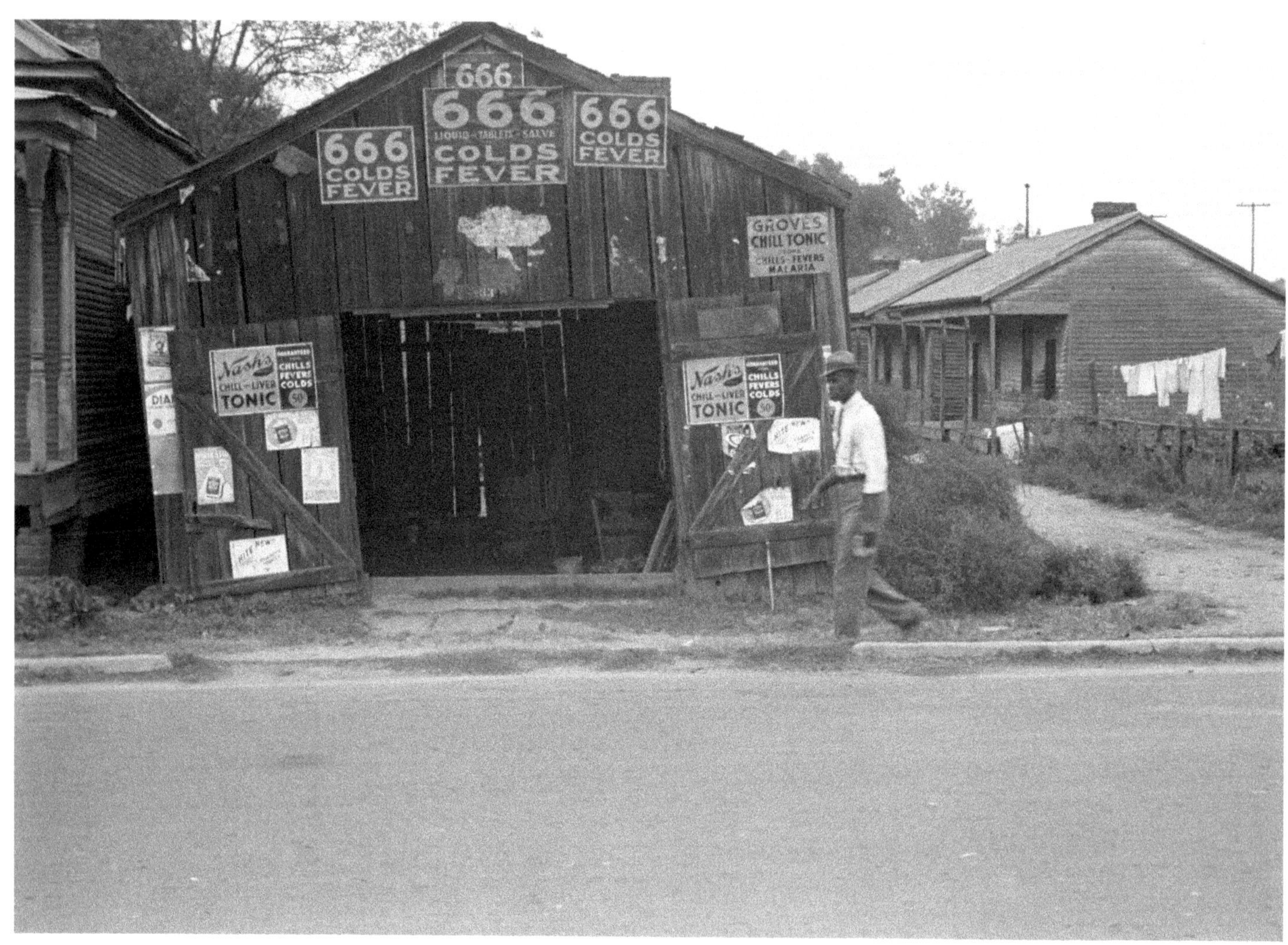

This old shed at Natchez is crowded with medicinal advertisements in October 1935, which tout the wonders of popular remedies of the day. One of them, Grove's Chill Tonic, claims that it "stops chills - fevers - malaria." The cold remedy 666 was widely relied on by cold sufferers and is still manufactured and marketed today.

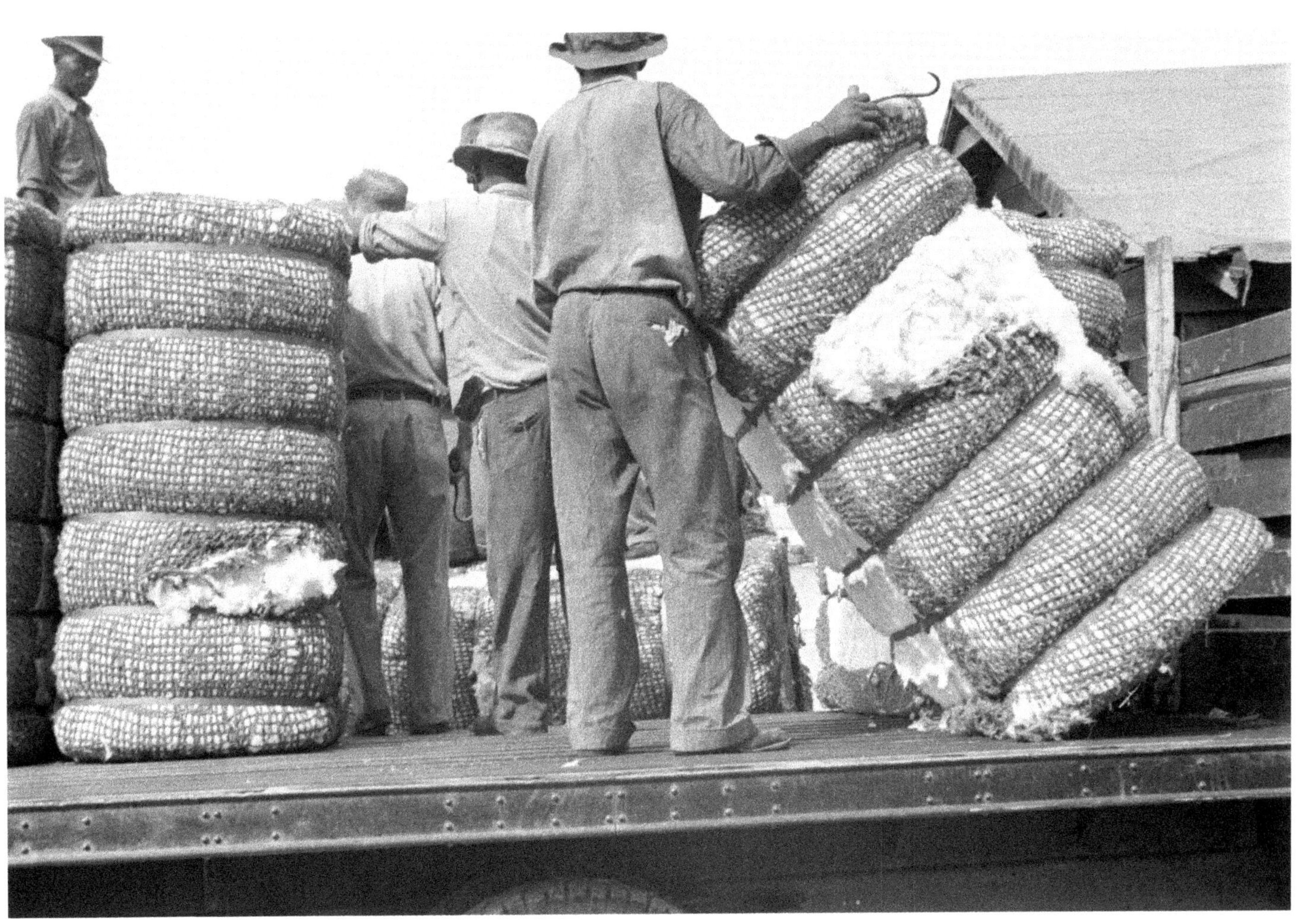

Cotton was still big business in Mississippi in October 1935. Workers in Natchez load cotton bales for export.

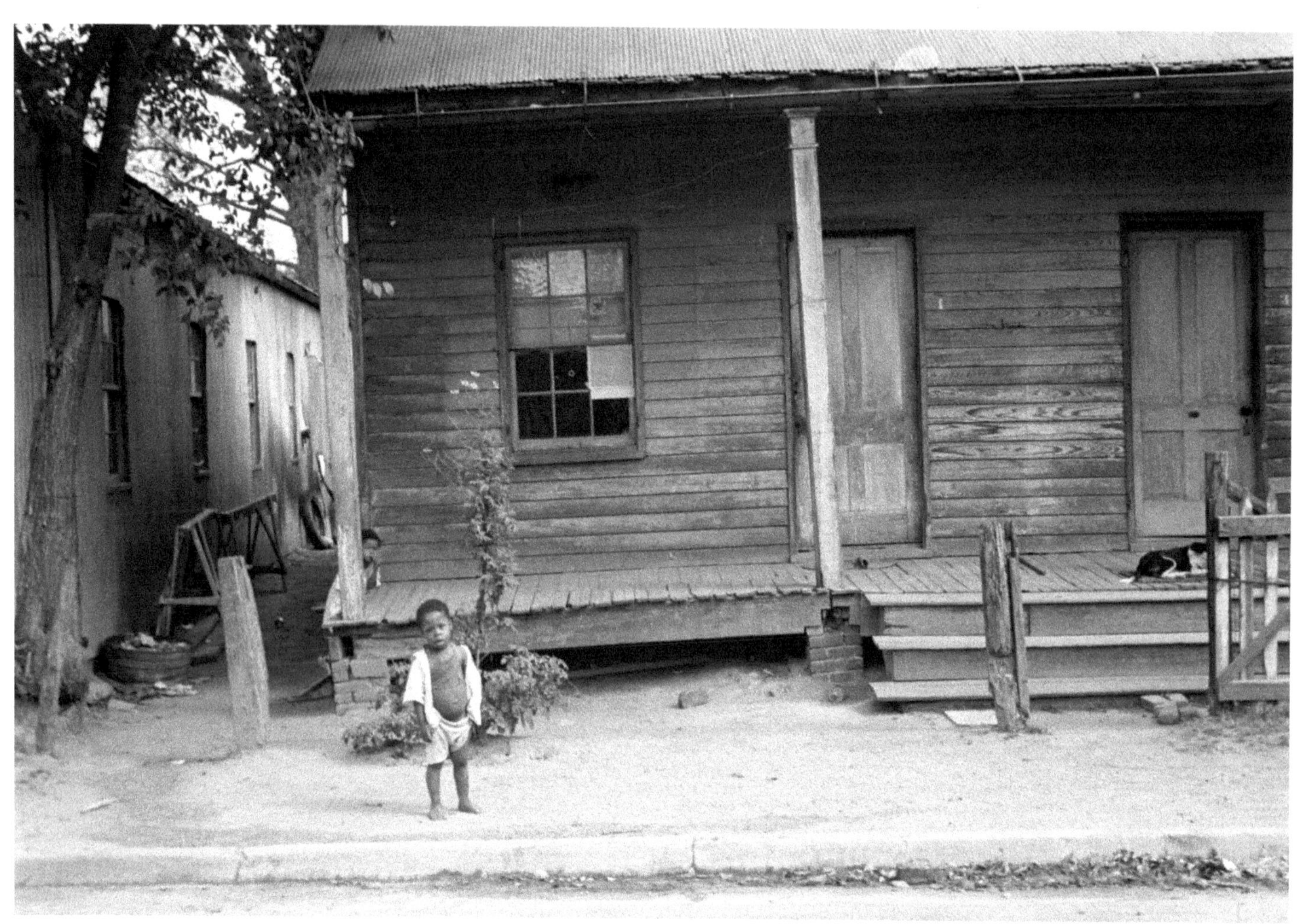

From mansions to shacks, Natchez has been home to a diverse array of citizens. These children stand in front of a badly run-down house in 1935 as a black-and-white pup naps on the front porch. The Great Depression was peaking, leaving many Americans on very hard times.

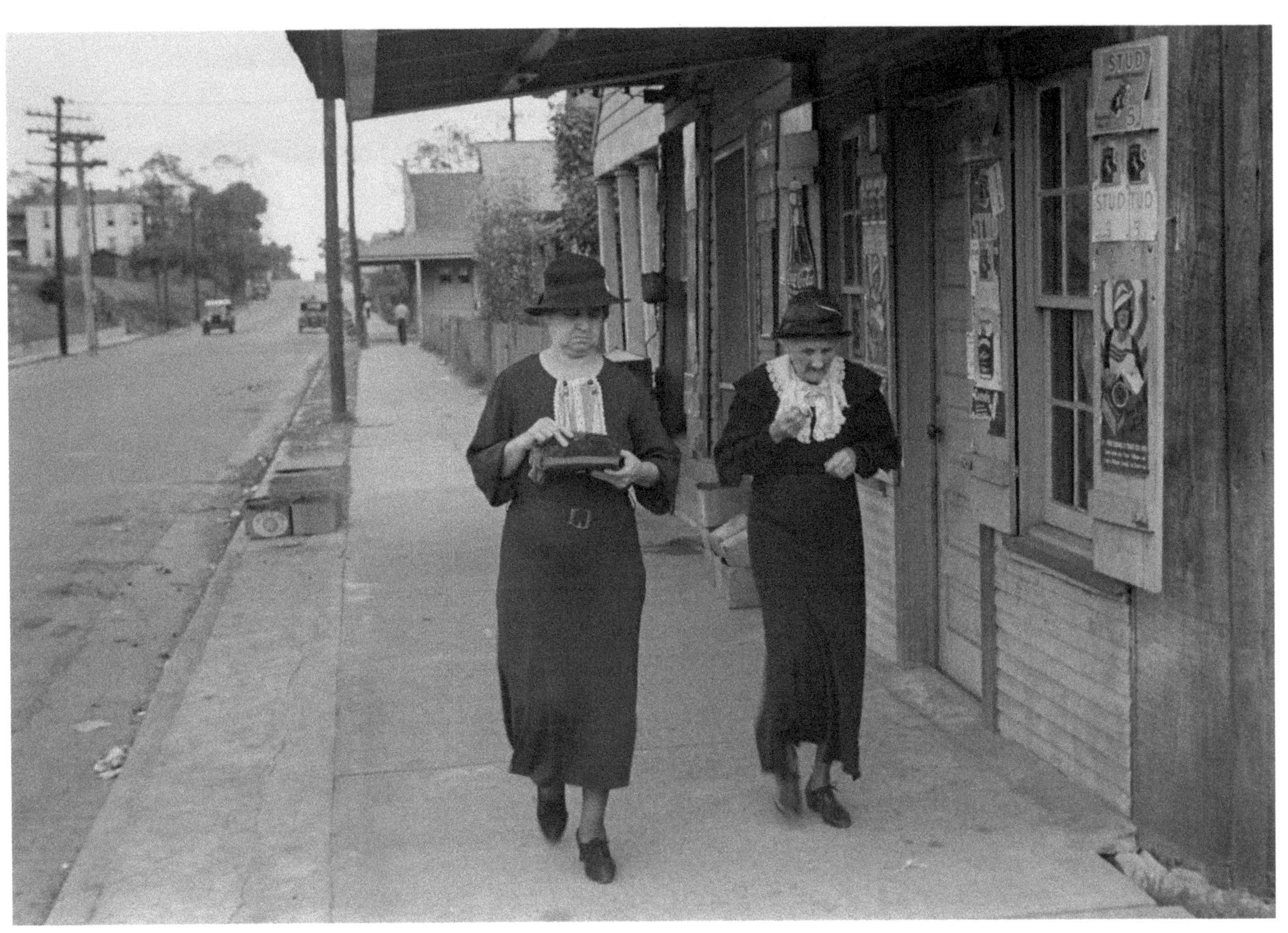

Two ladies of Natchez take a shopping trip on a seemingly deserted city street in 1935. Despite the hard times, Americans strove to dress neatly.

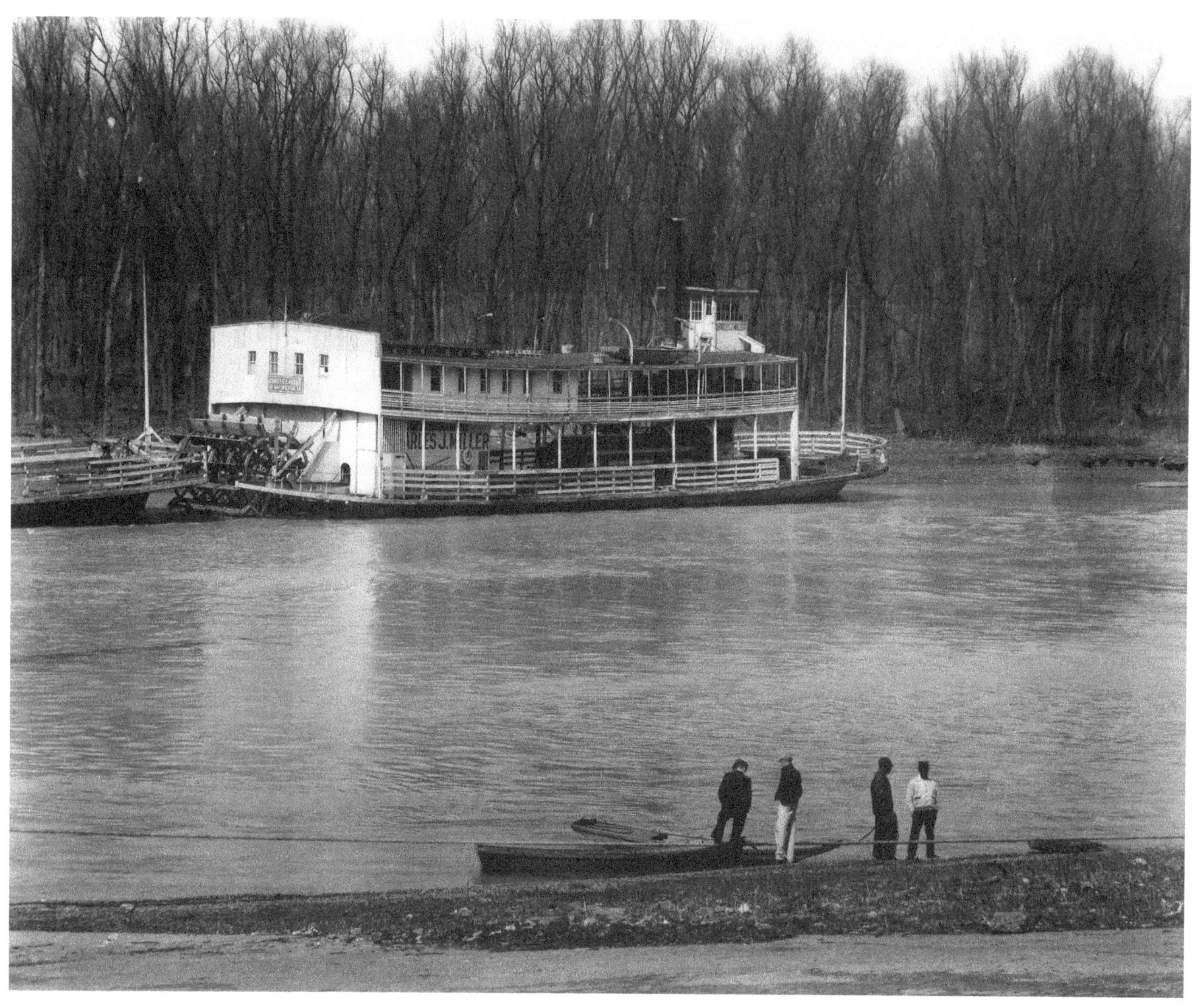

At Vicksburg in February 1936, the *Charles J. Miller* ferries river traffic while locals loiter at river's edge.

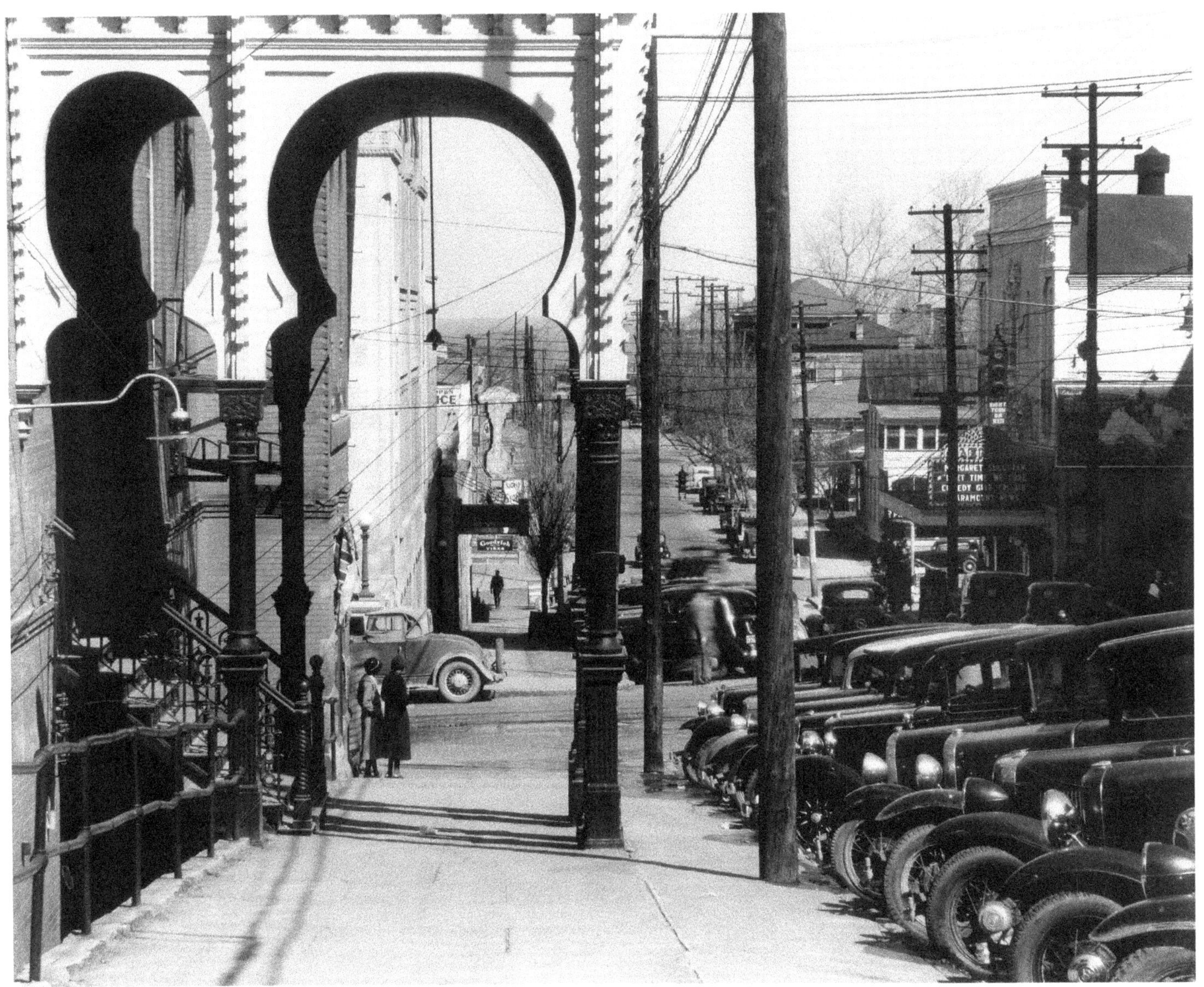

The scene at Vicksburg in March 1936. Most of the parking spaces seem to be taken as two ladies stand at the corner waiting to cross the busy street. In the distance a theater marquee advertises *Next Time We Love,* starring Margaret Sullavan and James Stewart.

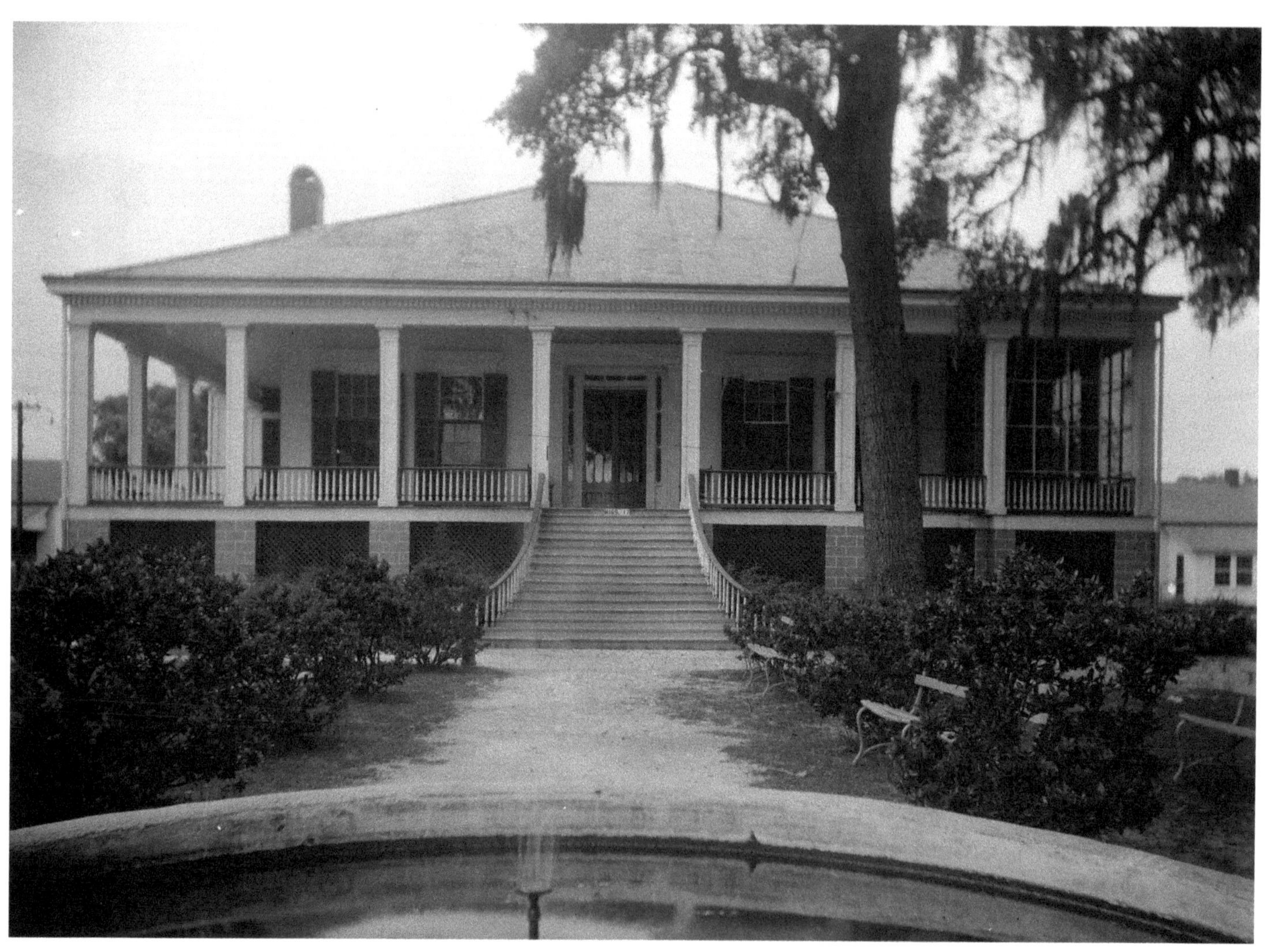

Beauvoir was the beautiful retirement home of Jefferson Davis, the first and last president of the Confederate States of America. Located in Biloxi, the home sits on the north side of Highway 90 and faces the Gulf of Mexico. The historic home is shown here as it appeared on April 22, 1936.

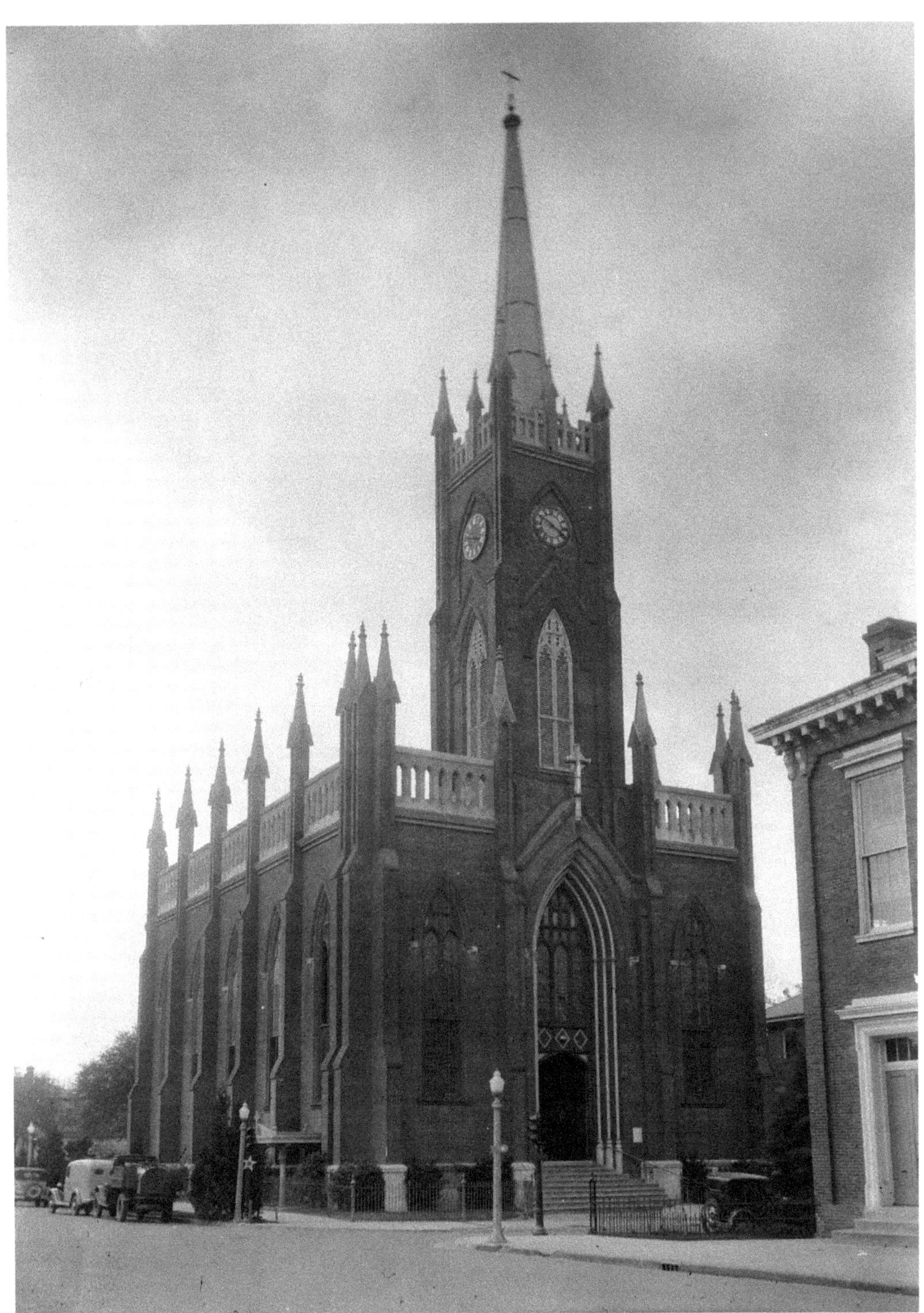

The lovely St. Mary's Cathedral in Natchez as it appeared March 28, 1936. The cathedral's cornerstone was laid February 24, 1842, and the church was dedicated on December 25, 1843. Consecrated on September 19, 1886, it remained the Cathedral of the Diocese until 1977.

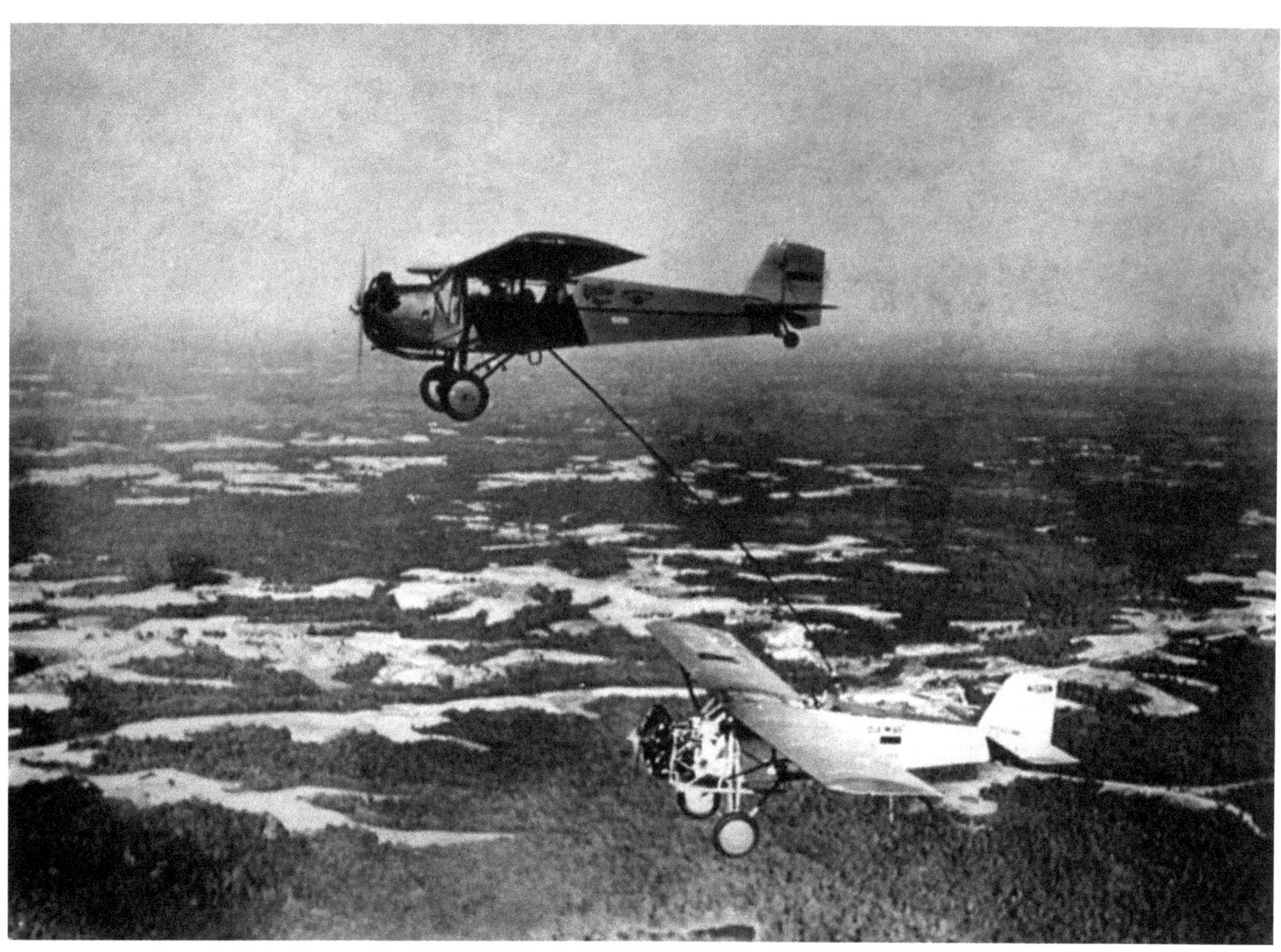

On July 1, 1935, a world record was set by the Key brothers, Al and Fred, of Meridian. The brothers perfected a daring mid-air refueling technique, shown in progress here, that enabled them to keep the *Ole Miss* in flight for more than 27 days. The aviation pioneers captured the attention of the entire world with this accomplishment.

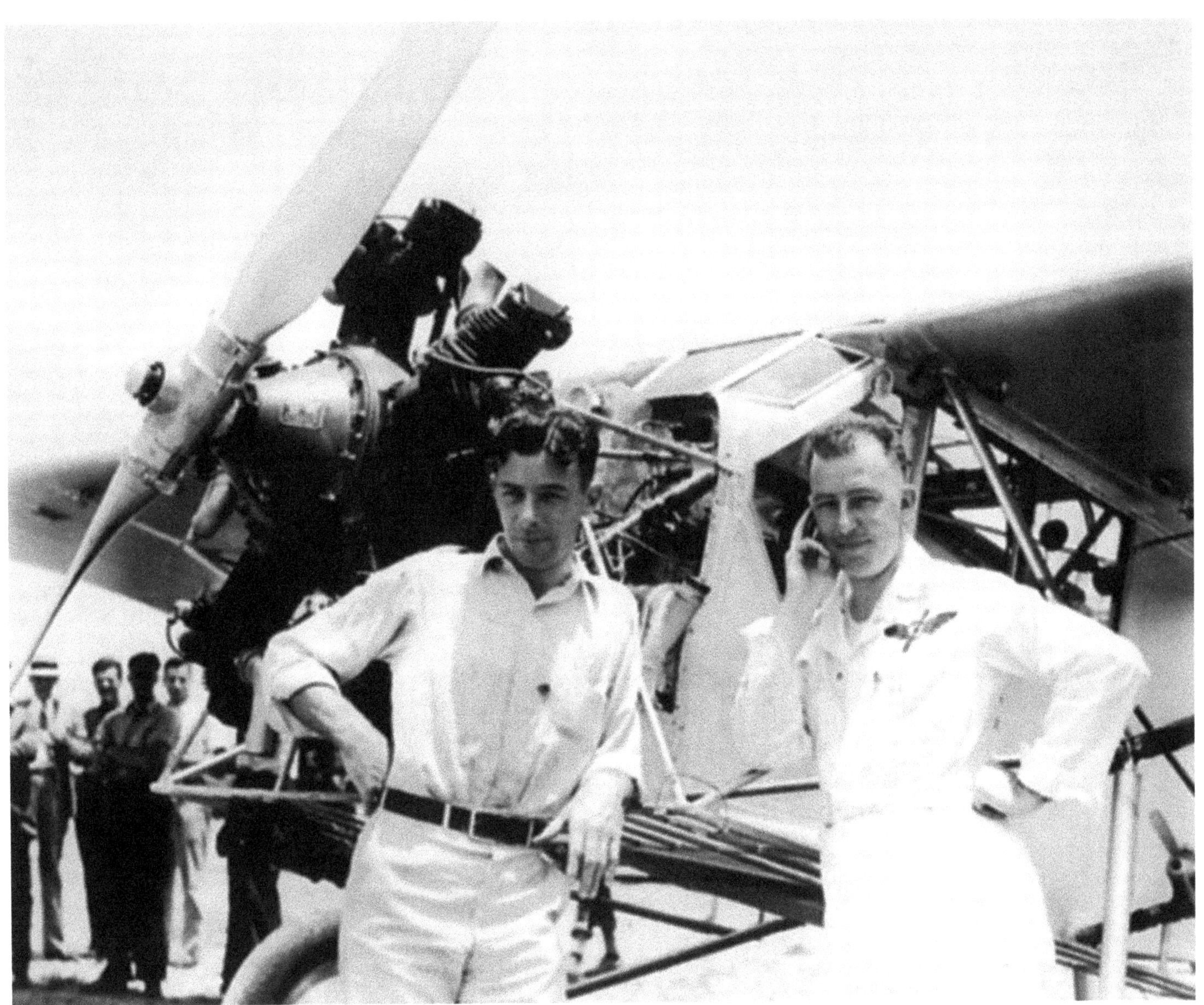

Fred and Al Key pose with their history-making plane *Ole Miss* on July 1, 1935, welcomed by 30,000 spectators. They were in the air for more than 27 days, trumping the old record of 23 days. With mechanic Anthony Hunter, they conceived several innovations to make the historic flight possible. The plane was accepted as a permanent exhibit by the Smithsonian Institution in 1955.

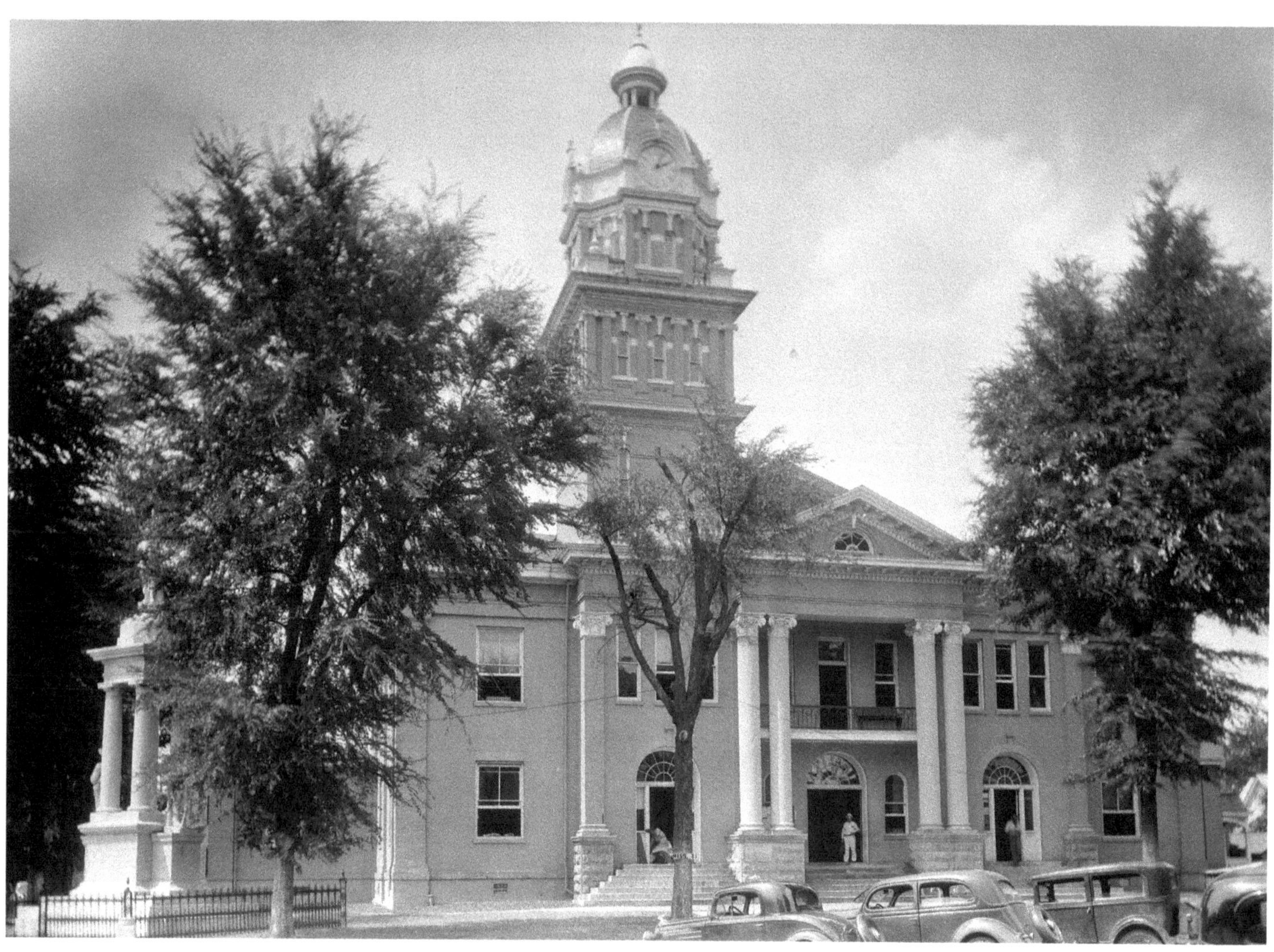

The impressive Lowndes County Courthouse, built in 1847, is shown here on June 10, 1936. The courthouse is located at Columbus, the county seat.

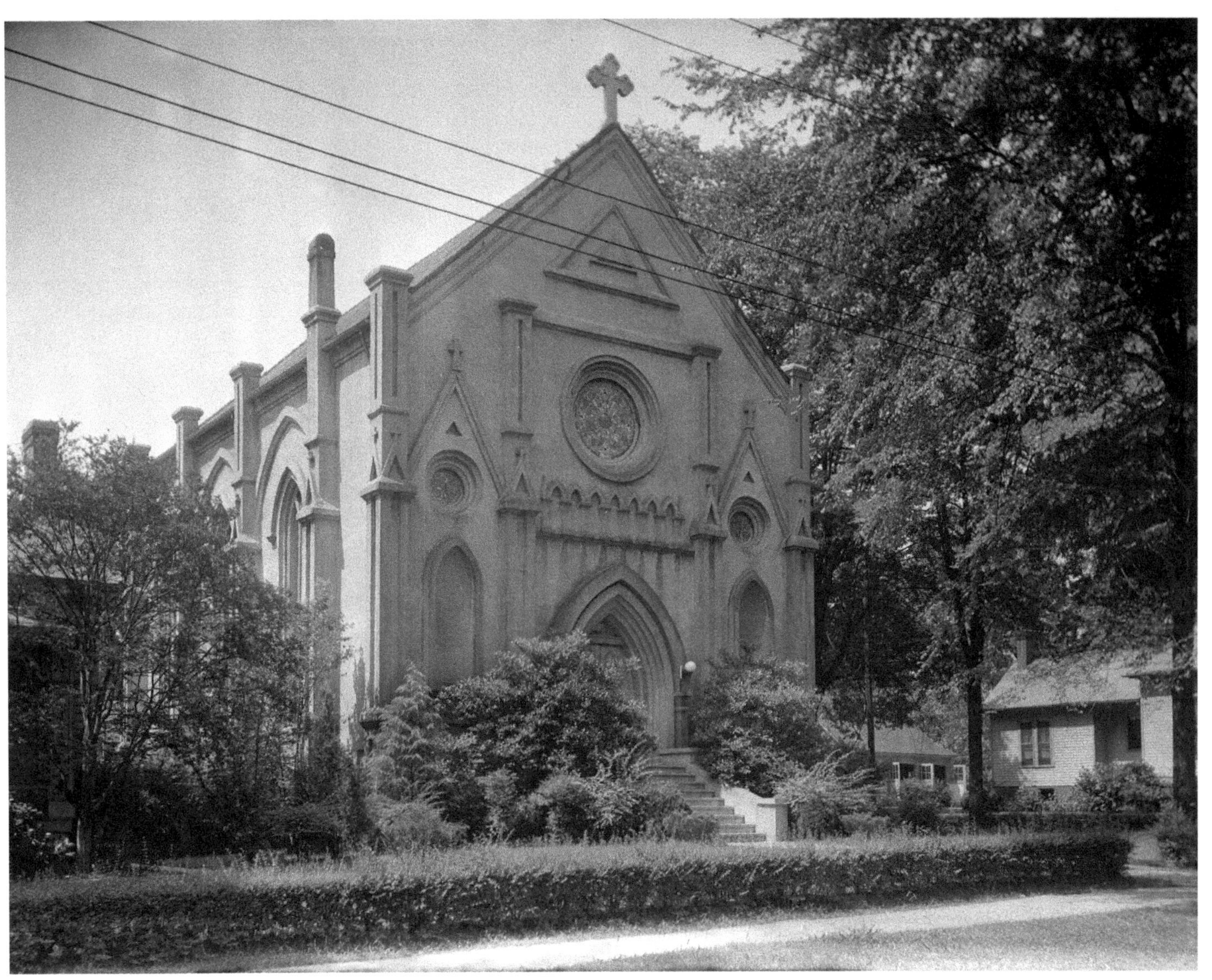

The Church of the Annunciation in Columbus laid their cornerstone on May 4, 1863. The church is the oldest in northeast Mississippi. This image was recorded on June 18, 1936.

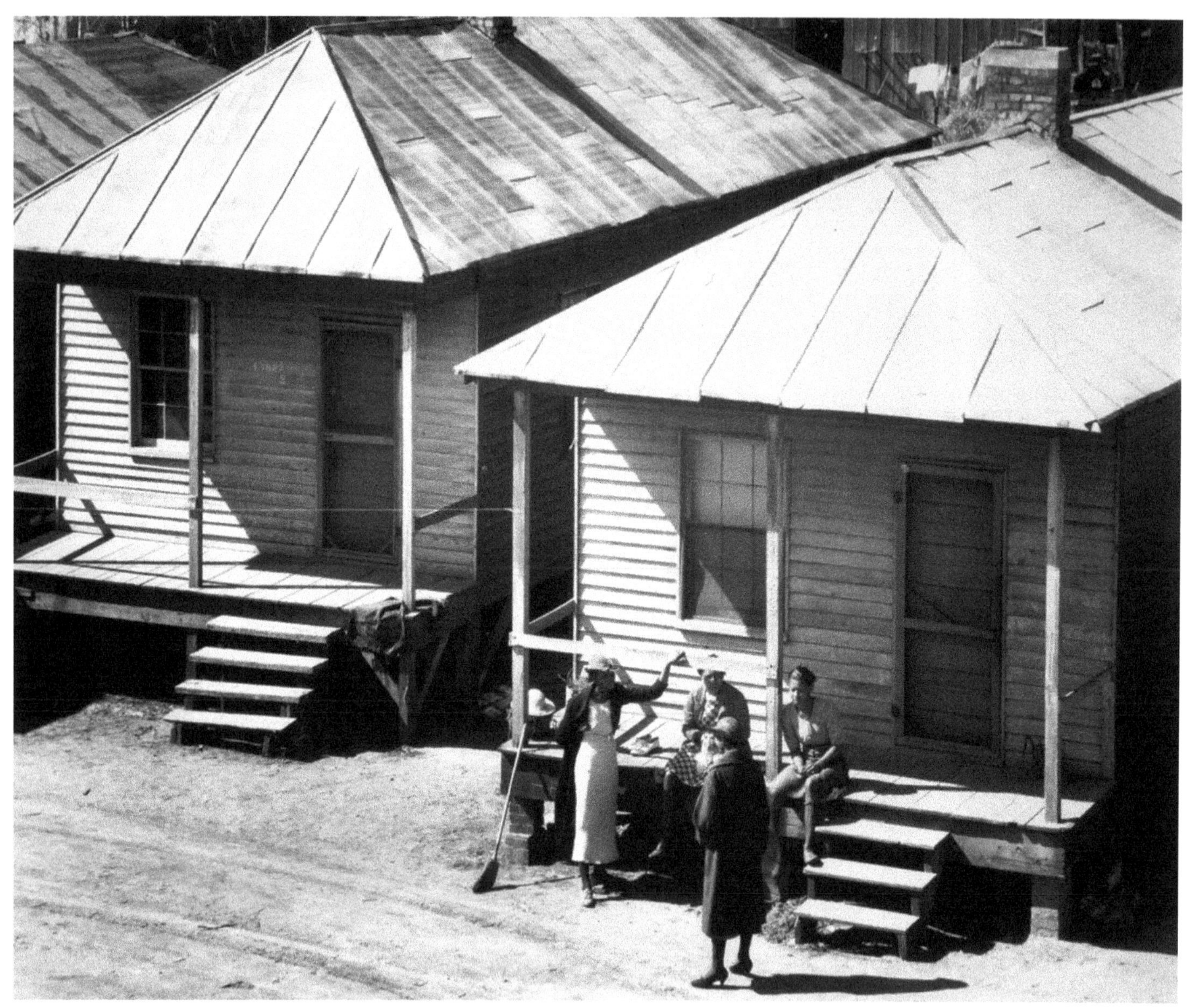

Neighbors gather to swap the local news in this small community in 1936 Vicksburg.

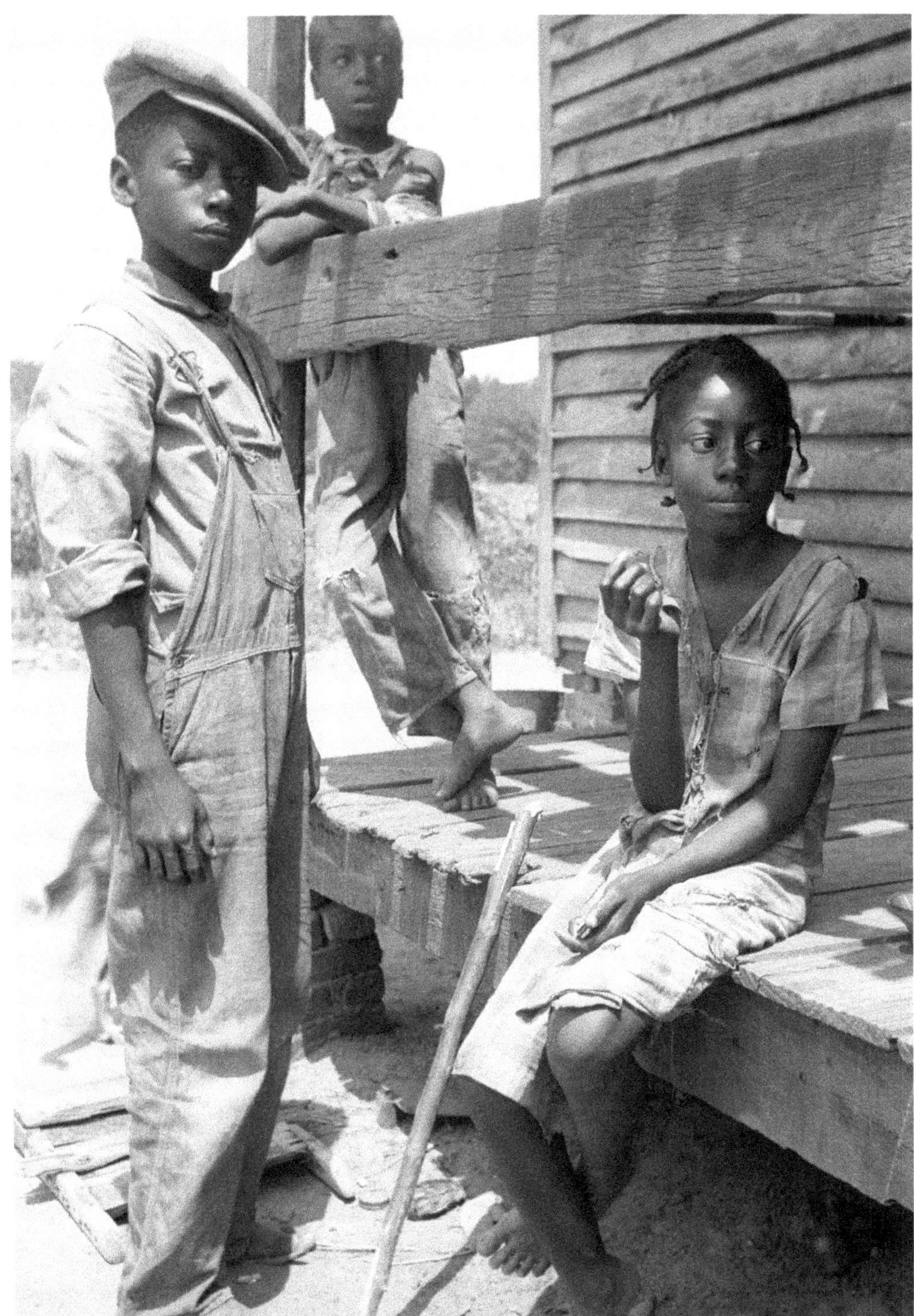

Children of sharecroppers gather porchside on a hot afternoon in July 1936, their routine probably interrupted by the photographer's visit. The rich bottomlands of the Mississippi Delta were suited to row crops, a field of which is just visible in the background at left. The lives of sharecroppers were never prosperous, and the expressions worn by these children suggest that life during the height of the Great Depression was particularly challenging.

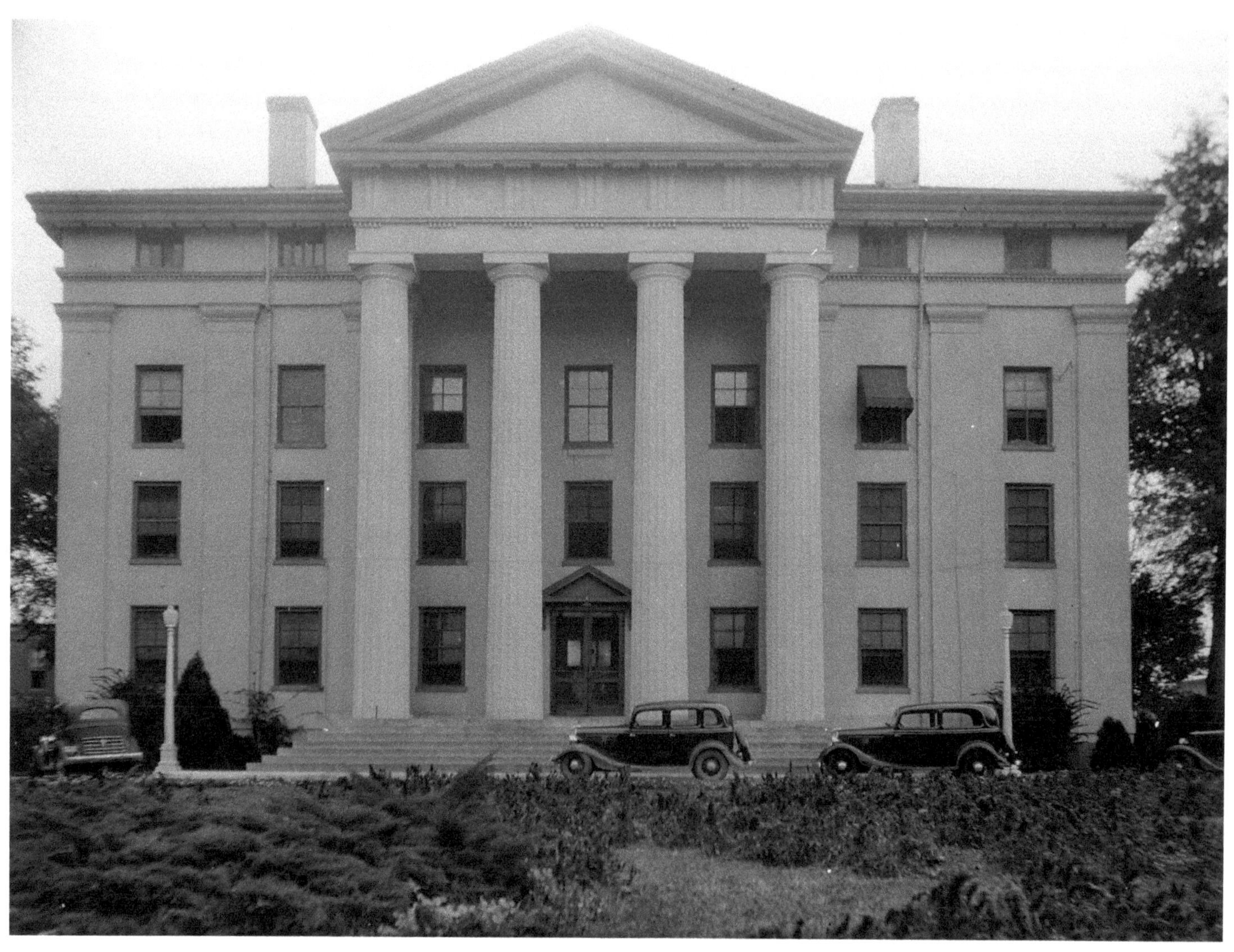

Shown here on September 7, 1936, Jackson's City Hall was built in 1847. During the Siege of Jackson in July 1863, Sherman's forces burned the city to the ground, sparing few of Jackson's public buildings. City Hall was among them, perhaps because it housed an army hospital during the war.

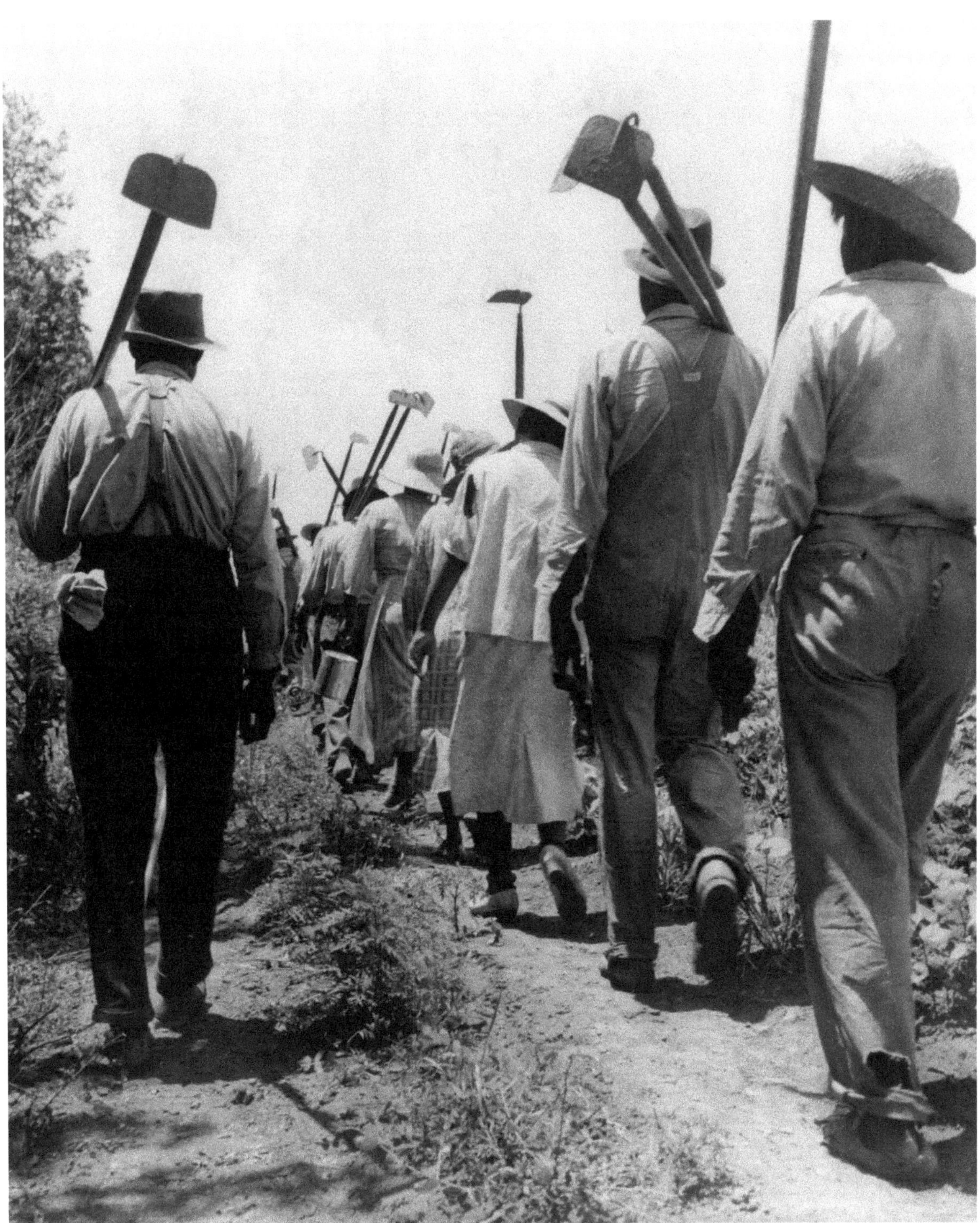

In summer 1937, laborers at Clarksdale, in Coahoma County, head for the cotton fields around six o'clock in the morning to begin a long day of hoeing cotton.

When the cotton was tall in Mississippi, workers began the workday early, before the heat of the sun began bearing down on them. Wide-brimmed hats and loose-fitting, light-colored clothing was the best apparel to keep the sun off. Field hands are shown here in 1937 hoeing a field of cotton to remove weeds and loosen the soil. Mechanized cultivation has long since replaced the need for most manual labor of this kind.

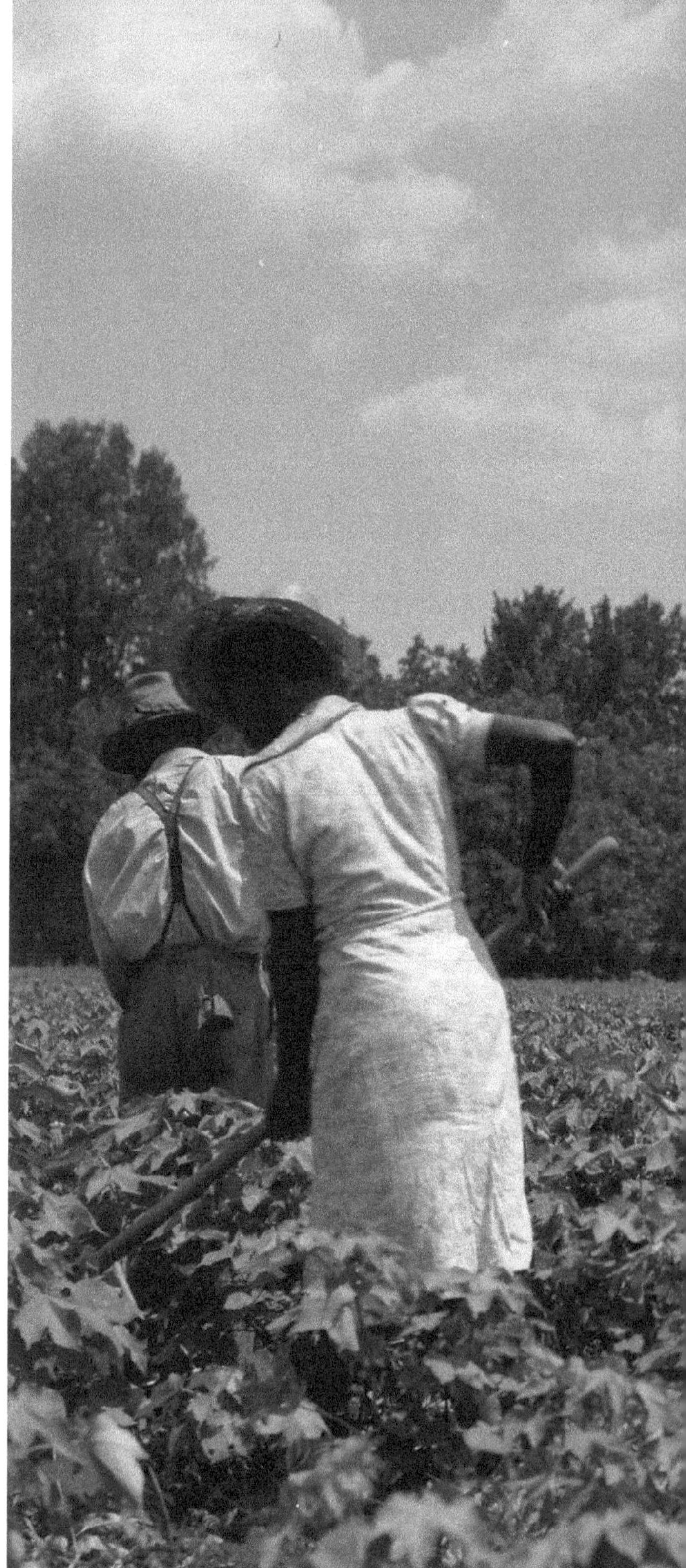

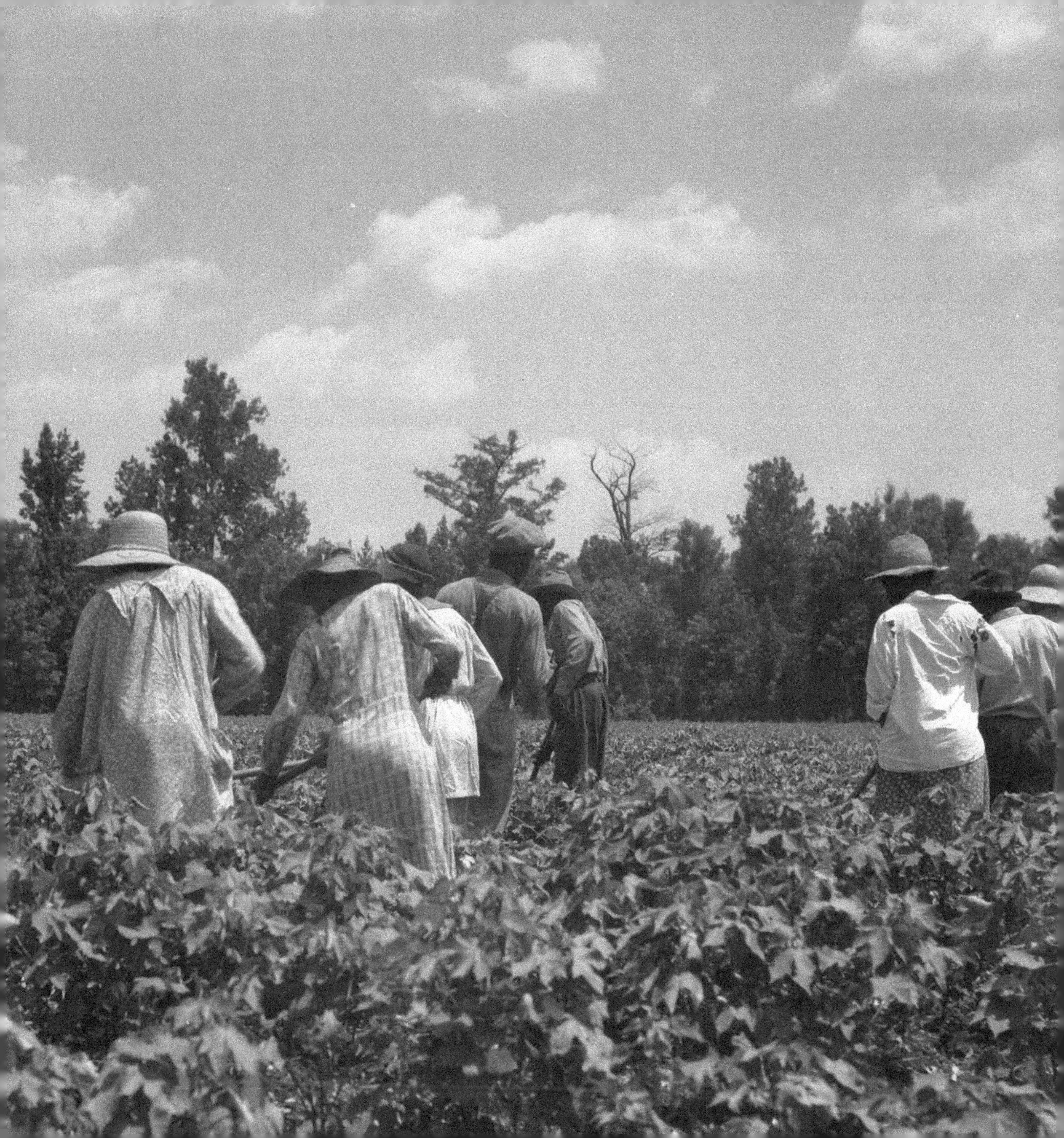

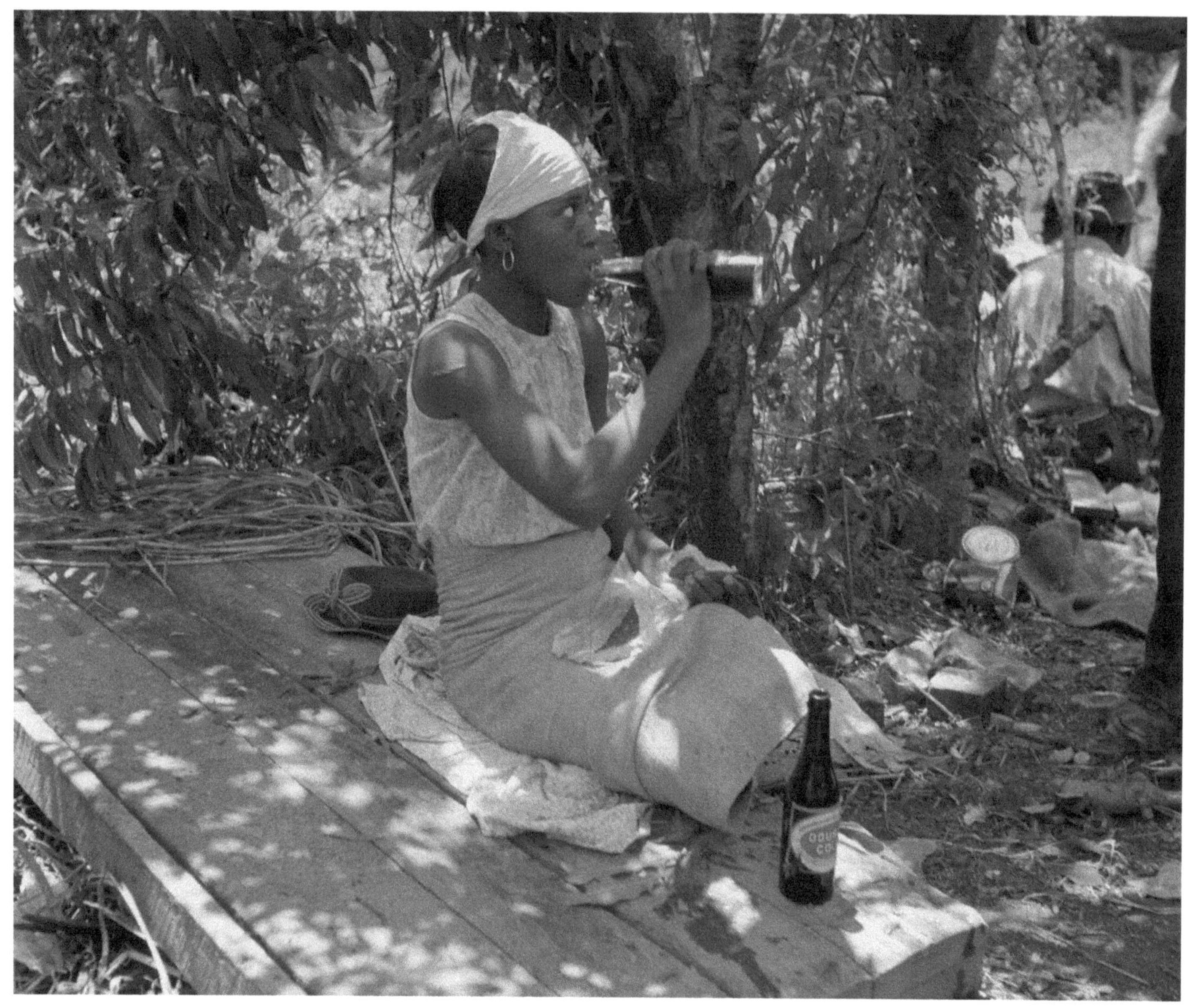

Field hands in a Mississippi Delta cotton field break for lunch under the shade of a tree. The young woman at front is having a Double Cola, a soft drink widely available in the South beginning in the 1930s.

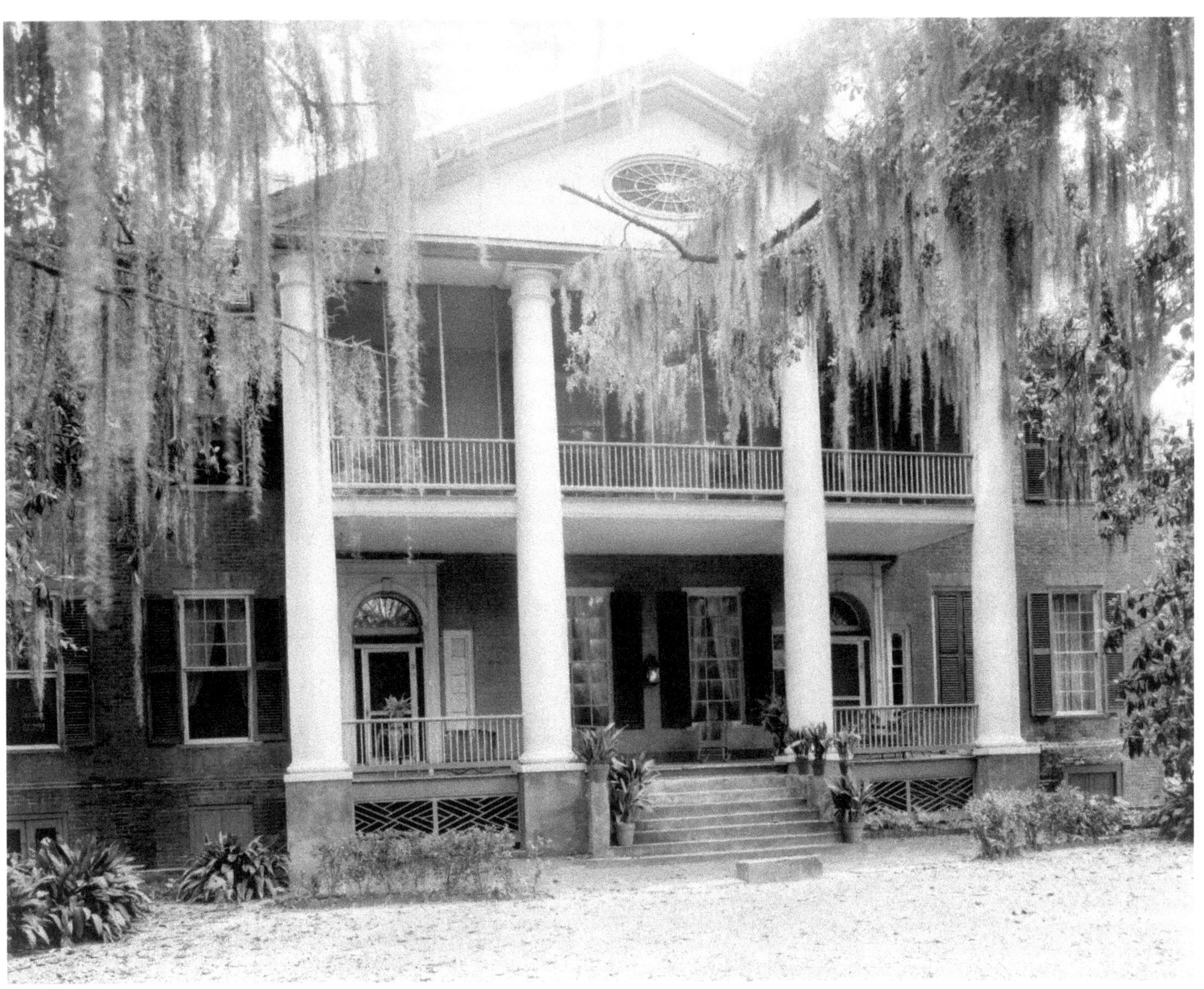

Spanish moss hangs from live oaks and magnolia, which adorn the yard of this elegant, timeworn Mississippi home in Adams County. The evergreen magnolia, filled with fragrant, white blossoms during part of the year, is abundant in the South and is particularly fond of the Magnolia State. The magnolia has been the state tree since 1938, and is also the state flower.

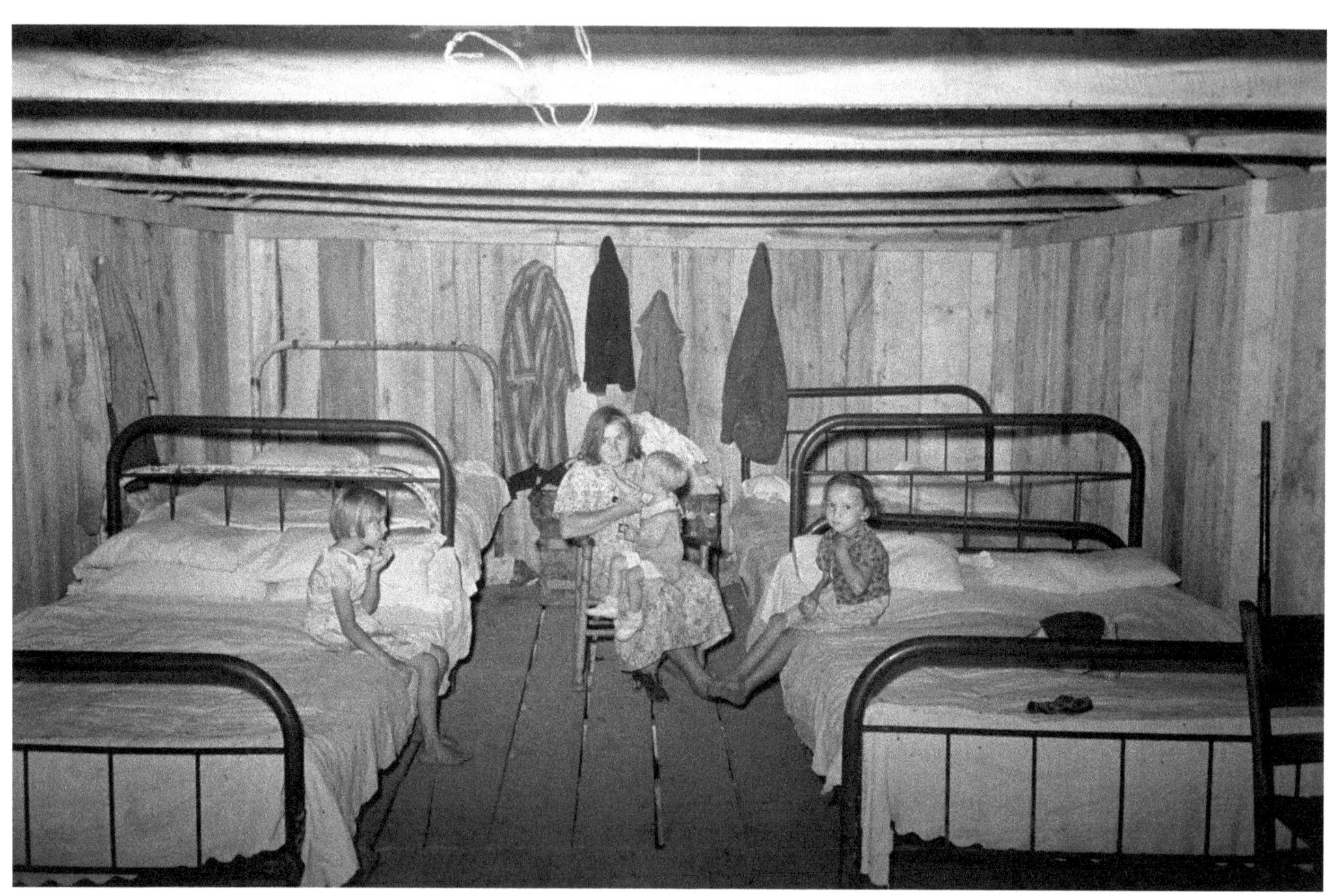

The spartan accommodations of sharecropper homes in Mississippi are apparent in this image from May 1938.

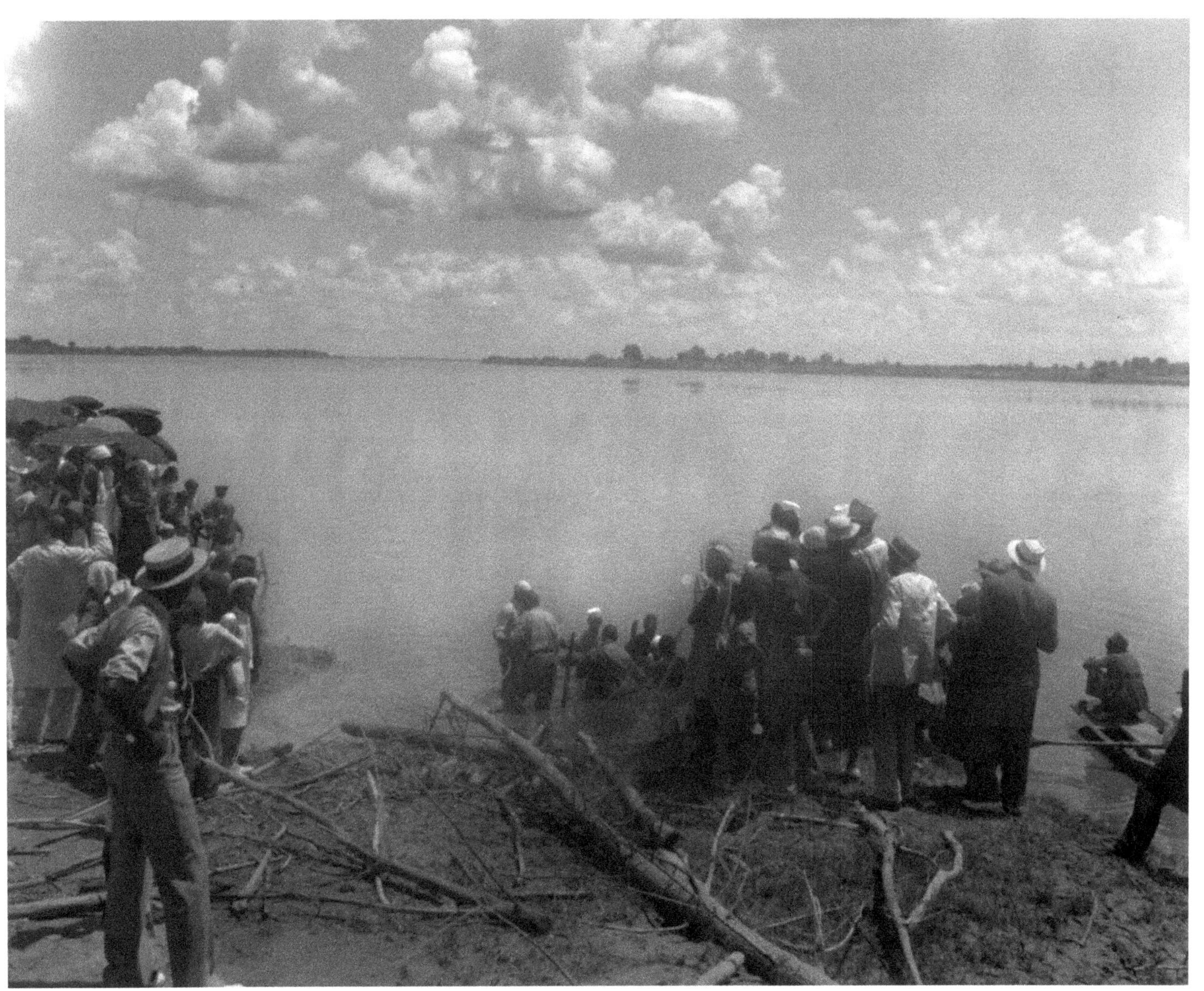

Church members gather at the Mississippi River to witness a baptism on May 29, 1938.

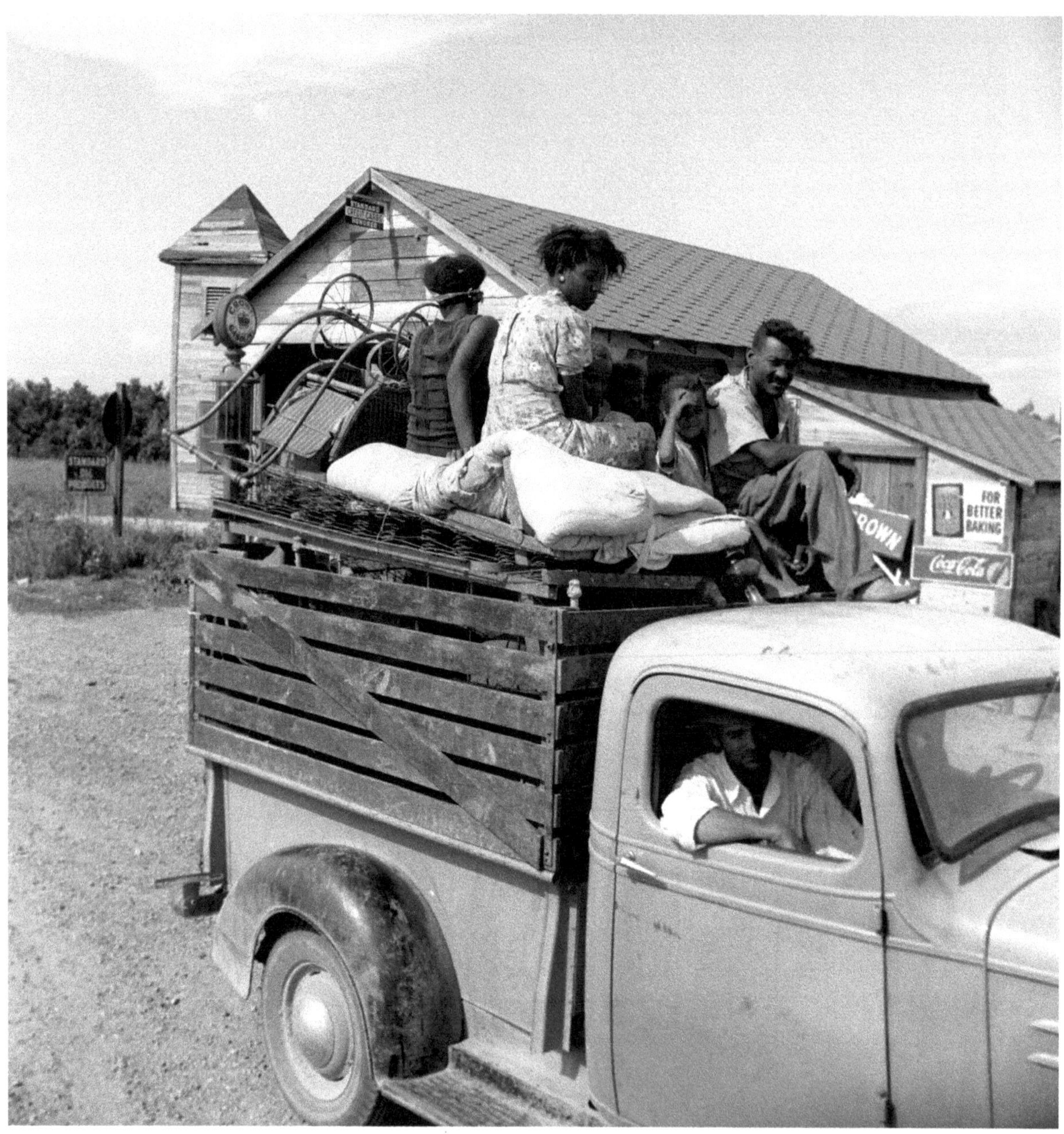

On moving day in June 1938, a laborer's family moves from Arkansas to Mississippi. The loaded truck is parked at a filling station along Highway 1 between Greenville and Clarksdale.

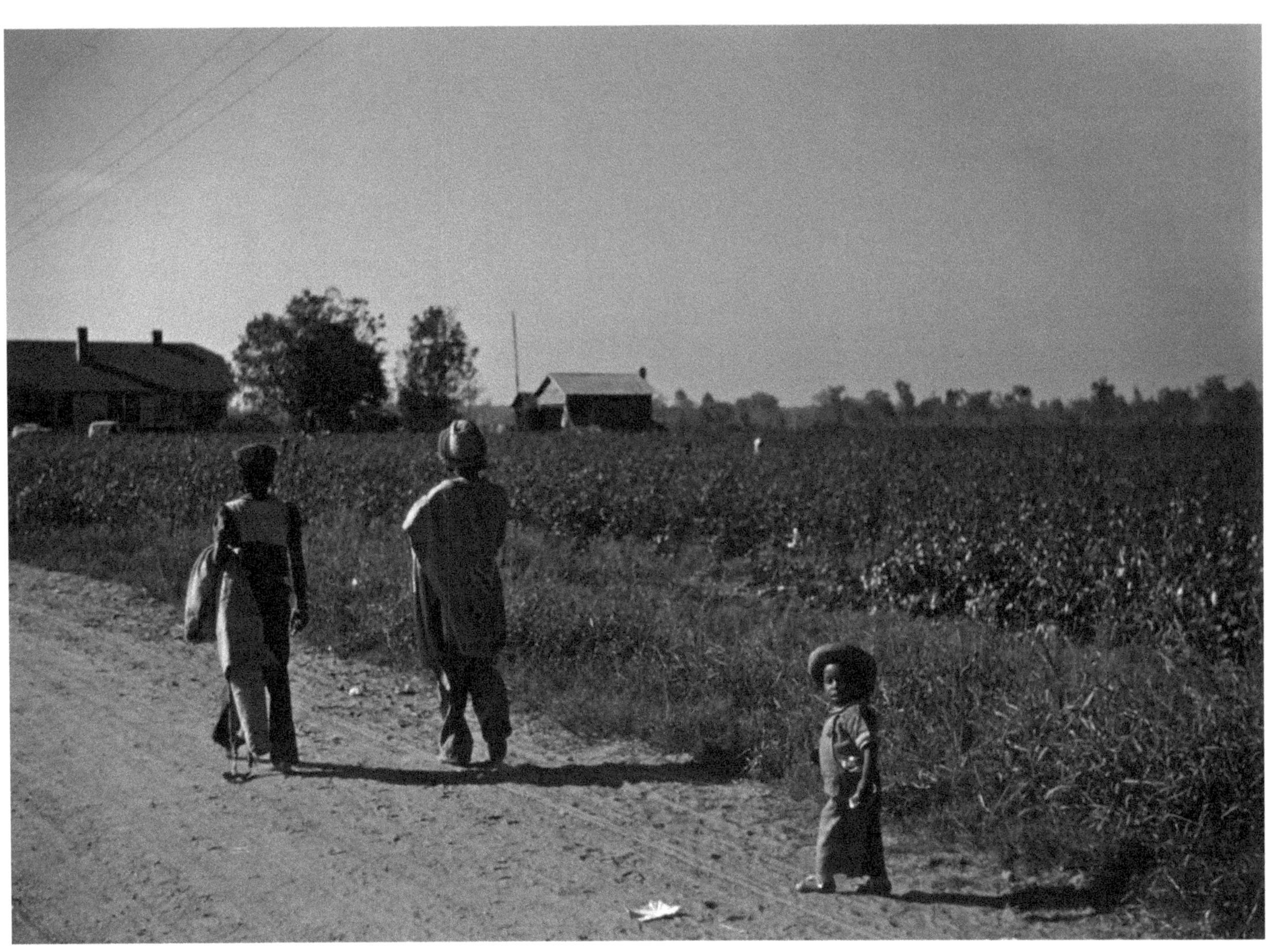

A child follows his parents up a lane at Marcella Plantation, at Mileston in Holmes County, in September 1939. A field of cotton is ripening in the background.

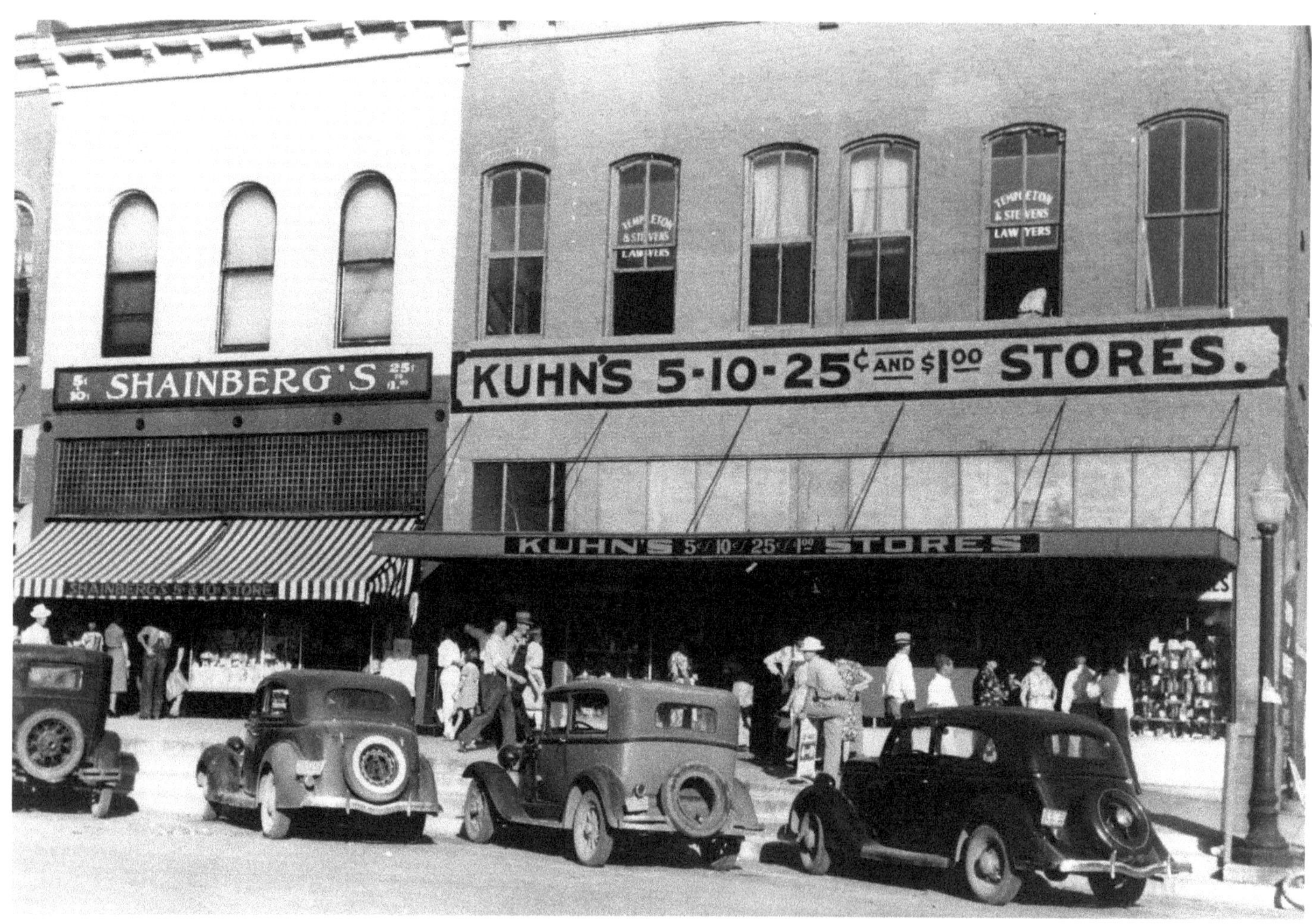

Shoppers fill the sidewalks of Lexington's Main Street on a Saturday afternoon in October 1939. Kuhn's and Shainberg's five and dimes are open for business. The "five and dime" had become a very popular kind of retail outlet throughout the nation.

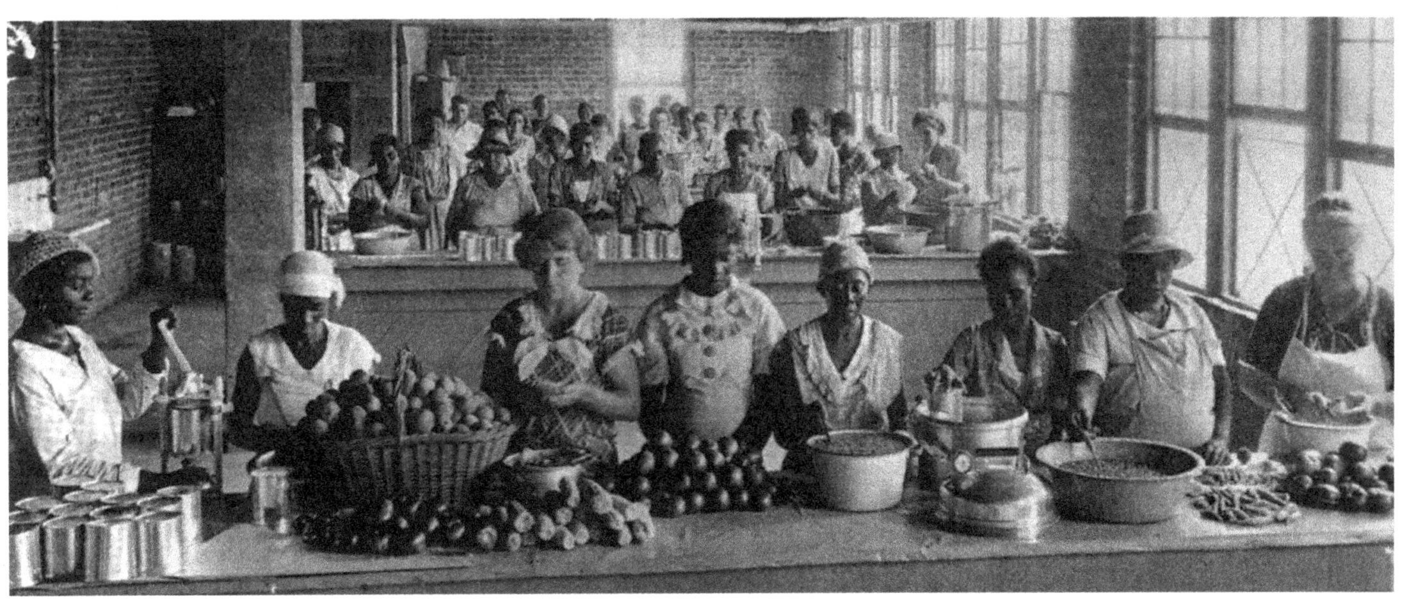

Women of east central Mississippi labor to process apples, corn, okra, and tomatoes at a Works Progress Administration canning factory during the Great Depression. Hard times have always brought forth the strong spirit and willingness to pull together implanted deep in the souls of all Mississippians.

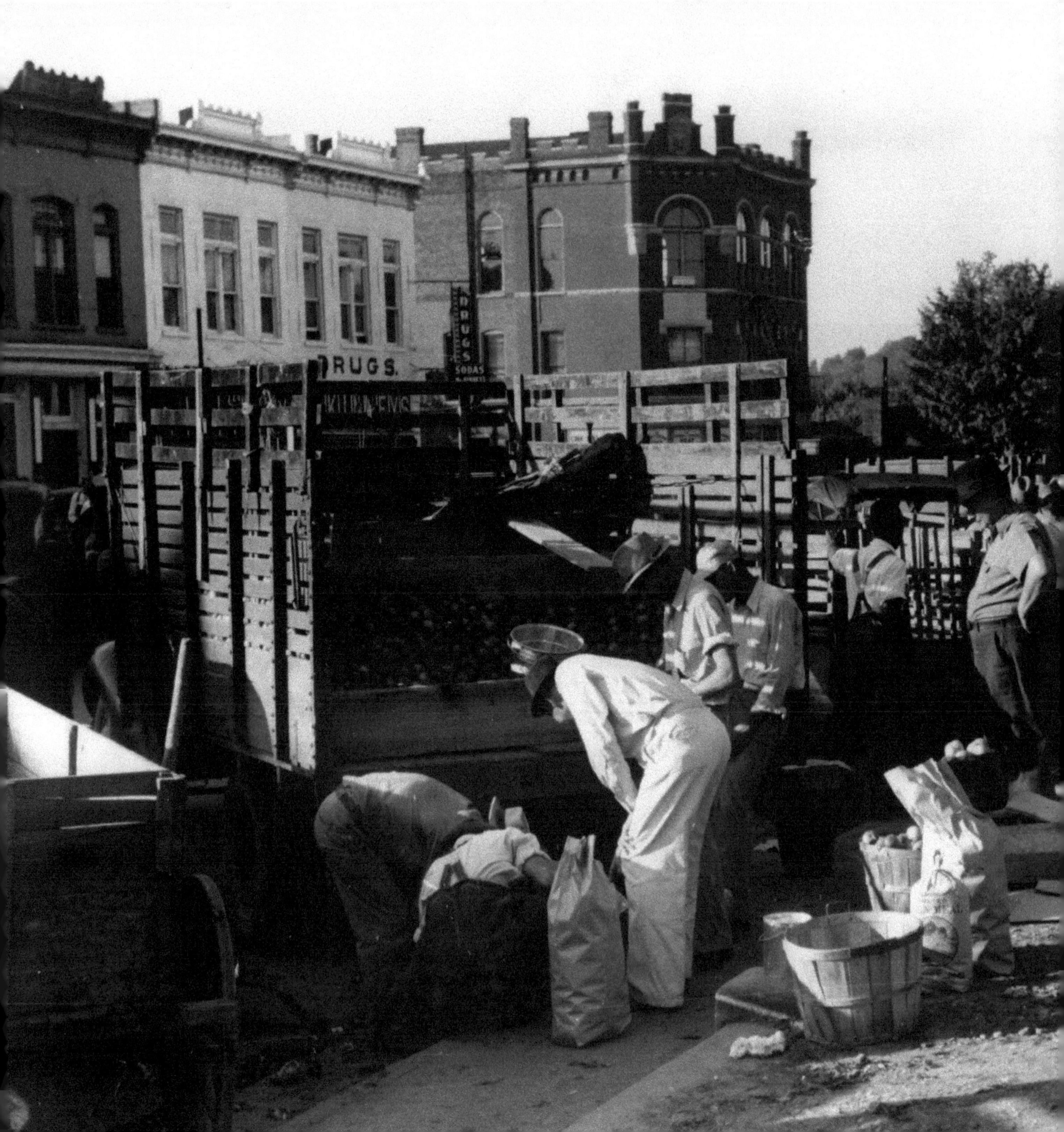
DRUGS.
DRUGS
SODAS

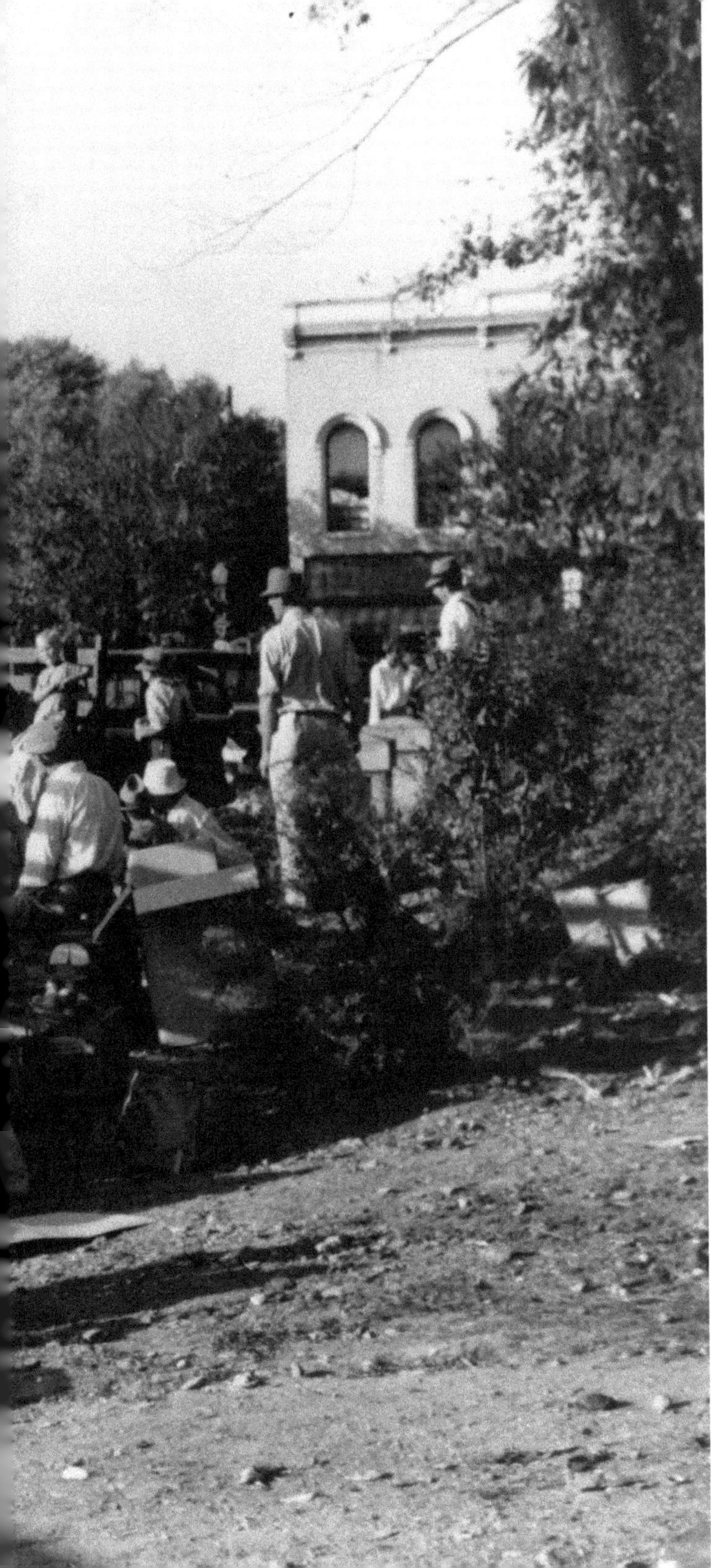

Main Street in Lexington was the scene of this open market for local produce. Farmers seem to have a bumper crop of apples available for sale on this Saturday afternoon in 1939.

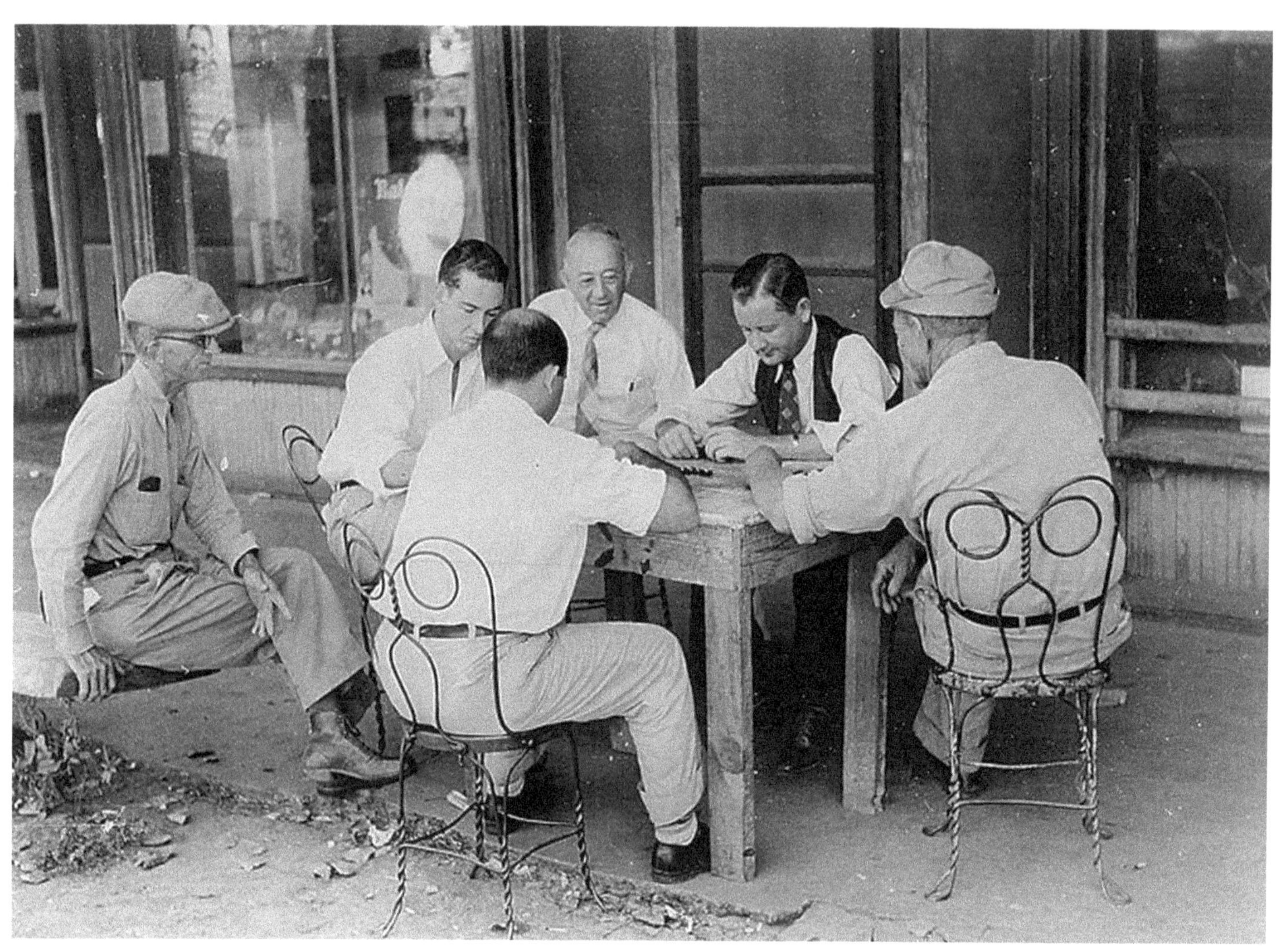

An intense afternoon game of dominoes is under way in 1939 as these men study their gaming options. Dominoes helped keep minds clear as Americans weathered the final years of the depression.

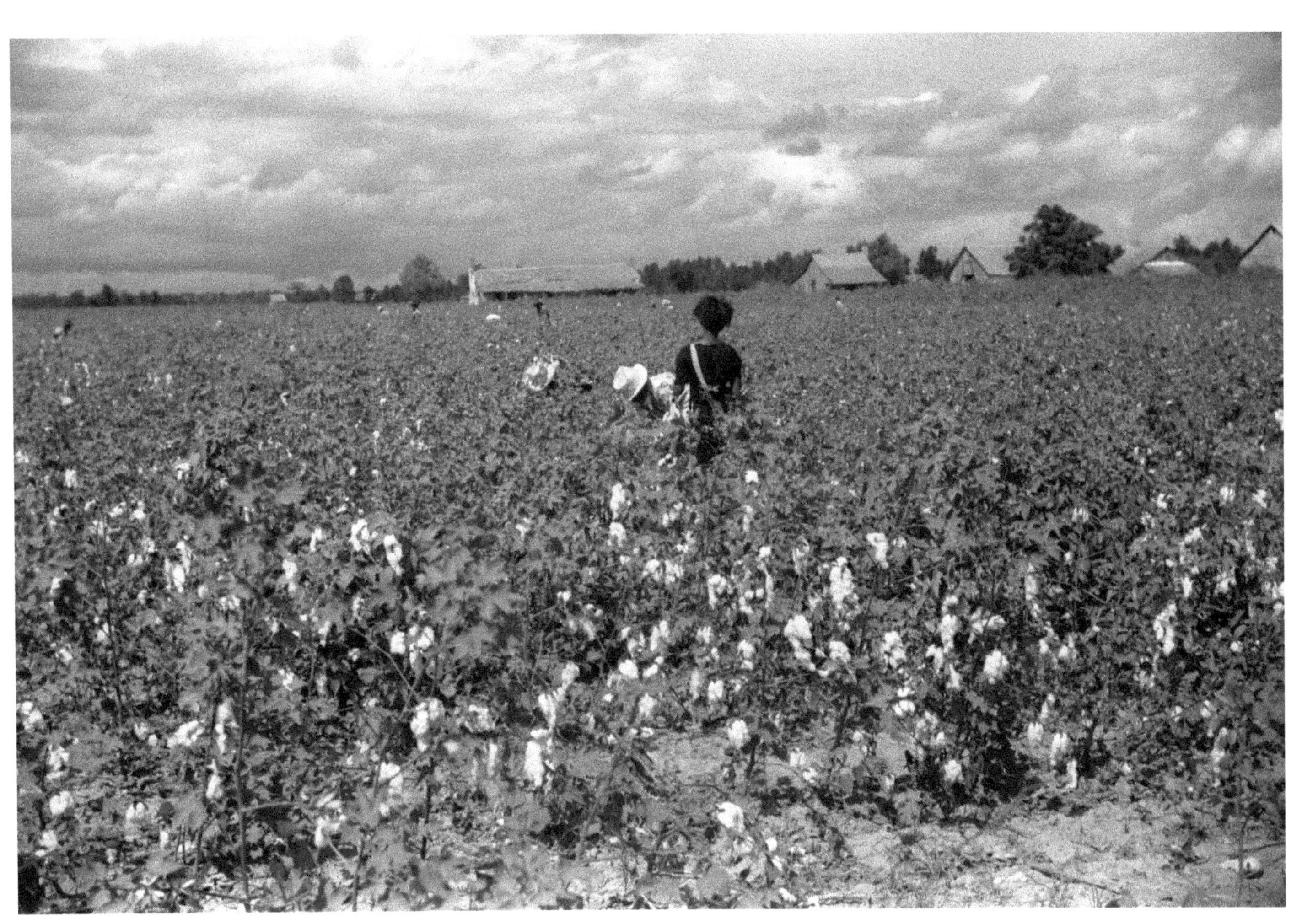

It's cotton-picking time in October 1939 at Nugent Plantation, in Benoit.

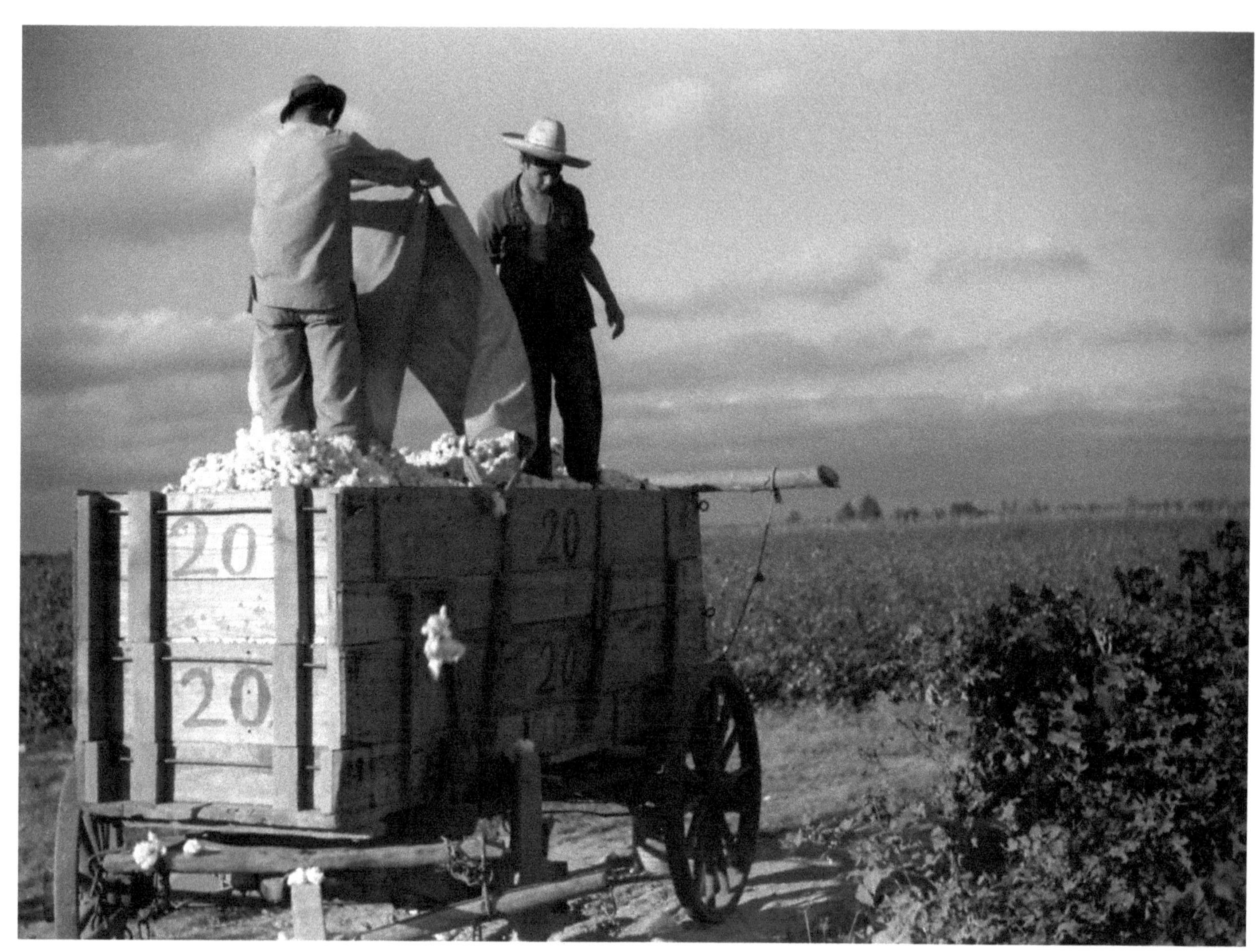

Laborers fill a wagon with cotton in a field at Knowlton Plantation, in Perthshire.

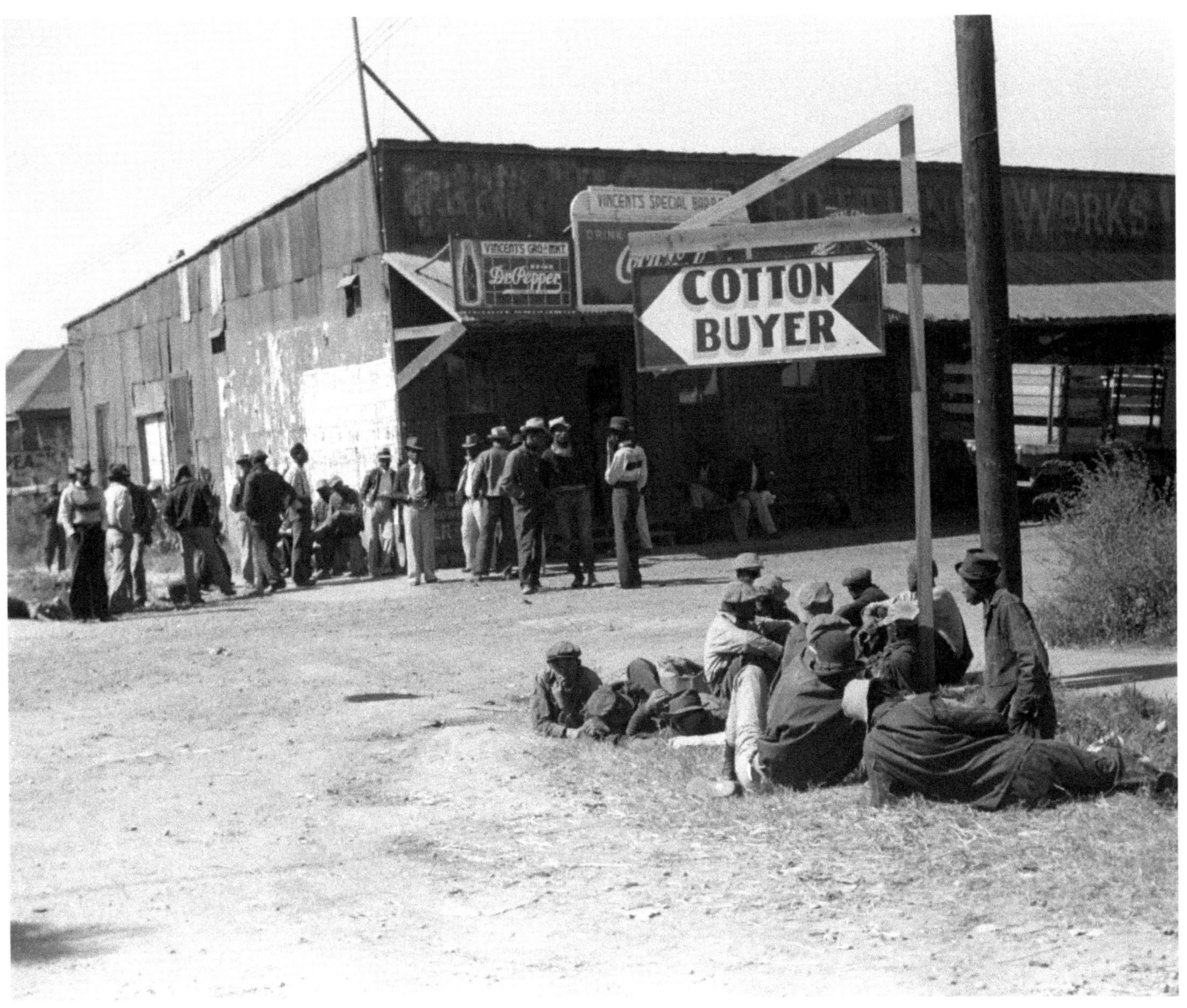

Locals of Belzoni, in Washington County, idle away a Saturday in 1939, perhaps awaiting the cotton buyer.

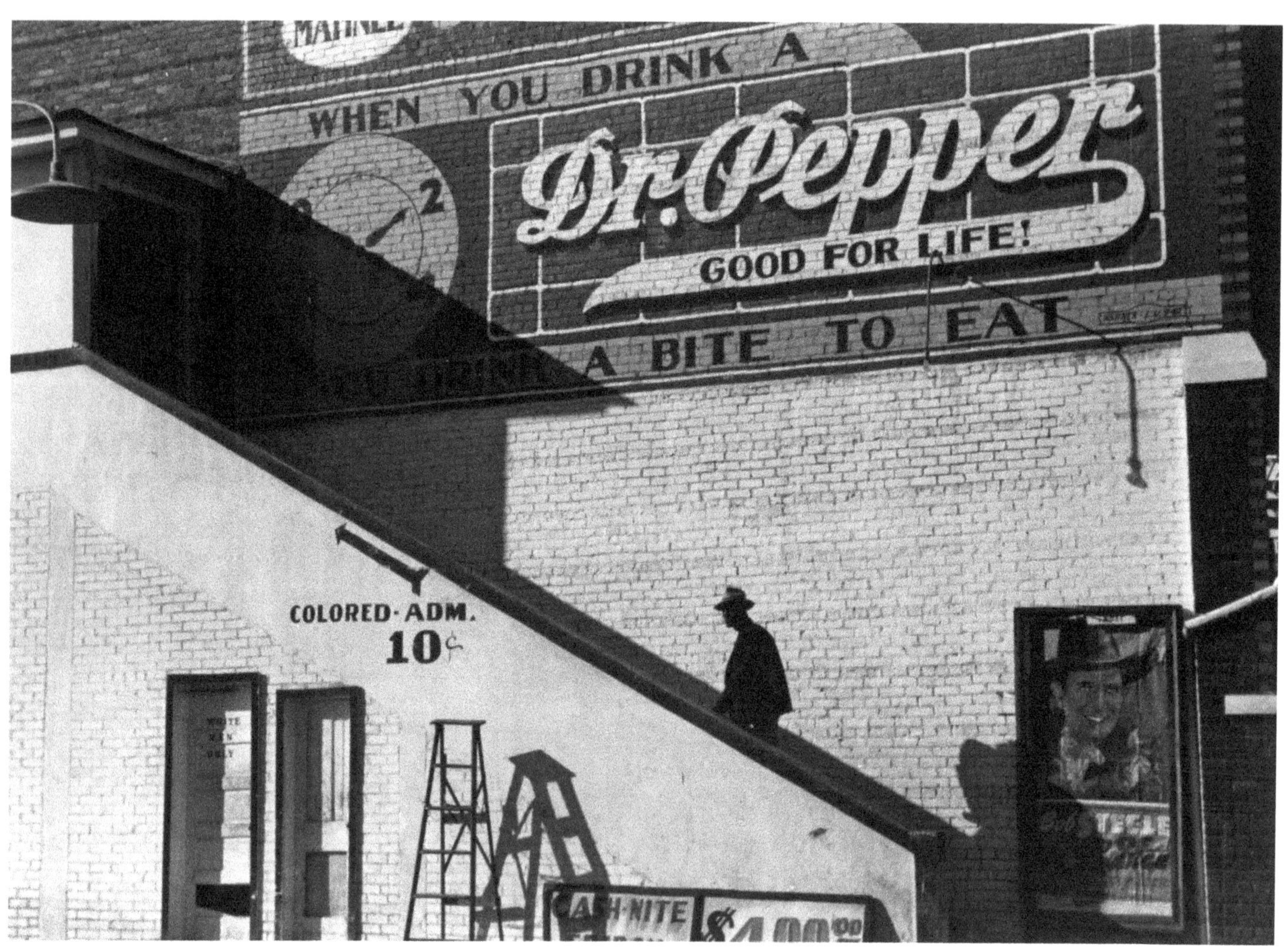

A Bob Steele western attracts a Belzoni moviegoer, who climbs the stairs to a Saturday matinee during the era of segregation.

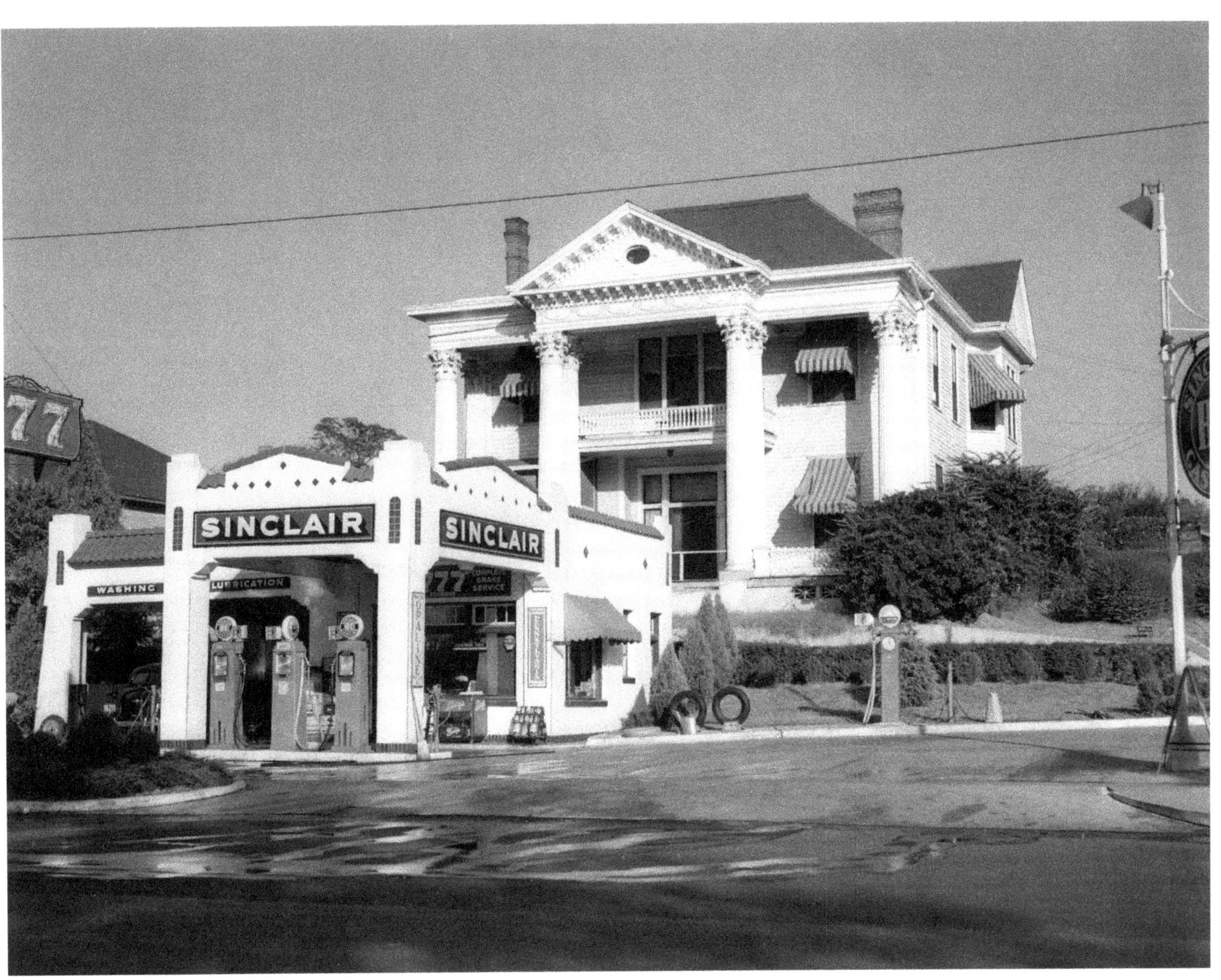

In November 1939 at Jackson, a Sinclair filling station occupies the land that would have been, in an earlier day, the front lawn of the historic home at rear. Filling stations of the era were carefully designed, often featuring terra cotta roofing and other refinements. The photographer's question, perhaps, is whether the architecture of this station both mimicks and compliments the stately columns, handsome portico, and other features of the aging mansion.

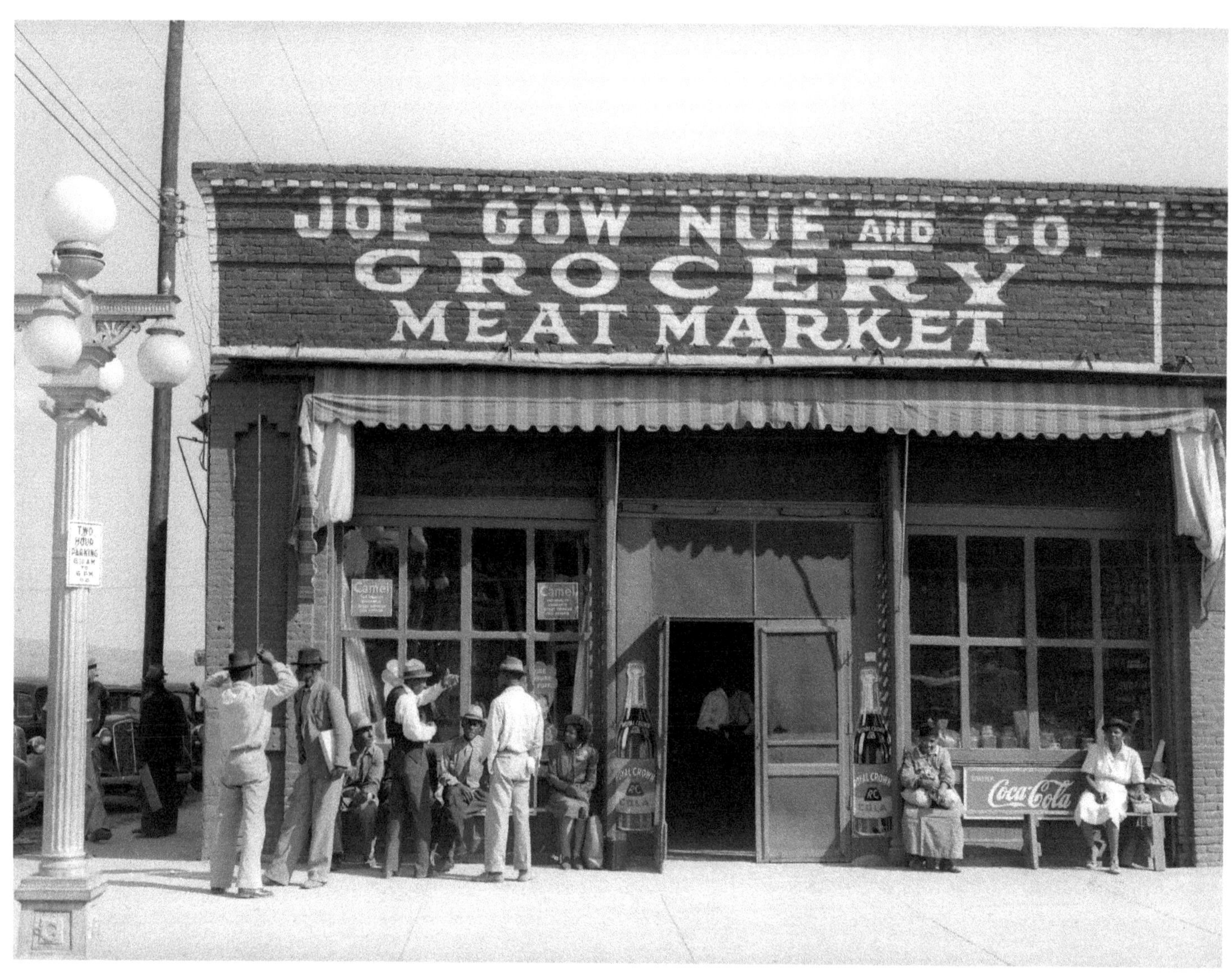

Joe Gow Nue and Company Grocery and Meat Market is open for business in November 1939. Signage limits parking to two hours, and a window ad announces that Camel is the "quality cigarette every smoker can afford."

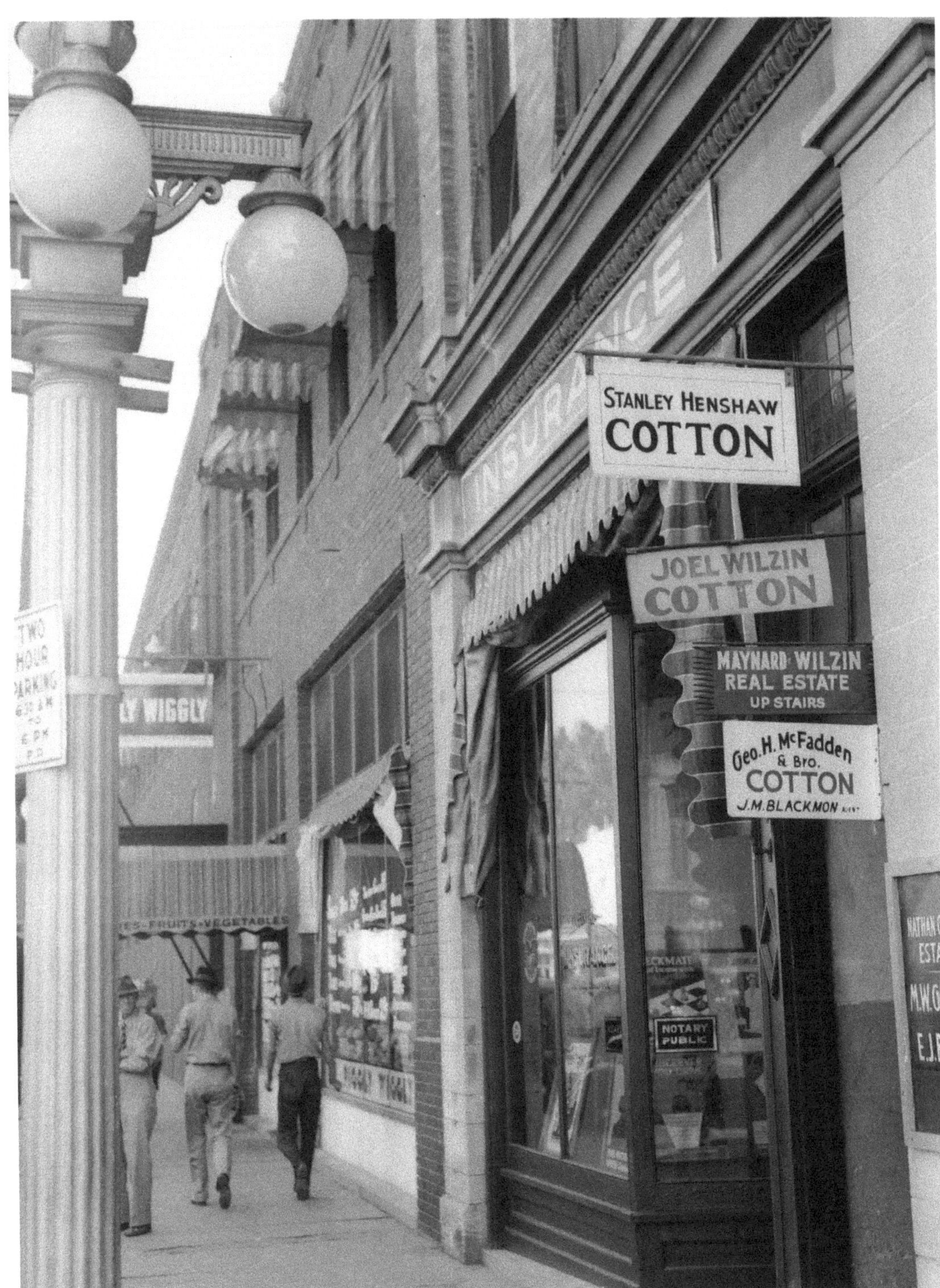

In November 1939, it is all about cotton on Cotton Row Street in Leland.

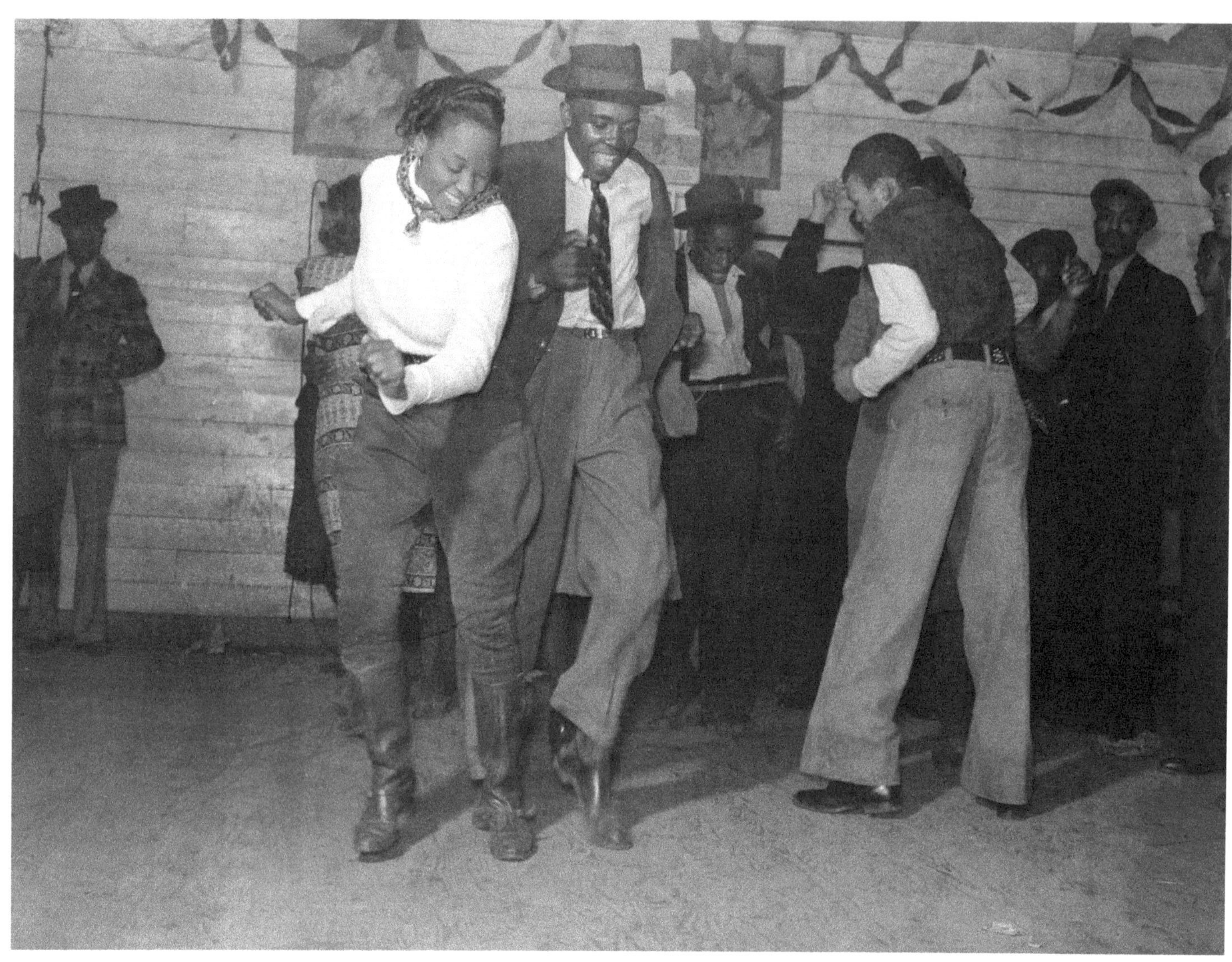

A Saturday evening in November 1939 at a juke joint near Clarksdale finds these patrons hard at play, jitterbugging. Wearing their best clothes, all participants seem to be having a very good time.

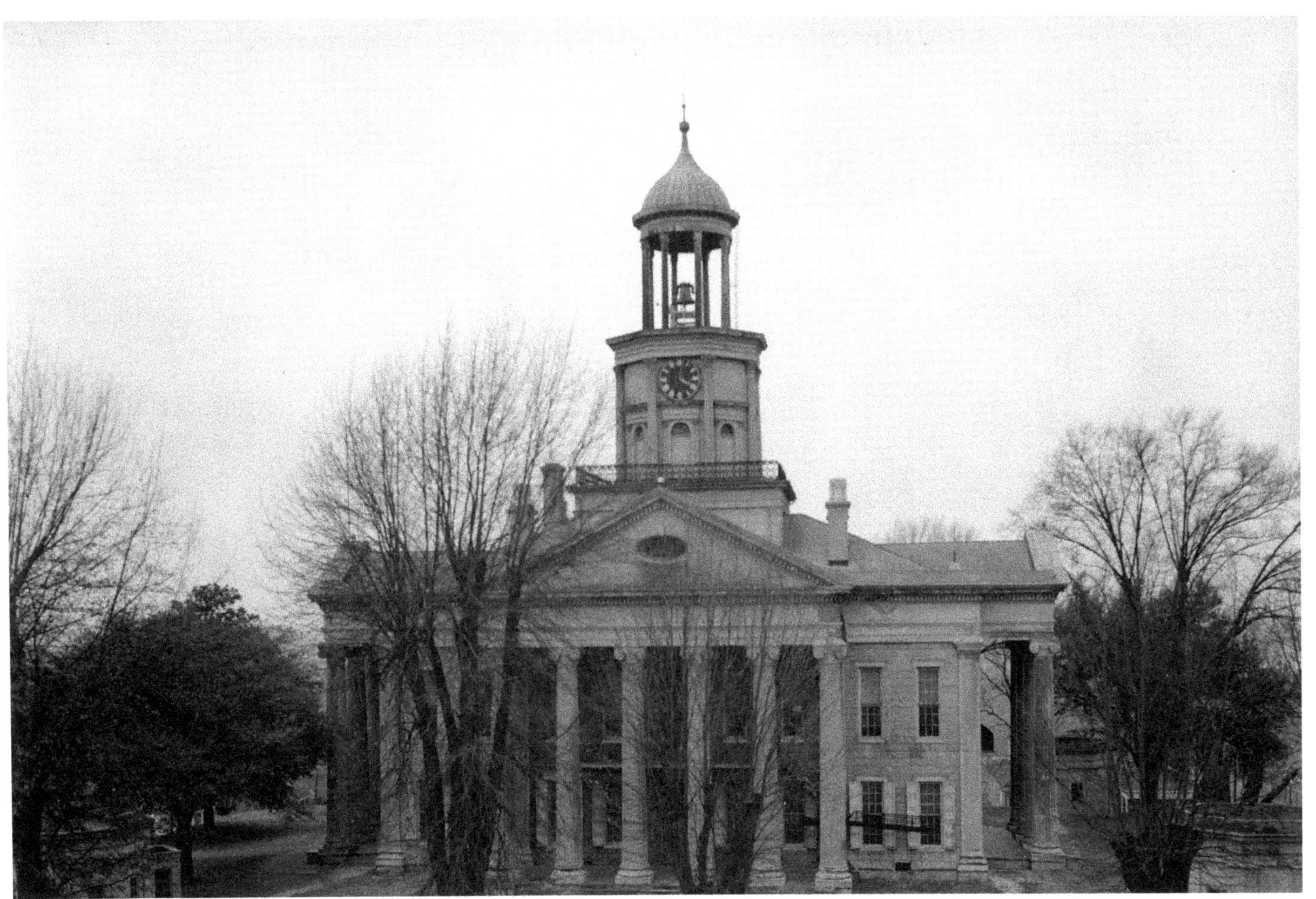

This is the Warren County Courthouse at Vicksburg as it appeared February 19, 1940. Dedicated June 16, 1858, the structure survived the 47-day siege during the Civil War, and it was here that the forces of General Grant brought down the Confederate flag at the fall of Vicksburg.

The Old State Capitol, shown here at 100 North State Street in Jackson, was another of the few structures to survive when Union forces under General Sherman torched the city during the Civil War. The structure is an excellent example of Greek revival, conceived and erected on a monumental scale. The Capitol was the seat of government for the State of Mississippi from 1839 to 1903, when it was replaced with the new capitol.

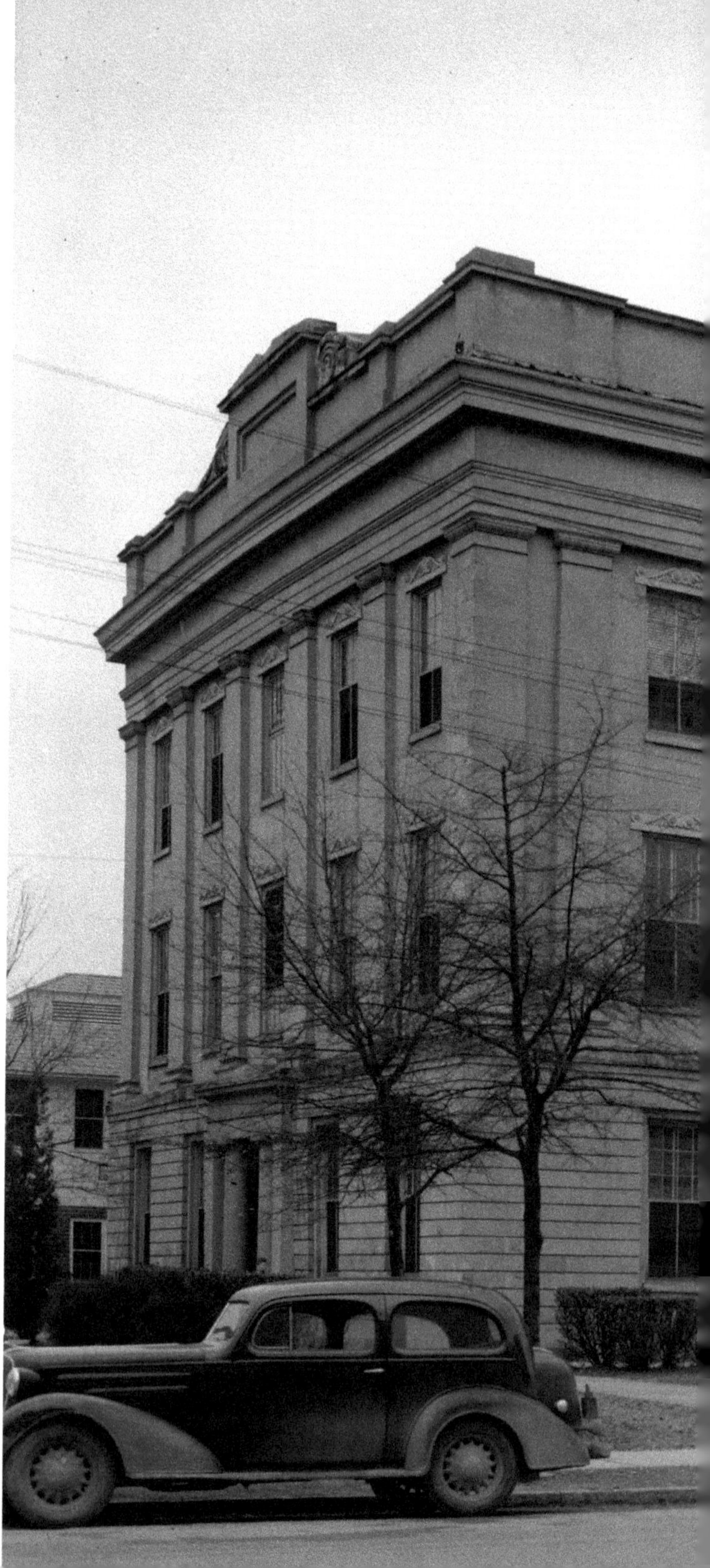

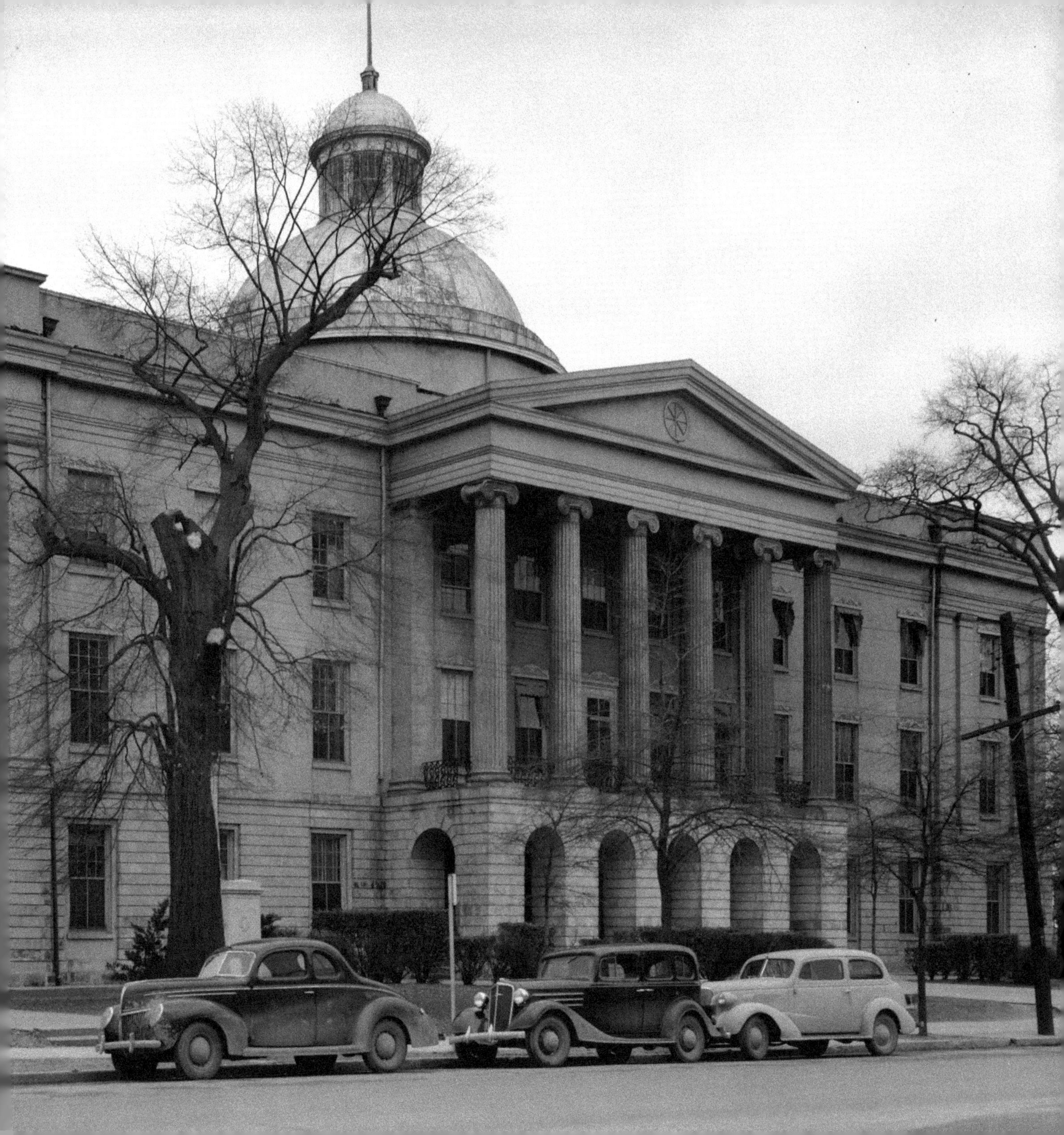

Stanton Hall at Natchez as it appeared in February 1940. The princely mansion, once owned by Irish immigrant Frederick Stanton, is one of the grandest in Mississippi. The massive white palace with immense Corinthian columns and wrought-iron fencing encompasses a full city block downtown.

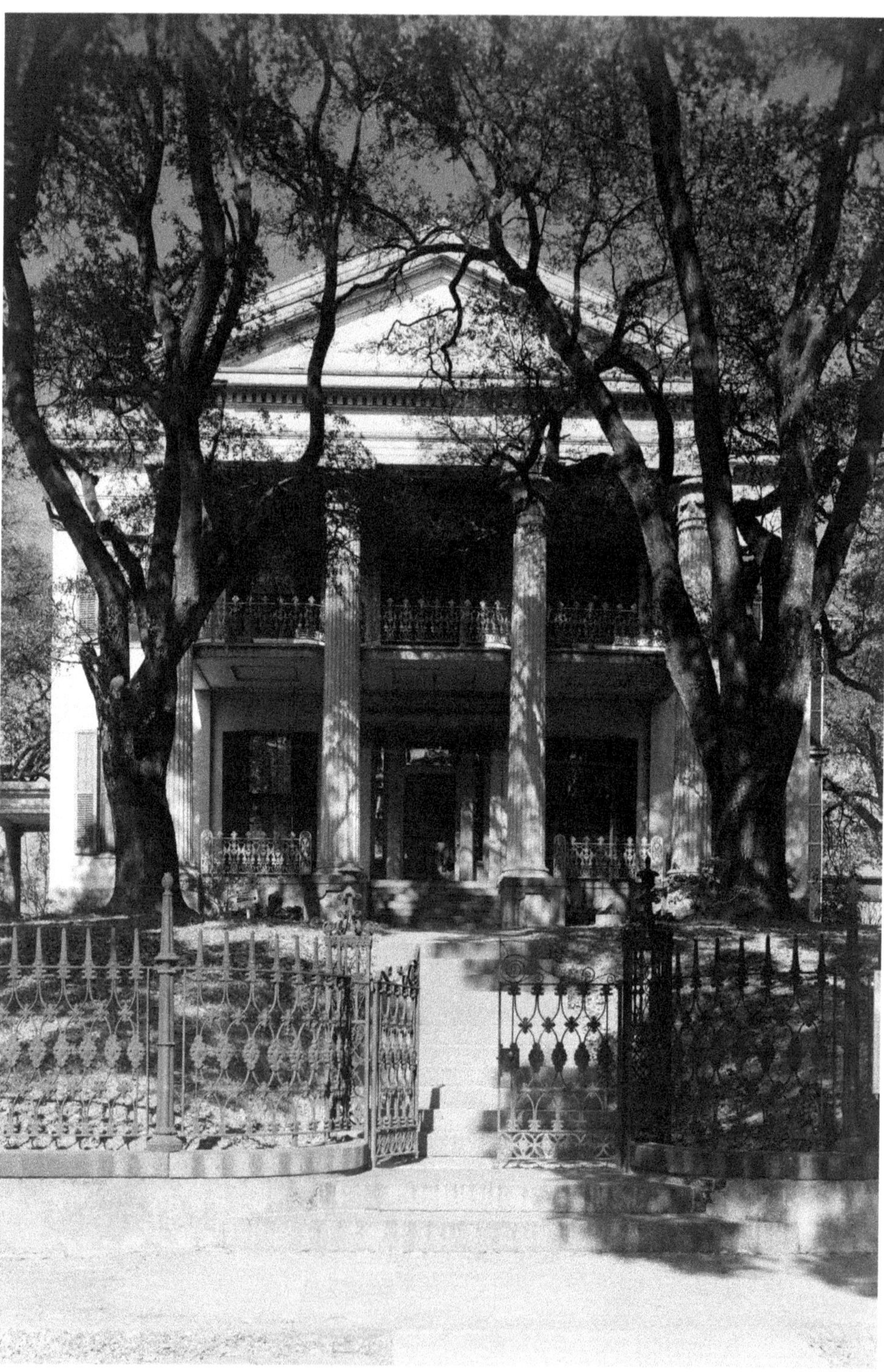

War in Europe and Struggles at Home

(1940–1970s)

Mississippians reacted to the news of the attack on Pearl Harbor in 1941 as a call to action. Thousands of young men joined the armed forces, and citizens who remained at home contributed to the war effort with campaigns to raise money through war bonds. They collected scrap metal, rubber, and other materials for recycling. Mississippians and Americans across the nation accepted the rigors of the rationing of gasoline, tires, and certain food staples as a call to patriotism. Women stepped in to fill the void in many ways, primarily in factory and production work. Ingalls Shipbuilding and new military bases created thousands of new jobs.

The war years ended the Great Depression. The Mississippi economy as well as the economy of the entire nation benefited. The dominance of agriculture in Mississippi also ended as wartime industries bequeathed to the state permanent footing as a competitive provider of industrial and professional services. A popular tune of the war era went, "How ya gonna keep 'em down on the farm after they've seen Pairee?" It was true. The farm boys who left Mississippi for the Pacific and European theaters of war returned as trained, responsible workers ready for new challenges and better paychecks.

After World War II ended in 1945, the sleepy southern state awoke to different ideas and perspectives. Racial tensions arose as African-Americans sought equality and an end to their longstanding second-class citizenship. NAACP leaders organized protest marches, conducted in towns and communities throughout the state in the 1950s. Southern Christian leadership joined with these efforts. In the end, a poignant day for racial equality came when African-American James Meredith was admitted as a student to the University of Mississippi in 1966.

As the people of the state united and worked together, Mississippi's storied history of perseverance prevailed. With strong leadership tempered by the voices of reason, Mississippians were able to show the world how to overcome great obstacles and how to find common ground, and to establish a flow of accord among the different identities in American culture as deep and as strong as the flow of the great river of our beloved state.

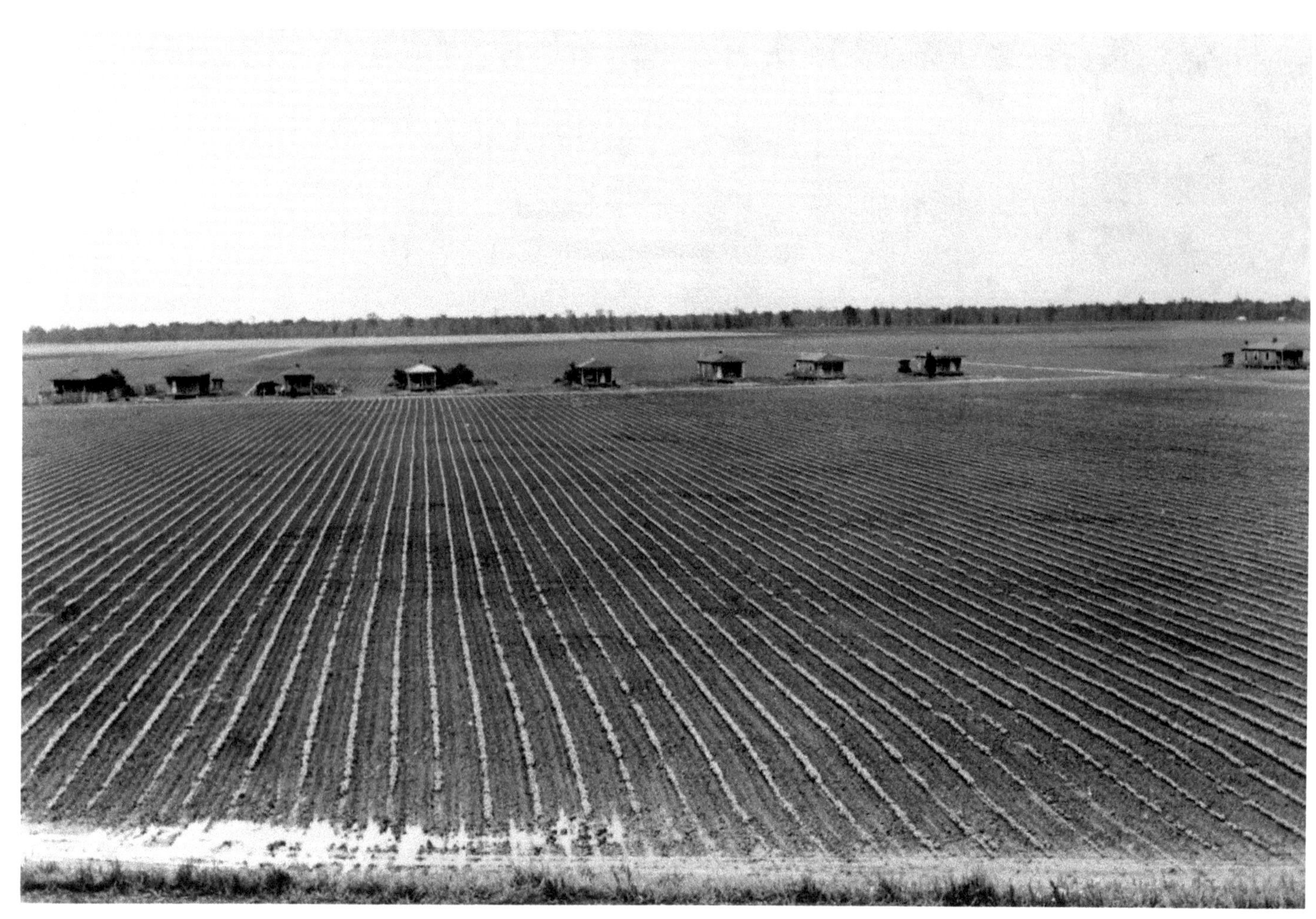

In May 1940, the tenant houses on this farm located at Rolling Fork, in Sharkey County, sit as neatly in line as the rows of cotton in the front of each one. Despite boll weevil infestations in foregoing decades, cotton remained a key to Mississippi agriculture.

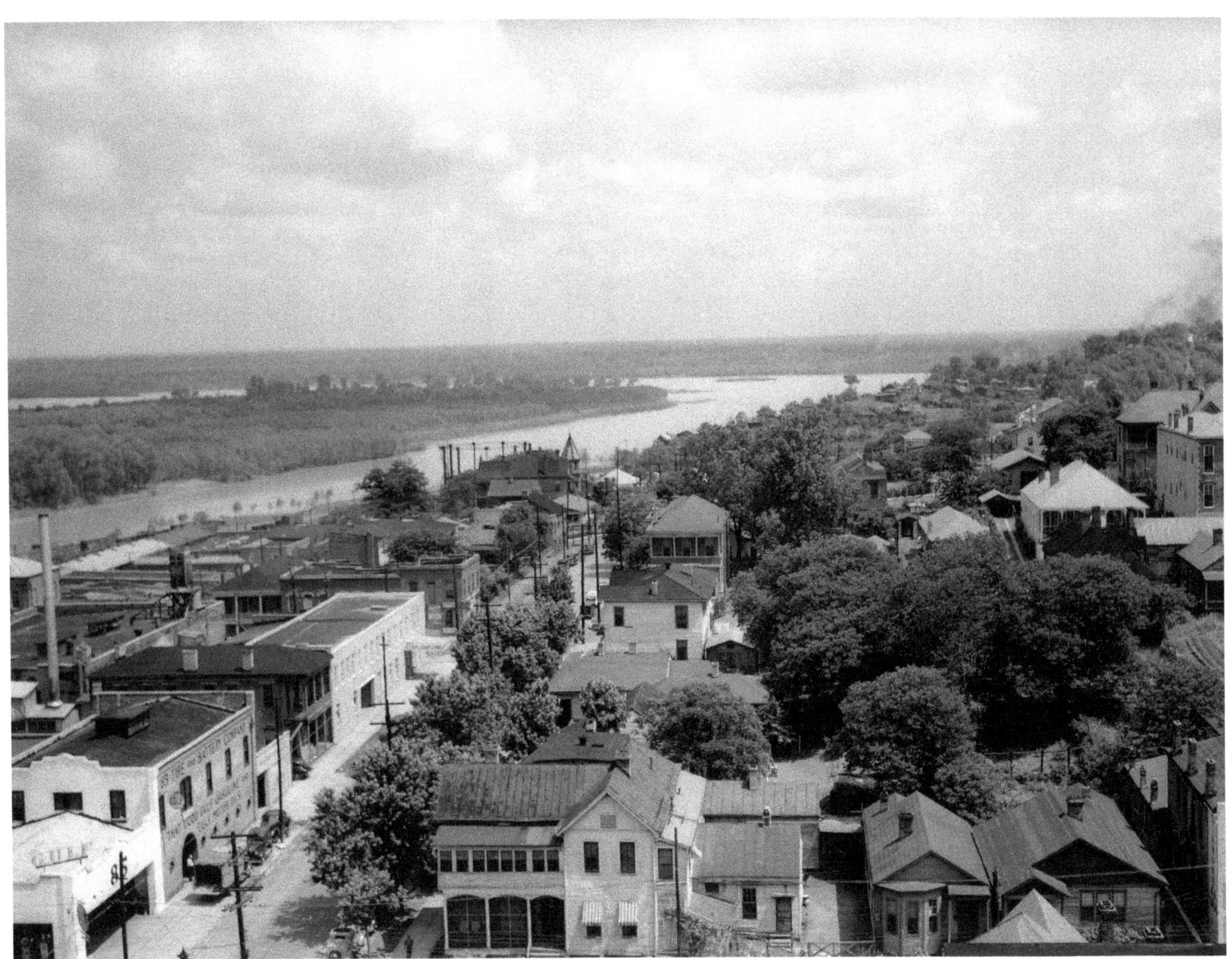

An arm of the Mississippi River snakes through Vicksburg in this bird's-eye view from May 1940.

Following Spread: On a partly cloudy day in August 1940 at Port Gibson, in Claiborne County, a horse-drawn wagon loaded with shoppers saunters through the business district, surrounded by automobiles. Occupied as early as 1729 and chartered as a town on March 12, 1803, Port Gibson is Mississippi's third-oldest settlement. The town has many historic buildings including the Windsor Ruins, which consist solely of 23 enormous columns. Windsor was Mississippi's largest antebellum estate. Although it survived the Civil War, it did not escape the ravages of a fire that broke out in 1890.

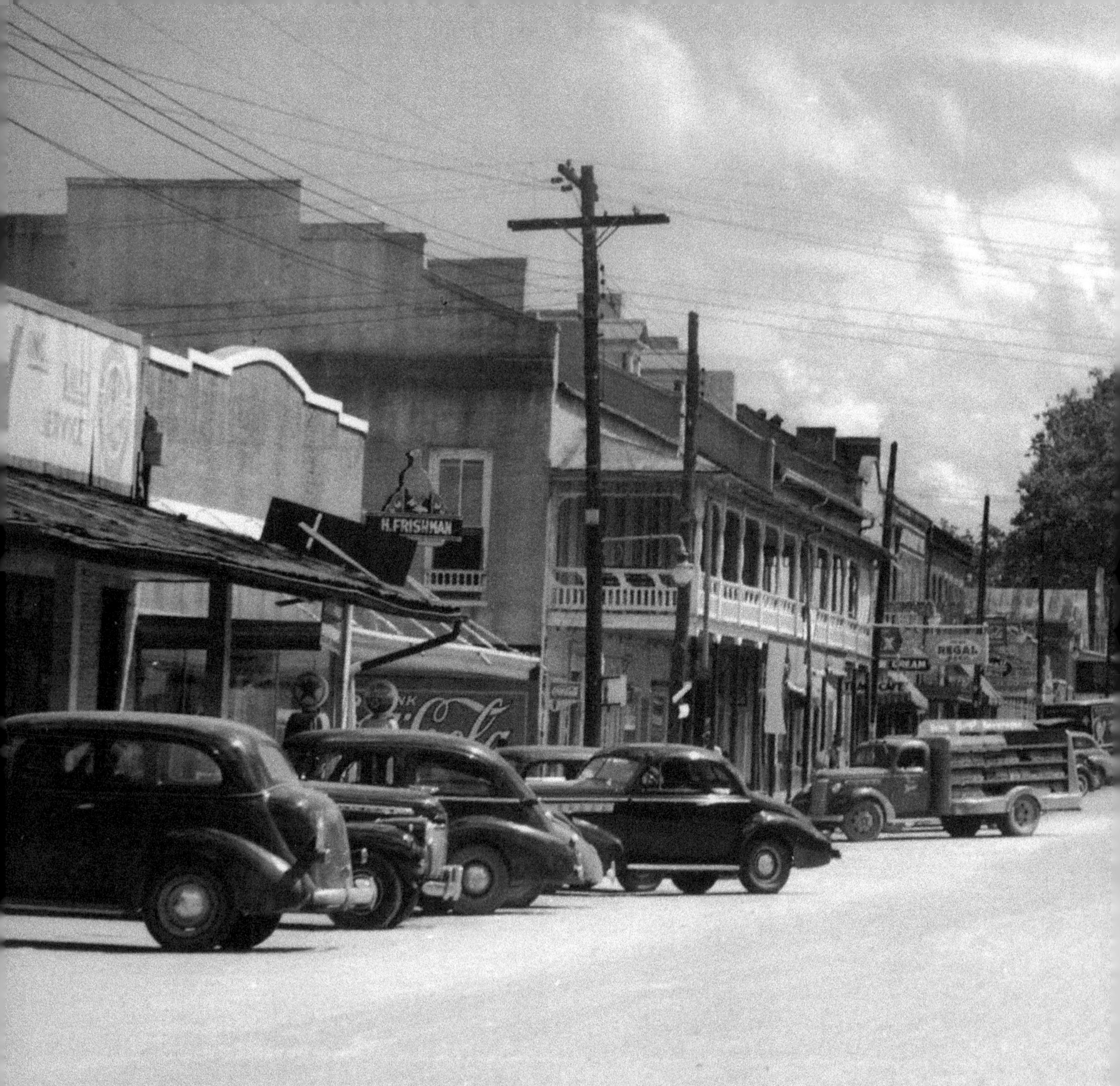

H. FRISHMAN
REGAL

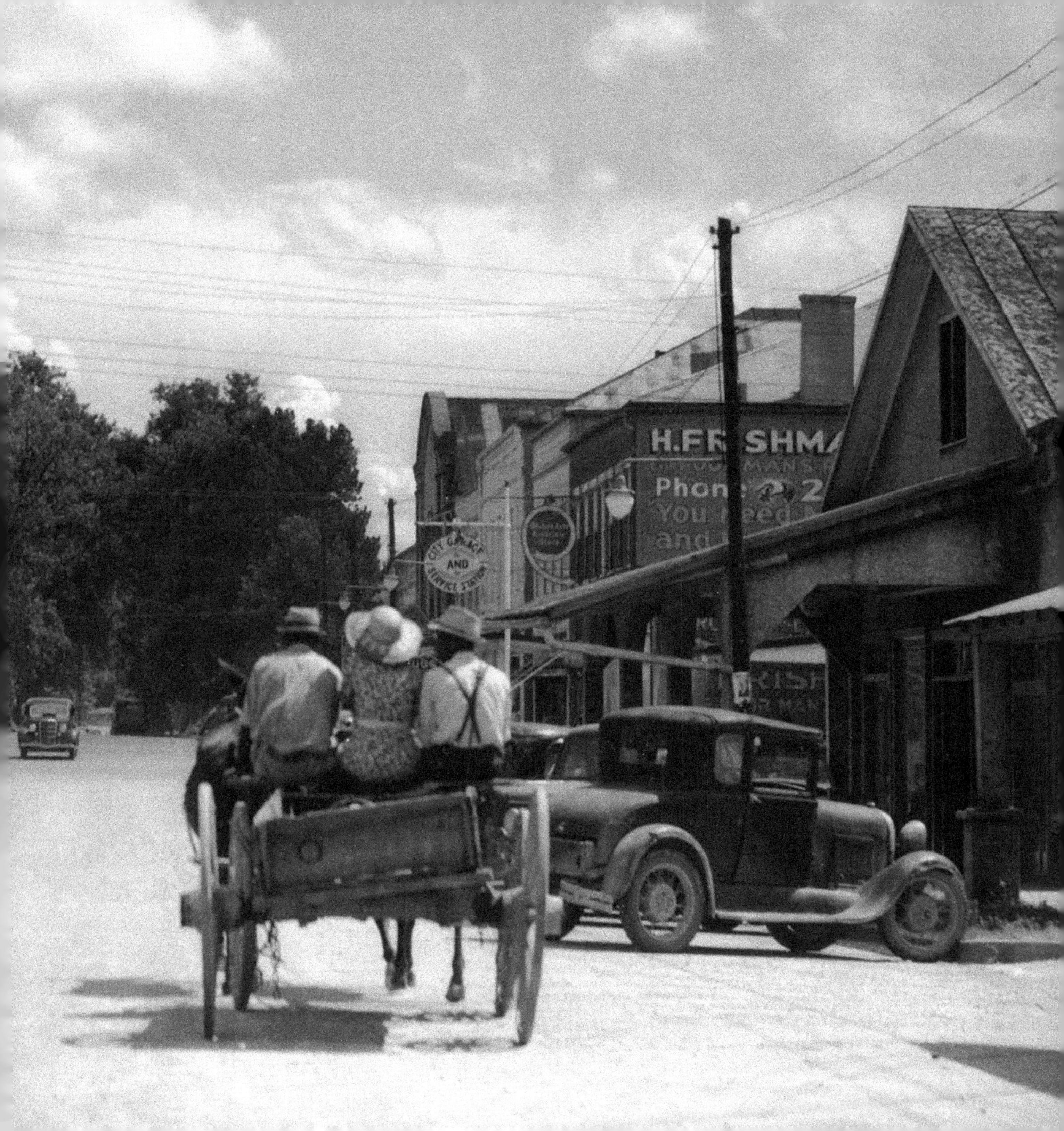
H.FR SHMA
Phon 2
You eed
and
CITY GARAGE
AND
SERVICE STATION

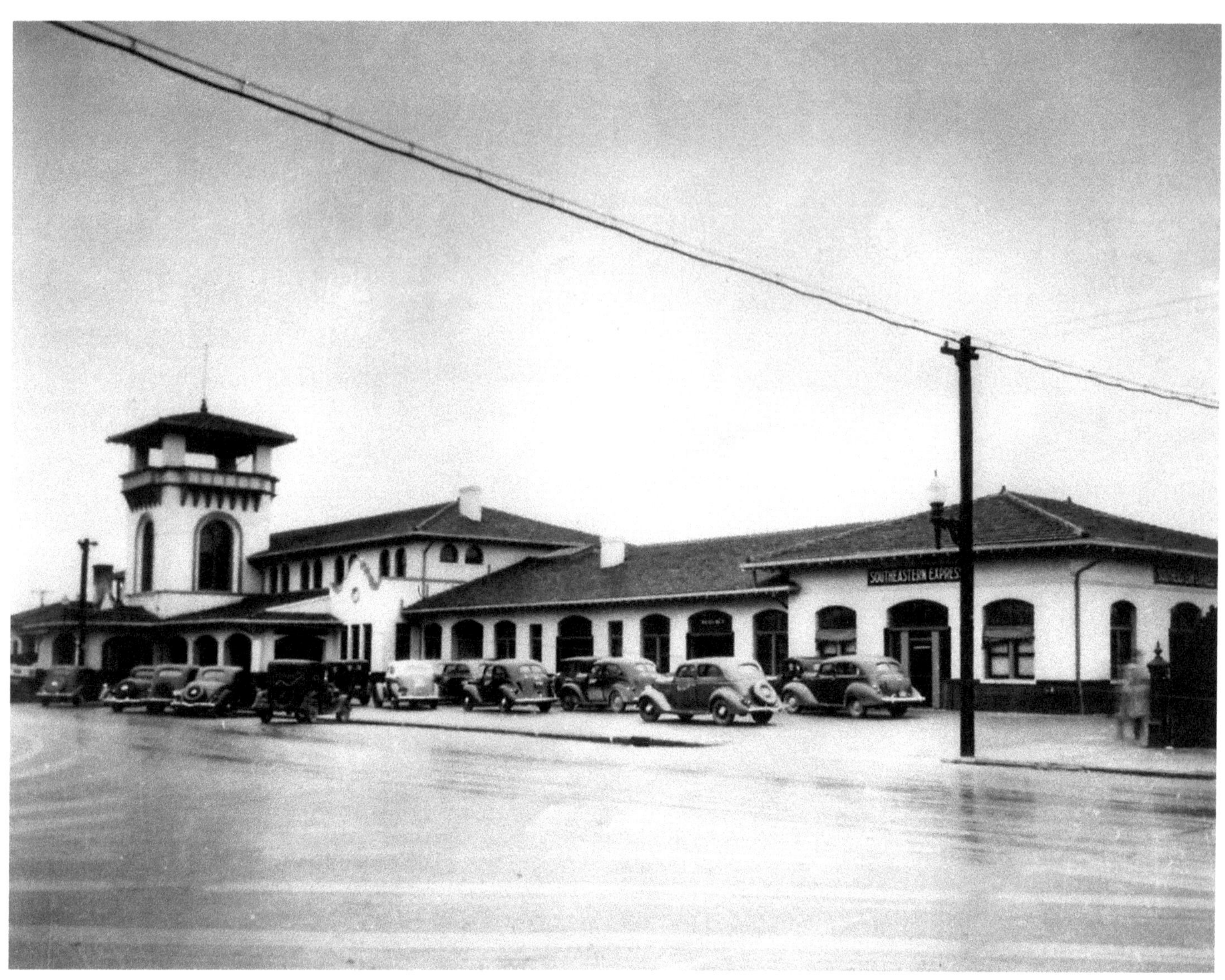

The Union Passenger Station in Meridian, built at a cost of $250,000 in the old Spanish mission architectural style, was fully operational by 1907. The station fronted three city blocks, and three train sheds next to the depot accommodated dozens of passenger trains each day. Railroads were pivotal to the growth and development of east central Mississippi.

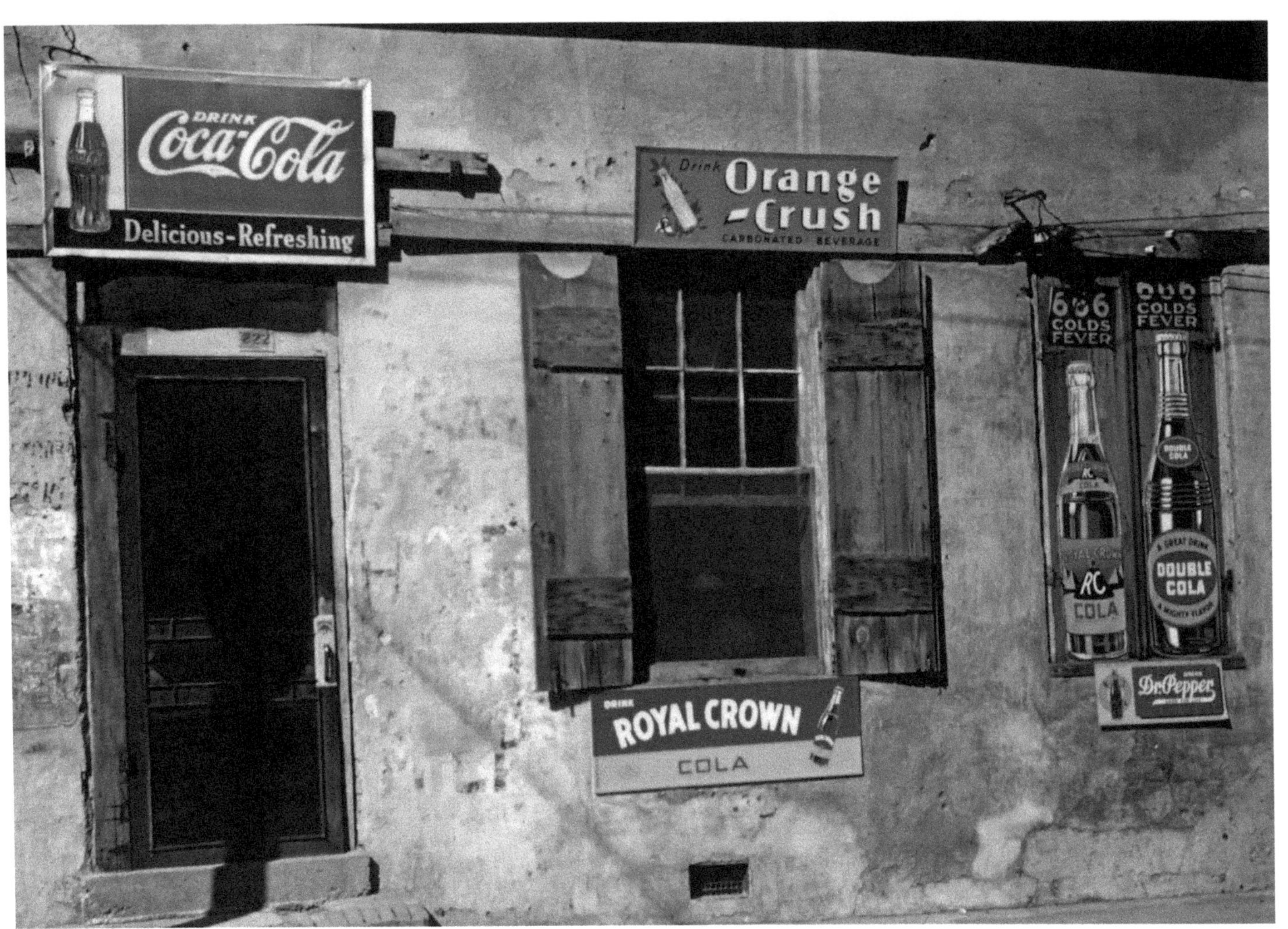

Signs of the times for August 1940 on a storefront in Natchez.

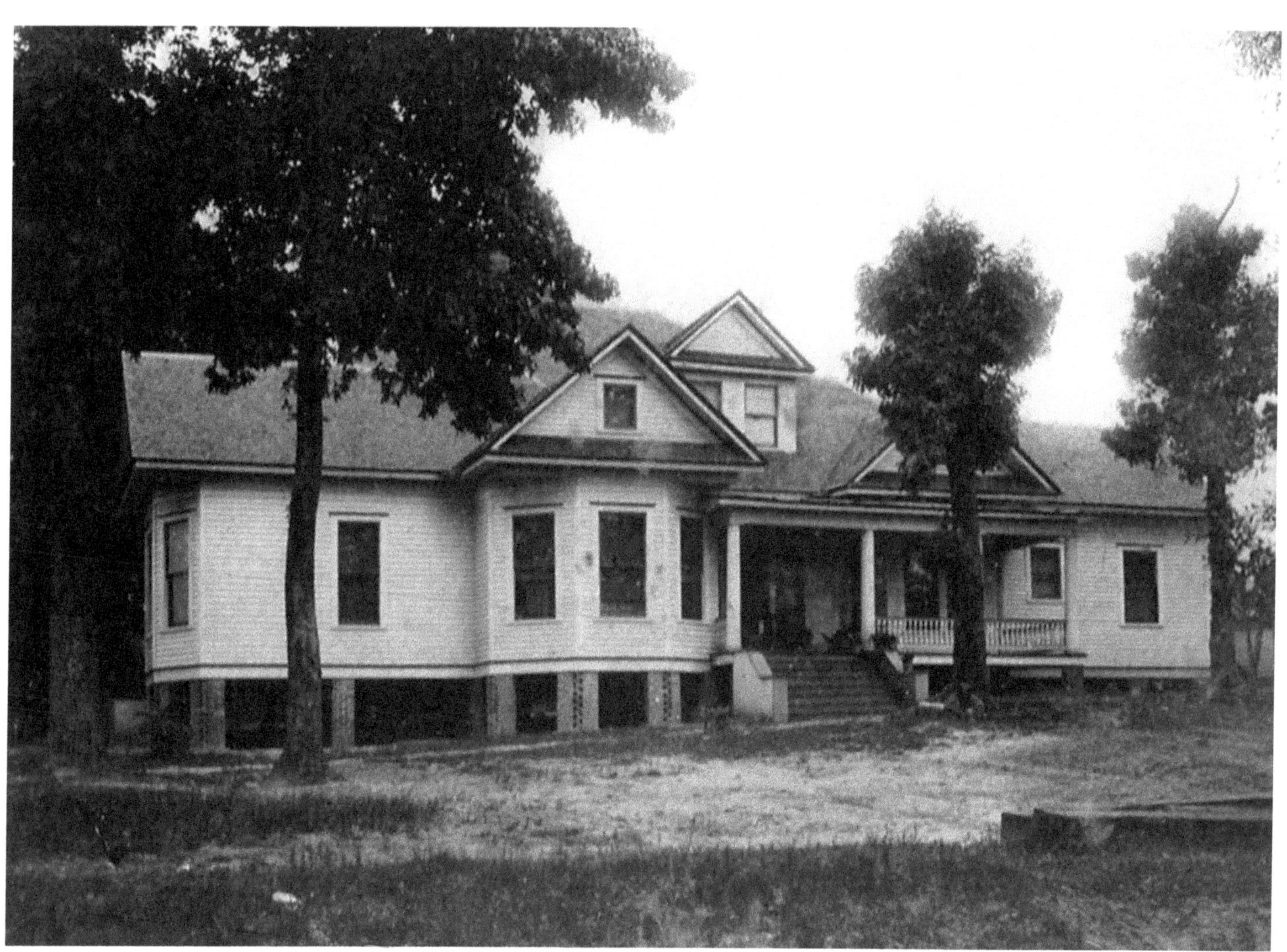

This house at Toomsuba, in Lauderdale County, once provided a lovely home for a large family. Bolstered by the timber business, the hamlet of Toomsuba was a thriving community during the late 1800s and into the 1900s with churches, schools, and a lively atmosphere.

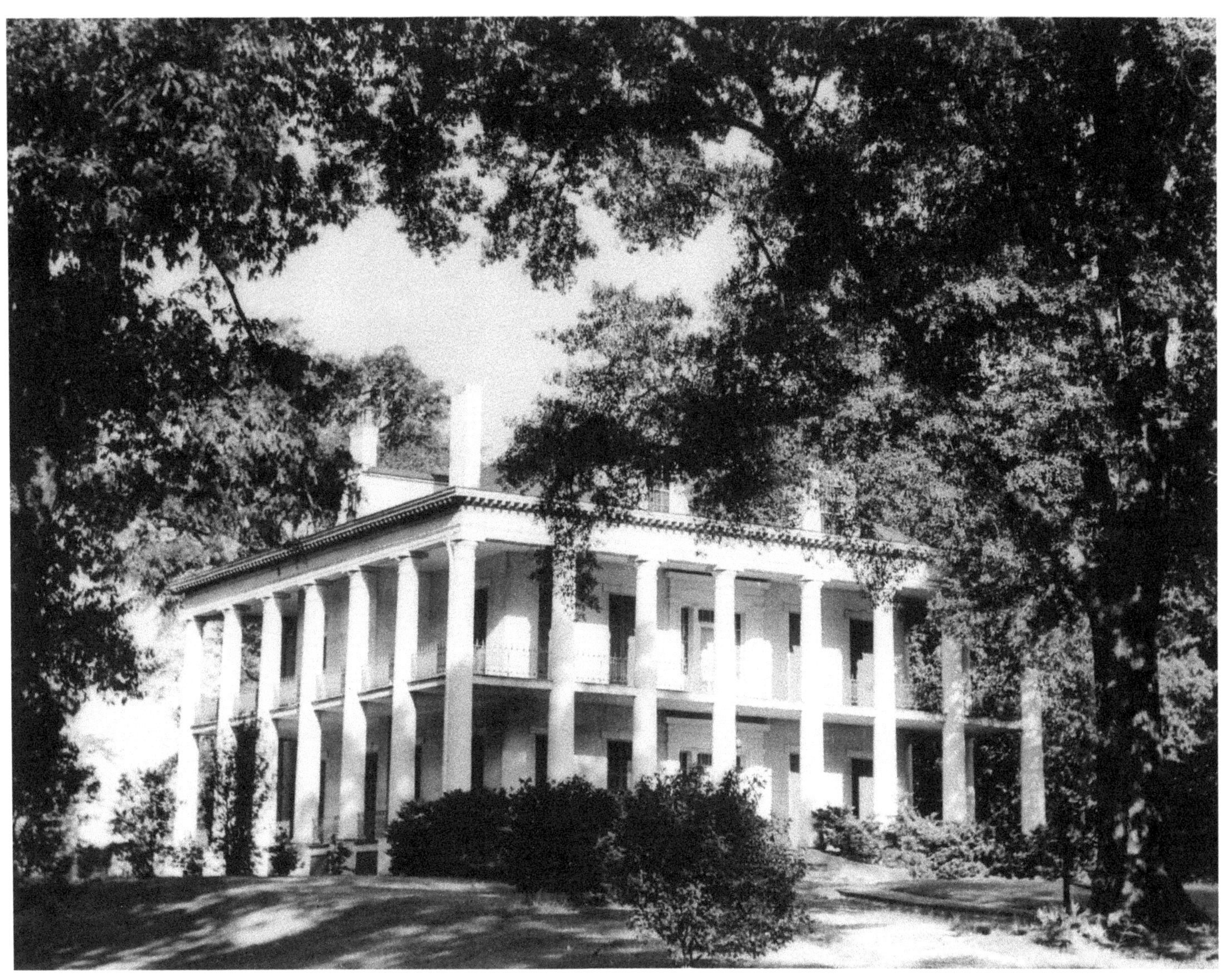

Shown here in 1940, this lovely antebellum Greek revival house is located at Natchez. The stately home was built in 1856 and is the last surviving example of a fully colonnaded house in Mississippi. Alfred Vidal Davis purchased the house for $30,000 in 1859 and gave it the Scottish name Dunleith.

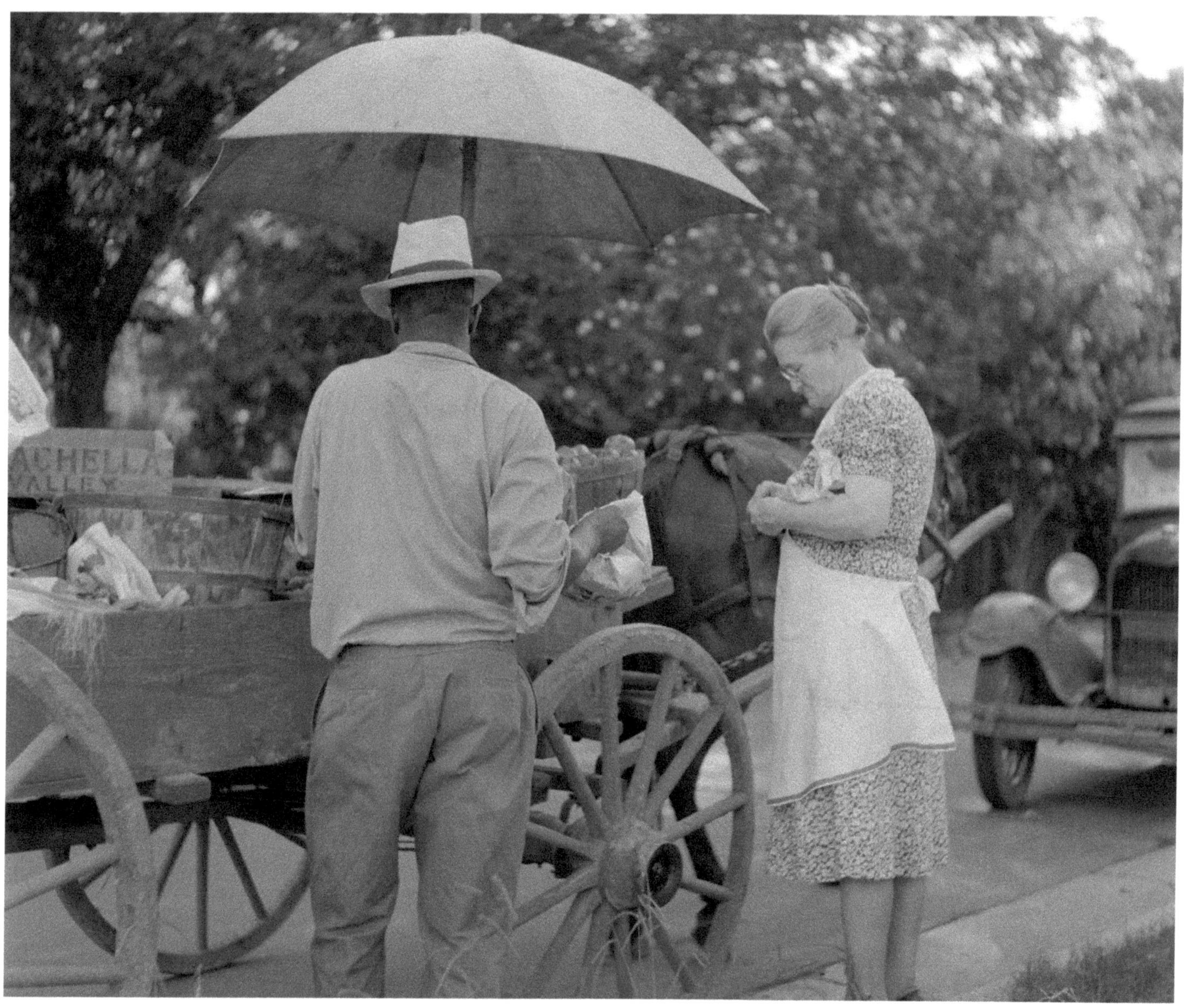

"Peas, beans, 'maters, and corn" calls the vegetable man in this Natchez neighborhood. The grandmotherly customer counts her pennies carefully as she buys fresh vegetables for the family.

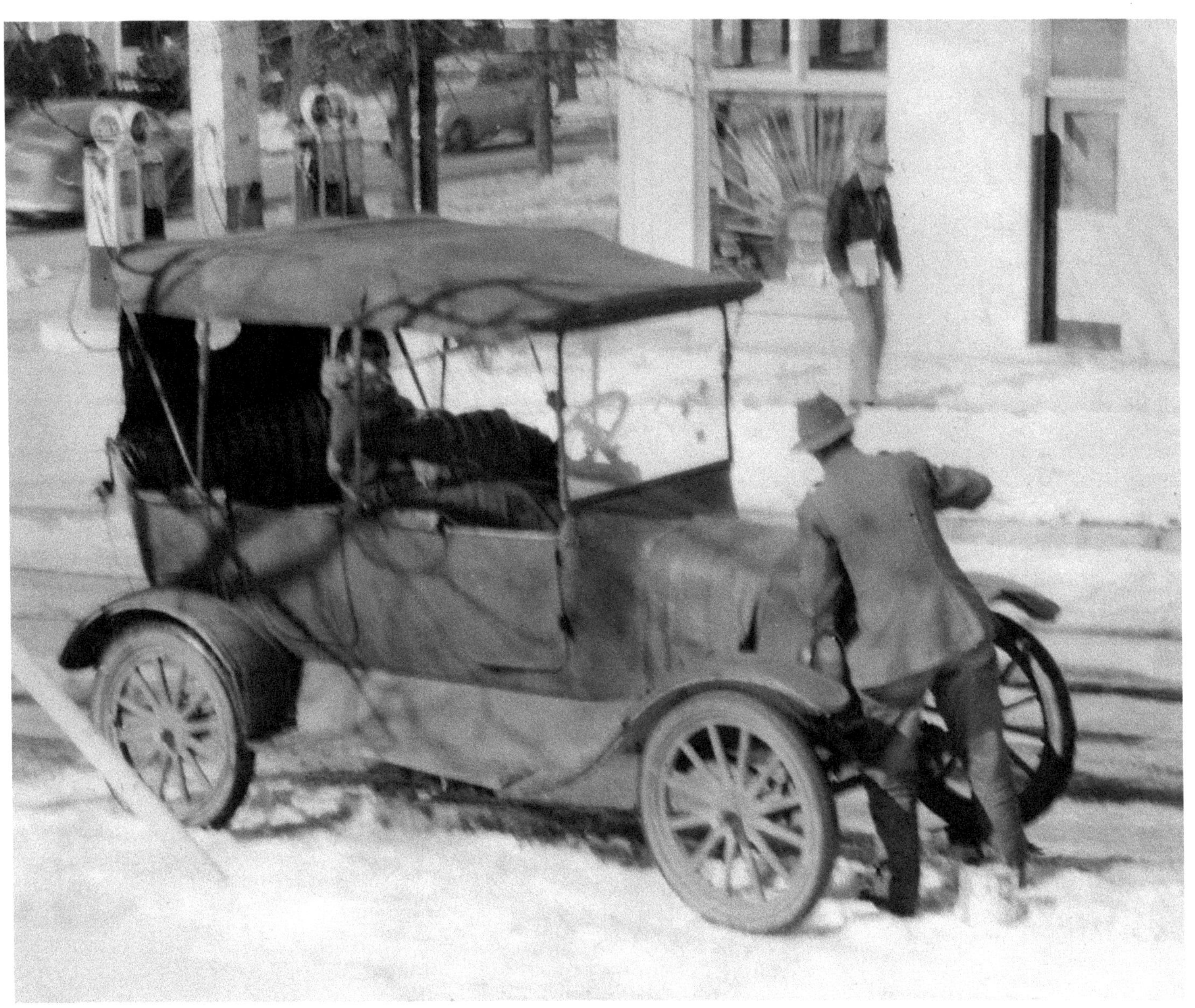

Time for an engine check on this cold day in the 1940s.

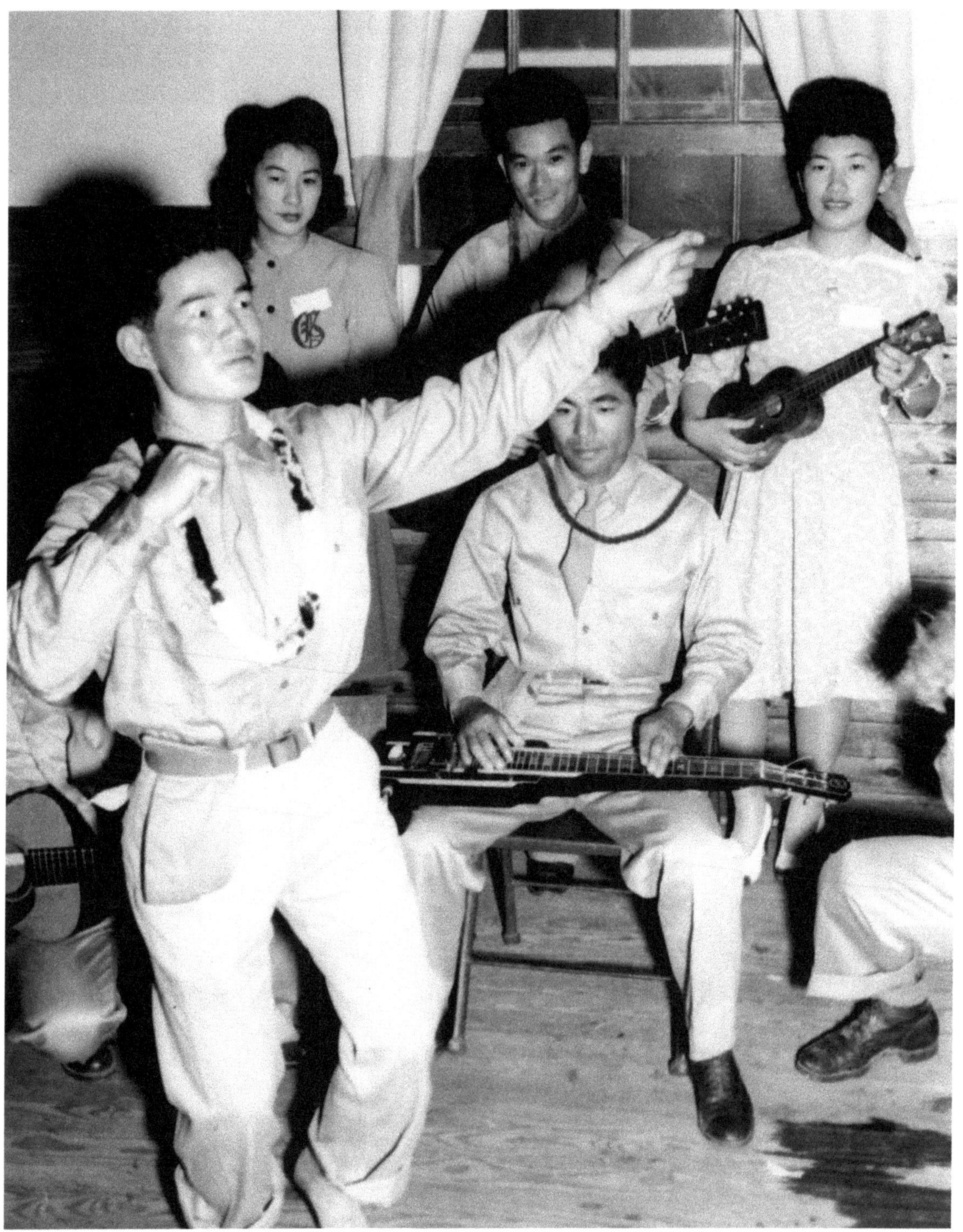

An off-duty scene of fun and frivolity breaks out at Camp Shelby in Hattiesburg in June 1943. The dance was held for service personnel stationed here. As Americans of Japanese descent, the soldiers were members of the 442nd Combat Team, and the girls hailed from the Jerome and Rohwer Relocation Center in Arkansas, an internment camp. At front, Private Harry Hamada tries the hula as the band plucks the lap steel guitar and the ukulele.

Sailors say their goodbyes at the Union Station railroad terminal in Meridian during World War II. Servicemen were leaving loved ones and family to serve their country—some never to return. The two sailors and young woman are all smiles, filled with hope that happier days lay ahead.

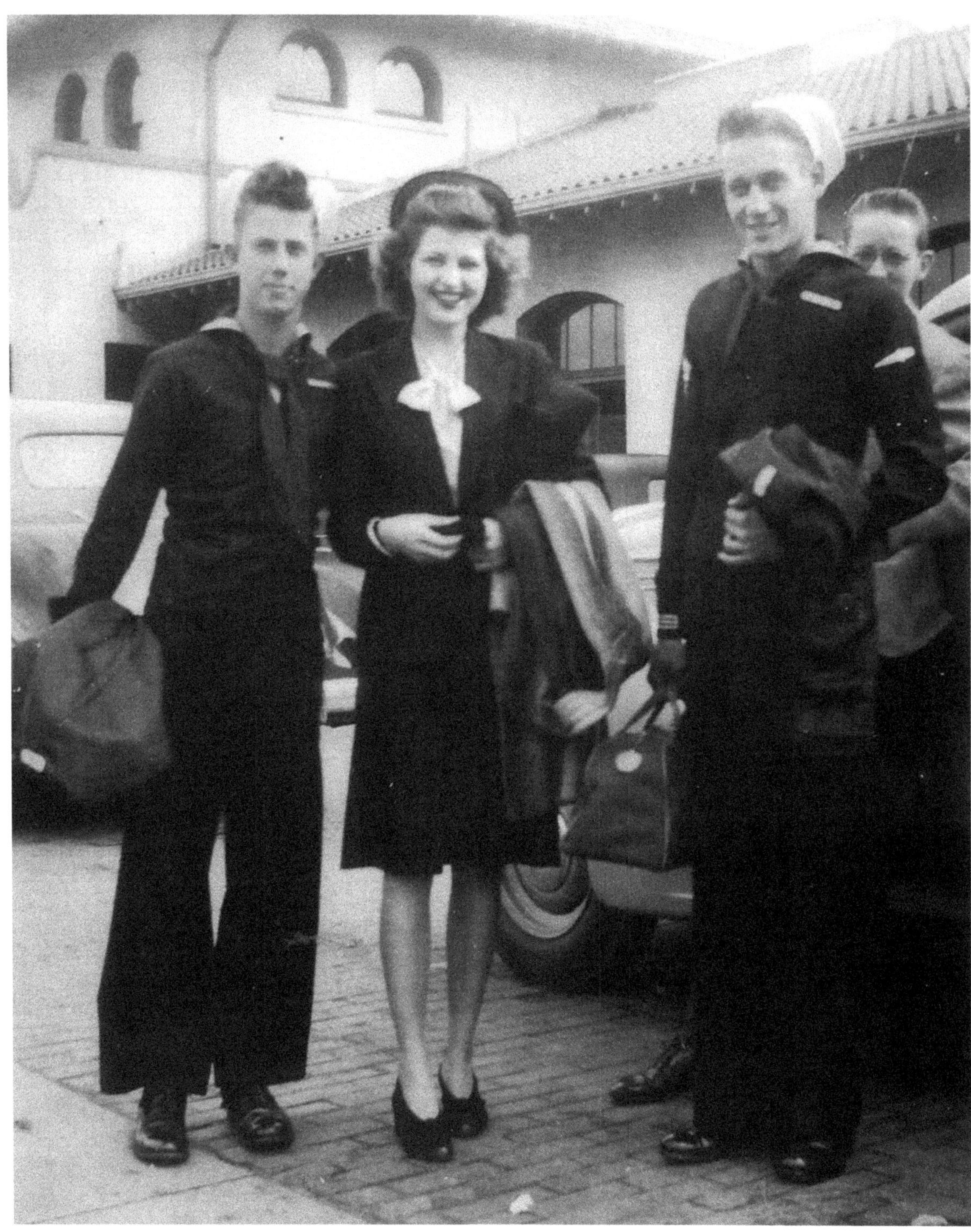

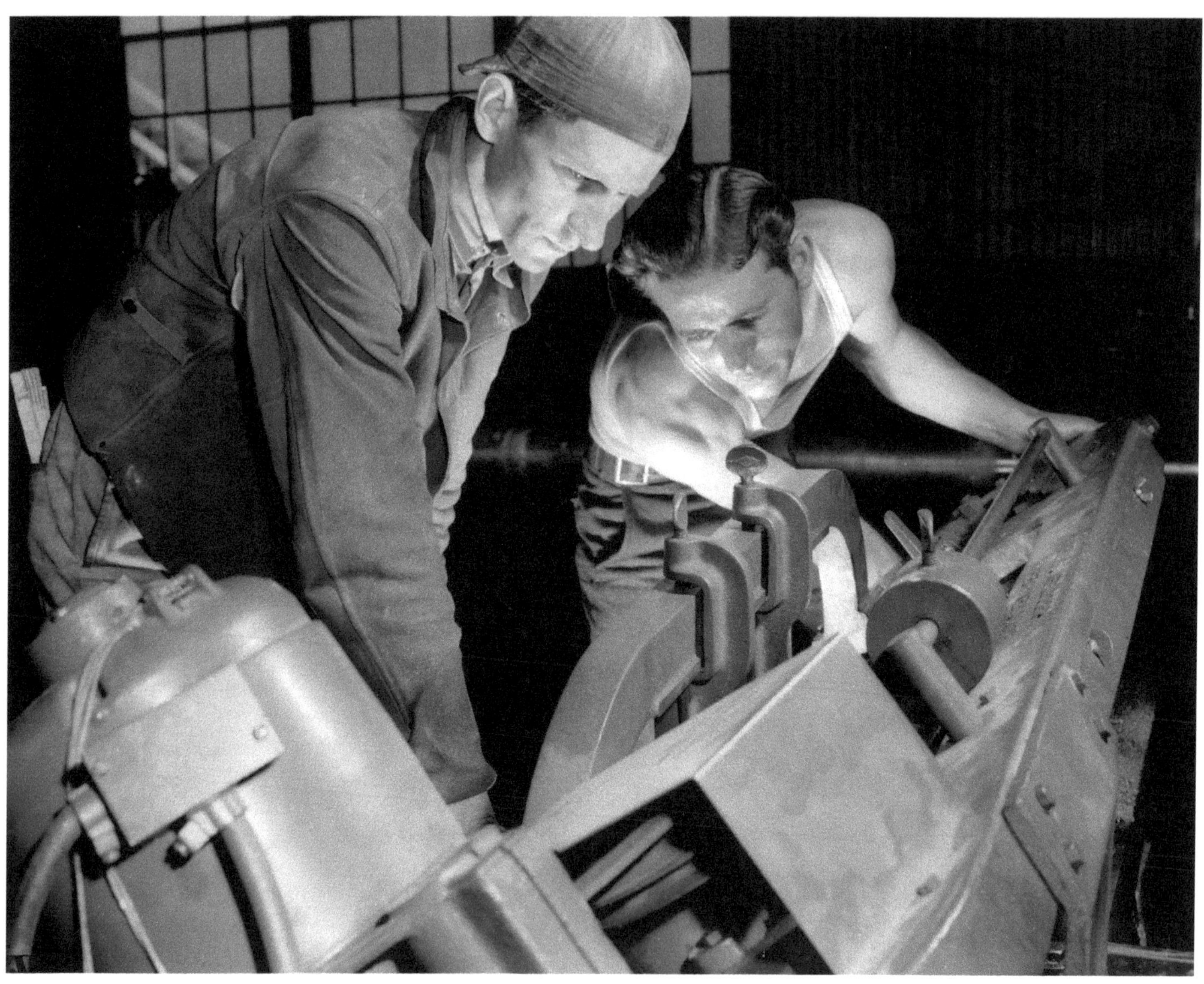

Established at Pascagoula in December 1938, Ingalls Shipbuilding became one of the largest industrial employers in the nation during World War II. Wartime job opportunities brought a basic change in the character of the state's rural population as droves of Mississippians left the farm to train for jobs with employers like Ingalls. These men are working at Ingalls in May 1942, just five months after the attack on Pearl Harbor.

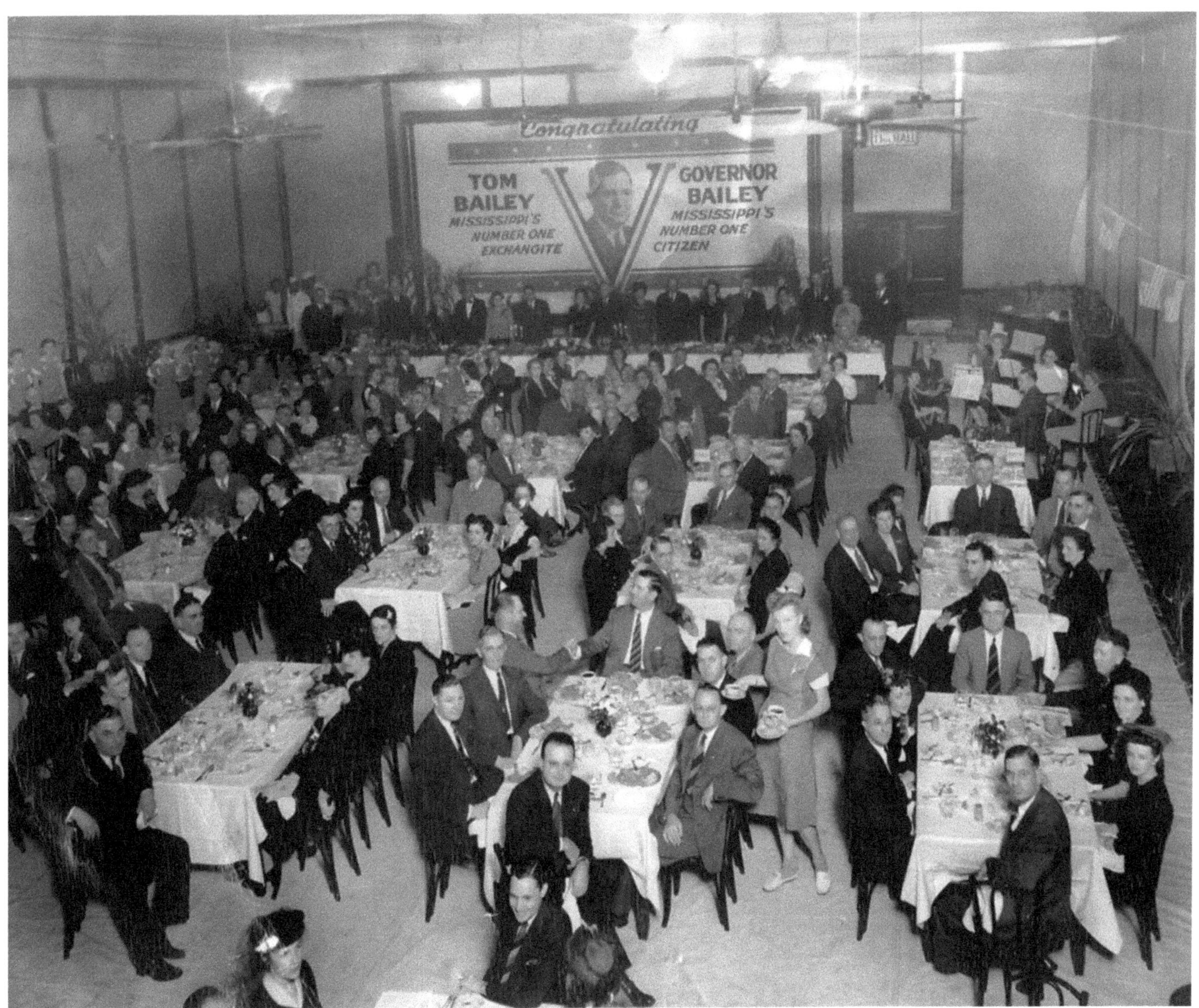

Governor Thomas Lowry Bailey is feted at a Meridian Exchange Club meeting during the 1940s. A resident of east central Mississippi, Bailey was elected to the legislature in 1915 and served there more than 20 years. He was Speaker of the House by 1927 and served as Mississippi governor from 1944 until his death in 1946. Bailey supported a progressive Mississippi with improvements to education, agricultural methods, and medical care.

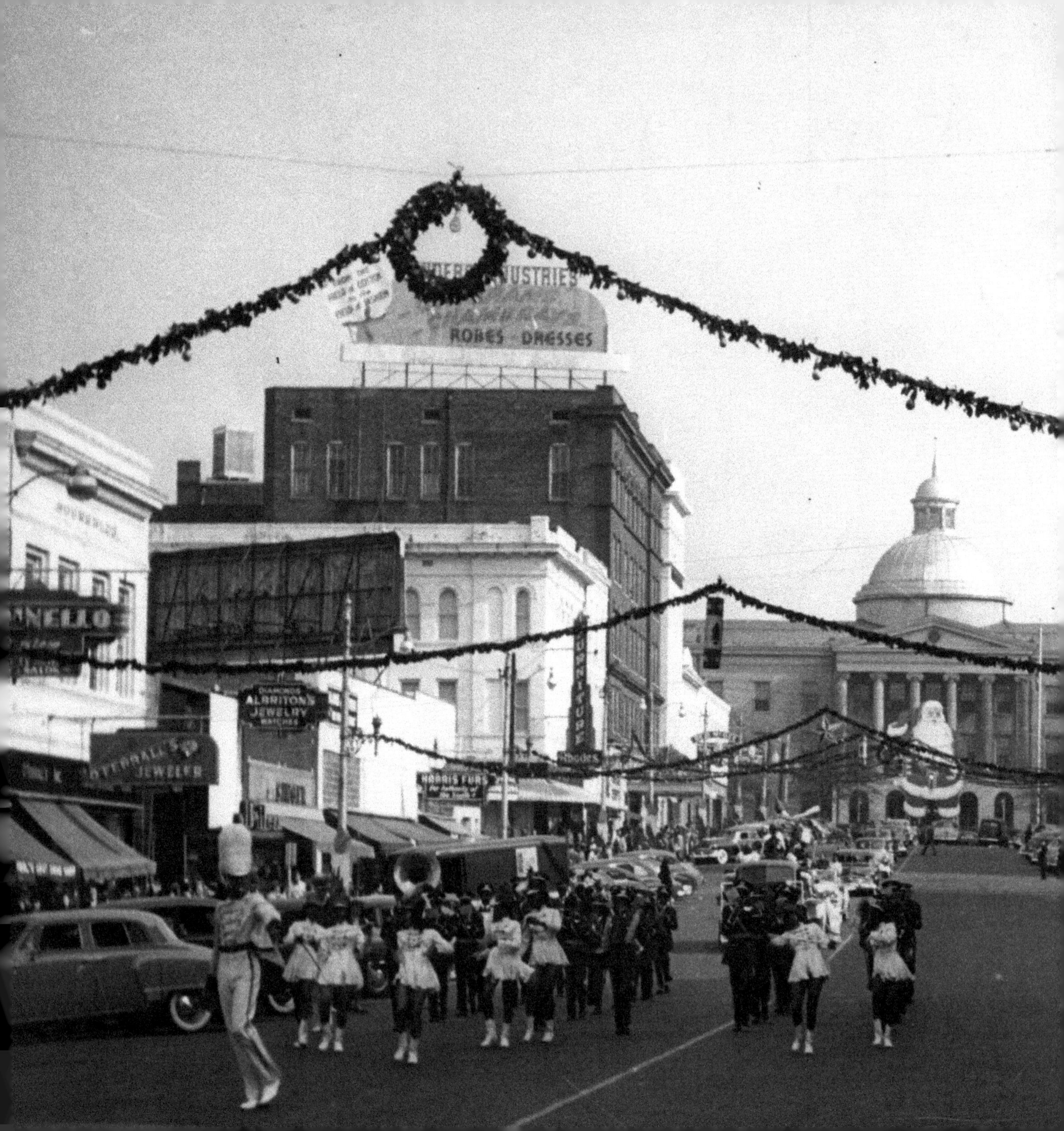

ROBES DRESSES
ALBRITON'S
JEWELRY
JEWELER
HARRIS FURS

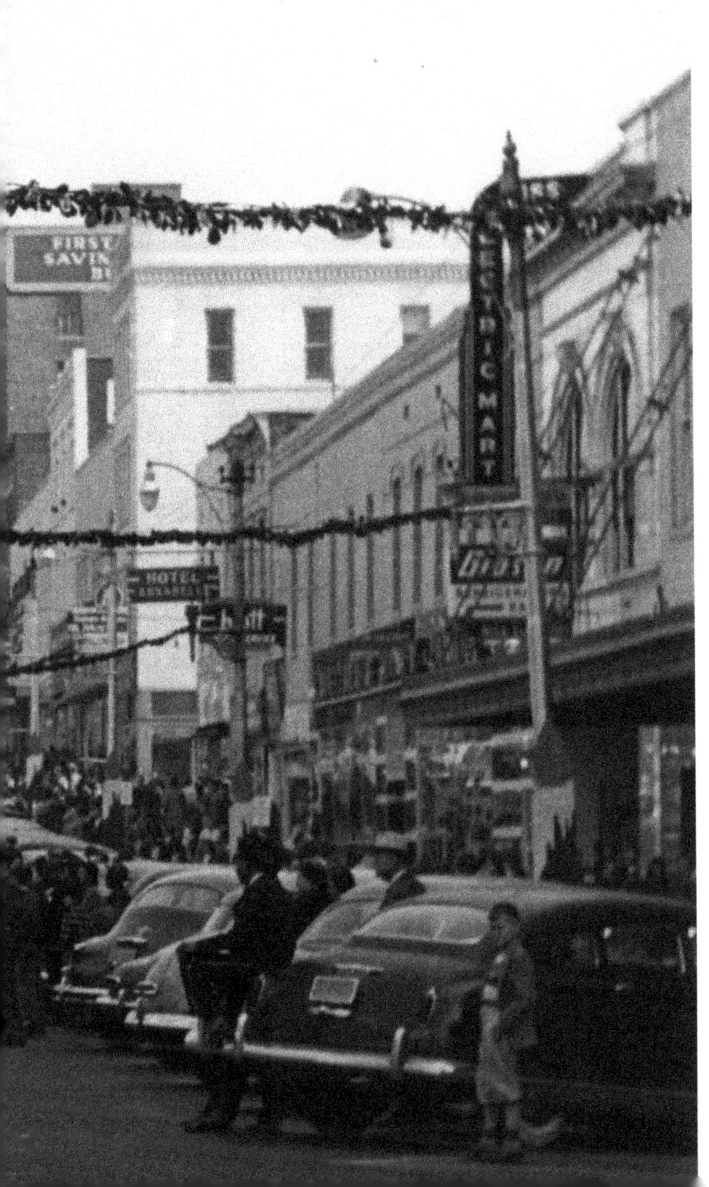

This is football parade day in December 1950 in Jackson. Shown on Capital Street is the marching band of Jackson College (today known as Jackson State University). An enormous image of Santa Claus and other Christmas regalia adorn the area in front of the Old State Capitol at rear.

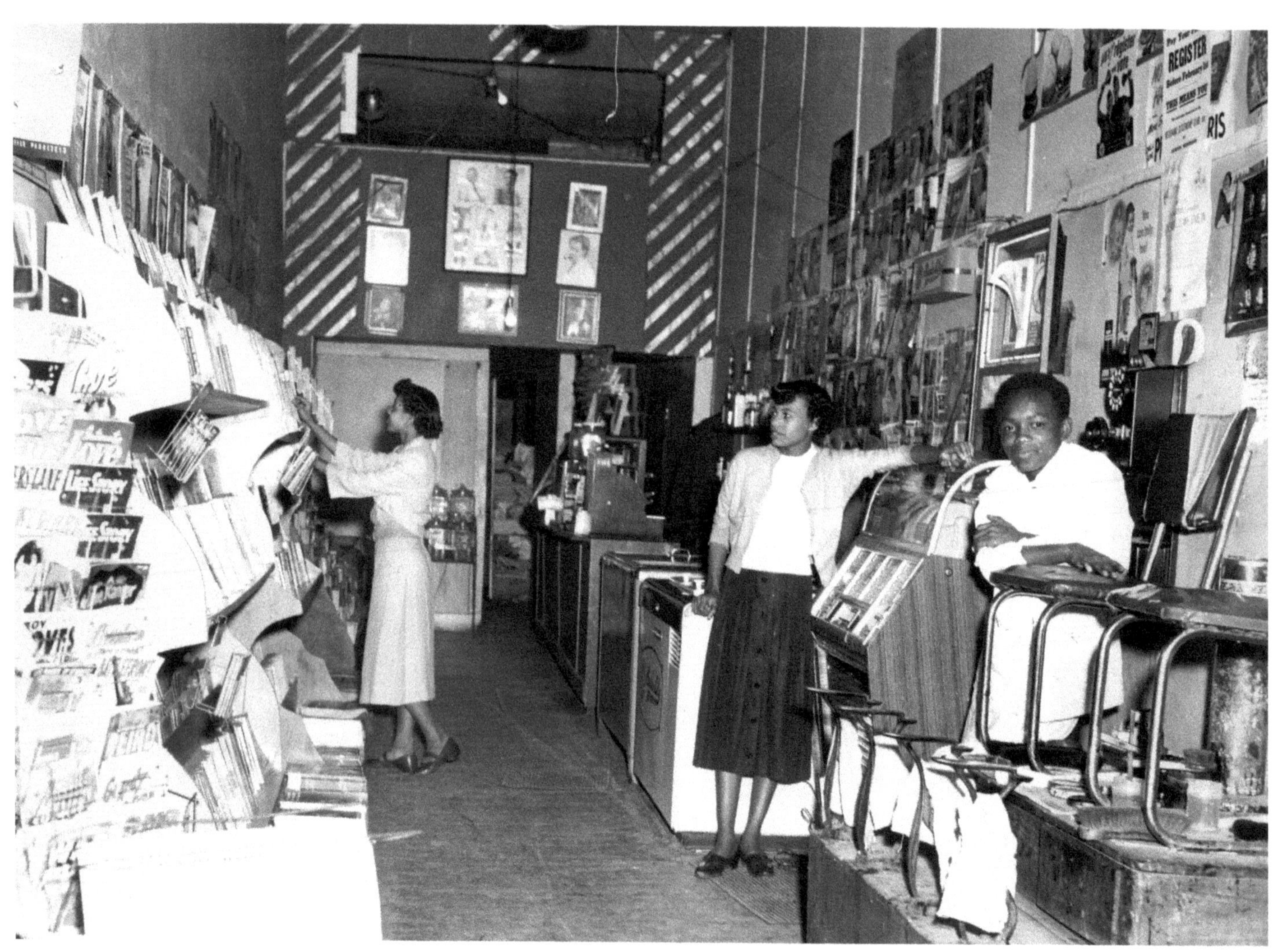

A busy day is in progress in the 1950s at the Farish Street Newsstand and Studio in Jackson. Shown are two clerks waiting to greet customers and one woman selecting a magazine.

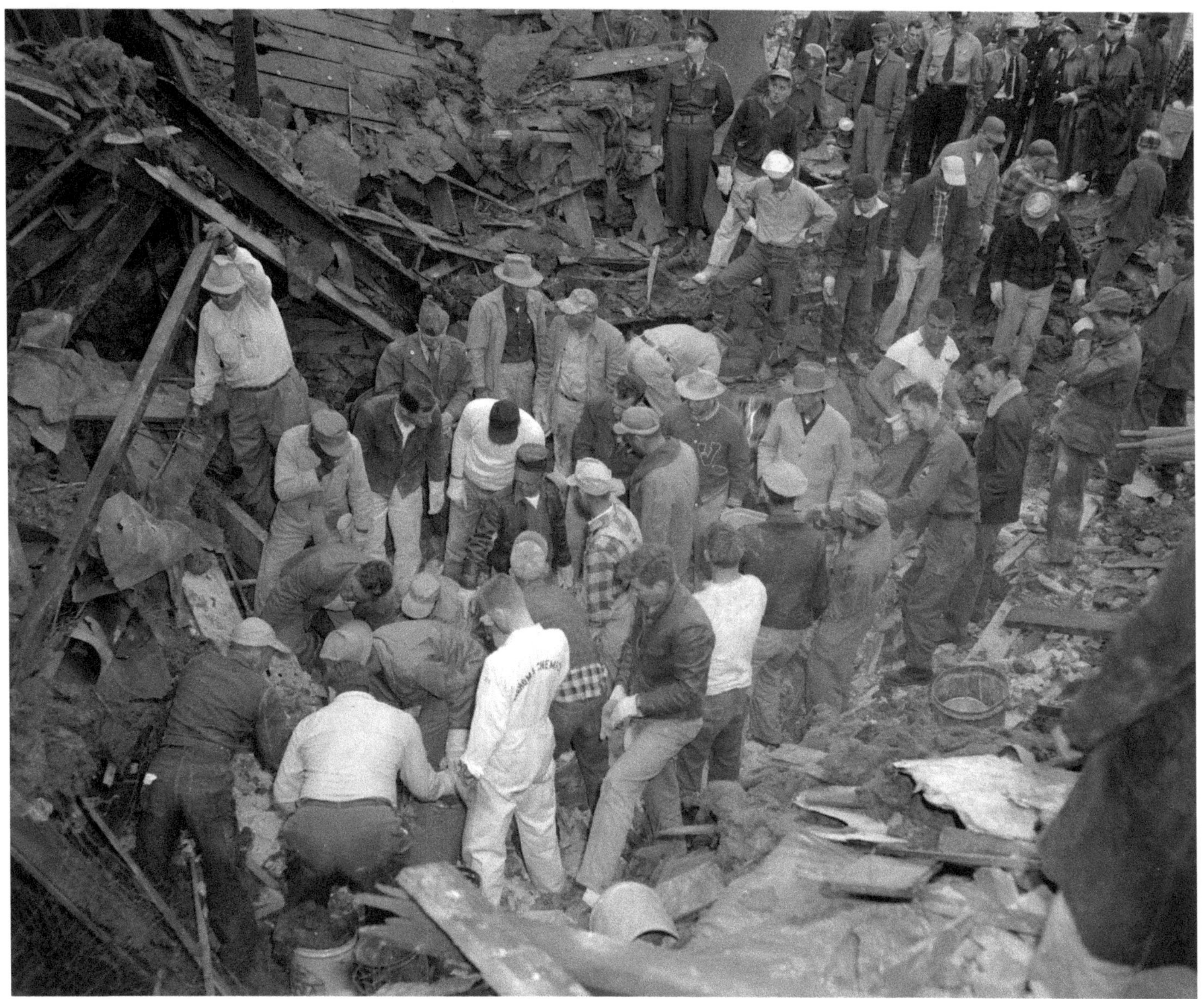

Rescue efforts are ramping up following the December 5, 1953, F5 tornado that killed 38 people and destroyed many structures in Vicksburg. Mississippi ranks second among the states for tornado fatalities and third for injuries. In 1953, 22 tornadoes whirled through the state, causing 39 deaths, 310 injuries, and damages of $66,466,880.

Following Spread: At least four tornadoes hit Vicksburg on December 5, 1953. Twelve blocks of the city's business district suffered extensive damage, the city's gas line was broken, and fires broke out throughout the area.

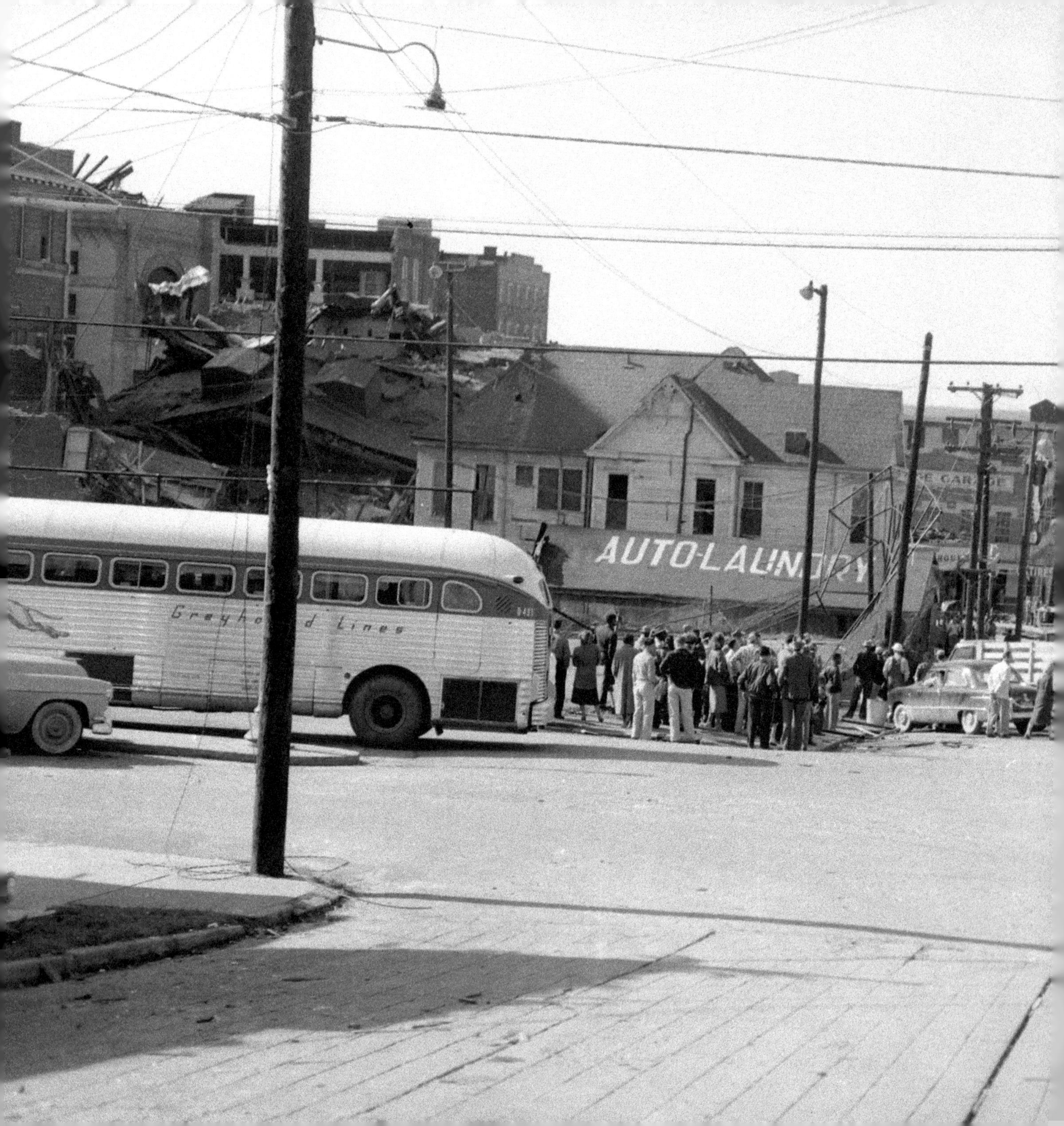
AUTO-LAUNDRY

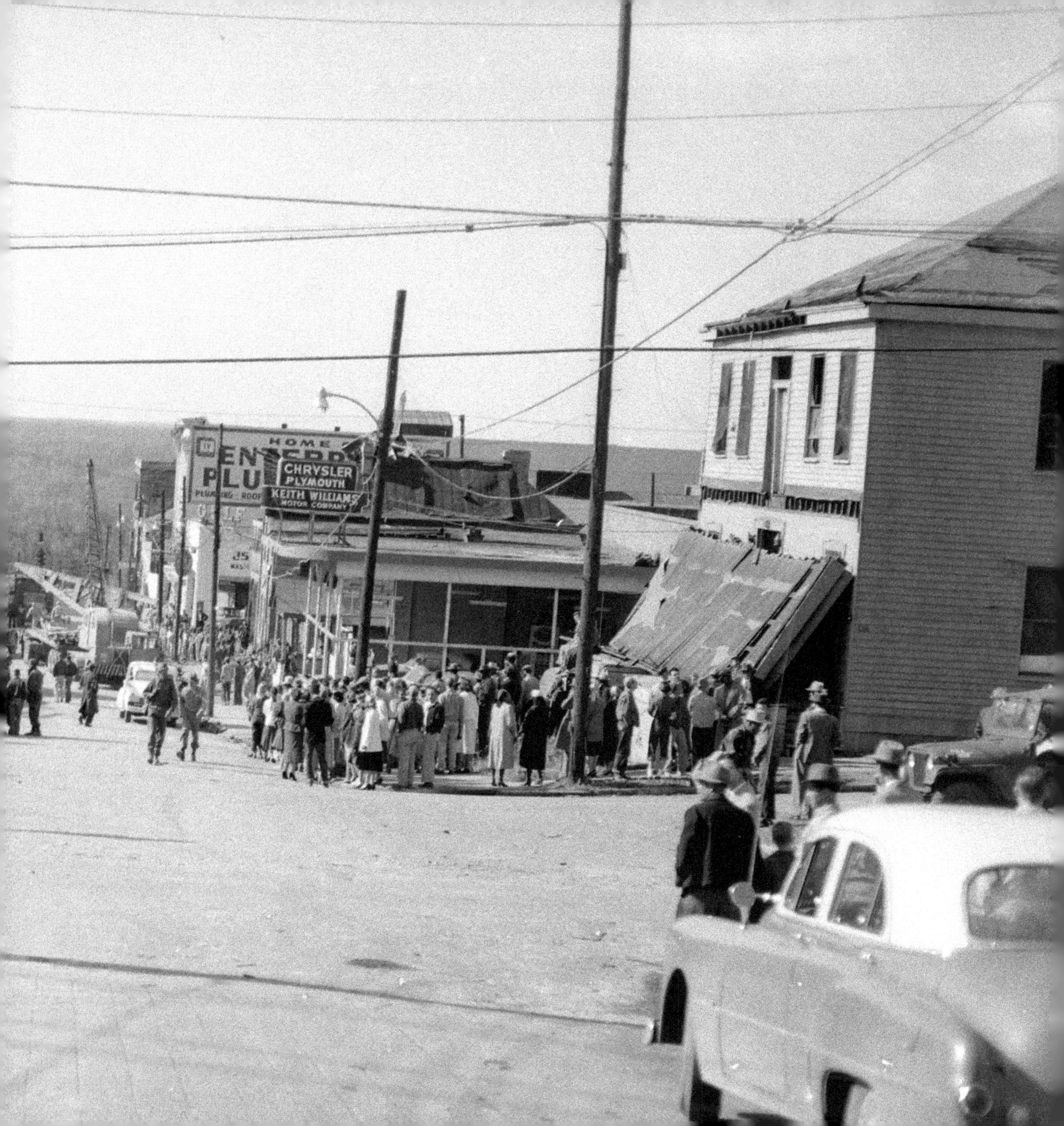
CHRYSLER
PLYMOUTH
KEITH WILLIAMS
MOTOR COMPANY

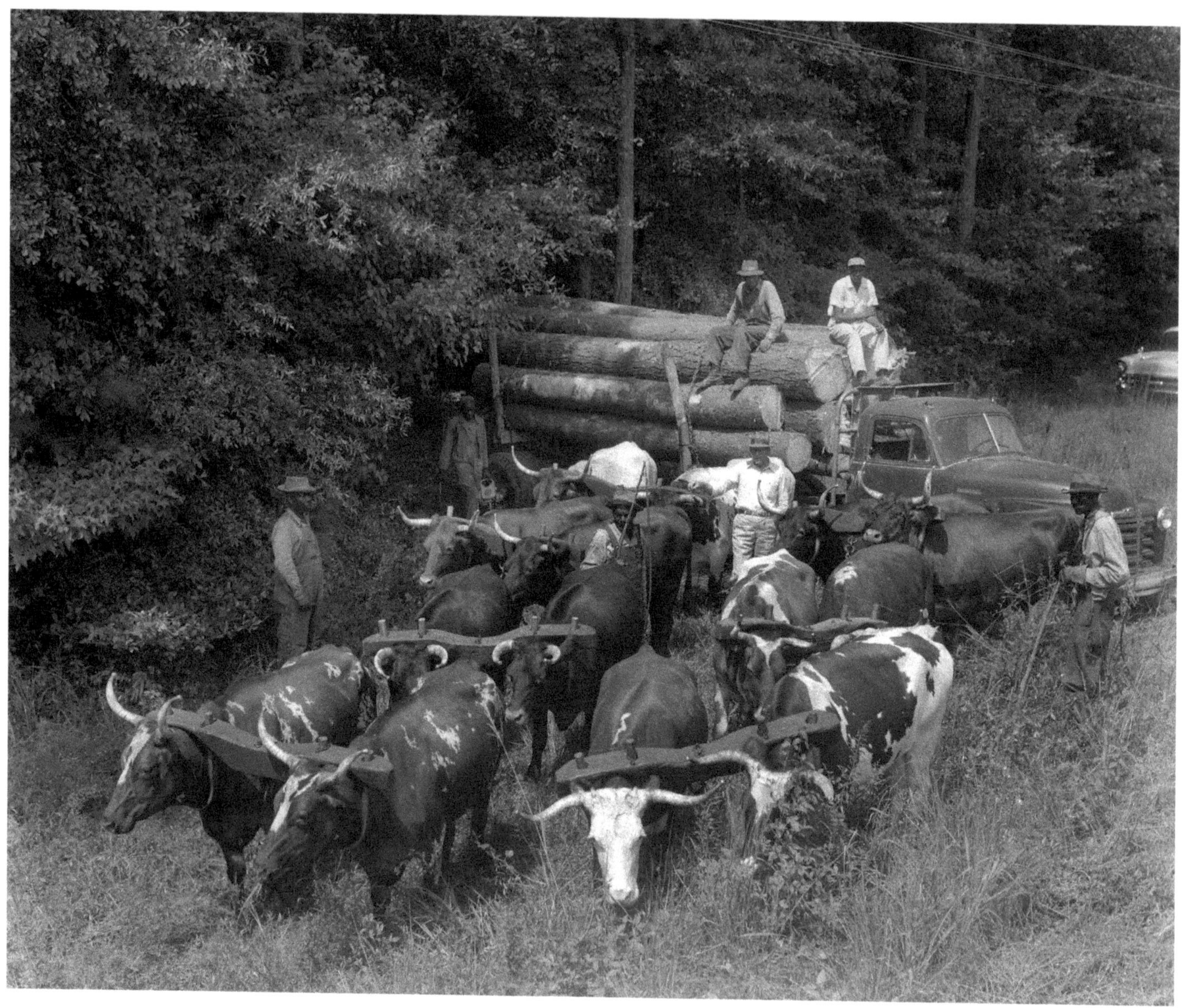

Deep in the Piney Woods region of southeast Mississippi, loggers lead seven teams of yoked longhorns to a truck in 1958. Logging was the original impetus for the establishment of many communities in Mississippi and continues as a leading industry in the state. Many of the original logging roads became major highways with the passage of time. The Piney Woods area gets its name from the longleaf pine tree that grows there.

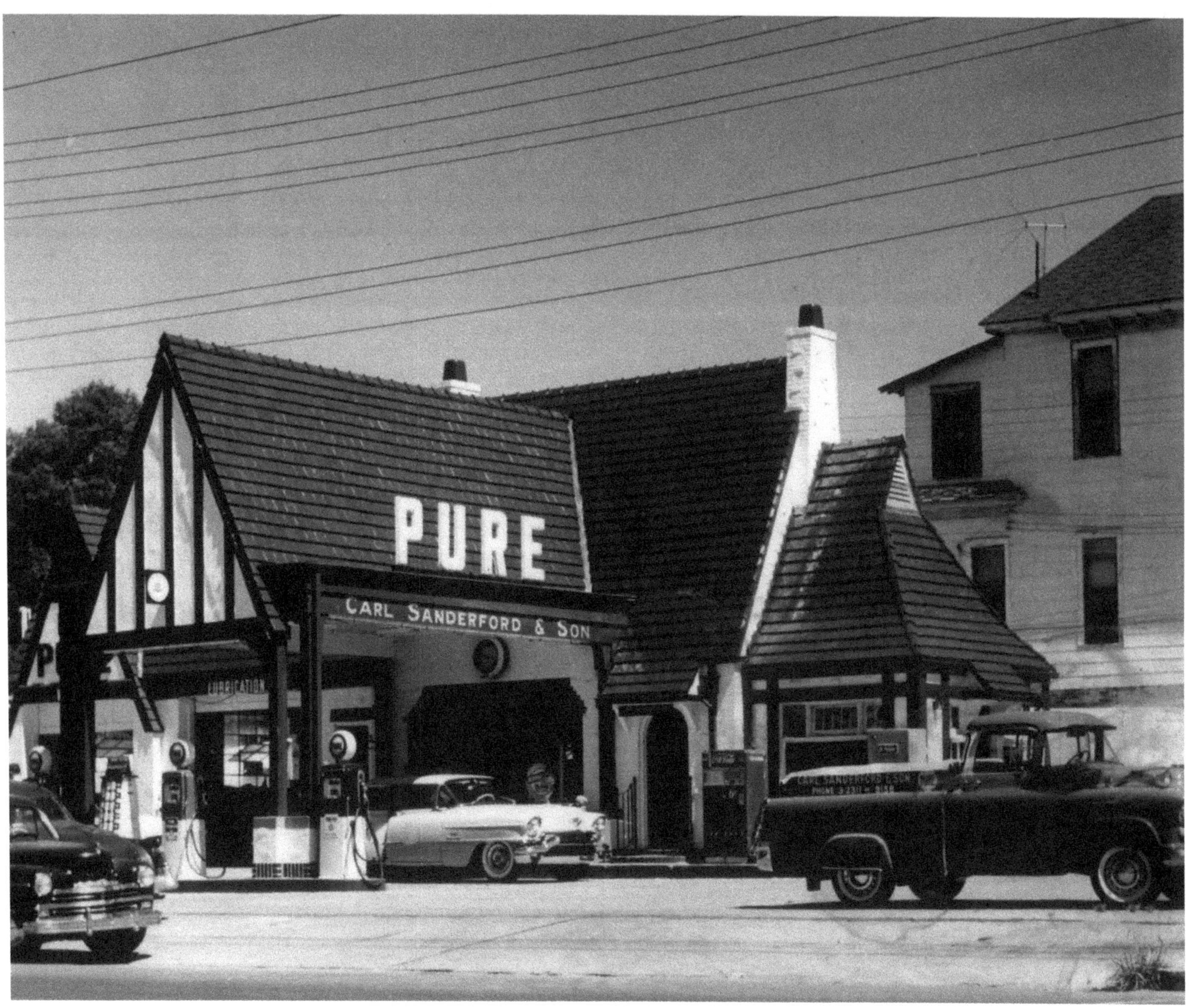

Carl Sanderford and son are "hitting on all eight" as proprietors of this booming full-service filling station in the 1950s. Once upon a time, American automobiles were often manufactured with eight-cylinder engines as a standard feature.

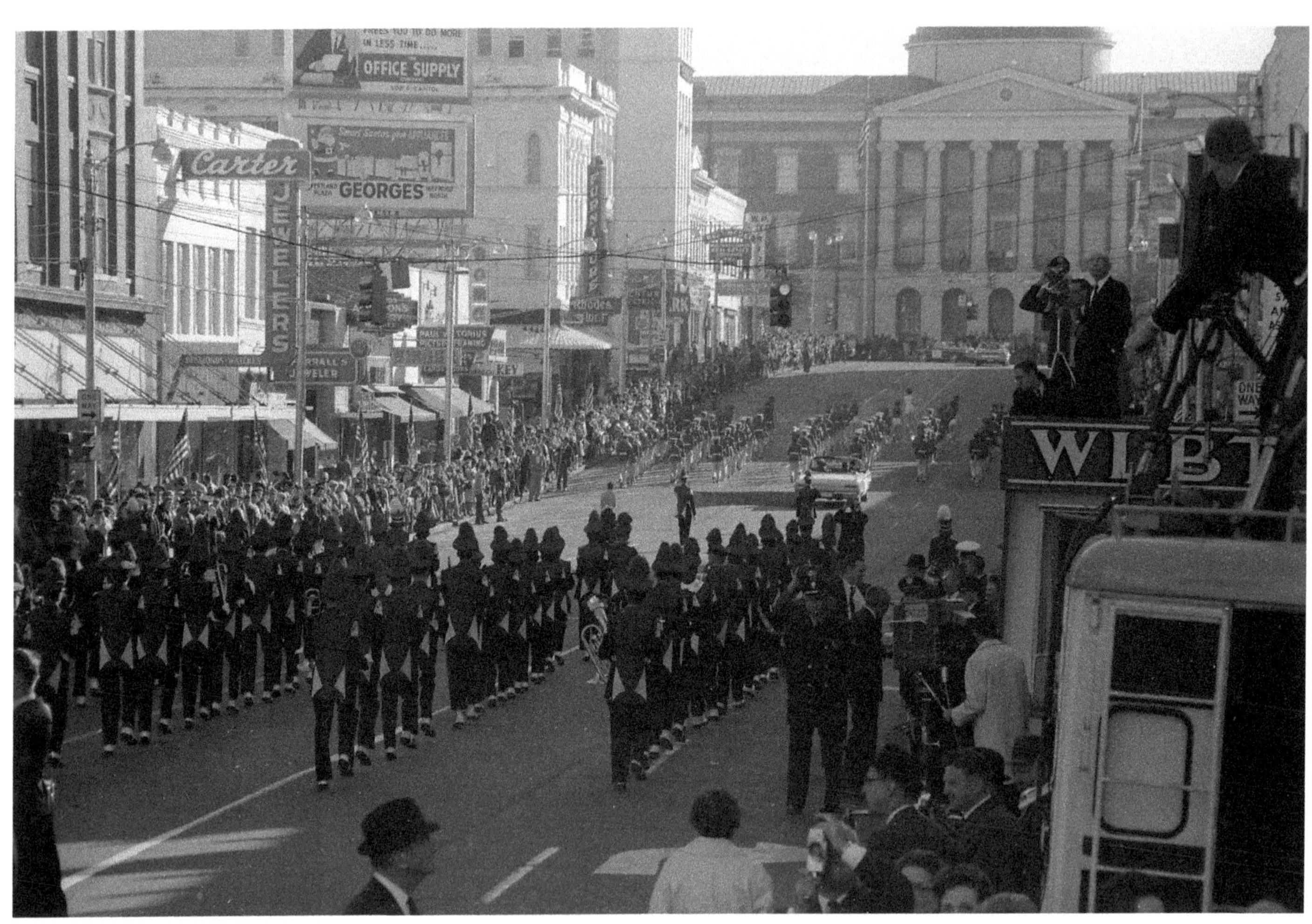

Inaugural parade of Governor Paul B. Johnson, Jr., January 21, 1964, in downtown Jackson. The Old Capitol is visible in the background.

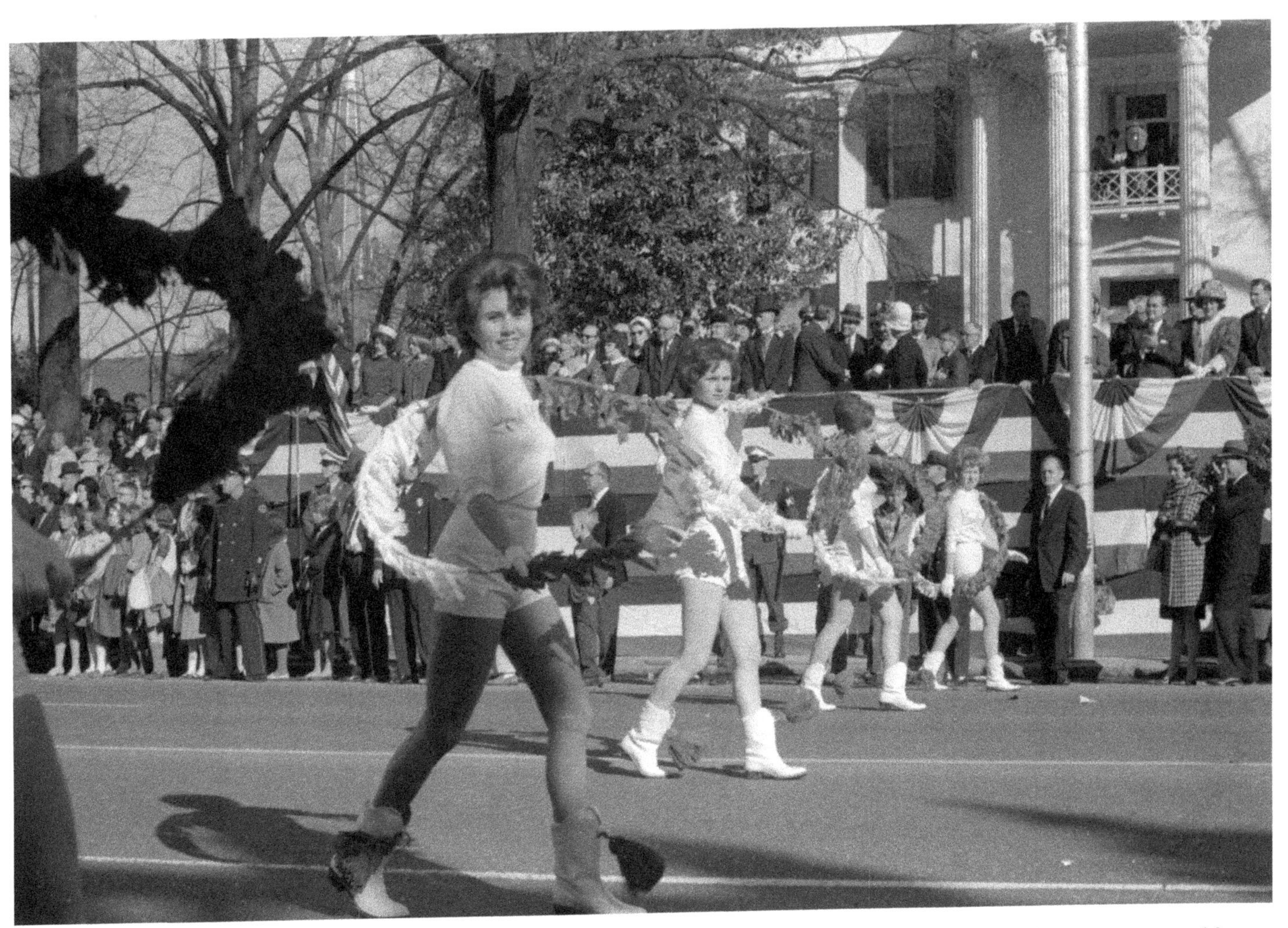

Governor Johnson's inaugural parade was replete with marching bands and pretty majorettes. Johnson was a son of former Mississippi governor Paul B. Johnson, Sr., and had served in the South Pacific with the U.S. Marine Corps during World War II. "Stand Tall with Paul" was his campaign slogan, and "Pursuit of Excellence" was his term's theme.

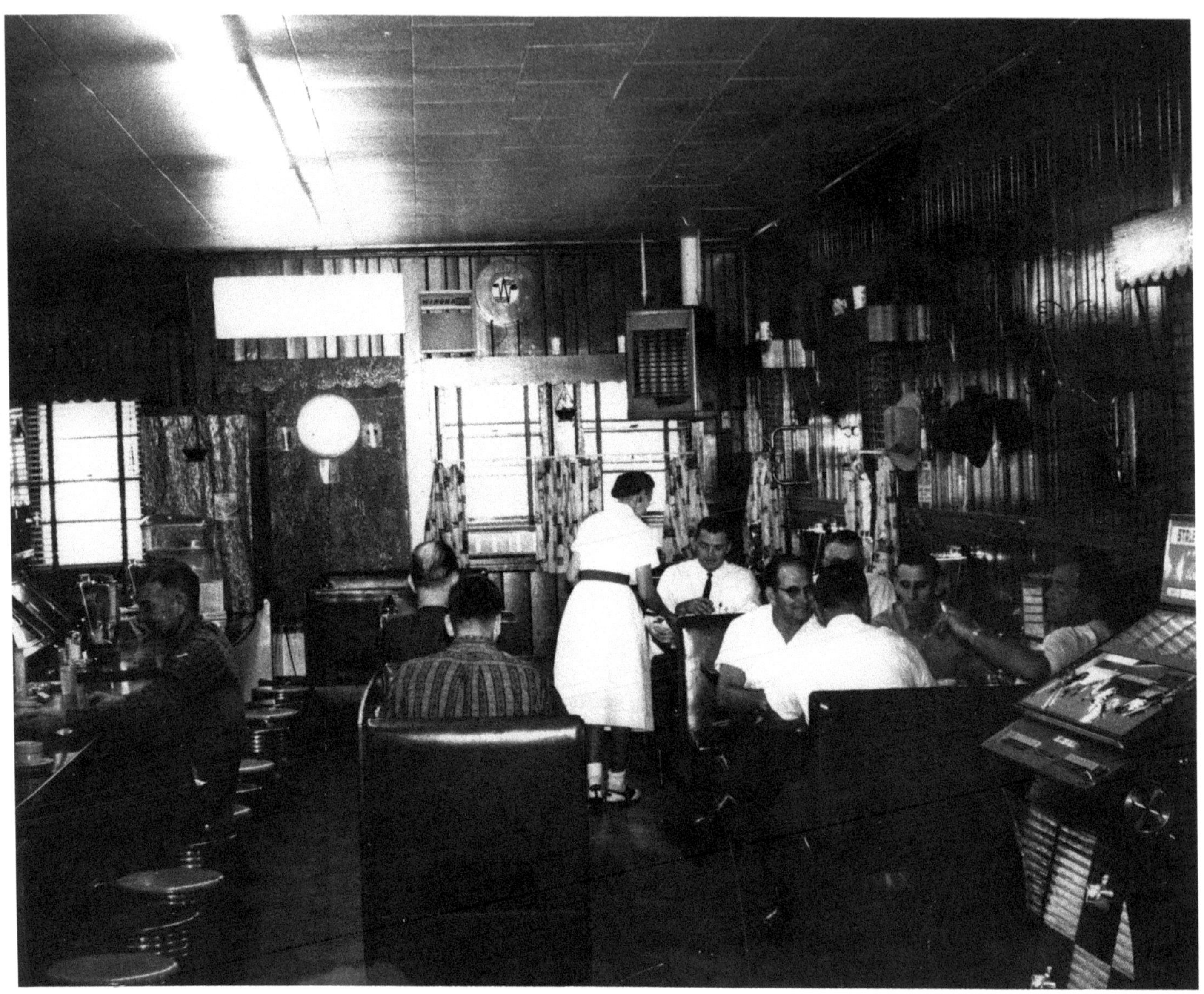

This is the Continental Trailways Bus Station and Staley's Cafe at Winona, in Montgomery County, in 1961. The red-topped, stainless-steel stools running neatly along the counter were typical of cafe appointments across the nation during the 1950s and 1960s. A jukebox is visible at right.

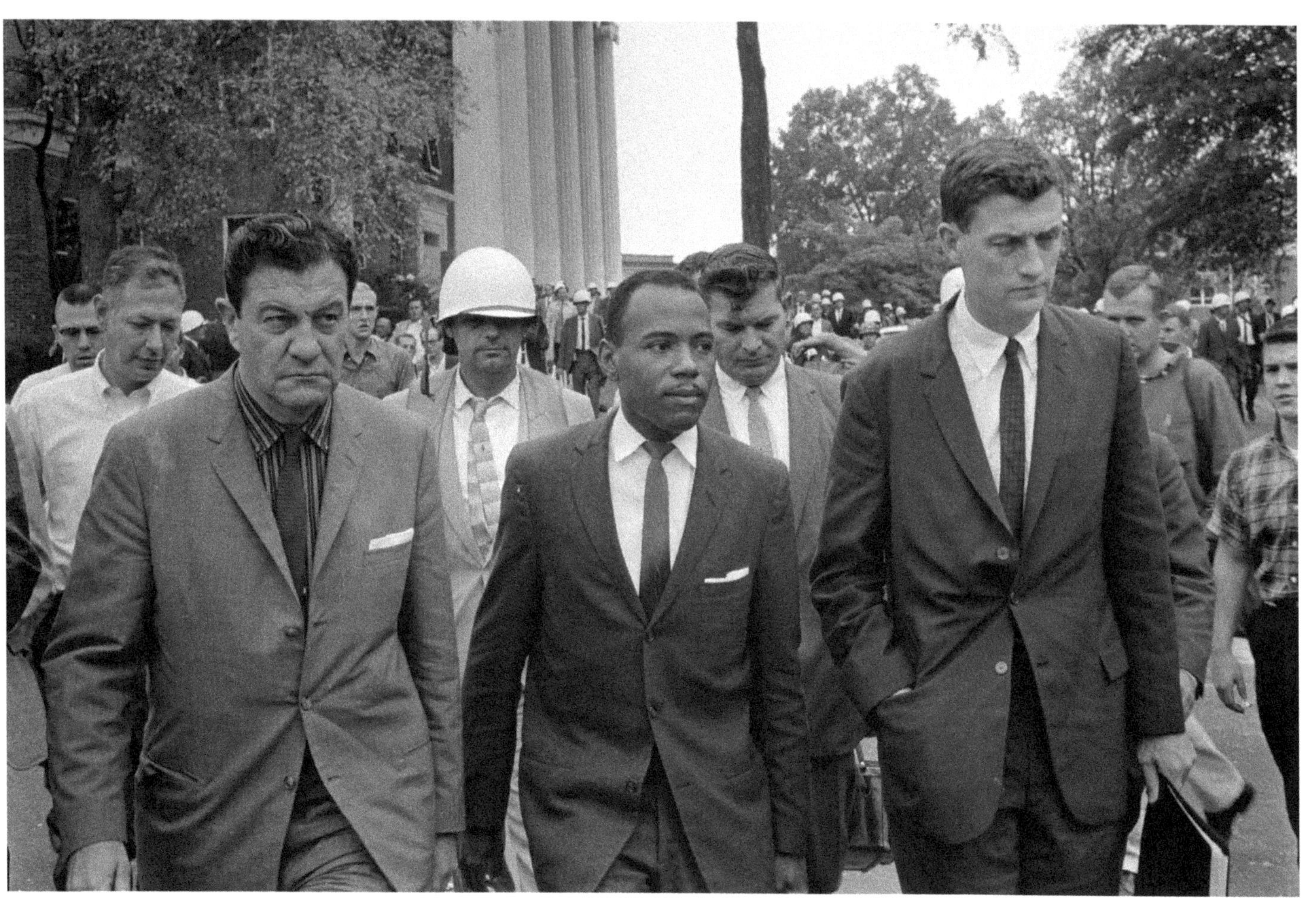

James Meredith walks to class at the University of Mississippi at Oxford, escorted by two U.S. marshals. An Air Force veteran, he applied to Ole Miss 24 hours after the inauguration of John Kennedy, eventually gaining admission in October 1962.

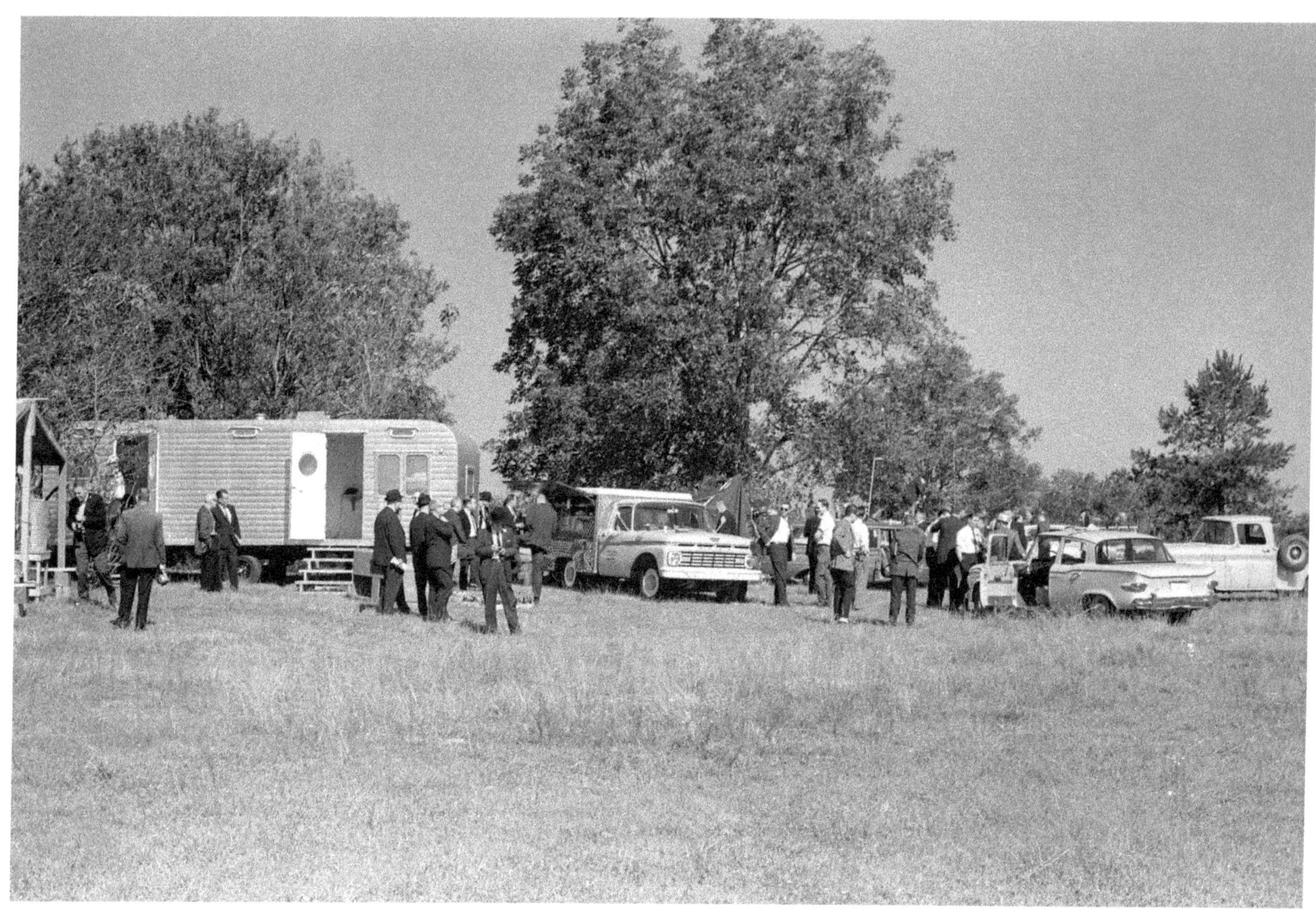

The Tatum Salt Dome, in Lamar County, became the site of a nuclear test on October 22, 1964. At 10:00 A.M., the federal government detonated an underground nuclear device. Residents felt three separate shocks, and observers watched as the surface of the earth undulated like ocean waves. This detonation, and the one that followed two years later at the same site, were the only nuclear tests conducted on U.S. soil east of the Rocky Mountain states.

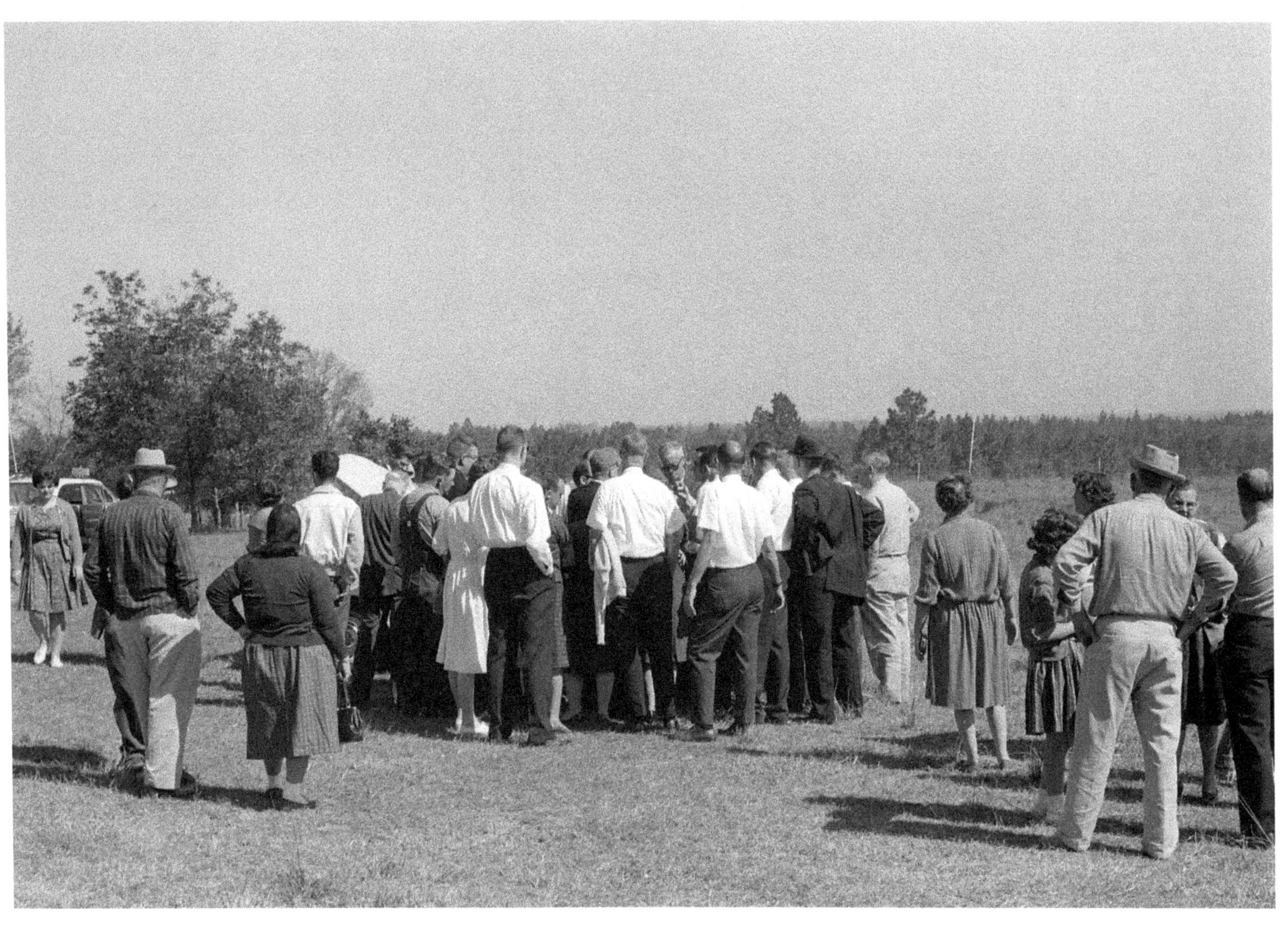

Atomic bombs were in the news in October 1964. Only one week before the Mississippi test, newspapers had reported that Communist China had detonated its first atomic bomb. For residents in Lamar County, however, no news story was watched more closely than the plans for nuclear testing in Mississippi.

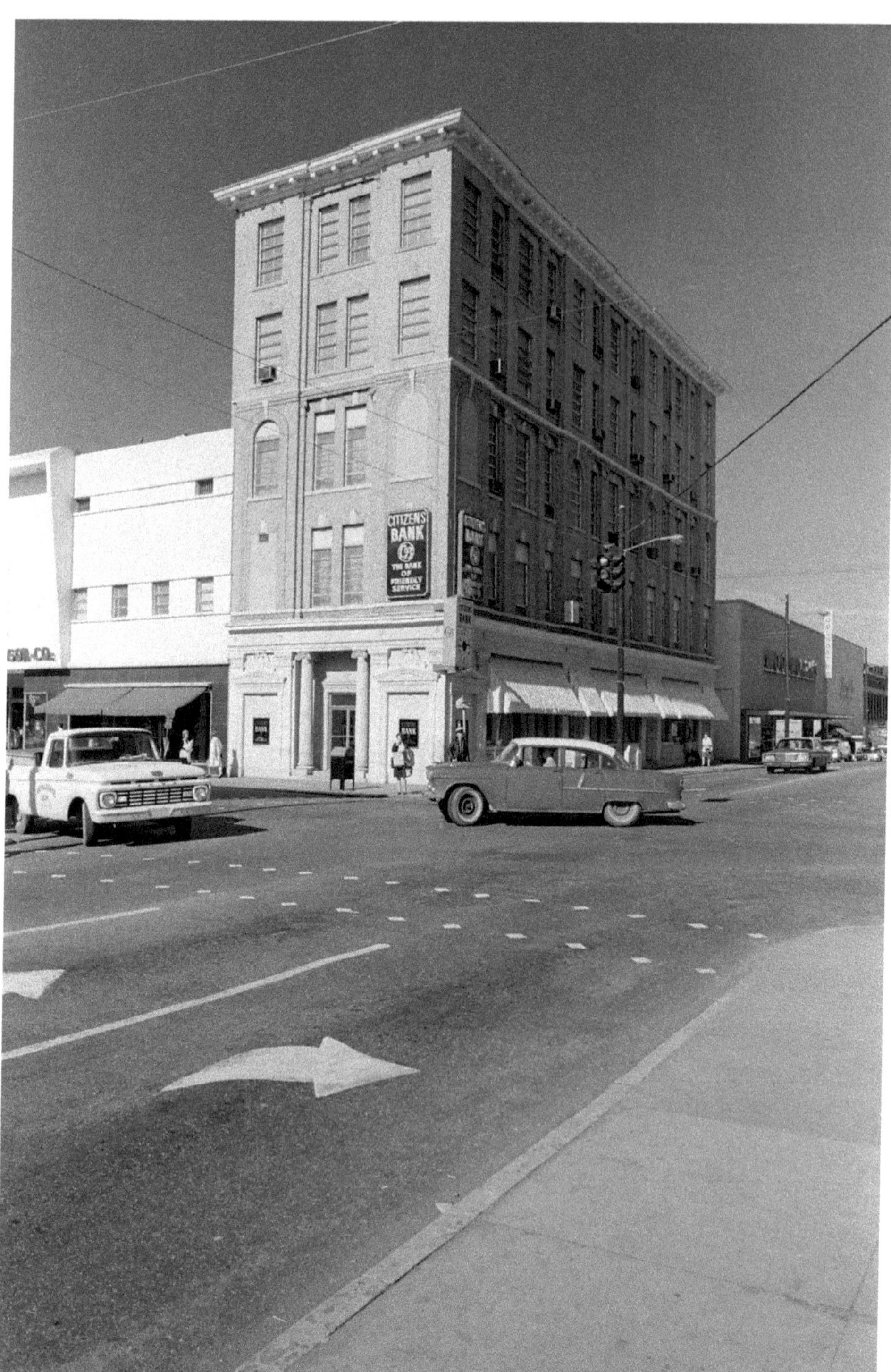

Citizens Bank is open for business at 601 Main Street in Hattiesburg in 1965. Woolworth's, down the street, was dominant across the nation as a chain of retail five and dimes, a status enjoyed by the company throughout much of the twentieth century.

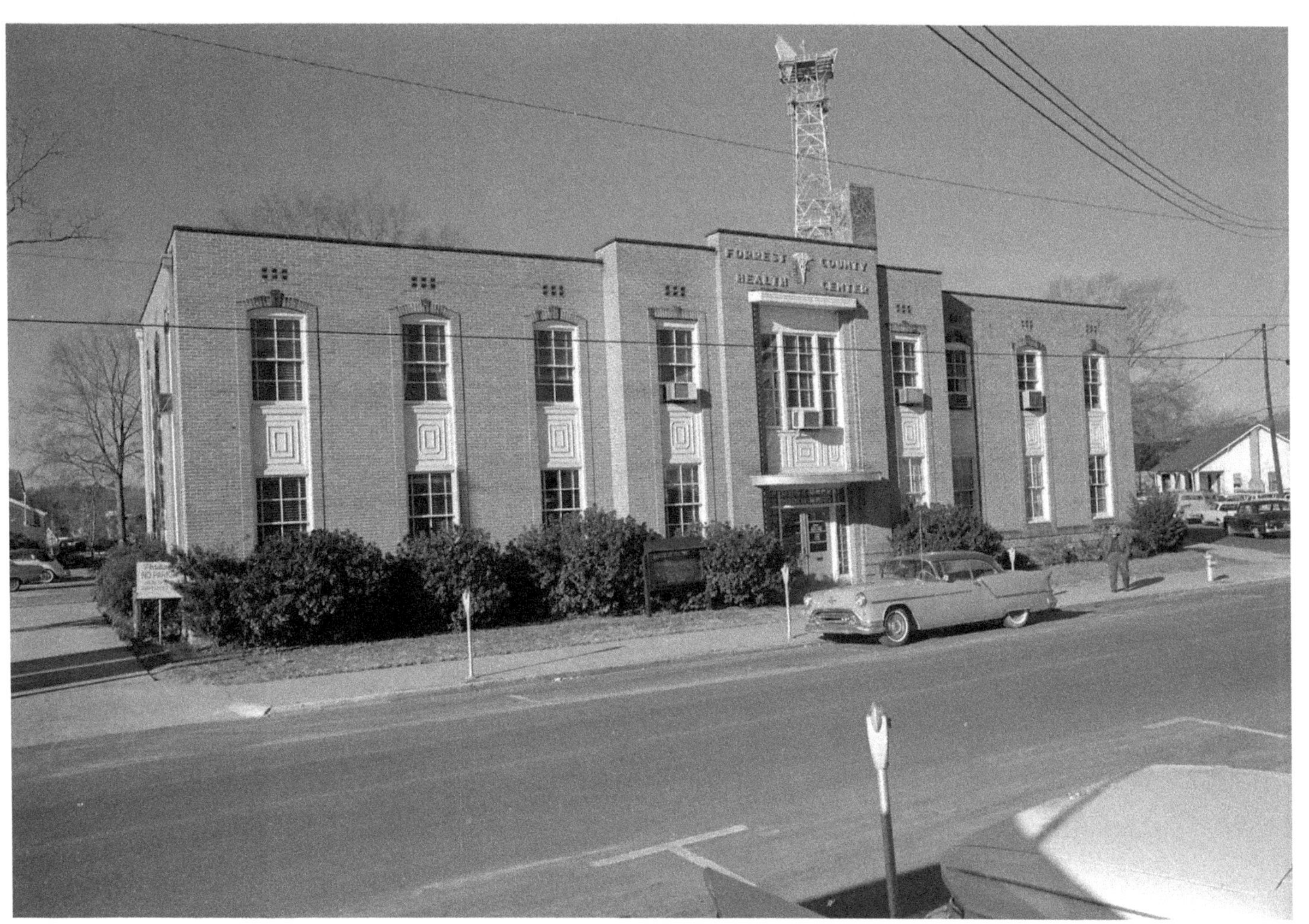

This is the Forrest County Health Department in Hattiesburg, in 1965.

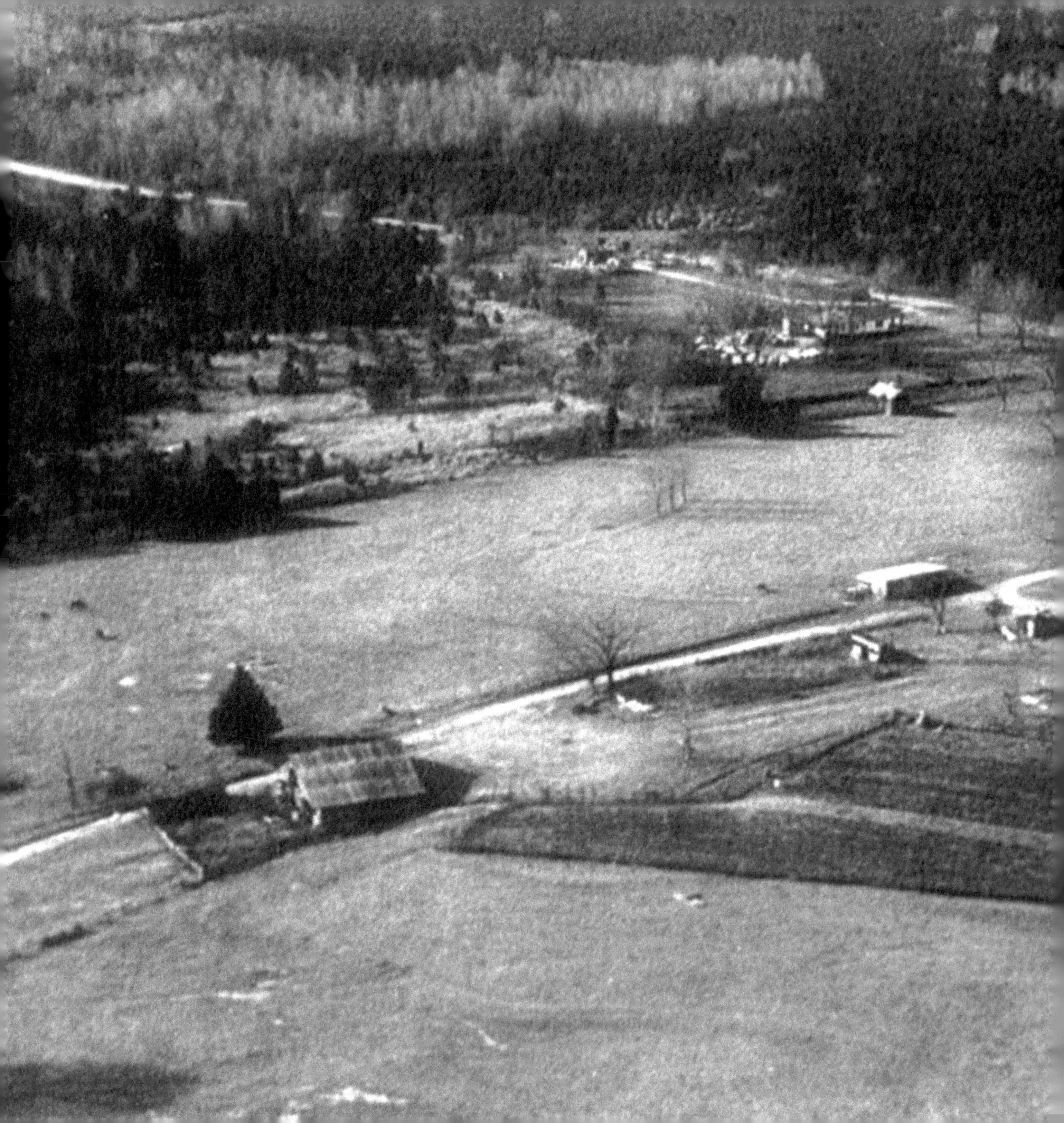

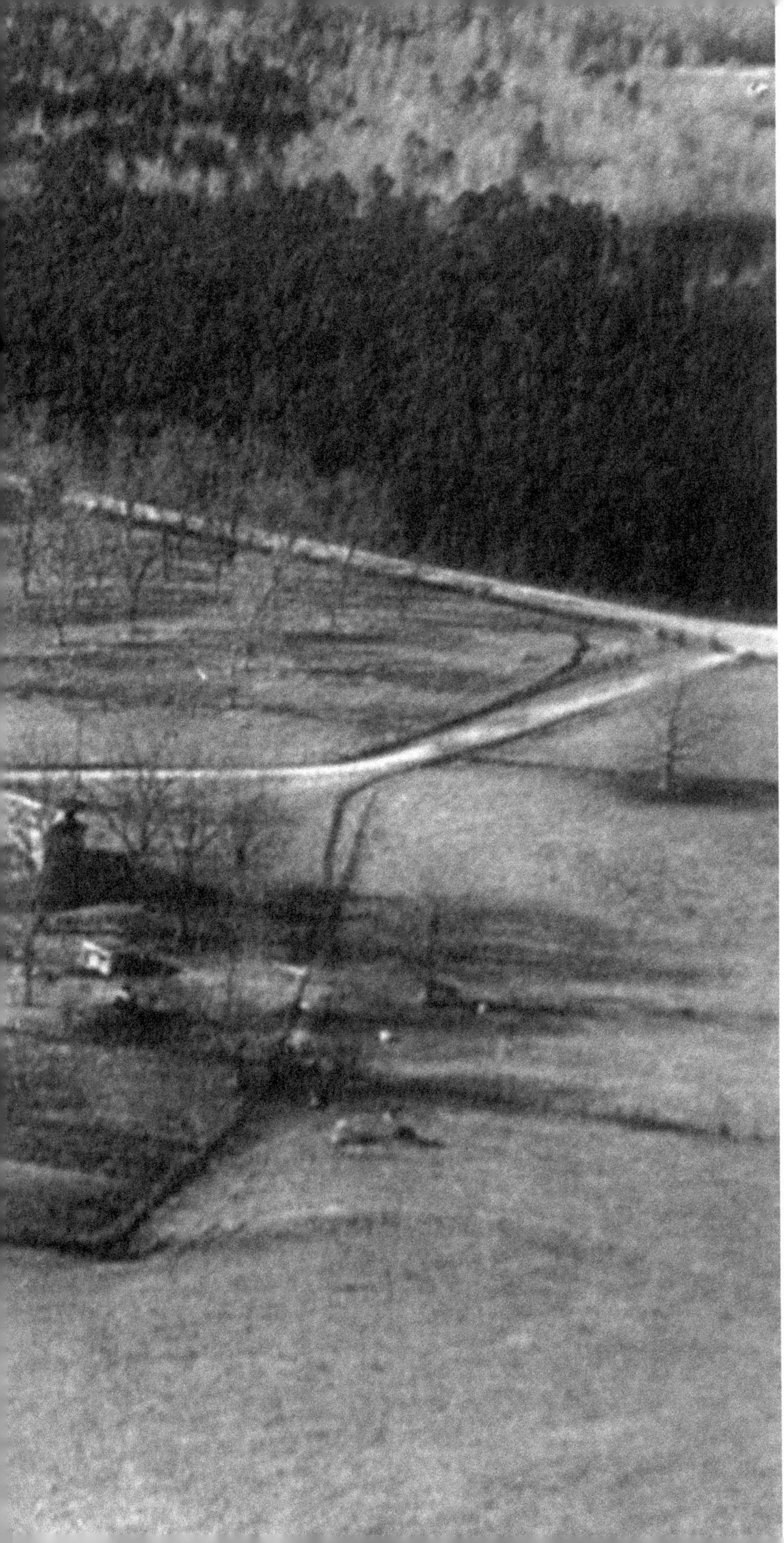

The Welch Plantation near Alamucha is shown from the air in the 1960s. Before the Civil War, the plantation held 3,000 productive acres planted in crops such as cotton, a blacksmith shop, smokehouse, horse-powered cotton gin, and more than 60 slaves. The spacious home, patterned after the colonial style of the day, featured wide verandas with columns that reached the upper porches.

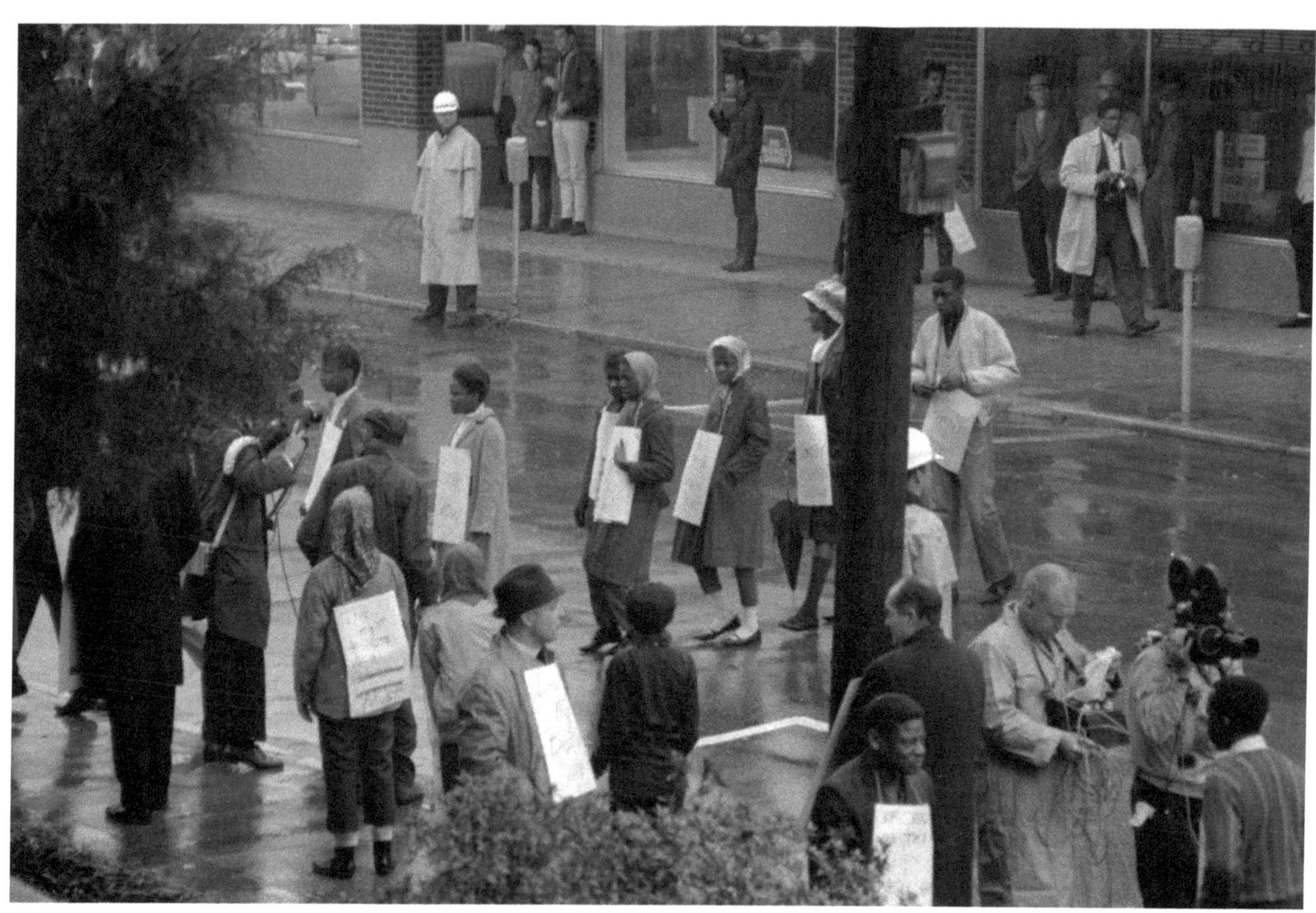

"Freedom Day," January 22, 1964, in Hattiesburg, as demonstrators march in front of the Forrest County courthouse. During Freedom Summer in 1964, the Hattiesburg–Palmers Crossing project was the headquarters for all civil rights activity in the 5th Congressional District of Mississippi. With more than 90 volunteers and 3,000 local participants, it was the largest and most active site in the state.

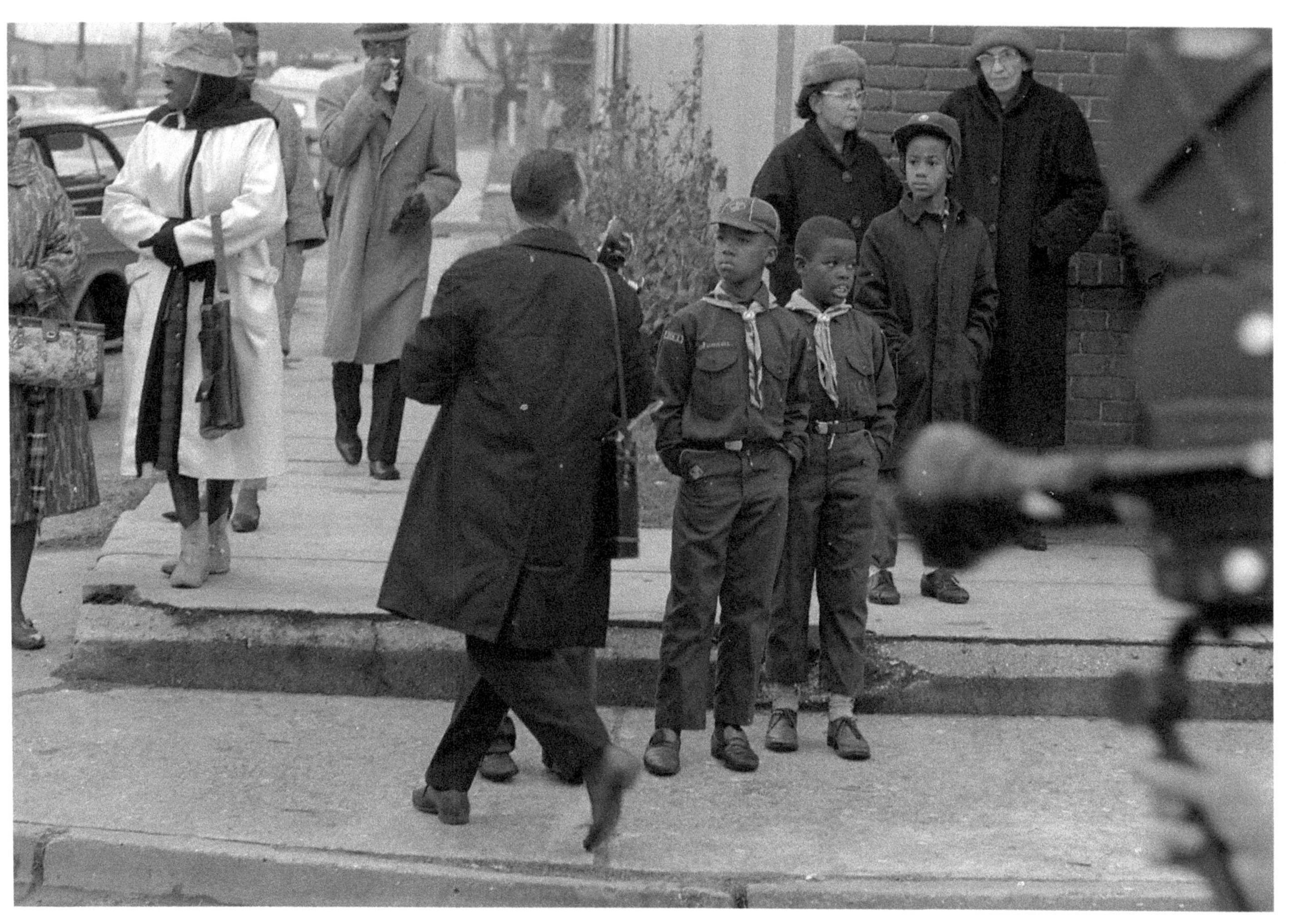

Demonstration on the morning of Vernon Dahmer's funeral, January 15, 1966, in Hattiesburg. Dahmer, a successful businessman and farmer, died as a result of a firebomb to his home on the night of January 10. As president of the Forrest County NAACP, he led voter registration drives in the 1960s. On his deathbed he repeated the words, "If you don't vote, you don't count."

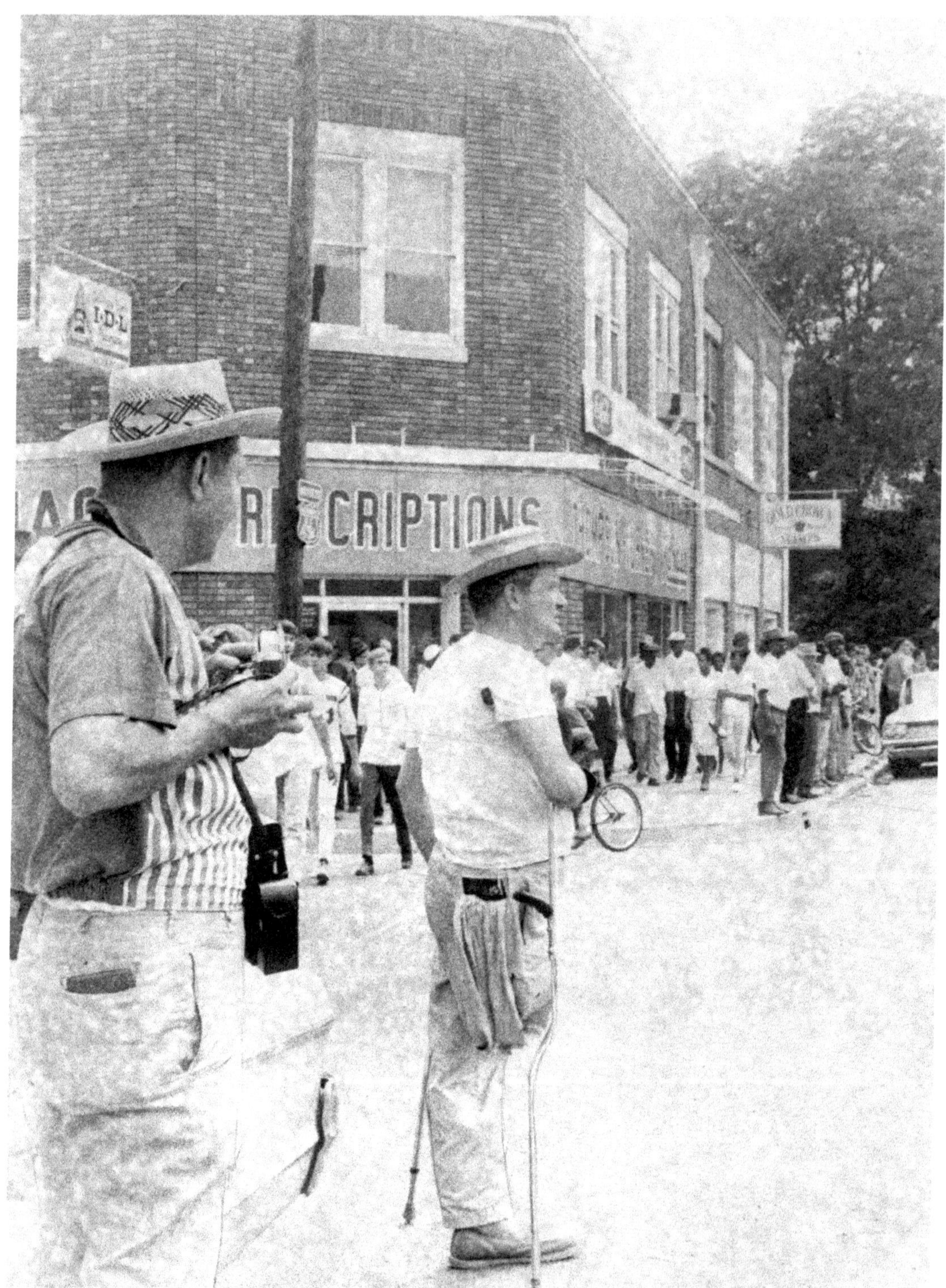

The Meredith Mississippi March took its name from James Meredith, who became the first black student to attend the University of Mississippi. On June 5, 1966, Meredith began a walk from Memphis, Tennessee, to Jackson, Mississippi, to encourage African-Americans to register to vote. It is estimated that between 2,500 and 3,000 black Mississippians were registered during the march.

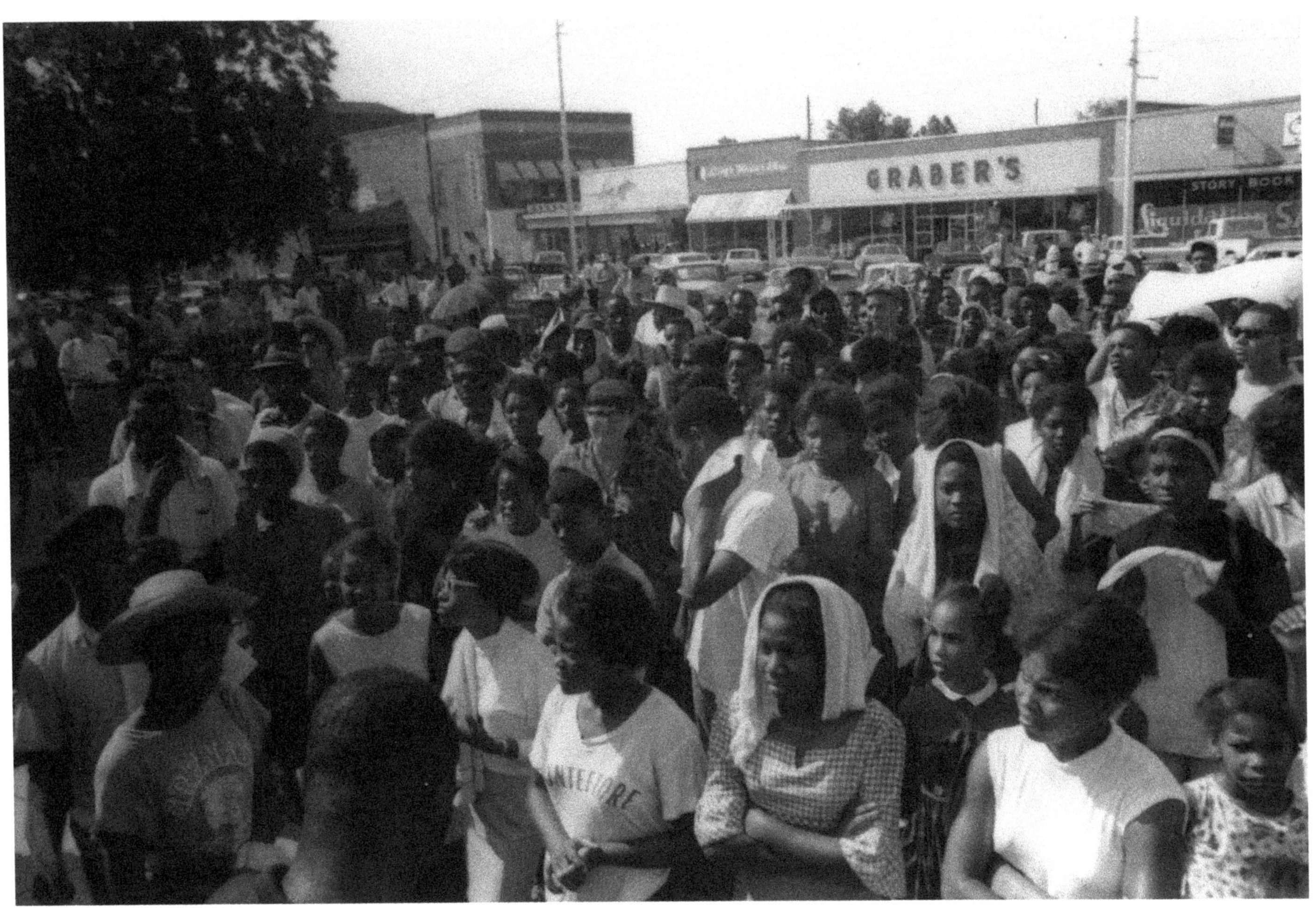

Civil rights demonstrations in Grenada, July 14, 1966. In the afternoon, 220 marchers went uptown and entered the town square, where they proceeded to the courthouse for a rally. The marches were repeated every day for three months: A mass meeting in the evening, then a night march to the square with a rally near the courthouse.

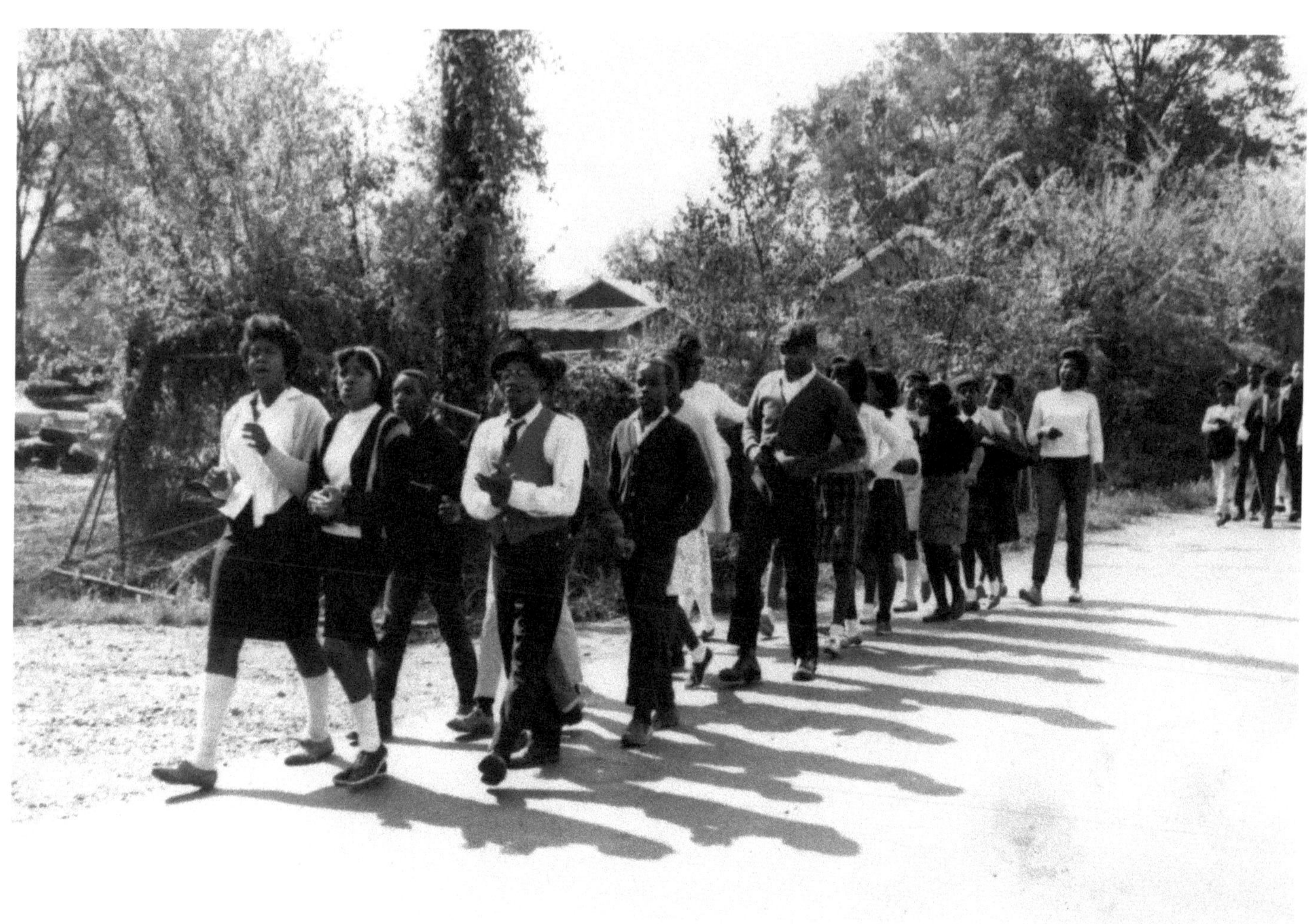

Major Wright, an active member of the Southern Christian Leadership Conference, is shown here marching during the 1966 Grenada boycott. The SCLC was an American civil rights organization, and the first president was Dr. Martin Luther King, Jr.

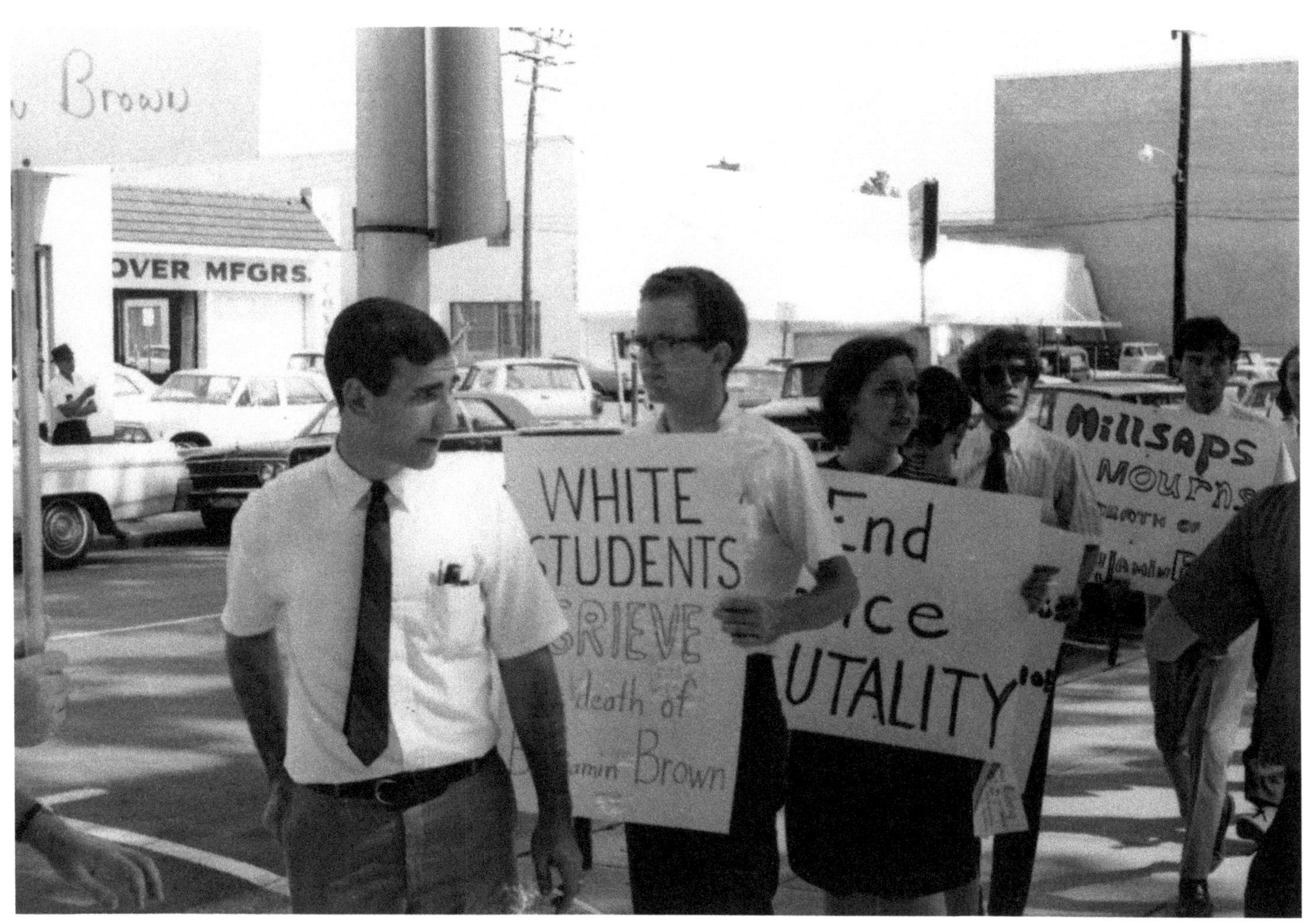

At Millsaps College in Jackson, students protest the death of Jackson State University student Ben Brown, an African-American who was killed May 10, 1967, by Jackson city police when a student demonstration turned violent. As demonstrators began throwing rocks and bottles at police, the officers answered with shotgun blasts, killing Brown, who was present at the protest near the Jackson State campus, but reportedly not participating.

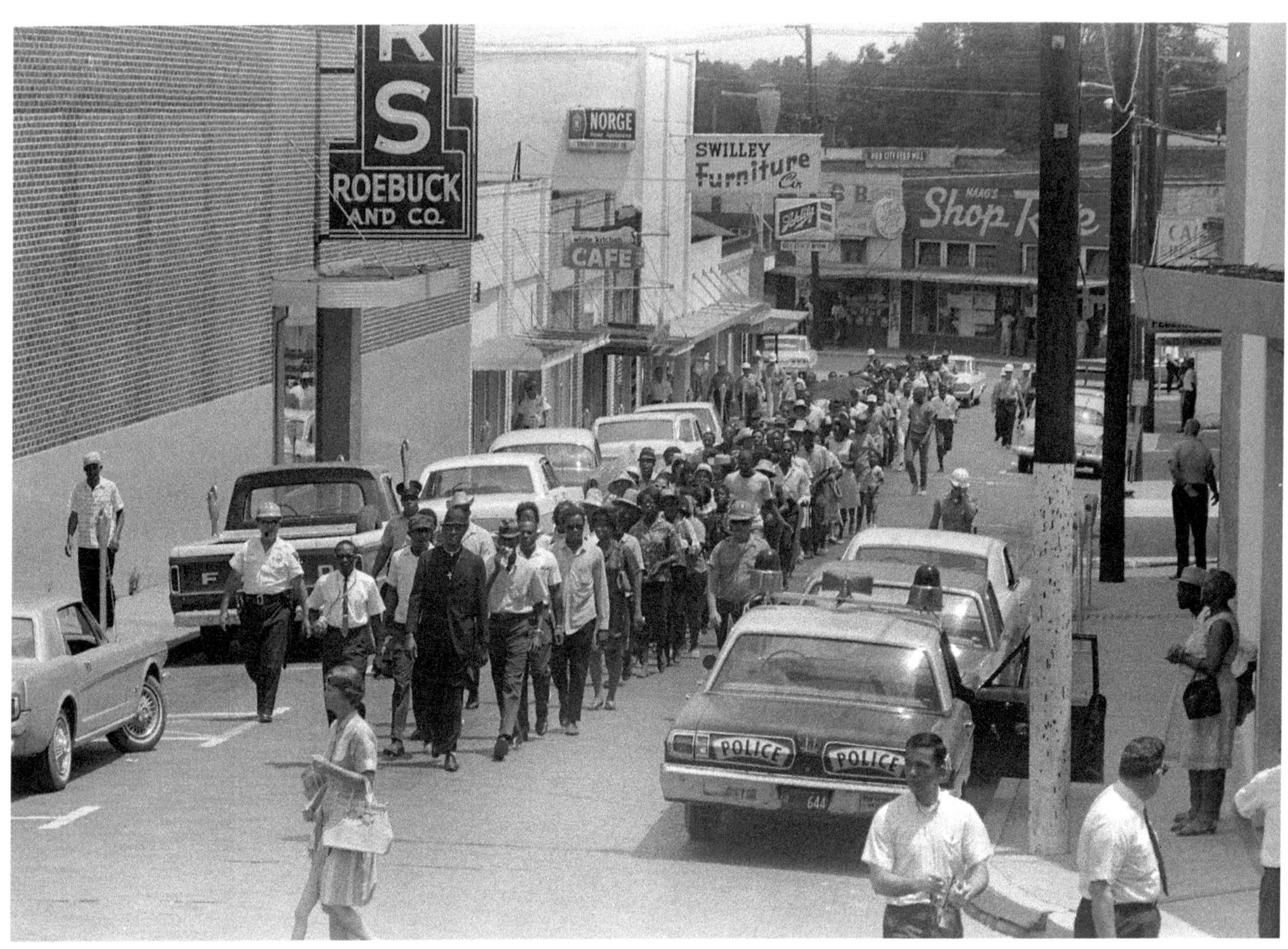

A civil rights demonstration held July 29, 1967, in Hattiesburg, protested the shooting of Lonnie Charles McGee by patrolman Willie McGilvery. An economic boycott of city buses and businesses was also in progress.

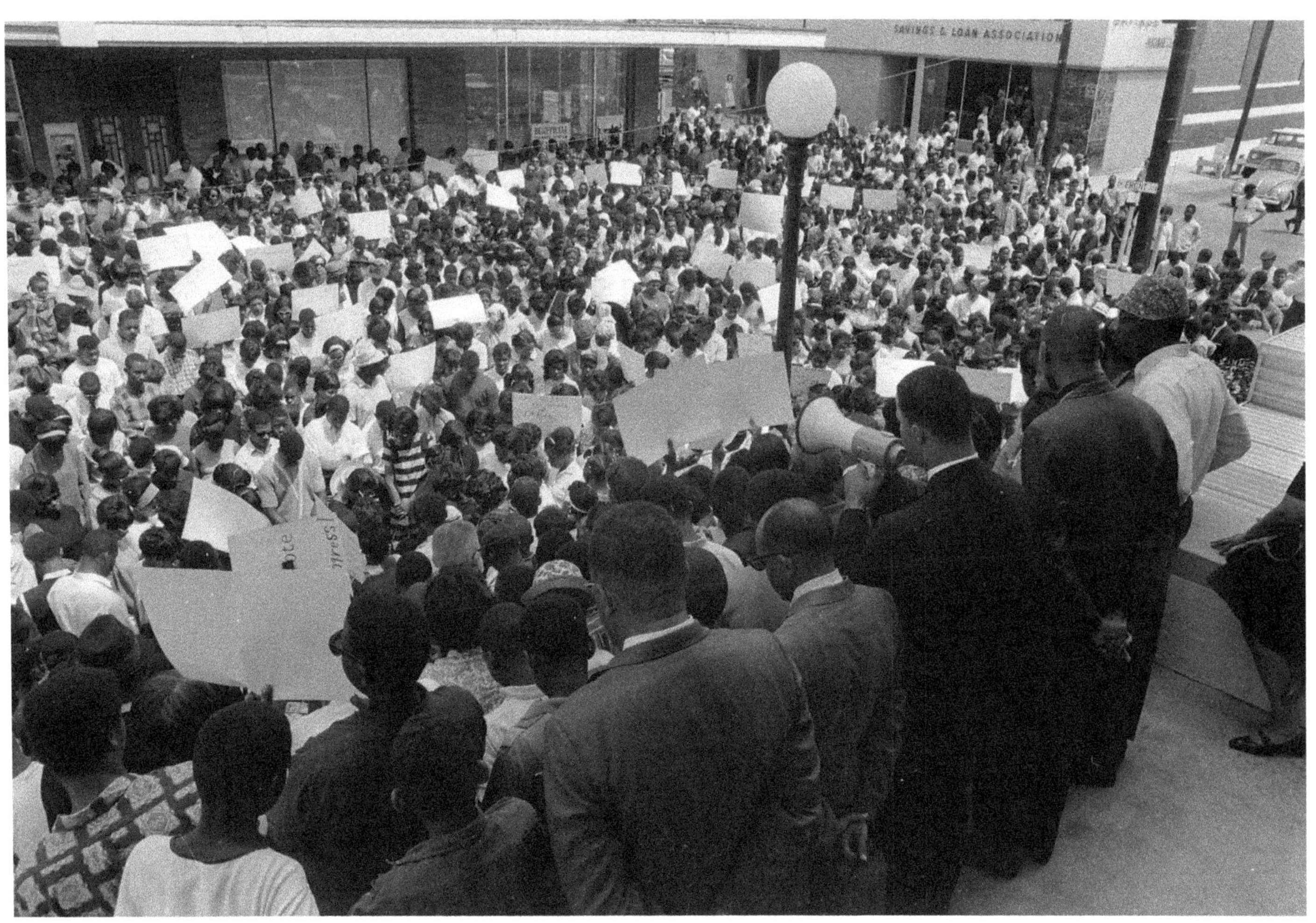

Thousands marched in memory of Dr. Martin Luther King, Jr., on April 8, 1968, in Hattiesburg. The march coincided with a weeklong boycott of schools and white-owned businesses and three days of workplace boycotts.

President Gerald Ford waves to a crowd at an election campaign stop in Biloxi in September 1976. Jimmy Carter won the election and carried Mississippi, the last Democratic presidential candidate to win Mississippi to the present day.

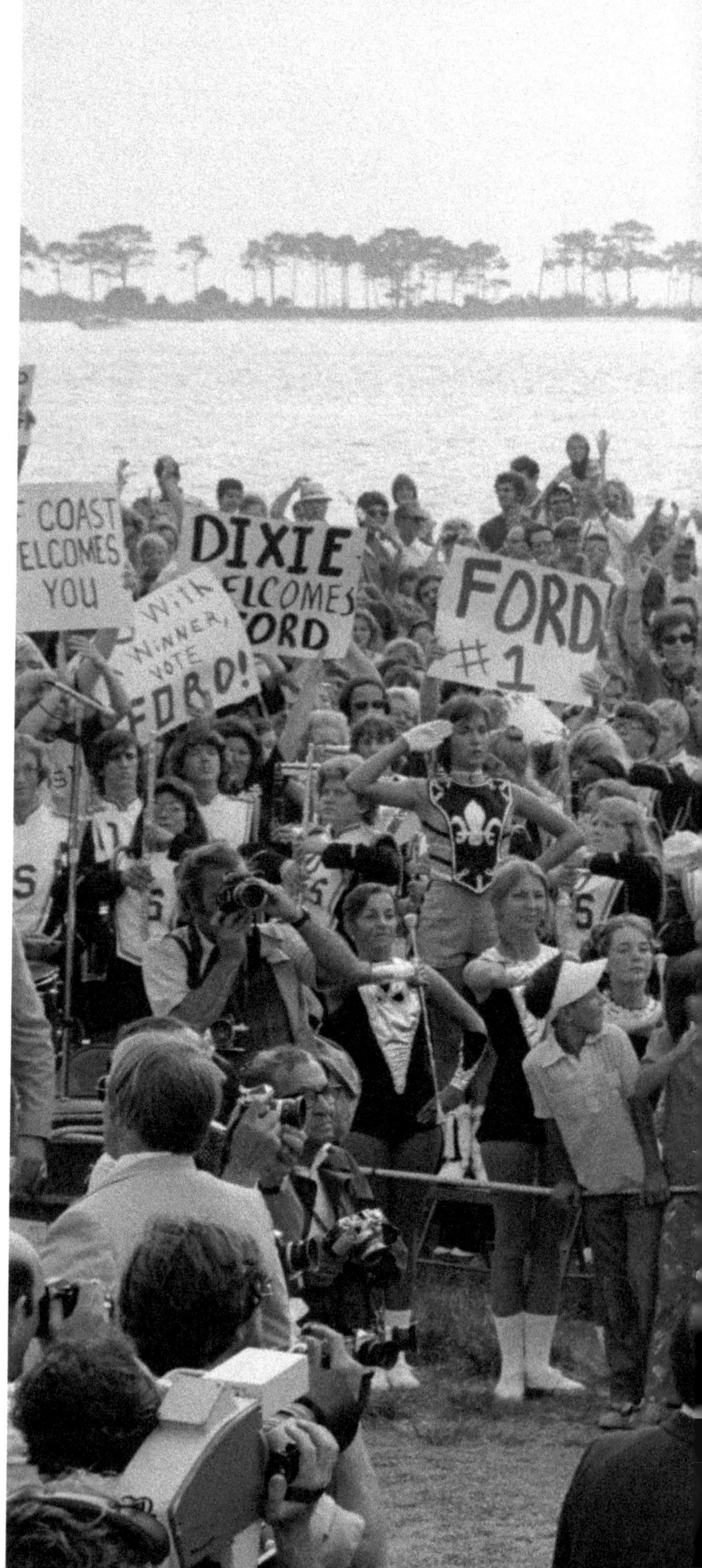

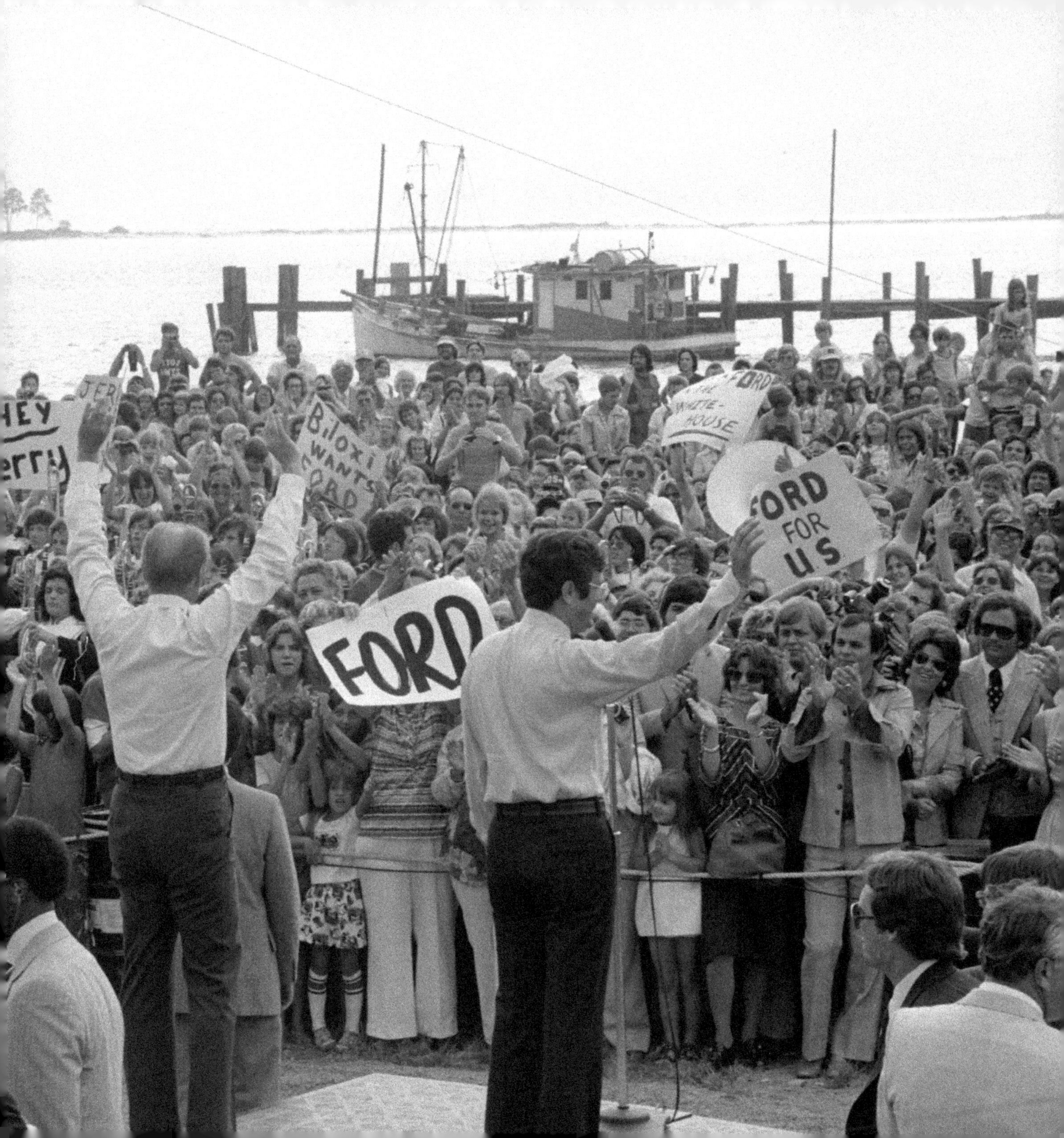

HEY
Biloxi WANTS
FORD FOR US
FORD

Notes on the Photographs

These notes, listed by page number, attempt to include all aspects known of the photographs. Each of the photographs is identified by the page number, photograph's title or description, photographer and collection, archive, and call or box number when applicable. Although every attempt was made to collect all data, in some cases complete data was unavailable due to the age and condition of some of the photographs and records.

ii **Big Black River Station**
Library of Congress
LC-DIG-cwpb-01013

vi **Steamboats 1860s**
Library of Congress
LC-DIG-cwpb-01012

x **Soldier at Chickasaw Bayou**
Library of Congress
LC-DIG-cwpb-01014

2 **Corinth Train Station**
Library of Congress
LC-USZ62-132591

3 **Battle of Corinth Aftermath**
Library of Congress
LC-B811-1291(P&P)

4 **Battle of Corinth Aftermath no. 2**
Library of Congress
LC-DIG-cwpb-01438

5 **Civil War Tin-clad Side-wheeler**
Library of Congress
LC-USZ62-113172

6 **Battle of Chickasaw Bayou Aftermath**
Library of Congress
LC-DIG-cwpb-00446

7 **Big Black Battlefield**
Library of Congress
LC-DIG-cwpb-00519

8 **Siege of Vicksburg Earthworks**
Library of Congress
HABS MISS, 75-VICK.
V, 3

9 **Pearl and State Streets in Jackson**
Mississippi Department of Archives and History
Seutter Collection
PI/1985.0032
96982-01

10 **Interior of Jackson Church**
Mississippi Department of Archives and History
Seutter Collection
PI/1985.0032
97127-01

11 **Jackson Church, 1870**
Mississippi Department of Archives and History
Seutter Collection
PI/1985.0032
97109-01

12 **Covered Bridge Across the Pearl River**
Mississippi Department of Archives and History
Seutter Collection
PI/1985.0032
97024-01

13 **Bridge Collapse**
Mississippi Department of Archives and History
Seutter Collection
PI/1985.0032
97029-01

14 **Jackson Citizens out for a Lark**
Mississippi Department of Archives and History
Seutter Collection
PI/1985.0032
97061-01

15 **Jackson Church and Locals, 1870**
Mississippi Department of Archives and History
Seutter Collection
PI/1985.0032
96977-01

16 **Capital Street in Jackson**
Mississippi Department of Archives and History
Seutter Collection
PI/1985.0032
97009-01

17 Jackson's First Christian Church
Mississippi Department of Archives and History
Seutter Collection
PI/1985.0032
96953-01

18 The Von Seutters
Mississippi Department of Archives and History
Seutter Collection
PI/1985.0032
97112-01

19 The Von Seutter Garden
Mississippi Department of Archives and History
Seutter Collection
PI/1985.0032
97017-01

20 Spengler's Corner
Mississippi Department of Archives and History
Seutter Collection
PI/1985.0032
96968-01

21 A Biloxi School
Library of Congress
LC-USZ62-95509

22 Sullivan Boxing Match at Richburg
Library of Congress
LC-USZ62-62328

23 Marks Rothenberg in Meridian
Lauderdale County Mississippi History and Archives

24 Cypress Forest Passenger Train
Library of Congress
LC-D43-T01-1575

25 The Kittrell Family, 1889
Lauderdale County Mississippi History and Archives
1899 Kittrell Family and shotgun style house

26 Dahomey Cotton Refinery
Library of Congress
LC-USZ62-93669

27 Meridian Federal Building and Post Office
Lauderdale County Mississippi History and Archives
Early (1901-1907) Meridian Post Office

29 Downtown Meridian, Late 1800s
Lauderdale County Mississippi History and Archives
Artesian well

30 Meridian Grand Opera House Interior
Lauderdale County Mississippi History and Archives

31 Meridian Grand Opera House Interior No. 2
Lauderdale County Mississippi History and Archives

32 Vicksburg Levee
Library of Congress
LC-D4-73349

34 Amory-Bigbee Bridge, 1899
Library of Congress
HAER MISS, 44-COLUM. V, 3

35 Dunn's Falls
Lauderdale County Mississippi History and Archives
Dunn's Falls

36 Stern-wheeler Lafourche
Library of Congress
LC-USZ62-91216

38 Main Street in Hattiesburg
Library of Congress
LC-USZ62-78627

39 Site of Old Fort Bayou at Ocean Springs
Library of Congress
LC-DIG-ppmsca-18161

40 Meridian Piano Parlor
Lauderdale County Mississippi History and Archives
Piano Parlors

41 Beachside at Bay St. Louis
Library of Congress
LC-DIG-ppmsca-18160

42 Old Capitol at Jackson
Library of Congress
LC-USZ62-113139

43 Sykes Chapel School Schoolchildren
Library of Congress
LC-USZ62-113945

44 George Ohr Pottery Shop
Library of Congress
LC-D4-13536

45 Mississippi Delta Workers
Library of Congress
LC-USZ62-91504

46 Timber Haulers
Lauderdale County Mississippi History and Archives
ulpwooders with wagon and oxen

47 Longhorn Cattle and Cowherds
Lauderdale County Mississippi History and Archives
Early 1900's–Men with longhorn cattle

48 Jackson Panorama
Library of Congress
pan 6a13653

50 Steam Engines with Lumber Crew
Lauderdale County Mississippi History and Archives
1905 Wayne County train crew at Robinson Lumber

51 **Vicksburg and Greenville Packet Company Steamboats**
Library of Congress
LC-DIG-det-4a13373

52 **Harbor at Gulfport**
Library of Congress
LC-D4-det-4a09951

53 **Vicksburg Battlefield Panorama**
Library of Congress
pan 6a13663

54 **Hattiesburg Church Baptismal Service**
Library of Congress
LC-USZ62-89115

55 **Emanuel Baptist Church Beginnings**
Library of Congress
LC-USZ62-77085

56 **Millsaps College in Jackson**
Library of Congress
pan 6a07020

58 **Williams Home at Yazoo City**
Library of Congress
LC-USZ62-89677

59 **Meridian's Highland Park**
Lauderdale County Mississippi History and Archives
Highland Park, Early 1900's

60 **Mississippi River Dry Dock**
Library of Congress
LC-D4-72265

61 **Pass Oyster Packing Company**
Library of Congress
LC-DIG-nclc-00867

62 **Pass Oyster Packing Company no. 2**
Library of Congress
LC-DIG-nclc-00869

63 **Pass Oyster Packing Company no. 3**
Library of Congress
LC-DIG-nclc-00857

64 **At Meridian Storefront, 1911**
Library of Congress
LC-DIG-nclc-02061

65 **Mayor E. H. Dial**
Lauderdale County Mississippi History and Archives
Golden Age Meridian Mayor Dial

66 **McComb's Cotton Mills Workers**
Library of Congress
LC-DIG-nclc-02077

67 **Laurel Schoolhouse, 1911**
Library of Congress
LC-DIG-nclc-02034

68 **Two Boys in Tupelo**
Library of Congress
LC-DIG-nclc-00880

69 **Trolley to Highland Park**
Lauderdale County Mississippi History and Archives
Trolley to Highland Park

70 **Yazoo City Yarn Mills**
Library of Congress
02097u

71 **Magnolia Cotton Mills**
Library of Congress
LC-DIG-nclc-01875

72 **Tupelo Homes**
Library of Congress
LC-DIG-nclc-02049

73 **Magnolia Mills Family**
Library of Congress
LC-DIG-nclc-02092

74 **Boler's Inn**
Moore's Boler's Inn Private Collection

75 **Engine no. 261 at Biloxi**
Library of Congress
LC-USZ62-93736

76 **Booker T. Washington**
Library of Congress
LC-DIG-ppmsca-13307

77 **Vicksburg National Memorial Reunion**
Library of Congress
pan 6a27341

78 **Queen Kelly Mitchell Funeral Hearse**
Lauderdale County Mississippi History and Archives
Queen Kelly's funeral

79 **A&M College Regimental Parade**
Library of Congress
pan 6a07007

80 **Pass Christian Public School**
Library of Congress
LC-DIG-nclc-01032

81 **Patriotic Sunday Outing**
Library of Congress
LC-USZ62-45947

82 **St. Joseph's Academy at Bay St. Louis**
Library of Congress
LC-DIG-nclc-01044

84 **Camp Shelby Military Base, 1918**
Library of Congress
LC-USZ62-88089

85 **Camp Shelby Bridge Construction**
Library of Congress
LC-USZ62-88092

86 **The Mississippi Riflemen, 1918**
Lauderdale County Mississippi History and Archives
ww 1 ms riflemen copy

88 **Breaking Ground for Civic Improvements**
Lauderdale County Mississippi History and Archives
1920's, Government officials start a new business

90 Stanton Hall at Natchez
Library of Congress
LC-USZ62-88468

91 Weidmann's Restaurant, 1926
Lauderdale County
Mississippi History and Archives
Weidmann's Restaurant

92 Special Train at McComb
Library of Congress
LC-USF344-007929-ZB

94 Fire Department
Lauderdale County
Mississippi History and Archives

95 Grand Opera House
Lauderdale County
Mississippi History and Archives

97 Flood of 1927 at Natchez
Library of Congress
LC-USZ62-129412

98 Flood of 1927 at Greenville
Library of Congress
LC-USZ62-75850

99 Flood of 1927 Food Line
Library of Congress
LC-USZ62-53838

100 Flood of 1927 at Greenville No. 2
Library of Congress
LC-USZ62-75847

101 Flood Refugees on Barge
Library of Congress
LC-USZ62-129391

102 Flood Refugees at Birdsong Camp
Mississippi Department of Archives and History
1927 Flood Collection
PI/1992,0002
97135

103 Flood of 1927 at Anguilla
Mississippi Department of Archives and History
PI/1992.0002
78038

104 Flooded Intersection at Greenville
Mississippi Department of Archives and History
1927 Flood Collection
PI/1992.0002
97142

105 Flood of 1927 Vaccinations
Library of Congress
LC-USZ62-117316

106 Flood of 1927 at Leland
Mississippi Department of Archives and History
1927 Flood Collection
PI/1992.0002
97161

107 Flood of 1927 at Rolling Fork
Mississippi Department of Archives and History
1927 Flood Collection
PI/1992.0002
97175

108 Flood of 1927 at Vicksburg
Library of Congress
LC-USZ62-129417

109 Vicksburg Tent City
Mississippi Department of Archives and History
1927 Flood Collection
PI/1992.0002
97189

110 Vicksburg Tent City No. 2
Library of Congress
LC-USZ62-123851

111 Drought Relief Provisions for Farm Family
Library of Congress
LC-USZ62-101920

112 Drought Relief Lunches for Duncan Schoolchildren
Library of Congress
LC-USZ62-101922

113 Boy Scouts at Cleveland
Library of Congress
LC-USZ62-101903

114 Isaac Pringle House
Lauderdale County
Mississippi History and Archives
1933 photo of the home of African American Confederate Soldier

115 Historic Natchez Building Front
Library of Congress
LC-USZC4-1795

116 Signage on Natchez Shed
Library of Congress
LC-USF33-006093-M5

117 Cotton Bales
Library of Congress
LC-USF33-006095-M2

118 Depression Era Children
Library of Congress
LC-USF33- 006093- M3

119 Two Ladies of Natchez
Library of Congress
LC-USF33-006093-M4

120 Vicksburg River Ferry
Library of Congress
LC-USF342- 001308-A

121 Busy Day at Vicksburg, 1936
Library of Congress
LC-USF342-008049-A

122 Jefferson Davis Retirement Home in Biloxi
Library of Congress
HABS MISS, 24-BILX, V, 1–3

123 St. Mary's Cathedral in Natchez
Library of Congress
HABS MISS, 1-NATCH, 14

124 Key Brothers Aviation Record
Lauderdale County
Mississippi History and Archives
Key Brothers Airplane

125 Fred and Al Key
Lauderdale County
Mississippi History and Archives
Key brothers, aviation pioneers

126 Lowndes County Courthouse at Columbus
Library of Congress
HABS MISS, 44-COLUM, 1

127 Church of the Annunciation at Columbus
Library of Congress
HABS MISS, 44-COLUM, 12

128 Vicksburg Neighbors Confab
Library of Congress
LC-USZC4-1794

129 Sharecropper Children, 1936
Library of Congress
LC-USF34-009435-E

130 Jackson City Hall
Library of Congress
HABS MISS, 15-JACK, 9

131 Farm Laborers at Clarksdale
Library of Congress
LC-USF34-017464

132 Hoeing Cotton, 1937
Library of Congress
LC-USF34-017289-C

134 Breaking for Lunch
Library of Congress
LC-USF34-017460-E

135 Magnolias and Spanish Moss
Library of Congress
LC-USZ62-115699

136 Interior of Sharecropper Home
Library of Congress
LC-USF33-011567-M4

137 Mississippi River Baptism
Library of Congress
LC-USZ62-49648

138 Moving Day
Library of Congress
LC-USF34-018952-E

139 Farm Living at Mileston
Library of Congress
LC-USF35-156

140 Main Street at Lexington
Library of Congress
LC USF33-030590 M3

141 Depression Era Canning Factory Workers
Lauderdale County
Mississippi History and Archives
Women of Depression at work

143 Saturday at Lexington Farmers Market
Library of Congress
LC-USF33-030587-M3

144 Dominoes Players
Library of Congress
LC-USF347-030540-M1-A

145 Cotton Field Harvest at Benoit
Library of Congress
LC-USF33-030583-M3

146 Cotton Harvest at Perthshire
Library of Congress
LC-USF33-030561-M1

147 Saturday in Belzoni
Library of Congress
LC-USF33-030660-M4

148 Segregated Theater
Library of Congress
LC-USF33-030577-M2

149 Filling Station Architecture at Jackson, 1939
Library of Congress
LC-USF34-052296-D

150 Joe Gow Nue Market
Library of Congress
LC-USF34-052450-D

151 Cotton Row Street in Leland
Library of Congress
LC-USF34-052506-D

152 Clarksdale Jitterbuggers
Library of Congress
LC-USF34-052594-D

153 Warren County Courthouse at Vicksburg
Library of Congress
HABS MISS, 75-VICK, 7

154 Old State Capitol at Jackson, 1930s
Library of Congress
HABS MISS, 25-JACK, 3

156 Stanton Hall at Natchez, 1940
Library of Congress
HABS MISS, 1-NATCH, 21

158 Rolling Fork Tenant Houses
Library of Congress
LC-USF34-053771-D

159 Bird's-eye View of Vicksburg
Library of Congress
LC-USF34-053775-D

160 Port Gibson, 1940
Library of Congress
LC-USF34-054859-D

162 Union Station at Meridian
Lauderdale County
Mississippi History and Archives
Original Meridian Train Depot

163 Signs of the Times
Library of Congress
LC-USF35-115

164 House at Toomsuba
Lauderdale County
Mississippi History and Archives
Old home at Toomsuba

165 Dunleith at Natchez
Library of Congress
LC-USF34-054827-C

166 Vegetable Vendor at Natchez
Library of Congress
LC-USF34-055058-E

167 Cold Day Engine Check
Lauderdale County
Mississippi History and Archives
Old car filling station

168 Camp Shelby Frivolity, 1943
Library of Congress
LC-USZ62-89915

169 Union Station Good-byes
Lauderdale County
Mississippi History and Archives
WW II Soldiers at Union Train Station

170 The War Effort at Ingalls Shipbuilding
Library of Congress
LC-USE6-D-005393

171 Governor Bailey Celebration
Lauderdale County
Mississippi History and Archives
MS Governor Tom Bailey

172 Football Parade in Jackson, 1950
Mississippi Department of Archives and History
Sovereignty Commission
10-35A-0-14-1-1-1ph

174 Farish Street Newsstand in Jackson
Mississippi Department of Archives and History
Sovereignty Commission
1-14-0-5-2-1-1ph

175 Vicksburg Tornado Rescue Efforts, 1953
Mississippi Department of Archives and History
Moncrief Collection
815

176 Scene of Destruction at Vicksburg
Mississippi Department of Archives and History
Moncrief Collection
818

178 Logging in the Piney Woods, 1958
Mississippi Department of Archives and History
Moncrief Collection
814

179 Sanderford Filling Station
Lauderdale County
Mississippi History and Archives
Sanderford filling station

180 Governor Johnson Inaugural Parade
Mississippi Department of Archives and History
Moncrief Collection
863

181 Governor Johnson Inaugural Parade no. 2
Mississippi Department of Archives and History
Moncrief Collection
98

182 Staley's Cafe at Winona
Mississippi Department of Archives and History
Sovereignty Commission
2-65-0-63-1-1-1ph

183 Meredith and Marshals
Library of Congress
LC-U9-8556-24

184 Tatum Salt Dome Nuclear Test
Mississippi Department of Archives and History
Moncrief Collection
187

185 Tatum Salt Dome Nuclear Test no. 2
Mississippi Department of Archives and History
Moncrief Collection
184

186 Citizens Bank in Hattiesburg
Mississippi Department of Archives and History
Moncrief Collection
297

187 Forrest County Health Department at Hattiesburg
Mississippi Department of Archives and History
Moncrief Collection
291

189 Welch Plantation at Alamucha
Lauderdale County
Mississippi History and Archives
Plantation home at Alamucha

190 Demonstrators at Hattiesburg
Mississippi Department of Archives and History
Moncrief Collection
70

191 Vernon Dahmer's Funeral
Mississippi Department of Archives and History
Moncrief Collection
406

192 The Meredith March
Mississippi Department of Archives and History
Sovereignty Commission
1-91-0-7-1-1-1-dph

193 Demonstrators at Grenada
Mississippi Department of Archives and History
Sovereignty Commission
9-37-0-2-9-1-1ph

194 Grenada Boycott Marchers
Mississippi Department of Archives and History
Sovereignty Commission
8-19-1 51-1-1-1ph

195 Millsaps College Protesters
Mississippi Department of Archives and History
Sovereignty Commission
3-11-0-25-2-1-1fph

196 **Demonstrators at Hattiesburg no. 2**
Mississippi Department of Archives and History
Moncrief Collection
478

197 **Demonstrators at Hattiesburg no. 3**
Mississippi Department of Archives and History
Moncrief Collection
686

198 **Gerald Ford Campaign Address**
Library of Congress
LC-DIG-ppmsca-08528

HISTORIC PHOTOS OF MISSISSIPPI

Imagine a ride with the Mississippi mockingbird as it soars through the Mississippi skies. Beginning in the land of Elvis at Tupelo, one moves down to the Piney Woods of East Central Mississippi where the ground is covered with fragrant pine straw and where Choctaw moccasins once walked the trails. Then turn south where the ocean waves swell upon sandy beaches and sea gulls hover and squawk in the breeze. Continue onward to the mansions of historic Natchez and the cotton fields of the Mississippi Delta where the blues reigns supreme. Finally, swoop down toward Old Man River, the majestic Mississippi, and skim across its yellow waters. The waters have seen war and defeat, loss and love, heartbreaks and triumphs. No sentiments need speaking. Only the sweet songs of the mockingbird are required to understand a land whose beauty is second only to the strength of its people. Through nearly 200 images printed in vivid black-and-white, with brief introductions and captions, *Historic Photos of Mississippi* takes the viewer on a flightpath to key points of interest in historic Mississippi.

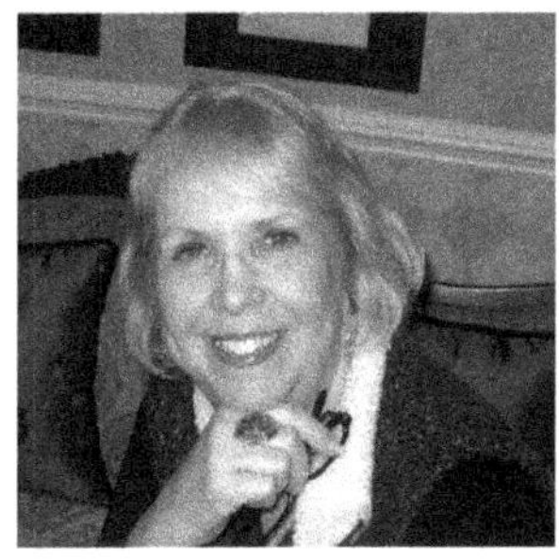

Anne B. McKee is a literary and performing artist. She is listed on the Mississippi Artist Roster sponsored by the Mississippi Arts Commission. McKee contributes to the arts community in her roles as a storyteller, humorist, public speaker, writer, creator of historic literary events, and work on Mississippi heritage projects. She teaches creative writing workshops and serves as a guest playwright for several community theaters. One of the joys of her life is to teach school students through her originally written program "Loving Mississippi," in which she uplifts the accomplishments of famous Mississippians. Native to the state, McKee's love and support for Mississippi began in childhood as she sat at the knees of relatives to learn the Mississippi story—a story for her that is always new and fresh. Be it a short story, poem, play, or presentation, McKee's work is always about Mississippi, its good people, and its natural beauty.

WWW.TURNERPUBLISHING.COM

www.ingramcontent.com/pod-product-compliance
Lightning Source LLC
LaVergne TN
LVHW060611110826
845154LV00003B/70
9781684420841